Photoshop®
Elements 2 Bible

Photoshop® Elements 2 Bible

Laurie Ulrich

WILEY

Wiley Publishing, Inc.

Photoshop® Elements 2 Bible

Published by
Wiley Publishing, Inc.
111 River Street
Hoboken, NJ 07030
www.wiley.com

Copyright © 2004 by Wiley Publishing, Inc., Indianapolis, Indiana

ISBN: 0-7645-4391-1

Library of Congress Control Number: 2003114877

Manufactured in the United States of America

10 9 8 7 6 5 4 3 2 1

1O/RW/RS/QT/IN

Published by Wiley Publishing, Inc., Indianapolis, Indiana
Published simultaneously in Canada

WILEY

About the Author

Since the late 1990s, **Laurie Ulrich** has authored and co-authored more than 20 books on computers, software, and their creative and effective use. Recent publications include *Restoring and Retouching with Photoshop Elements 2*, and *The Photoshop Complete Reference*, establishing her expertise in photo restoration and creating original graphics for print and the Web. In addition to writing computer books, Laurie teaches at local universities, corporate training centers, and for her own clients — she has trained more than 10,000 people to use computers and software since the early 1980s, and will be training many more, as her training expands to online and CD-based courses in early 2004. Laurie also runs her own firm, Limehat & Company, Inc., providing general computer consulting with a focus on marketing and making effective use of the Web.

Despite the obvious focus on computers, Laurie also finds time for her husband, Robert Fuller (who wrote Chapter 18 in this book), and for her family, which includes three cats and several humans. You can read more about Laurie at www.planetlaurie.com, where you can find links to her other Web sites and information on causes near and dear to her heart.

Credits

Acquisitions Editor
Tom Heine

Project Editor
Kenyon Brown

Technical Editor
Dennis Short

Copy Editor
Jerelind Charles

Editorial Managers
Robyn Burnett
Rev Mengle

Vice President and Executive Group Publisher
Richard Swadley

Vice President and Executive Publisher
Barry Pruett

Project Coordinator
April Farling

Graphics and Production Specialists
Lauren Goddard
Joyce Haughey
Jennifer Heleine
Lynsey Osborn
Heather Ryan

Quality Control Technician
Brian H. Walls

Proofreading and Indexing
TECHBOOKS Production Services

*This book is dedicated to my new family, especially
Aunt Nan (Anna Stickney) and Aunt Jean (Laura Jean Bowling),
who are truly wonderful and who, along with my new father-in-law,
William Fuller, have made me feel very loved and welcome.
Coming from a very small family, I'm happy to be joining a family
that includes too many people to possibly list here. I am truly blessed.*

Preface

If you already purchased this book, you probably flipped through it in the bookstore or looked at the sample pages or a description of the book online before making your purchase and feel sure this was the right book for you. You looked at the table of contents, you may have scanned the index, and hopefully, you took a look at some of the chapters, checking out specific topics to see how I cover them. The color section, a series of 32 full-color images, might also have grabbed you. While I'm quite sure this *is* the right book for you, if you're still undecided and are standing there in the bookstore or reading this page online, consider these points:

+ The Bible series is a justifiably respected series, with many deserving best-sellers in its booklist. This book will hopefully follow in their footsteps, and the author and several editors and production people at Wiley worked hard to make this book a good one.

+ The author (me) has written several books on Photoshop and Photoshop Elements and has been teaching people to use these applications and others like them for quite some time.

+ I also use this application daily in my own work, so I know it pretty much "like the back of my hand."

+ While I know the application thoroughly, I do learn new facets about Photoshop and Photoshop Elements nearly every time I embark on a new project, which makes me both respectful of the software and its powers, and humble in terms of my own knowledge. How does this help you? Because rather than assuming I know everything and closing my mind, I'm open to all sorts of new ideas and techniques and see any opportunity — any task, any student, any artwork I see — and take full advantage of what I can learn from it. Further, when I figure out something new, I'm excited about it and I share it. So this book is filled with things I'm excited about and that I'm happy to share with you!

So, I hope you'll add this book to your personal library, and if you already have, that you're enjoying the book and find it useful. I've enjoyed writing it and have tried to keep many different types of users in mind as I've been writing. From the total novice to the person who's been poking around, trying different things on his or her own, I think this book provides the thorough coverage you need. If you're already quite experienced with Photoshop Elements, you'll find this book can serve as a great reference for the features you don't use often or that you haven't completely mastered. If you use Photoshop at work (where budgets are much larger than yours might be) and have purchased Elements for use at home, this book will help you navigate the differences — commands that are in different places, tools that don't exist in Photoshop, and so on. This truly is a book intended for any Photoshop Elements user.

What is Photoshop Elements?

Photoshop Elements has been called "Photoshop Lite." It's a somewhat scaled-down version of Photoshop, the industry standard for photo retouching, creating original artwork, and for optimizing graphics intended for use on the Web. Photoshop Elements contains virtually all the same tools in the toolbox that you find in Photoshop, and a few that I wish were part of Photoshop—the Selection Brush and the Red Eye removal tool, being just two examples.

So what's missing? *Actions*, for one thing, which are automated procedures you can record (a lot like a macro in a word processor or spreadsheet program) that perform a series of steps in an order you specify. You also won't find a Channels palette, and the ability to format type is quite limited—no kerning, tracking, or leading tools are available. Some of the dialog boxes are simplified, offering a little less flexibility to do things like adjust the size and shape of a beveled edge, or the nature of a drop shadow. The reduced set of Type tools and the lack of blending options for layers are probably the things I miss most, having gotten used to having them at my disposal in Photoshop. However, given that I now often default to using Photoshop Elements (even though I have Photoshop loaded on my computers, too), I must not miss them *that* much, right?

Of course the biggest selling point for Elements is the price tag. Instead of paying $600 or more for Photoshop, you can get Elements for $99. This puts the product in the budget of more people, from home users who want to scan vintage family photos or make duplicates of their wedding pictures (without paying a photographer or printing shop to do it) to growing businesses in need of graphics for marketing materials, both printed and online.

How This Book Is Organized

As I said, this book is intended for Elements users of all skill and usage levels. It's a big book, following in the Bible tradition of covering every nook and cranny of the software. At over 600 pages, you should find coverage of every tool, command, and palette in the application, plus lots of ways to use them in combination and/or in non-traditional ways. The book is divided into six parts, plus a Color Section:

Part I: Photoshop Elements 2 Defined

Part II: Repairing, Restoring, and Retouching Photographs

Part III: Creating Your Own Works of Art

Part IV: Working with Type

Part V: Sharing Your Elements Creations on Paper and Online

The book also includes two appendixes.

Each part (other than the Color Section) consists of at least two chapters. You find both discussion and step-by-step coverage in each chapter, and plenty of images to help you follow what I'm explaining, and to help you envision the techniques and their outcomes more effectively.

Color Section

The Color Section consists of 32 color images, demonstrating the use of a variety of Elements tools and features, including several of the Filters, some used in combination for interesting results.

These images are just a small sampling of the kind of things you'll be able to do after reading this book. To be honest, you'll be able to do many of them after reading just parts of this book. Many people, when faced with a 600+ page book, only read the parts that interest them immediately — the chapters on topics that have perplexed them or that pertain to features they've never tried on their own before. Even if you don't read this book cover-to-cover or don't try every feature described, you'll be able to achieve great things with your scanned photos, original artwork, and graphics for both print and the Web.

Conventions

For consistency's sake, each chapter contains procedural coverage, found in the form of STEPS, headed sections that list a series of tasks that the reader can perform to achieve a specific goal. Throughout the steps, images are inserted to help the reader make certain that he or she is following along properly. There is also a good deal of expository text, in the form of a friendly discussion of the topics at hand. This text is peppered with appropriate icons, heralding the presence of Tips, Notes, and Cautions:

 Tips are generally short paragraphs, each imparting a quick concept to the reader. If there's an aside that I'd whisper to you while sitting with you at the computer, showing you how a particular feature works, that's what you'll find in a tip.

 Notes are a bit longer than tips and contain general information related to or relevant to the subject at hand. Rather than being additional information on how to do something, Notes often tell you when or why to do something.

Caution icons warn you about potential problems you may encounter, and how to avoid making mistakes.

Final Thoughts

I really do hope you enjoy this book, and that it helps you accomplish great things with Elements. The list of functions Elements can help you to do — from restoring treasured photos to creating animated graphics for your Web site — is considerable, and the size of this book is proof of that. Don't be intimidated by the book's length (although there are longer books in the Bible series), and don't be intimidated by Elements. While there are a lot of "bells and whistles" in the software, and a lot of tools and features in the workspace, you don't have to use them all. You may never use many of the commands, tools, and other features in the application, and that's fine. You should use the software for what you need it to do, and unless you're just plain curious about the other features, it's just fine if you never use them. I think you'll have a lot of fun if you do go exploring beyond the specific tools you absolutely need, but it's up to you. Elements is not a complicated application, and hopefully, with this book, you'll agree that it's a great piece of software and you'll accomplish great things with it.

If you run into any questions about how Elements works, or need further clarification of anything you've read in this book, please feel free to contact me at `laurie@planetlaurie.com`. You can also visit my Web site for information about my other Elements and Photoshop books and to find out more about me and my personal and professional background. I look forward to hearing from you!

Acknowledgments

I'd like to thank Tom Heine, who gave me the opportunity to write this book. I imagine Tom probably tore out a good deal of his hair waiting for the book to be completed, as there were a few unavoidable delaying events that all decided to happen in the final weeks of the project. I really appreciated Tom's patience and encouragement throughout the process. Others at Wiley who must be thanked for their invaluable assistance include my project editor, Kenyon Brown, technical editor, Dennis Short, copy editor, Jerelind Charles, and the talented production staff. It requires more than an author to produce a book — editors provide an objective vision, help maintain technical accuracy, clean up the text, and work together to tie everything together. The production staff creates the tools that help readers navigate the book — the table of contents and the index — and they make sure the book's elements — text, images, tips, notes, and so forth. . . are all in the right places. These seemingly small details are really quite big in terms of the quality of a book, and I appreciate these people more than I can say.

I must also thank my contributor, husband, and best friend, Robert Fuller. Robert took time out from writing his own book to help me with this one. He wrote Chapter 18 (on optimizing images for the Web), and he did a great job. I hope you'll all check out Robert's book, *HTML in 10 Simple Steps or Less*, to which I contributed three parts, because I'm such a nice person.

Finally, I must thank my agent, Margot Maley Hutchison, for being an unflagging and supportive guide through the often hazardous waters of the publishing industry and for being a really great person. I feel quite fortunate to have her in my corner.

Contents at a Glance

Preface ix
Acknowledgments xiii

Part I: Photoshop Elements 2 Defined 1
Chapter 1: All About Photoshop Elements 2 3
Chapter 2: Getting to Know Photoshop Elements 17
Chapter 3: Making Photoshop Elements Your Own 57

Part II: Repairing, Restoring, and Retouching Photographs 75
Chapter 4: Opening, Scanning, and Capturing Photos 77
Chapter 5: Selecting and Masking Content for Editing 97
Chapter 6: Photographic Housekeeping 123
Chapter 7: Mastering Color and Light 165
Chapter 8: Changing Image Size 203

Part III: Creating Your Own Works of Art 223
Chapter 9: Drawing and Painting with Elements 225
Chapter 10: Using Layers to Control Image Content 255
Chapter 11: Using the Shape Tools 273
Chapter 12: Applying Fills and Styles 291
Chapter 13: Using Filters and Special Effects 309

Part IV: Working with Type 383
Chapter 14: Adding Text to Images 385
Chapter 15: Applying Type Styles and Effects 405

Part V: Sharing Your Elements Creations on Paper and Online . . . 421
Chapter 16: Saving Your Elements Images 423
Chapter 17: Printing Your Artwork and Photographs 441
Chapter 18: Turning Images into Web-Safe Graphics 473

Appendix A: Keyboard Shortcuts to Speed Your Elements Activity . . . 489
Appendix B: Finding Photoshop Elements Tools on the Web . . . 493
Appendix C: Restoring and Preserving Your Original Images. 505

Index 527

Contents

Preface ix

Acknowledgments xiii

Part I: Photoshop Elements 2 Defined   1

Chapter 1: All About Photoshop Elements 2 3

Understanding What Elements Does 3
    What Can You Do with Elements? 3
    What Can't You Do with Elements? 11
Do You Need Photoshop Instead? 13

Chapter 2: Getting to Know Photoshop Elements 17

Understanding the Photoshop Elements Workspace 17
    Identifying Workspace Elements 18
    Sizing the Workspace 23
Finding the Right View for Specific Images and Tasks 25
    Using the View Menu's Options 28
    Displaying the Ruler 29
    Using the Grid 30
Using the Elements Toolbox 32
    Working with Tools 32
    Repositioning the Toolbox 32
    Using Keyboard Shortcuts 34
    Working with Tool Alternates 34
Customizing Tools through the Options Bars 35
    Understanding Common Options 35
    Using the More Options Button 37
Viewing and Working with the Docking Well and Palettes 44
    Displaying and Moving Palettes 51
    Reattaching Palettes to the Well 52
    Rearranging Palette Tabs in the Well 52
Getting Help, Hints, and Working with Recipes 53

Chapter 3: Making Photoshop Elements Your Own **57**

Customizing Photoshop Elements 57

Establishing General Preferences 58

    Choosing a Color Picker 59

    Establishing Common Keyboard Shortcuts 60

    Setting Up General Options 61

Controlling Save Settings 62

Choosing Cursor and Display Options 64

How Will Transparency Look? 67

Selecting Measurement Tools 68

    Choosing Your Rulers and Type Units 69

    Setting Column Size 69

    Establishing a Default Resolution for New Documents 69

Establishing Grid Settings 70

Setting Up Plug-Ins and Scratch Disks 71

Establishing Memory and Image Cache Settings 73

Part II: Repairing, Restoring, and Retouching Photographs   **75**

Chapter 4: Opening, Scanning, and Capturing Photos **77**

Opening an Existing Image 77

Creating New Images by Scanning Printed Art 81

    Making Sure Your Scanner Is Set Up Properly 82

    Using the Import Command to Capture Images 84

Specialized Scanning 90

    Scanning in Color and Black and White 90

    Scanning Damaged or Low-quality Images 92

Capturing a Photo with a Digital Camera 93

Performing a Basic Save 93

    Saving an Image for the First Time 93

    Saving New Versions of an Existing Image 95

Chapter 5: Selecting and Masking Content for Editing **97**

Mastering Elements' Selection Tools 97

Selecting Geometric Shapes 99

Selecting Free-Form Areas 101

    Closing Your Free-form Selections 102

    Adding to, Subtracting from, and Combining Selections 104

Painting a Selection 107

Selecting by Sampling 109

Modifying Selections 111

Creating Layers from Selections 113

Cutting, Copying, and Deleting Selections 115
    Sharing and Moving Selections Between Images 115
    Getting Rid of Selected Content 117
Masking Areas of an Image. 118
    Creating a Mask 118
    Saving a Mask Selection 120

Chapter 6: Photographic Housekeeping 123

Enhancing the Quality of Photographs 123
    Adjusting Sharpness and Blur 123
    Using Filters to Enhance Detail 128
Repairing the Signs of Wear, Tear, and Age 136
    Getting Rid of Scratches, Scuffs, and Tears 136
Replacing and Editing Content 150
    Selecting, Moving, and Removing Content 152
    Covering Up Unwanted Content and Filling In Holes 154
    Creating a Patterned Background with the Pattern Stamp 155
Eliminating Red Eye Automatically 158
Manual Options for Red Eye Removal 161

Chapter 7: Mastering Color and Light 165

Selecting Foreground and Background Colors 167
    Restoring Default Colors 167
    Swapping Foreground and Background Colors 168
    Sampling Colors from Existing Content 169
Applying Special Color and Light Effects 171
    Making Color Corrections 171
    Using the Color Variations Window 178
    Correcting Light Levels 180
    Using Auto Color Correction 183
    Working with Brightness and Contrast 183
    Using the Auto Contrast Command 186
    Using the Levels Command 187
Making Overall Adjustments Automatically 189
    Working with Quick Fix 189
    Using Auto Levels 190
Using Adjustment Layers to Improve an Image 190
Working with Modes 191
Using Special Color Effects 196
    Equalizing an Image 197
    Working with Gradient Maps 197
    Inverting Colors 200
    Using the Posterize command 200
    Setting Thresholds 201

Chapter 8: Changing Image Size **203**

Resizing Your Image 203
Adjusting Pixel Dimensions and Depth 204
Changing the Image Print Size 205
Changing the Canvas Size 206
Increasing or Decreasing Canvas Size 206
Cropping Away Unwanted Edges 208
Cropping with the Crop tool 209
Cropping Manually 212
Transforming Your Image and Layers 213
Rotating Layer Content 214
Resizing Your Layers 216
Skewing Image Content 218
Distorting the Image 219
Changing Image Perspective 220

Part III: Creating Your Own Works of Art   **223**

Chapter 9: Drawing and Painting with Elements **225**

Working with the Paintbrush 225
Selecting the Brush Size and Preset Options 226
Working with Brush Modes 229
Setting Brush Opacity 232
Working in Airbrush Mode 234
Accessing More Options for Your Brush 236
Designing Custom Brushes 237
Painting Tips 240
Using the Impressionist Brush 242
Drawing with the Pencil Tool 245
Choosing a Pencil Preset and Size 245
Using Auto Erase 247
Working with the Erasers 248
Using the Standard Eraser 249
Working with the Background Eraser Tool 250
Erasing Specific Colors with the Magic Eraser 253

Chapter 10: Using Layers to Control Image Content **255**

Mastering the Layers Palette 255
Creating a New Layer 256
Creating a New, Blank Layer 257
Creating a Layer from Existing Content 258
Creating a Type or Shape Layer 260
Hiding and Displaying Layers 261

Duplicating a Layer 263
Changing Layer Properties 265
Rearranging Layers 266
Deleting a Layer 267
Moving Layers between Files 268
Linking and Merging Layers 269
    Linking and Unlinking Layers 269
    Merging and Flattening Layers 270

Chapter 11: Using the Shape Tools **273**

Using the Shape Tool 273
    Drawing Simple Geometric Shapes 274
    Drawing Polygons 277
    Drawing Custom Shapes 279
    Drawing Lines 280
Working with Shape Layers 281
Creating Shapes with the Selection Tools 284
Manipulating Shapes 286
    Transforming Shapes 287
    Moving Shapes 289

Chapter 12: Applying Fills and Styles **291**

Filling Selections and Layers with the Paint Bucket 291
    Applying a Pattern Fill 293
    Creating Your Own Patterns 296
Working with Gradient Fills 298
    Choosing Gradient Colors 300
    Selecting a Gradient Preset 300
    Applying Directional and Shape Gradients 301
    Using the Gradient Editor 302
Applying Layer Styles 305
    Customizing Layer Styles 306
    Removing Layer Styles 307

Chapter 13: Using Filters and Special Effects **309**

Viewing Your Filter and Effect Choices 309
    Displaying Filters and Effects by Category 311
    Viewing Filters and Effects as a List 311
Working with Filters and Effects 313
    Applying Filters that Mimic Artistic Media 315
    Blurring and Sharpening Effects 335
    Working with Filters that Distort Image Content 341
    Applying Noise Filters 350
    Applying the Pixelate Filters 353
    Using the Render Filters 357

Using the Stylize Filters 361
Working with Texture Filters 367
Using Video and Other Filters 371
Applying Special Visual Effects 375
Applying Effects 378
Creating Specialized Frames 381

Part IV: Working with Type   383

Chapter 14: Adding Text to Images 385

Creating a Type Layer 385
Activating the Correct Type Tool 387
Typing Your Text 388
Choosing the Right Font, Size, and Color 391
Selecting and Reformatting Text on the Type Layer 392
Warping Text 394
Changing Text Orientation 400
Editing Paragraph Content 401
Checking Your Text for Spelling Errors 402

Chapter 15: Applying Type Styles and Effects 405

Working with Layer Styles 405
Navigating the Layer Styles Palette 407
Applying a Layer Style 408
Working with Text Effects 412
Displaying Text Effects Thumbnails 416
Applying a Text Effect 417
Tweaking Text Effects 418
Removing Text Effects 419

Part V: Sharing Your Elements Creations on Paper and Online   421

Chapter 16: Saving Your Elements Images 423

Saving Your Photoshop Elements Files 423
Resaving and Creating Multiple Image Versions 428
Saving Your Image as a PDF 431
Creating a PDF Slideshow 433
Attaching an Image to an E-Mail Message 438

Chapter 17: Printing Your Artwork and Photographs **441**

    Applying Your Artwork to Paper 441
    Choosing the Right Printer 445
        Understanding the Inkjet Printer 446
        Looking Inside a Laser Printer 446
        Working with Dye-Sublimation Printers 446
    Printing Your Image 446
        Previewing Your Printout 447
        Working with Page Setup 455
        Setting the Print Quality 457
    Printing the Image 458
    Choosing a Print Layout 459
        Printing a Contact Sheet 460
        Using Picture Package 464
    Printing a Panoramic Picture with Photomerge 468

Chapter 18: Turning Images into Web-Safe Graphics **473**

    Understanding the Web Optimization Process 473
    GIF? JPEG? PNG? Choosing the Right Web Graphic Format 473
        Graphic Interchange Format 473
        JPEG File Interchange Format (JPEG) 474
        Portable Network Graphics (PNG) 475
    Using the Save for Web Command 476
    Optimizing Images into GIF and PNG-8 Formats 478
        Optimization Presets 479
        Custom GIF and PNG-8 Optimization Settings 480
    Optimizing Images into JPEG and PNG-24 Formats 485
        Optimization Presets 485
        Custom JPEG and PNG-24 Optimization Settings 486
    Resizing Images 487
    Creating Animated GIF Images 487

Appendix A: Keyboard Shortcuts to Speed
              Your Elements Activity **489**

Appendix B: Finding Photoshop Elements Tools on the Web **493**

Appendix C: Restoring and Preserving Your Original Images **505**

Index 527

Photoshop Elements 2 Defined

Chapter 1
All About Photoshop
Elements 2

Chapter 2
Getting to Know
Photoshop Elements

Chapter 3
Making Elements
Your Own

All About Photoshop Elements 2

✦ ✦ ✦ ✦

In This Chapter

Identifying Elements' strengths

Deciding if Elements can do what you need to do

Choosing between Photoshop and Photoshop Elements

✦ ✦ ✦ ✦

Photoshop Elements' most important role is bringing the power of the world's most deservedly popular photo retouching program (Photoshop) within the budgetary reach of most of the world's computer owners. This means that everyone, not just photographers, Web designers, and graphic designers can afford the software (Elements is normally available for under $100), and can take advantage of its many features.

Understanding What Elements Does

Unlike the "lite" versions of other applications, Elements provides most of Photoshop's key features, most in the same form and with the same options that you find supporting them in Photoshop. Some features are "missing," but you have workarounds for most of them, enabling you to achieve similar results without the exact tools as they appear in Photoshop. Elements also has a few tools and features that Photoshop *doesn't* have, and that the Adobe designers will hopefully make part of Photoshop in its next release — a paintbrush-like selection tool is my personal favorite from the Elements toolbox.

What Can You Do with Elements?

The list of functions you *can't* do with Photoshop Elements would be a much shorter list, and you can find that in the next section of this chapter. For now, the list of functions you can do, along with visual examples of those things, follows:

✦ **Scan photographs.** With a scanner attached to your computer, you can take printed photos (or any other artwork for that matter), and scan them directly into Elements. You can do this simply to be able to print copies of a photo on photo-quality paper, or so that you can resize, crop, or retouch the scanned image.

✦ **Restore damaged photos.** Think that precious and only-remaining photo of your great grandmother is damaged beyond repair? Think again. Elements toolbox contains tools that allow you to recreate lost portions of the image, bring details out the darkness, and restore depth and detail that's been lost to sunlight, dryness, mildew, and rough handling. Figures 1-1 and 1-2 are before and after versions of the same photo — in the first figure, you see a photo that looks ready for disposal. In the second figure, that same photo is ready for framing.

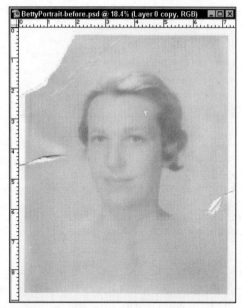

Figure 1-1: Before: A torn, scratched, and faded photo seems beyond saving.

Figure 1-2: After: A little restoration goes a long way with Photoshop Elements.

✦ **Adjust the color and contrast in photos and other images.** Whether your flash was too bright or it never went off, you can fix the contrast and light levels. You can also remove a color cast (such as a greenish or yellowish tinge that's taken over an older print or Polaroid™, and you can add or remove color that's too faded, too bright, or just wrong. Figures 1-3 and 1-4 are examples of the sort of corrections Elements can make — selected areas in each image have been fixed — the first one in terms of lighting, and the second in terms of color.

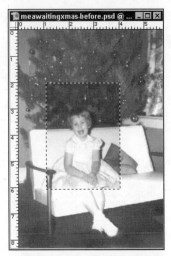

Figure 1-3: Let there be light? Well, maybe not so much.

Figure 1-4: It's not easy being green, but it is easy to get rid of unwanted green casts in a photo.

✦ **Create graphics in Web-safe formats.** Any artwork you create in Elements, be it a drawing, painting, or photo you retouched or made your own through the use of special effects, can become a graphic for the Web. Web browsers require the use of a small set of file formats, and good sense dictates that those images load quickly so as not to bore your site visitors. Elements makes it easy to pick the right format for your Web-bound graphics, and to make sure they load quickly without losing visual quality in the bargain. Figure 1-5 shows an image being optimized for the Web in Elements' powerful Save for Web dialog box.

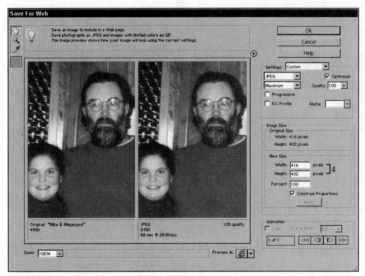

Figure 1-5: From stats on how long the image will take to load to tools for setting image quality and color, the Save for Web dialog box makes it easy to create Web-safe graphics.

✦ **Colorize black and white (grayscale) photos.** Remember how Ted Turner "colorized" all those great black and white movies? Some people loved the change, and others hated it. You can be the judge when it comes to your black and white photos, and if you want to add color — a splash in one spot or over the entire image — you can do so quite easily with Elements. Figure 1-6 shows a black and white photo that now looks like it was taken with color film — back in the 1800s!

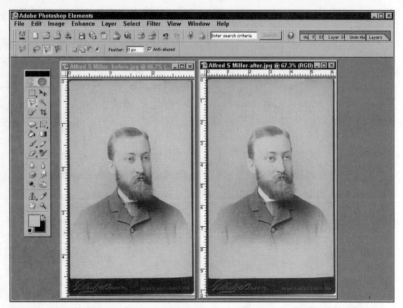

Figure 1-6: Formerly drab and lifeless, this old man is now a colorful character.

✦ **Create original artwork.** You have an idea, a vision, and you want to create a picture, a shape, a design of some sort. Can Elements help you? Yes — with paint brushes, pencils, special effects and filters, and tools for drawing shapes of just about any description. Figure 1-7 shows just such an original design, something you could make without even stretching Element's capabilities.

✦ **Design Web page backgrounds and navigational tools.** From a visually-appealing "wallpaper" for your Web page to a series of tabs or buttons, you can use Elements' tools to create a pattern, draw a button or tab, and place instructional text on anything you create. Figure 1-8 shows a row of navigational tabs that was created in Elements. After they are placed in a Web page, you can convert each tab to a *hotspot* — a hyperlinked section of the image, pointing to another page or site.

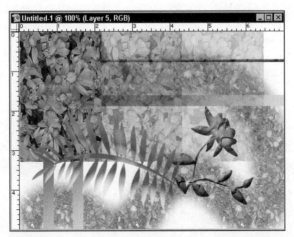

Figure 1-7: Anything you can imagine can be rendered with Elements brushes, pencils, and special effects features.

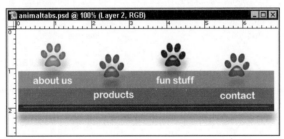

Figure 1-8: Create your own custom Web page buttons and tabs with Elements.

✦ **Add text to photos and other images.** A picture's worth a thousand words, or so the saying goes. If you need to augment the message in your photo or other picture, Elements' Type tool stands ready to give you text in any font, size, color, and style (see Figure 1-9). There are even special type effects that will make your text stand out — from making it look three-dimensional to creating the look of see-through, plastic letters. You can also cut away content from your image in the shape of text, using a type mask. The possibilities are nearly unlimited.

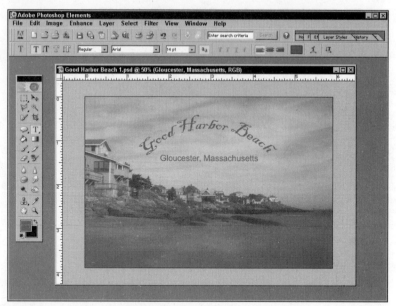

Figure 1-9: Add a caption, title, or use type as a decorative component in your image.

✦ **Apply special effects to photos and drawings.** You can turn photos into paintings or drawings, turning the pixels that make up your realistic image into brush or pencil strokes, watercolor, or the look of pastels, smudged to perfection. As shown in Figure 1-10, where part of the image is still a photo, and the other half has been turned into a painting, you can turn a relatively boring photo into an alleged work of art with a simple menu selection.

Figure 1-10: Choose just about any artist's medium for your Elements filter, converting a photo (or any drawing in any style) into something that looks painted or drawn by hand.

What Can't You Do with Elements?

Photoshop Elements is not intended for creating crisp, sharp line art. Elements is not a vector-based illustration tool, and its bitmap method of creating and retouching images does not yield the kind of sharp edges and clean lines that some artwork requires. Applications such as Adobe's Illustrator or CorelDRAW! are better tools for that kind of art, but if Elements is the only tool at your disposal, you can still create very nice line art, much like the image seen in Figure 1-11. The same image, created in Illustrator, appears in Figure 1-12. See much difference? Probably not. For some very high-quality print jobs, however, the latter image will be the more desirable, but if you're designing for the Web or for personal use (printed on an inkjet printer, for example), the former image will probably do just fine.

Figure 1-11: A logo with colored shapes and straight lines, created in Elements

Figure 1-12: The same logo, created in Illustrator

Tip

What are vector and bitmap images? *Vector* images are made up of mathematical information — the length of a line, the depth of a curve, the angle of a corner, the space between two sides of a closed shape. A *bitmap* image is made up of a group of pixels, each one a particular color, making up the appearance of text, lines, and shapes. Photos are best rendered in a bitmap-based product, such as Photoshop or Photoshop Elements, where as a piece of line or clip art would probably be better designed in a vector-based application, such as Illustrator or CorelDRAW!.

Another thing you probably don't want to do in Photoshop Elements is page layout. Tools such as QuarkXPress and PageMaker are better suited to creating a magazine or book layout, placing text and image placeholders around on the page to determine how the page components will work together visually. While you can do this in Elements, no tools specifically are designed for these jobs in the application. The aforementioned Quark and PageMaker are created specifically for page layout tasks, and have the proper tools ready and waiting.

Do You Need Photoshop Instead?

Good question. If you look at the Photoshop workspace and compare it to the Elements workspace (see Figures 1-13 and 1-14, respectively), you'll see that they're quite similar. At first glance, they're nearly identical. The choice between the products, therefore, will be determined by the details.

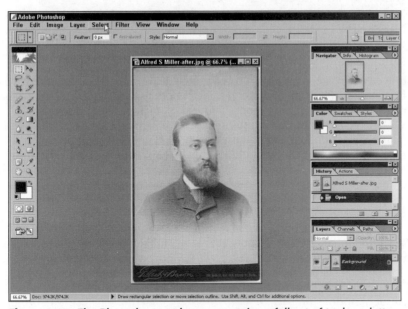

Figure 1-13: The Photoshop workspace contains a full set of tools, palettes, and an options bar for virtually every tool and feature.

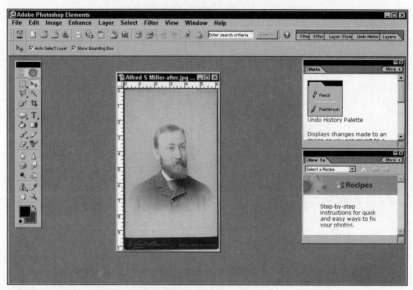

Figure 1-14: So does the Elements workspace, with a few minor exceptions

So getting down to those details, you have a few features in Photoshop that you won't find in Elements. One of the first ones people notice is the Channels palette, which is conspicuously missing from Elements' docking well. What does the Channels palette do? It allows you to break your image down into colors — red, green, and blue (for an RGB image) or cyan, magenta, yellow, and black (for a CMYK image) and to isolate the different colors in channels. After being isolated, you can tinker with a particular channel to achieve various retouching effects. Figure 1-15 shows the Channels palette in Photoshop, and a photograph with just the red channel displayed.

You have ways to work around this in Elements, however, as you'll discover. The Type formatting tools are also somewhat limited in Elements, but not in such a way that the average user would find them lacking. Some of the dialog boxes for various filters and special effects are also somewhat pared down, and someone who has become quite adept with Photoshop may feel slightly limited or controlled by the reduced set of options offered for some tools in Elements. As a user of both products, and as someone who creates mostly Web graphics and print content for informal projects, I have yet to find any of these "limitations" significant enough to say I'd only use Photoshop. In fact, due to some of the simplified tools, sometimes it's faster for me to work in Elements, despite my having spent more years as a Photoshop user.

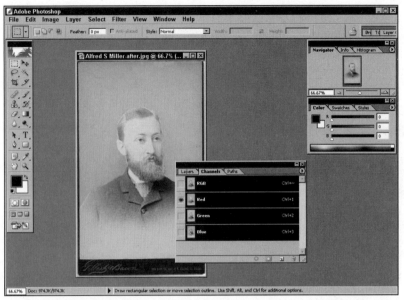

Figure 1-15: Some Photoshop users would miss the Channels palette, which is absent from Elements.

What does this all mean? If you're a professional photographer, creating work for magazines, books, or for use in television or other visual media, you may want to use Photoshop so that you have every possible tool and option for those tools at your fingertips. While even a professional photographer won't use every tool in Photoshop's arsenal every day, having them available can be reassuring. If, on the other hand, you're a Web designer, graphic artist, or a growing business or home user, Elements has everything you'd ever need to do just about anything you'd ever want to do with photographs, scanned images of any description, or original drawings. Of course, if you have several hundred dollars to spend on your photo retouching and Web graphics software, go ahead and buy Photoshop, and know that you have the world's most popular and powerful photo retouching software in your hands. If $100 or less sounds more like your ballpark, with Elements you have the right tools, the right price, and now, the right book.

✦　　✦　　✦

Getting to Know Photoshop Elements

✦ ✦ ✦ ✦

In This Chapter

Learning to navigate
in the Elements
workspace

Choosing the right
view for specific tasks

Working with menus
and tools

Mastering the use
of palettes and
options bars

Getting the help
you need

✦ ✦ ✦ ✦

The Photoshop Elements workspace is both structured and flexible, functioning well for a variety of people with a variety of working styles.

Understanding the Photoshop Elements Workspace

The workspace default configuration, as seen in Figure 2-1, can be manipulated and resized to meet your needs for different tasks and different types of images, but leaves the key features on-screen in easy reach. This flexibility makes it easier to perform common activities and commands.

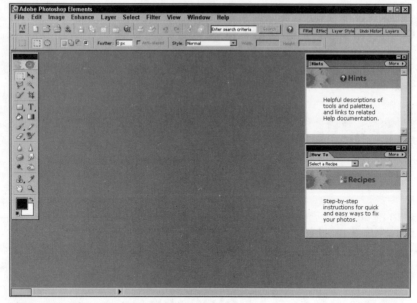

Figure 2-1: There's a lot going on, but you can move and size the tools to meet your needs and keep you organized.

Identifying Workspace Elements

The Elements workspace consists of six sections:

✦ The toolbox (see Figure 2-2) contains 24 buttons and a set of tools for choosing foreground and background colors. It also offers selection, painting, cloning, retouching, fill, zoom, and navigation tools. Buttons with a triangle in the lower-right corner contain alternate tools, such as a variety of erasers or free-form selection tools. To see the alternate tools, click and hold the button down for a second, and the other buttons appear in a small fly-out toolbar, as shown in Figure 2-3.

✦ The options bar varies for each tool (see the Brush tool's options in Figure 2-4), though some tools have very similar option bars due to tool similarities. Options come in the form of drop-down lists, check boxes, and radio buttons, each controlling how the selected tool works.

Figure 2-2: Twenty-four buttons and color control tools give you a comprehensive set of weapons for your image-editing arsenal.

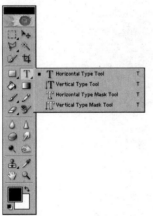

Figure 2-3: With all the alternate buttons, you have a total of 41 tools at your disposal.

Figure 2-4: Customize the way individual tools work with the options bars.

Tip

You can move the options bar down into the open area of the workspace if you drag it by its handle, located at the far left end of the bar.

✦ The menu bar isn't much of a mystery — you simply click the menu names and then make a choice from the commands that display in the menu (see Figure 2-5). The commands that will spawn a dialog box are followed by an ellipsis (...). If there is no ellipsis, the command will go to work automatically, no questions asked. If you don't like what happens when you issue a command, you can Undo anything by choosing Edit⇨Undo, or by using the Undo History palette.

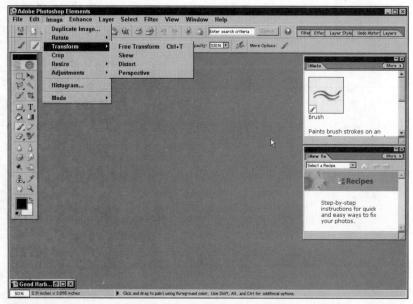

Figure 2-5: Menu commands are stored in logical groups for file management, customization, editing images, working with selections, and applying special effects.

✦ The shortcuts bar offers tools for common file-management and related tasks, such as opening files, saving files, importing, and printing, as shown in Figure 2-6. You also find quick access to two very useful features — the Quick Fix and Color Variations commands. As the name "shortcuts bar" implies, this bar is there to help you gain faster access to actions you do frequently.

Figure 2-6: You have quick access to common features on the shortcuts bar, which you find just below the menus.

✦ The palette well contains eight tabs, each representing a different palette. You can display the palettes by clicking the tabs, and then as desired, drag the palettes down onto the workspace, as shown in Figure 2-7. Just drag the palette by its tab, and release it after you free it from the palette well. After separated from the palette well, the palette has its own title bar, and you'll notice a More button — click it to see a list of commands pertaining to the palette's function and the portions of the image that the palette controls.

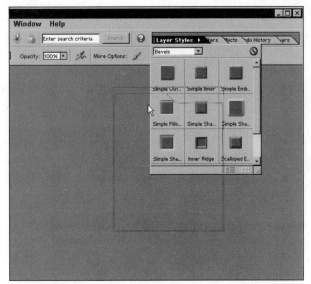

Figure 2-7: Keeping palettes within reach but out of the way, the palette well is a handy section of the workspace.

✦ The palettes themselves appear in two places in the default workspace: eight reside in the palette Docking Well, and the Hints and How To palettes reside on the open workspace area. These last two palettes aren't hidden in the palette well because the software's designers assumed you want quick access to help, and made the palettes context-sensitive — they display information on whatever tool or feature you activate at any given time, as shown in Figure 2-8.

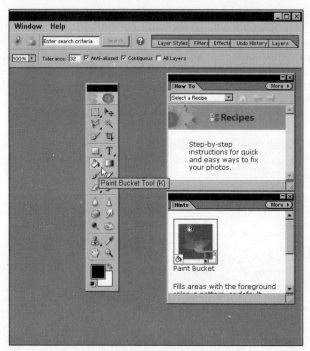

Figure 2-8: Whether docked in the well or free-floating, palettes can be moved, resized, and closed as needed.

The six workspace sections provide and support all the tools you might need to perform just about any job that you'd imagine doing in Elements — drawing, painting, erasing, adding light, adding shadows, smudging, blurring, sharpening, filling an area with color — the list goes on and on.

Tip   Photoshop Elements allows you to manipulate a very comprehensive set of Preferences, enabling you to customize your environment, tools, and display settings. Read Chapter 3 to find out how to make Elements your own.

Sizing the Workspace

You may find that you prefer working with Elements maximized, which means that it takes up the entire screen. This provides the largest possible workspace, but it also hides any other on-screen elements — Desktop icons, other open applications, and so on. If you work with Elements maximized, you'll have to use the Task Bar to access other open applications, to open applications that aren't active already, and to display the Desktop so that you can use the shortcuts that are stored there.

To maximize the Elements worksheet, double-click the title bar or click the Maximize button (see Figure 2-9) in the upper-right corner of the Elements window. If the window is already maximized, using either of these techniques restores the window to a smaller size, such as shown in Figure 2-10.

If this button is a single box, you're already maximized.

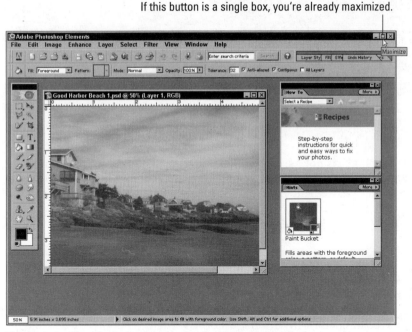

Figure 2-9: The Maximize button (to the right of the title bar)

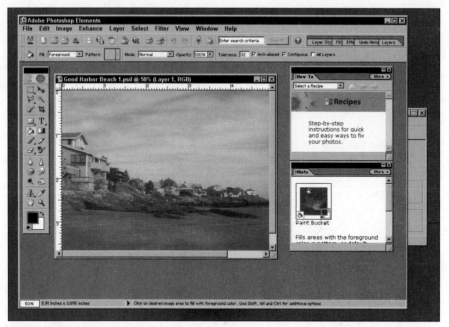

Figure 2-10: Not quite the size of the screen, you can still see the Desktop and another open window from another application.

If your workspace is not maximized, you can drag its edges to make it taller, shorter, wider, or narrower. Just point to an edge (see Figure 2-11), and when your mouse turns to a two-headed arrow, drag. Dragging inward reduces the window's size, dragging outward increases it. If you drag from a corner, you can resize both horizontally and vertically in a single drag.

After you resize, you may want to move some of your palettes, the toolbox, and the image window around to achieve the most efficient workspace arrangement. This is much like shuffling stacks of paper, your phone, your pencil cup, your calendar, and so forth, on your physical desktop. You can use the Window⇨Reset Palette Locations to bring your toolbox, Hints, and How To palettes back into their default locations, positioned relative to the window's size.

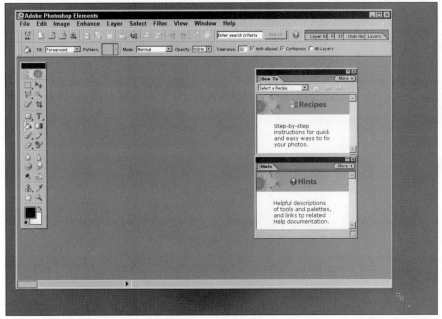

Figure 2-11: The two-headed arrow tells you you're ready to resize the workspace.

Finding the Right View for Specific Images and Tasks

Photoshop Elements gives you several views of your image—several sizes, actually, or visual distances from the image. You can zoom in so close that you can see every pixel, or out far enough to see the image in the size it will print or so that the entire image is visible on-screen, despite the fact that the image might be much larger than the viewing area within the workspace.

Most of your viewing options are found in the View menu (see Figure 2-12), but you can zoom in and out in a variety of ways, as well:

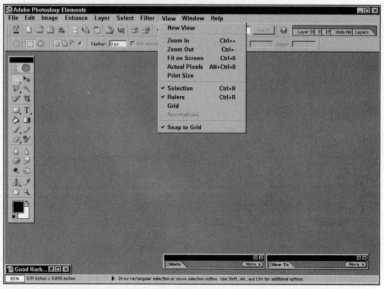

Figure 2-12: Choose from several view options for the active image.

✦ Press Ctrl + + (the plus sign) to get closer to the image, or press Ctrl + - (minus sign) to zoom out.

✦ Use the Zoom tool to click on or marquee to a particular spot. Figure 2-13 shows the image zoomed in on by clicking, and then as a marquee is drawn with the Zoom tool, a very specific area of the image is brought in very close.

✦ Use the Navigator palette (see Figure 2-14) to zoom in by dragging the slider and moving the red box (in the thumbnail, inside the palette) to focus on a particular part of the image.

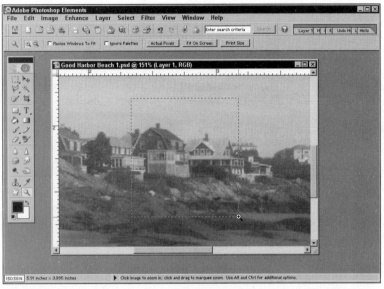

Figure 2-13: Zoom in or draw a box around the area you want to focus on.

Figure 2-14: Navigate to the spot you want to zoom in on and then set your zoom with a slider or by entering a percentage.

✦ Adjust the Zoom percentage in the lower-left corner of the workspace (see Figure 2-15). Click in the displayed percentage and type to adjust the number or double-click the number to type a replacement.

Figure 2-15: Type the zoom percentage you want to use.

✦ Double-click the Zoom tool (magnifying glass) to view your image in Actual Pixels size, and double-click the Hand tool if you want to see your image in Fit to Page view.

Using the View Menu's Options

If simply zooming doesn't do the trick — perhaps you want to see the image in a particular way — as it will appear online (Actual Pixels) or on paper (Print Size) — you can use the View menu. Each of the view options moves you closer to or farther away from the image, based on the zoom level you're currently using. For example, if you've zoomed in very close to the image to do some fine editing, choosing Print Size will probably zoom you out — and the size you see is the size that the image will print. If you're at Print Size and you choose Actual Pixels, you'll probably zoom in a bit. One of the most useful views is Fit on Screen, especially for larger images. This sizes the image window so that you can see the entire image (no scrollbars) within the workspace.

Tip

You may need to move the toolbox or any floating palettes around a bit if you choose Fit on Screen. If the image is very big, fitting it on-screen may put it behind some of your on-screen tools. If this happens, simply move the on-screen tools aside as you work on the image, moving them so that you can see whatever portion of the image you're working on, and re-positioning them as you continue to edit other areas. If this becomes a pain, just zoom out until you can see the entire image and not have any of your palettes or the toolbox overlapping the image window.

Displaying the Ruler

The Ruler helps you measure your selections, the distance between shapes and lines that you're drawing, or to crop your image to a particular size. To display the ruler, follow these steps:

STEPS: Displaying the Ruler

1. Choose View⇨Ruler.

2. Adjust the zero point (which is set to the upper left corner of the image by default) by dragging from the intersection of the horizontal and vertical rulers (see Figure 2-16) and moving your mouse onto the image at the point where the two rulers' zero points should intersect.

Figure 2-16: Reset your zero points to help you measure your image or a portion thereof.

3. Choose the units that your ruler displays — inches, pixels, picas, and so on — from the Preferences dialog box. Choose Edit⇨Preferences and choose Units & Rulers from the submenu. In the resulting dialog box (see Figure 2-17), establish your ruler options.

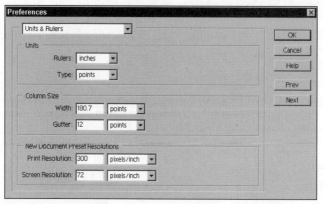

Figure 2-17: Work in inches for print work, or pixels for images bound for the Web.

If you no longer want to see the Ruler at any point, simply reselect View⇨Ruler. The ruler disappears until you reissue the command if and when you want to see the ruler again.

Using the Grid

The grid, shown turned on in Figure 2-18, is a series of evenly spaced coordinates connected by lines within the image window. To display the grid, choose View⇨Grid.

The grid helps you position elements of your image, especially if you have the View menu setting Snap to Grid turned on (it's on by default). With Snap to Grid turned on, you can easily position a series of shapes, all aligned manually *and* neatly, as shown in Figure 2-19.

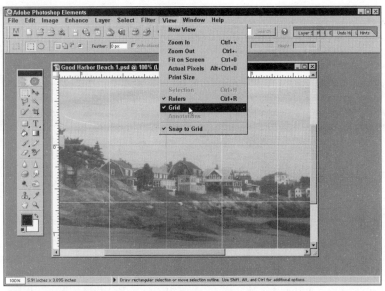

Figure 2-18: All these boxes and their intersections help you move and draw image content.

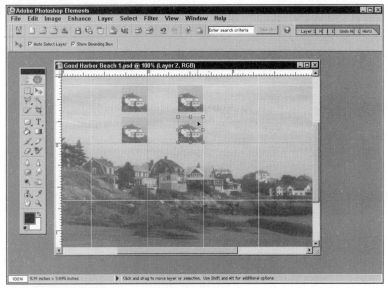

Figure 2-19: Drag your content and feel your mouse adhering to the grid if you have Snap to Grid turned on.

If for any reason you don't want to see the grid, simply reselect View➪Grid, and the check mark that indicates that the feature is turned on will disappear (you'll see it's gone if you redisplay the View menu). Snap to Grid can remain turned on, as it won't work if the grid is not displayed.

Note　　You can set the size of the grid using the Preferences dialog box. Choose Edit➪Preferences and choose Grid from the submenu. Within the resulting dialog box, you can set the color of the grid, and how many subdivisions appear within it. Of course the more subdivisions you have, the more precisely you can use the grid to position shapes and lines within the image. Find out more about all the Elements Preferences in Chapter 3.

Using the Elements Toolbox

The Elements toolbox works like any toolbar you've worked with in other applications — you just click on a tool to activate it, and then you can use it — to draw, retouch, erase, fill, type, adjust your zoom, or choose a color to paint with. Of course toolbars in other applications have their own set of tools that do other application-specific things — but the way you use the toolbar is simple and familiar.

Working with Tools

As soon as a tool becomes active, its optional settings appear on the appropriately named options bar. You can find the name of any tool by pointing to it with your mouse, which displays a tool tip, which includes the tool's name and the keyboard shortcut for that tool, as shown in Figure 2-20.

Repositioning the Toolbox

The toolbox can be moved on the workspace, enabling you to move it to the right, left, up or down, whatever's conducive to working in a particular image. If you're zoomed in on an area and will be using several different tools to do your editing/retouching, you can drag the toolbox right next to the area you're working on. Figure 2-21 shows the toolbox in a spot that obscures part of the image, but makes accessing tools that the user needs much easier.

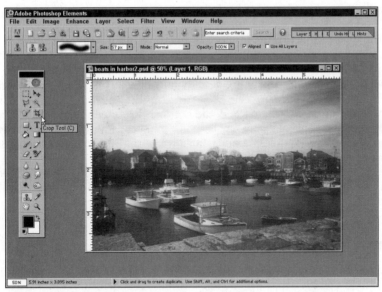

Figure 2-20: Tool tips help you remember tool names and the quick keyboard method of invoking them.

Figure 2-21: Move the toolbox to wherever it will do you the most good.

Using Keyboard Shortcuts

Of course the keyboard shortcuts for each of the tools make switching between tools quick and easy, and many of them are pneumonic, meaning that the keyboard shortcut letter is somehow related to the tool's name, such as B or Brush or I to activate the Eye Dropper. Well, that's more of a rhyming device, but you get the idea!

Note   You may not be able to commit all of the shortcuts to memory — especially those that aren't pneumonic or in any way linked to the tool name. Q for Sponge is not terribly memorable, for example, and neither is J for the Burn tool. You can refer to the handy Appendix A for a table of all the toolbox shortcuts, as well as keyboard shortcuts for menu commands and shortcuts bar tools. Viewing them all in one place can make it easier to memorize them, rather than trying to learn them by displaying the tool tips when you select the tools in the toolbox.

Working with Tool Alternates

To add a little complexity to the toolbox, however, several of the toolbox buttons house more than one tool. How do you know when a tool has alternates? When you see a small triangle in the lower right-hand corner of a button. For example, the Lasso tool button is also the home of the Polygonal Lasso and the Magnetic Lasso, as shown in Figure 2-22. All three of the tools that use that button have the same keyboard shortcut (L), which makes it easier to remember (L for any Lasso tool), but you do need your mouse to switch between versions of the Lasso tool.

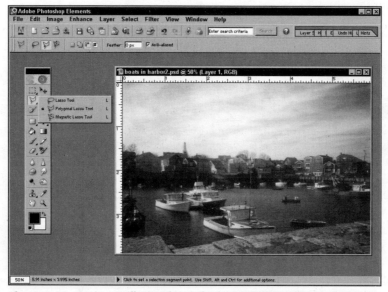

Figure 2-22: See a small triangle on the button? That tells you there are more buttons from which to choose.

After you switch to one of the alternate tools on a single button, that button version remains active—meaning that if you press the keyboard shortcut, you'll get the tool that's displayed. To switch to another version of that tool, use your mouse and click and hold the button down for a second, to display a fly-out menu of all the available tools for the button.

Tip   Want to check out the Adobe Web site? Click the sunflower at the top of the tool-box, and you're taken to Adobe online. Find out more about other online sources of Elements information in Appendix B.

Customizing Tools through the Options Bars

For each tool in the toolbox, you'll see a different set of options appear on the options bar as soon as a tool is activated. These options enable you to control how the tool works, making it do more or less, have more dramatic effects or more subtle effects, or simply change the size and shape of the tool in question. There are defaults for each setting, and the first time you use Elements, you'll see them in place. After you tweak the settings, however, you'll see your last settings in place when you click on a tool.

Of course for many situations, the defaults are just fine, if only because the most common uses for tools, in the most common scenarios, were used to determine what the defaults would be. If you need to make adjustments, however, all you have to do is click the drop-down lists to make new choices, click different check boxes or radio buttons, or enter new values into the various fields found in the options bars. The options vary by tool, as stated earlier, although you may find that some tools' options are very similar. Figure 2-23 shows the Rectangular Marquee tool's options bar, which is virtually identical to the Elliptical Marquee tool's options— for obvious reasons.

Understanding Common Options

Just as some of the selection tools have very similar options, so do any of the tools that work by painting or drawing—whether you're applying color with the tool or removing it. All of the brush-based tools, including the Brush, Smudge, Dodge, Burn, Sharpen, and Blur tools, have nearly identical options. You need to select brush size, and choose a brush shape/style (from a drop-down list of presets, as shown in Figure 2-24).

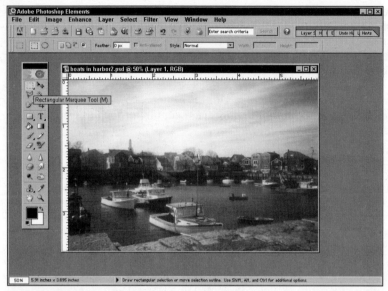

Figure 2-23: Tools that do the same sort of functions have similar options to choose from.

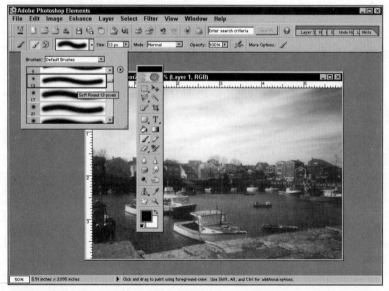

Figure 2-24: The options will be pretty consistent across a wide variety of brush-based tools.

Brush-based tools that change the nature of your image content (think of the Smudge, Blur, Sharpen, and Erase tools) require a Strength setting that allows you to determine how much of an effect the tool will have. Figure 2-25 shows the Strength setting for the Blur tool, which enables you to have very subtle blurring (with a low setting) or very dramatic blurring (with a high setting).

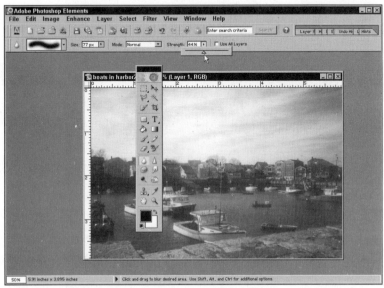

Figure 2-25: A lot of blur or just a little? Set the Strength for tools that change the nature of your image.

Using the More Options Button

On several of the tools' options bars, you'll see a More Options button, followed by a picture of the active button (see the Brush tool's More Options button in Figure 2-26). When you click this More Options button, a set of options for tweaking the way the tool works appears. These are options that go way beyond the basic options found in the options bar — for example, the Brush tool's added options include settings that make the brush strokes more strident (the Hardness setting), shaky (through the Jitter and Scatter options) and even Fade along the strokes themselves.

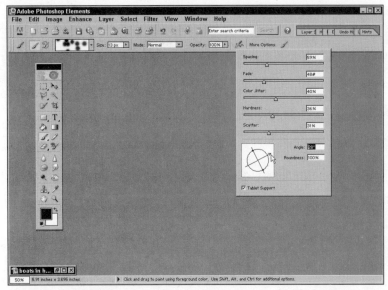

Figure 2-26: When they say "More Options," they're not kidding. You have significant options available for added customization of just about any tool.

You can make your changes to the settings that appear for the tool in question, and then go about using the tool. The first time you access the tool's More Options, you see the default settings — after that, you see the last settings used.

Tip
To return a tool to its defaults, right-click the tool's picture on the far left end of the options bar (while the tool is active). A shortcut menu consisting of two commands — Reset Tool and Reset All Tools — appears. Choose Reset Tool, and the defaults are restored.

Using Tool Presets

Just as the name implies, a "preset" is a pre-existing setting. Photoshop Elements has several of them, and you can apply them to most tools to create a quick change to the way the tool does whatever it's supposed to do. For example, if you change the Paint Bucket tool from Foreground (solid color) to Pattern Mode, you'll have a series of Pattern presets to choose from (see Figure 2-27).

To access more presets for any tool, click the arrow to the right of the preset button (see Figure 2-28) and choose from additional groups of presets. You can add them to the group you're already displaying in the drop-down list or change to a new group altogether.

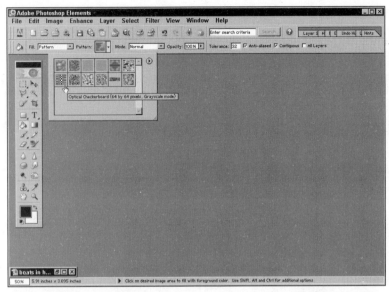

Figure 2-27: Preset patterns give you a nice selection of choices for the Paint Bucket's fill capabilities.

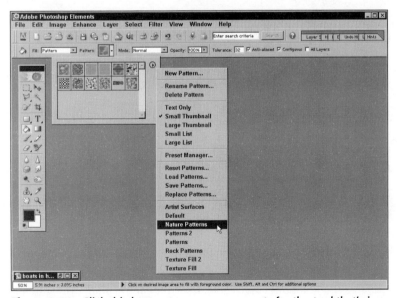

Figure 2-28: Click this button to see more presets for the tool that's in use.

Creating Custom Brush and Fill Presets

One of the really great aspects of Photoshop Elements is that despite the lower price, which one would assume might leave you with a very limited set of tools, you can customize the sizable group of tools you're given and even build new presets for brushes and fills. This means that all the preset options that you learned how to access in the previous section are just the tip of the iceberg — you can customize existing and create new presets for any brush or fill and save them for future use by making adjustments to the content, size, shape, style, and opacity settings for an existing preset and saving it with a new name. To do this, follow these steps:

STEPS: Creating a Brush Preset

1. Choose an existing brush preset to serve as the basis for your new brush.

2. Click the More Options button to display additional options for changing the brush shape, spacing, jitter, and other stroke attributes, as shown in Figure 2-29.

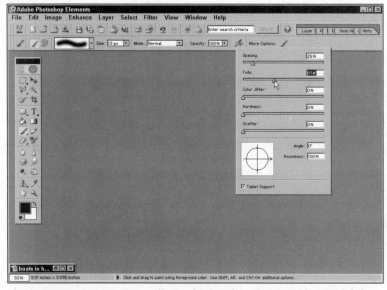

Figure 2-29: More Options offers additional settings you can tweak for your brush presets.

3. Make any desired adjustments. By clicking back on the main options bar, the More Options palette disappears.

4. As needed, pick a Mode for the brush.

5. Click the Brush Presets drop-down list and click the Options Menu button, shown in use in Figure 2-30.

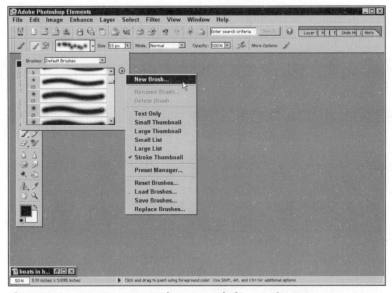

Figure 2-30: More presets and commands for creating new ones appear.

6. Select New Brush from the options menu.

7. In the resulting Brush Name dialog box (see Figure 2-31), type a name for your new brush. Choose a name that clearly describes the effect that the brush will impose, the texture it mimics, or the scenarios in which you might use the new brush. This makes it easier to choose it when you need it in the future.

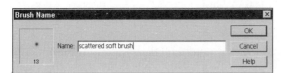

Figure 2-31: Name your new brush preset.

Note   Another way to create a brush preset! Select a portion of your image and choose Define Brush from the Edit menu. Name the brush, and you have a custom brush that appears in the current set of presets.

You can also create presets for pattern fills and gradients, adding to the fairly comprehensive set of fill presets that come with the software. Figure 2-32 shows the list of pattern-preset groups from which you can choose.

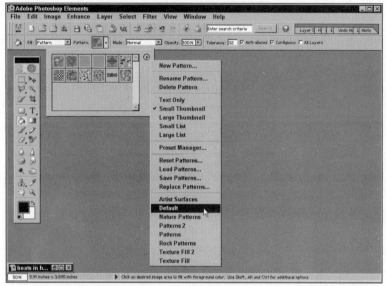

Figure 2-32: Natural and artistic pattern fills are readily available, but you may want your own fill to meet specific needs.

You can build a new fill preset based on an existing preset, or you can create one totally from scratch. The process is quite similar to creating brush presets — choose an existing pattern or gradient, make changes to its settings using the options bar for the fill tool (Paint Bucket or Gradient) and then click the Options Menu button to access the drop-down list of presets. Click New Pattern or New Gradient (from the resulting menu) and then name your preset. You find it there waiting for you the next time you want to apply your custom fill.

Another way to create a pattern or gradient fill is to base it on something you've drawn, or on a pattern that exists in a photo. Figure 2-33 shows just such a pattern, selected within a picture.

Figure 2-33: Create a new pattern based on existing content within your image.

To create a pattern from a selection within your image, follow these steps:

STEPS: Creating a Pattern from Existing Image Content

1. Select a rectangular area within your image, using the Rectangular Marquee.

2. Choose Edit⇨Define Pattern. The Pattern Name dialog box opens, as shown in Figure 2-34.

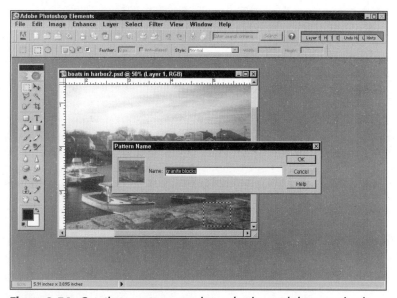

Figure 2-34: Creating a pattern requires selecting and then naming it.

3. Type a name for your pattern, choosing one that describes the nature of the pattern, or perhaps its intended use.

4. Click OK to create the pattern.

After the new pattern is created, it joins the default set of presets in the Pattern drop-down list on the Paint Bucket's options bar. Point to the pattern to see the name you gave it, as shown in Figure 2-35.

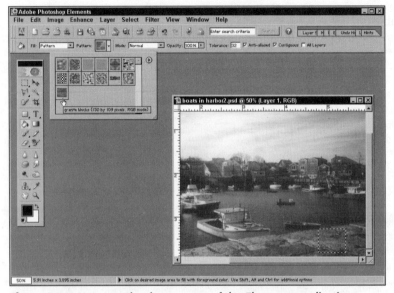

Figure 2-35: Your creation is now part of the Elements application.

Viewing and Working with the Docking Well and Palettes

Palettes are like dialog boxes, in that they elicit information, provide information, and give you the ability to adjust how something works or what will happen when a tool or command is used. For example, the Layers palette lists all the layers in your image, and allows you to name them, rearrange them, delete them, connect them to other layers, and determine which of the layers can be seen and which are hidden.

Other palettes contain options and commands, and these features vary by the palette and according to what's selected in the image at the time. There are eight palettes stored in the palette well, and then there are two more palettes that offer help and instructions. The Hints and How-To palettes aren't stored in the palette well, if only because the software's designers wanted to keep help open and available at all times. You can close them, however, if you find you rarely use them or they're in the way during your current session.

To get acquainted with the palettes, look at them one at a time:

✦ **Filters.** This palette contains special effects for images and/or type, falling into several categories, the same as those seen in the Filter menu. You can also create frames, to give your images an artistic border. To apply a filter, just double-click it (see Figure 2-36) or drag it onto the image. At that point, the filter is automatically applied to a selection within your image (if there is one) or without anything selected, to the entire image. If any options must be confirmed or changed before applying the filter, a dialog box will appear, as shown in Figure 2-37.

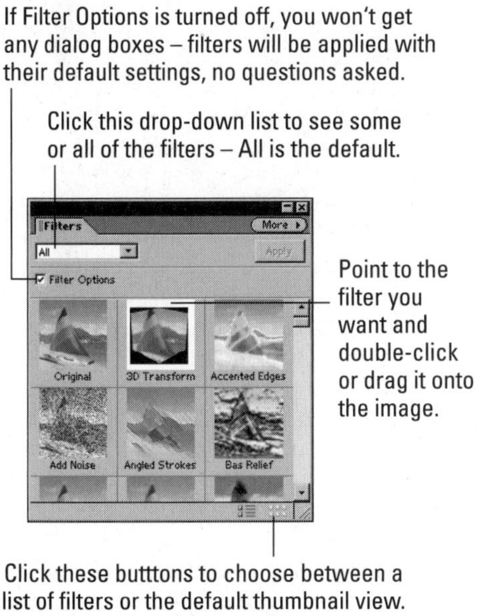
If Filter Options is turned off, you won't get any dialog boxes – filters will be applied with their default settings, no questions asked.
Click this drop-down list to see some or all of the filters – All is the default.
Filters
More
All
Apply
Filter Options
Original
3D Transform
Accented Edges
Add Noise
Angled Strokes
Bas Relief
Point to the filter you want and double-click or drag it onto the image.
Click these butttons to choose between a list of filters or the default thumbnail view.

Figure 2-36: Scroll through the thumbnails that show you what the filters do to a sample sailboat.

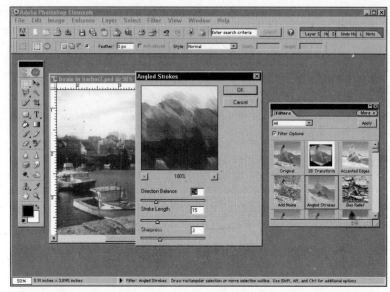

Figure 2-37: Filter options allow you to control the degree to which the filter affects your image, and/or the exact nature of the filter itself.

✦ **Effects.** You might not be able to spot the difference between Filters and Effects — on first glance, they look like identical palettes, as shown in Figure 2-38. However, the Effects palette offers a list of special effects with illustrative names, such as Brushed Aluminum, Cold Lava, and Lizard Skin, and are generally applied without your having to use a dialog box to control the results. Like Filters, the effects can be applied to the image or to type. You can view the Effects as a list or as thumbnails (see the buttons on the bottom of the palette), and you can choose which Effects to see, using the drop-down list at the top of the palette. All is the default, but you can choose to see Frames, Image Effects, Text Effects, or simple Textures. Textures make interesting fills, rather than being effects to apply to existing image content.

Tip   You might find that Textures make better fills than effects—you'd be better off applying something such as Asphalt or Bricks to a shape or layer than to existing photo or drawing content, where effects that enhance or distort content would be more appropriate.

Figure 2-38: Think you're seeing the Filters palette again? Not quite. Effects are quick and easy, applied without your needing to adjust any settings.

✦ **Layer Styles.** There are 14 Layer Styles categories (see them by clicking the drop-down list at the top of the palette), and each one has several options within it. Everything from drop shadows to glass and metal fills, the Layer Styles palette is one of the most useful palettes you'll work with, especially when you're creating original artwork for print or the Web. Figure 2-39 shows the list of categories, and you can see a portion of the Bevels category's options displayed in the palette. To apply a Layer Style, simply click it — to "unapply" it, click the Clear Style button.

The Clear Style button

Figure 2-39: From simple shadows to cool glass buttons, you can use Layer Styles to create subtle touches or dramatic fills.

✦ **Swatches.** The Swatches palette is similar to the display of paint chips at the home store. Because it's on a computer, however, you can change swatch sets, and you have seven different sets, in addition to the default set, from which to choose. You can use the displayed Swatches to choose a new Foreground color (click once on a swatch with the mouse) or Background color (press the Ctrl key and click on a swatch), or if you want to check the name of a color before applying it, simply point to a swatch and wait for the tool tip to appear, as shown in Figure 2-40.

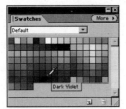

Figure 2-40: Pick a color, any color — on the Swatches palette.

Tip

Three different sets of swatches are for use on the Web, and several sets to meet your needs for printing your image through a PC or Mac. Click the drop-down list along the top of the palette (below its title bar) to see your choices.

✦ **Undo History.** Want to go back in time? If you just smacked your forehead and wished you hadn't done whatever you just did, the Undo History palette could be for you. While you can choose Edit⇨Undo (or press Ctrl + Z), you can undo a series of steps, in reverse chronological order, by clicking on the last step that you want to remain in place. When you do so, everything done since that point in time will be undone. You can undo your undo, by clicking on steps that you've undone (now appearing as dimmed and italicized). As you can see in Figure 2-41, the step you selected is highlighted in blue, reminding you how far back in time you've gone.

Figure 2-41: Time travel for graphic artists is found in the Undo History palette.

Tip Want to go back to the beginning of time? Click the Open state, the first one in the palette. To eliminate the possibility of any undone step being redone, click the More button or right-click on any step listed in the palette and choose Clear Undo History.

✦ **Navigator.** This palette's name gives you a good idea how it can be used. You can use this palette to adjust your magnification (Zoom) with the slider or by clicking the buttons (that look like little mountains on either side of the slider), and you can enter a Zoom percentage. You can also pan around with the red box and choose which part of the image is visible within the image window. Of course, only if the image is larger than the current size of the image window can you use the red box (see Figure 2-42, where the red box appears as a gray box on the image thumbnail) to pan to an area of the image.

Figure 2-42: Navigate to the portion of your image you want to focus on and then zoom in on it.

✦ **Info.** If you need to know the levels of particular colors in a particular pixel in your image, click on that pixel with the Eyedropper tool, and the RGB levels for that color appear in the Info palette, as shown in Figure 2-43. If you also need to select a rectangular area that's an exact measurement, watch the W (width) and H (height) fields as you drag your mouse to draw the shape. Release the mouse when the right dimensions are seen in the W and H fields. You can also use the X (horizontal position) and Y (vertical position) coordinates to let you know where on the image your mouse is when you point, select, paint, or use any tool that requires that you move your mouse over the image.

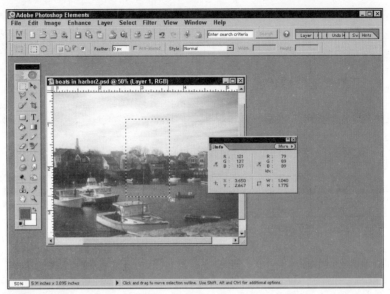

Figure 2-43: Statistics on size, position, and color can be found in the Info palette.

Tip   Click the More button in the Info palette and choose Palette Options. The resulting dialog box allows you to select a first color readout mode, a second color readout mode, and the measurement type (inches, pixels, and so forth) for measuring width and height and displaying mouse coordinates.

✦ **Layers.** Last, but certainly not least, the Layers palette may be the one you use the most as you develop original artwork and retouch existing photos. When you scan a photo or take a picture with a digital camera and import it into Photoshop Elements, you get a single layer called the Background. As you add content — type, shapes, lines, pasted content from within the same image or another image — new layers are or can be created, as shown in Figure 2-44. For example, pasted content is automatically on a new layer, but when you draw lines, shapes or use the Paint Brush or Pencil to add content, it's your choice as to whether or not the new content is on a new layer. Keeping changes on separate layers really helps you do more with Elements tools, as you'll learn in subsequent chapters in this book. Through the Layers palette, you can name layers, delete them, duplicate them, rearrange them, and choose whether or not they're hidden in the image window.

Figure 2-44: Keep everything on a separate layer for greater control over content, effects, and retouching tools.

Displaying and Moving Palettes

Opening palettes in the palette well couldn't be easier — simply click the palette's tab, as shown in Figure 2-45, where the Layer Styles palette has been opened. After it's opened, you can then drag the palette onto the workspace to make it a floating palette, or you can leave it attached to the palette well. If you opt to leave it attached to the palette well, it will close when you're not using it. If you make it a floating palette, it will remain open until you close it, and if you want to keep it open, you may have to move it around (drag it by its title bar) to keep it both close by for use and out of the way as you work. To close an open, floating palette, click the Close (X) button in the upper-right corner of the palette.

Figure 2-45: Click the palette's tab and see the palette's tools displayed.

Reattaching Palettes to the Well

Returning a floating palette to the palette well can be done in one of two ways — by setting it to go back there when you close it, or by dragging it by its tab (not its title bar, which you use to move it) back to the palette well and letting it reattach by proximity to the well.

To set a palette to automatically return to the well when closed, click the More button and choose Close Palette to Palette Well (see Figure 2-46). This doesn't close the palette at that moment, but tells Elements that when you do close it, you want it to go back to the well. To close the palette and see it return to the well, click the Close (X) button in the upper-right corner of the palette and watch it snap back into position.

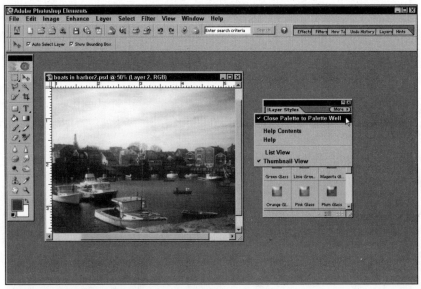

Figure 2-46: Get back where you belong! Make this choice from the More menu, and your palettes go back to the well when you close them.

Rearranging Palette Tabs in the Well

You can change the order of the palette tabs in the palette well by right-clicking them and choosing from the rearrangement commands — Move to the Left, Move to the Right, Move to the End, and Move to the Beginning (see Figure 2-47). This makes it possible to put them in an order that makes sense to you, based on use or alphabetical order if you think that will help you find them faster when you need them.

Figure 2-47: Make a move and rearrange your palette tabs as you see fit.

Note Palette well too crowded? If you have all the palettes stored there, it can be so crowded that you can't see all the tabs. To make more room, float some of the palettes you rarely use or know you won't use in this current session, and turn off the Close to Palette Well command. Then close the floating, unwanted palettes — they'll disappear from the workspace, and you'll have only the tabs you want (and now will be able to see them in their entirety) in the palette well. Don't worry that the closed palettes can't be retrieved — just select them from the Window menu when you're ready to use them again, and you can reattach them to the palette well as desired, or leave them floating.

Getting Help, Hints, and Working with Recipes

Photoshop Elements is not only more reasonably priced than Photoshop, it's intended to be more reasonably designed — simpler to use, more direct and intuitive in terms of the way tools are used and customized, and most of all, in terms of the accessibility of help. To help Elements achieve this goal of accessibility and quick help, the software designers put two palettes right on the workspace, open and floating, ready to be used:

✦ **Hints** (see Figure 2-48), where context sensitive help appears when you activate a tool, make a menu choice, or begin performing a task.

Figure 2-48: Just clicked on the Marquee selection tool? The Hints palette automatically displays tips for using that tool effectively.

✦ **How To** (see Figure 2-49), provides Recipes for a variety of tasks, from simple formatting of text to the more complex retouching of photos. Click the drop-down list that says Select a Recipe and choose from the list of 10 commands, the last one taking you to the Adobe Web site where new recipes can be downloaded.

Figure 2-49: Cook up a solution to just about any Elements activity with the How To palette's recipes.

Of course, even with these two handy on-screen tools, you also have access to Photoshop Elements' Help files. Just click the Help menu, and choose Photoshop Elements Help, or press F1. In the resulting Help window (see Figure 2-50), you can choose from a variety of ways to search the help database, including combing a contents view, or searching by keyword.

Click Search to enter keywords.

Look through main topics in the Content view of help.

Use the Index for an alphabetical search.

The Help articles that appear contain links to related topics.

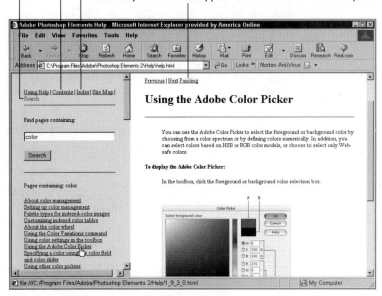

Figure 2-50: Elements' Help files appear in a separate window and give you several different ways to find the help you need.

✦   ✦   ✦

Making Photoshop Elements Your Own

✦   ✦   ✦   ✦

In This Chapter

Setting general preferences for the way Elements works

Customizing the way Elements looks and behaves

Making Elements more efficient

✦   ✦   ✦   ✦

L ike Photoshop, Photoshop Elements gives its users credit for having preferences and knowing what they like and need from a software application. Elements offers users a comprehensive set of Preferences that enable you to customize how the application works, how images and layers appear, how tools are displayed and accessed, how you interact with them, and how your files are saved.

Customizing Photoshop Elements

To access these tools for customizing Elements, simply choose Edit⇨Preferences and then make a selection from the submenu shown in Figure 3-1.

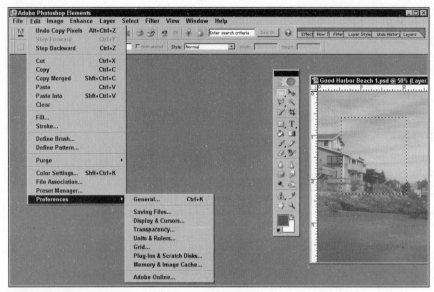

Figure 3-1: Access any one of Elements' eight different Preferences categories through the Edit⇨Preferences submenu.

Tip   You don't need to keep going back to the menu and selecting different Preferences submenu commands in order to change different aspects of how Elements works. Instead, you can choose any one of the submenu commands and then use the Previous and Next commands within the Preferences dialog box to move through the General, Saving Files, Display & Cursors, Transparency, Units & Rulers, Grid, Plug-Ins & Scratch Disks, and Memory & Image Cache versions of the Preferences dialog box.

Establishing General Preferences

The General version of the Preferences dialog box is shown in Figure 3-2. Through this dialog box, you can decide how key areas of Elements will operate — everything from how colors are selected to whether or not Elements remembers how you had your palettes arranged when you exit the application.

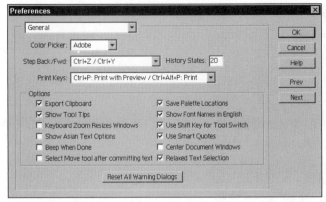

Figure 3-2: Customize several key elements of Elements' General operations.

Choosing a Color Picker

Through the General Preferences dialog box, you can choose which Color Picker you want to use — Photoshop Element's own (Adobe), shown in Figure 3-3, or a Windows version (shown in Figure 3-4), much like the one you see if you're setting colors for text and shapes in Microsoft Word or Excel, or if you're setting Display preferences in Windows.

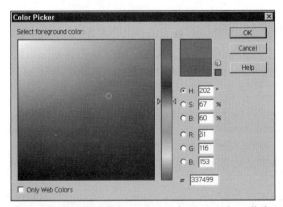

Figure 3-3: The Adobe color picker provides all the tools you need for selecting and adjusting colors.

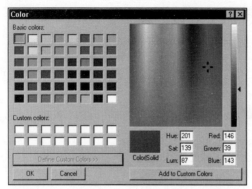

Figure 3-4: Feel more comfy with the picker you've been using through your Operating System (Windows or Macintosh)? You can stick with it if you like.

Tip   If you're using a Mac, the word "Mac" will appear in the drop-down list instead of "Windows." You might want to go with the operating system's color picker, if only because you're used to working with it. It offers much of the same functionality, but remember that Elements' Help files will assume you've gone with the Adobe picker, and any references to color will refer to that. The Adobe picker does have some benefits, too — there are more tools available inside it for making fine adjustments to color and working with a decidedly Web-safe palette.

Establishing Common Keyboard Shortcuts

Also through the General preferences dialog box, you can also decide which keys will take you backward a step (Undo) and forward a step. The default setting is Ctrl + Z (backward) and Ctrl + Y (forward), but you can select alternatives if you want. It's unlikely that you'll want to deviate from Ctrl + Z for Undo, given that that shortcut is probably the most commonly used shortcut in all software written for both Mac and Windows. Ctrl + Z is as common as Ctrl + S for save, which is another shortcut you should get to know and never change or assign to some other activity.

Tip   Want more than 20 History states (levels of Undo)? Enter a new number in that field. I have mine set to 100, which seems to suffice for even the most complex editing jobs. You may want to enter a higher number, and you're upper limit is 1000.

Your printing shortcuts can also be established here (see Figure 3-5, where the alternative is displayed in the drop-down list). You might want to switch and not use the defaults (Ctrl + P = Print with Preview, and Ctrl + Alt + P = Print) if the simpler and more ubiquitous shortcut (Ctrl + P) seems more familiar to you (it's the Print command in virtually all software applications) and if you don't care about seeing a Preview before printing your images. If you find that most of your print jobs benefit from doing a Preview first, however, leave the default in place so that you can get that important preview with the simpler shortcut.

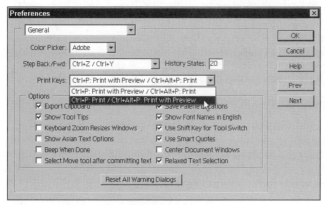

Figure 3-5: Pick a Print shortcut.

Note   Using a Mac? Replace Ctrl with Command and Alt with Option in any of the shortcuts discussed in this and the rest of the book's chapters.

Setting Up General Options

The Options list includes 12 different check boxes, some that are on by default, and others off by default. Most of their descriptions are fairly self-evident — "Beep When Done," for example, doesn't require too much explanation. On the other hand, "Select Move Tool After Committing Text" might not be completely clear to you. The list, and their uses:

✦ **Export Clipboard.** This means that whatever you've copied or cut to the clipboard will be available to other applications.

✦ **Show Tool Tips.** If you like being able to point to a tool in the toolbox or on the options bars and seeing the name and any keyboard shortcut for the tool, leave this one turned on.

✦ **Keyboard Zoom Resizes Windows.** When you zoom in or out on an image, if this option is on, the image window will resize appropriately.

✦ **Show Asian Text Options.** If you're working in an Asian country or your images will contain text that will use Asian characters, you might want to turn this option on.

✦ **Beep When Done.** For any command that takes a few seconds to complete — saving files, applying filters, resizing large images, for example — this can be a nice feature to turn on so that you're prompted when the procedure is complete.

✦ **Select Move Tool After Committing Text.** Typically, after you type a word or sentence and click away (to "commit" to the text), the Type tool stays active. If you turn this option on, however, the Move tool is automatically activated when you click away from freshly typed or edited text. This can be convenient if you typically transform or resize your text after committing to it, or if you move your text a lot.

✦ **Save Palette Locations.** If you've painstakingly arranged your palettes and toolbox so that they're right where you like them to be, leave this option on. The next time you open Elements, the workspace arrangement you made in your last session will appear, preserved for your new session.

✦ **Show Font Names in English.** If you speak English, leave this one on.

✦ **Use Shift Key for Tool Switch.** This one is on by default, and means that you can press the Shift key to switch between grouped tools — without having to press (or remember) the tools' single-letter keyboard shortcuts. Each press of the Shift key cycles you through the tools, and you can simply stop pressing Shift when you're on the tool you want to use.

✦ **Use Smart Quotes.** The quotes that curve in toward the text with which they're associated are called "smart quotes." The other kind of quotes look like the foot and inch marks (also know as "straight quotes") and are fine for numbers (where you're referring to measurements), but look very unprofessional when used in text. Leave this option on, but know that you can turn it off if you want to type measurements, after which you can turn it back on.

✦ **Center Document Windows.** This option is off by default, and pertains solely to the behavior of newly opened images. Instead of stacking them off-center (so you can see each image window's title bar), this option stacks them in a centered stack, the top-most window centered on top of the one below it, and so forth, down the stack. I'm not sure why this is even an option, other than that it makes a large group of simultaneously-opened windows take up less room on the workspace.

✦ **Relaxed Text Selection.** This option is on by default and allows you to click near text to select it.

Tip   Want a quick explanation of an option? Double-click the option text and a tool tip appears with a concise description of the option's purpose.

Controlling Save Settings

This version of the Preferences dialog box offers tools for controlling when images are saved, how they're saved (are the previews saved, how will file extensions be displayed), and how many files are displayed in the File⇨Open Recent submenu. As shown in Figure 3-6, you can use the two drop-down lists to choose Image Previews settings and a default File Extension, and work with the two File Compatibility options to determine how TIFF files are saved and whether or not compatibility with PSD is maintained when saving in PSD format. This figure shows the Saving Files dialog box with all of its settings in their default state.

When it comes to TIFF files, it's a good idea to leave this option (Ask Before Saving Layered TIFF Files) on, because leaving layers in a TIFF file can really increase file size. It can also preserve valuable edit-ability, so that you have to weigh your options and needs before making a choice here.

The option pertaining to PSD compatibility (Always Maximize Compatibility for Photoshop (PSD) Files) pertains to files that may be edited later in Photoshop, rather than in Elements. You want to leave this on if there's any chance that you or someone else who has Photoshop may open your Elements-created image in Photoshop.

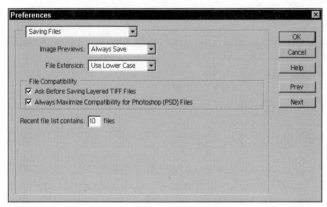

Figure 3-6: Customize how Elements saves your image files and how many recently used files appear in the File menu for quick access.

In addition, you can use the Recent File List Contains option to establish how many recently used files will appear in the File➪Open Recent submenu (see Figure 3-7). The default there is 10, but you can increase it to 30.

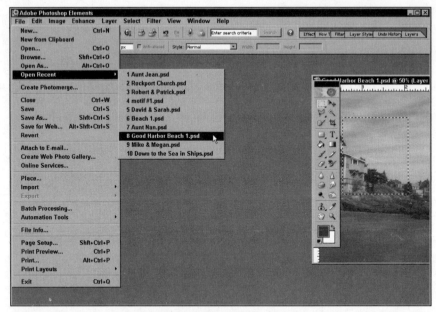

Figure 3-7: If you work with a lot of different files, a large number in the Recent File List Contains option will give you quick access to many of them.

Choosing Cursor and Display Options

The Display & Cursors preferences (see Figure 3-8) allow you to decide how your mouse pointer (or other pen pointer, if you're using one) looks while certain tools are in use. It also allows you to turn on Pixel Doubling, which makes images display faster by doubling the size of the displayed pixels and cutting the image resolution in half (only in terms of display—the file's pixel depth is not changed).

When it comes to your Painting Cursors, your choices are:

- ✦ **Standard**, which makes the pointer look like the tool that's in use (see Figure 3-9).
- ✦ **Precise**, which makes all cursors look like a crosshair, as shown in Figure 3-10.
- ✦ **Brush size**, which displays a circle that's the same pixel width as the size brush you've selected. Figure 3-11 shows a very large brush size.

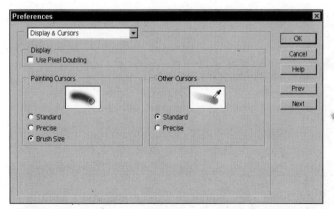

Figure 3-8: Customize your Elements' display and cursor settings.

Figure 3-9: Are you erasing or drawing? Your cursor can make that clear by appearing in the form of the active tool.

Figure 3-10: A crosshair can help you be more precise in your painting, drawing, and erasing.

Figure 3-11: No surprises in terms of the area affected by a painting tool when your cursor shows the brush size.

Tip Precise can be a good choice if you want to see the center of your brush (useful for choosing a starting position when painting, drawing, or erasing), which is represented by the center of the crosshair. This option is also good if you're sampling individual pixels or doing extremely precise editing, zoomed in to see individual pixels.

How Will Transparency Look?

When you created your image, you chose whether or not to make the background transparent (see the New dialog box in Figure 3-12). If you chose to make it transparent, the options in this version of the Preferences dialog box allow you to control how that transparency is displayed (see Figure 3-13). By default, the checkerboard display is set to Medium size, and the blocks in the checkerboard are a Light gray.

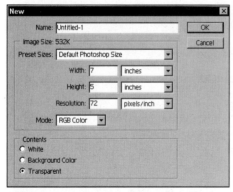

Figure 3-12: Choosing Transparent in the New dialog box means your Background will appear as a checkerboard, indicating transparency.

To change either the light or dark squares' colors in the checkerboard, click the Grid Colors drop-down list to choose from a series of presets, or click the colored boxes under the Grid Colors field — the Color Picker opens, and you can create your own entirely customized checkerboard, or if you pick the same color for both boxes, your transparency can look like a solid color.

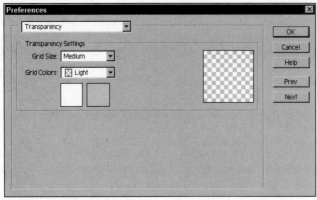

Figure 3-13: Customize how that transparency is displayed by choosing a checkerboard size and color.

Selecting Measurement Tools

If you'll be displaying rulers, this set of preferences is very handy — it enables you to choose what measurement method is used in those rulers. It also allows you to choose a default print and screen resolution for new images, so that you don't have to adjust these settings every time you start a new image, as shown in Figure 3-14.

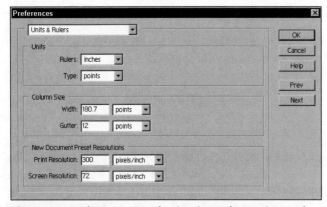

Figure 3-14: Choose your rulers' Units, Column Size, and New image resolution presets in the Units & Rulers Preferences dialog box.

Choosing Your Rulers and Type Units

You choose your ruler and type units simply by clicking the Rulers and Type drop-down lists — you can choose from pixels, inches, centimeters (cm), millimeters (mm), points, picas, or percent for the Rulers, and pixels, points, or millimeters (mm) for Type. The eventual use of your image can have a lot to do with your choices for the Rulers setting — if your image is Web-bound, you might want to use pixels, so that you're measuring your image the same way it will be viewed in a WYSIWYG Web design program (such as Macromedia's Dreamweaver or Microsoft's FrontPage), or the way it will be described in the HTML code that generates your Web pages. If your image is going to be viewed in print, pick the measurement units that you're most comfortable with, or that your commercial printer (if you're taking it out to be printed) prefers.

Setting Column Size

What is "Column Size?" It's a setting that you'll only need to tinker with if your image will be used in a layout program, such as QuarkXPress or PageMaker. These layout applications break pages into one or more columns, and by setting a column size for your image (or changing it from the default 180.7 points (Width) and 12 points (Gutter), you can make the image more compatible with the column setup that will be in use later in one of the layout programs.

Establishing a Default Resolution for New Documents

If you choose to set new defaults for new documents' resolution (for print and on-screen display), do so with care. Just like any other default you might set in any application (such as the default font and text size in your word processor), you want to know that the setting you're putting in place is going to be appropriate for the vast majority of situations.

Tip   When it comes to resolution, bigger is better. When setting up a new image and establishing its resolution, starting with a high number (at least 300 for print resolution), gives you more information to deal with in editing the image. You can always reduce resolution later, either manually, through the Image⇨Resize⇨ Image Size command, or through the Save for Web command (found in the File menu) that automatically reduces resolution as part of the optimization process, preparing images for use on the Web.

Establishing Grid Settings

The grid, hidden in your image by default, helps you position and resize image components on individual layers within your image. Of course, anything you want to move independently (such as a drawn shape, or a pasted element in a composite photo) must be on its own layer in order for you to move or resize it on its own. Figure 3-15 shows the grid displayed (by choosing View➪Grid), and a shape (on a Shape Layer) in transit.

In the Grid Preferences dialog box (see Figure 3-16) you can set the Color, Style, frequency with Gridline every, and number of Subdivisions in the grid. You might, for example, want to change the grid to a particular color so that it stands out on your image (don't worry, it doesn't print). If your image is very light — perhaps a picture of a bright, light blue sky with lots of white clouds — a dark-colored grid might be a good idea.

Figure 3-15: Display the grid so that you can see how it looks by default — then make changes as needed through Preferences.

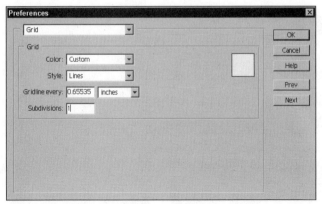

Figure 3-16: Choose your grid color, style, frequency, and the number of subdivisions in the grid.

Tip

The more gridlines you have, the more precisely you can position and resize items in your image. Tinker with the Gridline every and Subdivisions settings until you have the grid you need for the current image. You can reset the grid for other images later.

Setting Up Plug-Ins and Scratch Disks

In this version of the Preferences dialog box (see Figure 3-17), you can decide whether or not to include plug-ins from an additional directory, or to stick with the designated folder, `C:\Program Files\Adobe\Photoshop Elements\Plug-Ins`. You can also set up to four scratch disks, to help Photoshop Elements work within what might be not enough memory.

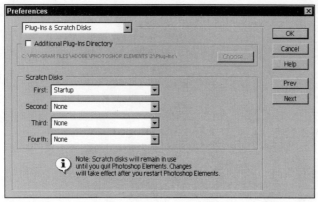

Figure 3-17: Though not likely to be of interest to a basic or new user, the ability to add new functionality through plug-ins and allocate space for more memory can be very useful.

Before you can make your choices in this dialog box (and you may never need to), it's good to know what's going on. Some definitions:

✦ Plug-ins are additions to the program that you can obtain from Adobe and third-party developers. These additions allow you to do more things, achieve greater functionality. You can find more about them at the Adobe Web site (www.adobe.com), or by doing an online search for "Photoshop Elements Plug-Ins." More plug-ins are designed for Photoshop than for Elements, but many of those designed for Photoshop do work in the Elements application, too.

✦ Scratch Disks are areas within your local hard drive, designated as free space to serve as virtual memory when you run out of RAM. This can become necessary when you have several images open at the same time, are working with images scanned or created at very high resolutions, or if you're applying several special effects to an already large image (large in terms of file size, not necessarily print dimensions). Through the dialog box, you can choose where the Scratch Disks (up to four of them) can be stored and accessed.

Tip   If you have more than one Scratch Disk designated (such as a D: drive, which is recommended, if you have two drives), you should run your operating system's defragmentation program frequently to make sure that the scratch disk areas remain contiguous.

Establishing Memory and Image Cache Settings

Yet another set of Preferences that require a little explanation before you can fully understand how and why you'd make changes to the options shown in Figure 3-18 — take a look at the Memory & Image Cache Preferences dialog box.

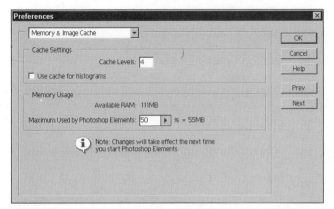

Figure 3-18: Speed up the display of images by adjusting your memory and image cache settings.

First, let me define *image cache*. Image cache is the section of hard drive space used for virtual memory. This will sound familiar from our discussion of Scratch Disks in the previous section of this chapter. By allocating space for the image cache, you speed up the on-screen redraw of images — after moving, resizing, or applying effects to an image — any action that makes the image recompose on-screen. The more levels you establish, the faster the redraws — so the default of four can be increased as needed. Make your changes, click OK, and then restart Elements to test the effects of your adjustments.

Second, the Memory Usage portion of the dialog box pertains to the amount of memory allocated for Photoshop Elements' use. The default is based on the amount of memory on your computer and can be increased as needed. Of course, you don't want to allocate all of your RAM to Elements, as chances are you'll want to run other applications at the same time, and your system does have its own utilities and so forth that are always running, and it needs memory for them, too. You'll see the Available RAM display in the dialog box — base your adjustments to the Maximum Used setting accordingly.

As stated, you won't see the results of your changes to image cache and memory usage until you restart Elements. You don't need to restart your computer, but you will need to exit Elements (File⇨Exit or press Alt + F4) and then restart the application.

✦   ✦   ✦

Repairing, Restoring, and Retouching Photographs

Chapter 4
Opening, Scanning, and Capturing Photos

Chapter 5
Selecting and Masking Content for Editing

Chapter 6
Photographic Housekeeping

Chapter 7
Mastering Color and Light

Chapter 8
Changing Image Size

Opening, Scanning, and Capturing Photos

✦   ✦   ✦   ✦

In This Chapter

Opening existing and recently used images

Scanning color images

Scanning black and white images

Capturing and opening digital camera images

Saving scanned and digitally captured images

✦   ✦   ✦   ✦

If you're not starting a new image from within a blank, new document window, you're opening an existing image. If that image was used recently, you may find it in the File menu, under File⇨Open Recent.

Opening an Existing Image

If you haven't used the image in a while, you'll have to navigate to it using the Open command, also found in the File menu. There are a few keyboard shortcuts to keep in mind, if you like to avoid using menus:

✦ Ctrl + O opens the Open dialog box, through which you can look for and open the file you wan to work on. Figure 4-1 shows the dialog box and a file about to be double-clicked and opened in an image window.

Figure 4-1: Fairly familiar to even novice computer users, the Open dialog box contains tools for specifying the type of file you're looking for, and for choosing from just about any location on your computer to look in.

✦ Shift + Ctrl + O opens the File Browser (this also opens if you choose File➪ Browse), which gives you the same end result as the Open dialog box (an open file), but gives you more tools to find the image for which you're looking. As shown in Figure 4-2, you get a Windows Explorer-like directory tree pane, a folder list, and a preview window to show you all the images in whatever folder you click on in the tree view, or that you select from the drop-down list at the top of the File Browser window. You can also access the More menu (see Figure 4-3), for file management and display tools, such as New Folder, and options for changing the size of the thumbnails that preview the images.

Figure 4-2: The File Browser window provides some convenient tools for searching for an image to open and edit.

Figure 4-3: Want more options? Click the More button.

✦ Alt + Ctrl + O issues the File⇨Open As command and opens the Open As dialog box. You use this command to take a file that's currently in one format and open it in another format. The Open As dialog box is virtually identical to the Open dialog box, except for the ability to use the Open As drop-down list to choose the format for the file to be opened.

There is no keyboard shortcut for File⇨Open Recent, but the convenience of having all your recently used files right there in a handy submenu (see Figure 4-4) makes up for the fact that you have to use the menu to get to it.

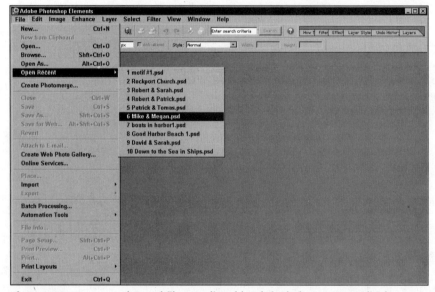

Figure 4-4: Ten recently used files are listed by default, but you can display up to 30 of them.

Tip

As discussed in Chapter 3, you can adjust the length of your list of recently used files by choosing Edit⇨Preferences and using the General options to increase or decrease the list.

After a file is open, you can do anything you want to it — you can print it, you can edit it, you can add to it, you can crop it, you can save it in a new format (see the last section of this chapter for saving instructions) and you can optimize it for use on the Web. While the image is open (see Figure 4-5), it resides in an image window, which you can move, resize, and close as needed.

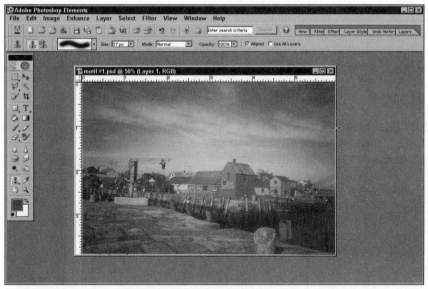

Figure 4-5: Resize the image window from any edge (look for the 2-headed arrow) or grab it by its title bar and move it anywhere in the workspace.

 Changing the view of your image (using the View menu to choose from Fit on Screen, Actual Pixels, or Print Size) you'll find that by default, the image window size changes, too.

 Want to keep an image open but out of sight? Minimize it by clicking the Minimize (dash) button in the upper-right of the image window. When you want to deal with the image again, double-click its title bar (it'll be squirreled away in the lower-left corner of your workspace), or click its Restore button to bring the image window back to the size it was before you last minimized it.

Creating New Images by Scanning Printed Art

Scanners have really had a dramatic impact on what you can do with an application such as Photoshop Elements. Prior to the inexpensive and wide availability of scanners, only photographers and high-end graphic artists could take printed photos, line drawings, or other original artwork and bring it into their computer for editing, resizing, and printing.

Now that scanners are within just about anyone's budget (many available for under $150), if you want to scan that old photo of your grandmother or the photo from your vacation, there's nothing stopping you. Of course, with a scanner, you aren't restricted to scanning printed photos and other artwork—you can scan your hand (to show far-away relatives your engagement ring), you can scan a piece of china, the lid of a painted box, your birth certificate, anything that can be placed on the scanner's glass "plate." You can also scan text, utilizing your scanner's OCR (*optical character recognition*) capabilities, but that creates a text file for use in a word processor.

The items you scan in order to create pictures—anything from a photo to a piece of jewelry you want to get appraised—will become graphic files rather than text files. Assuming you scan them into Photoshop Elements, you can save the scanned image in Elements' native format (PSD) or choose from any number of file formats, choosing the one that suits your intended purpose for the image.

So—text becomes a document, and photos, artwork, and objects become graphics. Is there anything else you need to know in order to perform a successful scan? Absolutely:

✦ You can scan part of an image, creating a new image by scanning only the area that interests you or that will fit within the intended display/print space.

✦ You can scan in color or in black and white, regardless of the nature of the original—in fact, it's often best to scan black and white photos as color, to give you more image data to work with in editing the image later. You fine more about scanning in both color and black and white later in this chapter.

✦ You can scan your images at a high resolution, creating a very large file, but preserving as much detail as possible, or you can scan at a low resolution, creating a smaller file with less fine detail. If you intend to do a lot of image editing—fixing blemishes, replacing missing content, rearranging things in the image—it's best to scan at a high resolution so that you have more information (pixels, colors) to work with in your editing. You can always reduce image resolution later if you need a small file size.

That's just the beginning, however. There's more to learn, from how to install a scanner on your computer (so that Elements "sees" it and lets you scan directly into Elements) to how to scan any sort of photo for the best editing, restoration, printing, and display options.

Making Sure Your Scanner Is Set Up Properly

Obviously, you need a scanner attached to your computer or attached to the network to which your computer is attached, in order to scan images. If you've just purchased a scanner, all you have to do is plug it in, restart Windows (or your Mac), and allow the operating system to detect the new device when it reboots. After the new device is detected, the operating system will prompt you for the CD that came with the scanner, and as soon as you insert the CD into your CD drive and click OK (or do whatever the operating system prompts you to do as soon as the CD's available), the installation process will begin.

The installation process informs not only the operating system, but all of your applications that a scanner is now available. This means that if you start Elements after installing your scanner, the File➪Import submenu includes the name of your scanner, as shown in Figure 4-6. Of course your scanner may be made by a different manufacturer than mine is, but you'll see your manufacturer's name and the scanner's model number in the submenu, and this then allows you to scan directly into Elements.

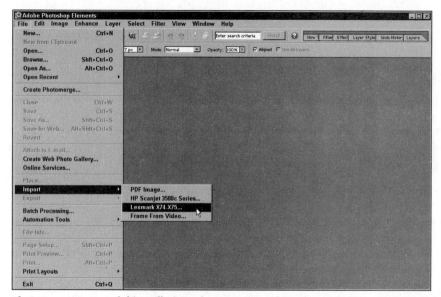

Figure 4-6: Successful installation of your scanner lets Elements know that you have a scanner and allows you to use it to send scanned images directly to Elements.

Tip   It's a worst-case, last resort option, but if you can't seem to make Photoshop Elements see your new scanner (and you know it's plugged in properly and you've installed its accompanying software), you might try reinstalling Photoshop Elements. Uninstall it first, which cleans out any reference to the software within your system, and then reinstall. When the installation occurs, the computer will inform Elements about the scanner, and Elements will be set up to make use of the scanner. You can see if it worked immediately by checking the File➪Import submenu.

Of course, after your scanner is set up and ready to go, you'll want to fire up your scanner's software (there should be a command for the software in your Startup menu, on the desktop, or in your program tray) and see what options you have. You'll probably have the ability to scan text, using the scanner's OCR (optical character recognition) capabilities, but those captures go to a word processor or text editor. When scanning photos or other artwork, the images are stored as graphic files, and Elements allows you to save them in a variety of formats, from Elements' native format (PSD) to a Web-safe format such as JPG. You'll know which format works best for your intended use of the image, or you can find out when it's time to save the file.

Note   Sending your artwork on disk, CD, or by e-mail to a professional printing company? Check with them first to ask what format they recommend for your final output (the type of paper, nature of display, and so forth) and which format (also known as *file type*) they prefer to work with.

Using the Import Command to Capture Images

When you're ready to scan an image, place it on the scanner's glass plate, following any symbol or picture instructions appearing along the edges of the plate, or referring to the scanner's instruction guide. If you're not sure which way to position the image so that it's "right side up," don't worry — you can always rotate the image later in Elements.

To begin the scan, simply choose File➪Import and then select your scanner from the submenu. This should start your scanner's designated software and allow you to do a few things:

✦ Preview the image to be scanned

✦ Select the portion of the image to scan, whether the whole image or just part of it

✦ Choose how the scan will capture the image — in color or black and white

Figure 4-7 shows the scanning software for one of my scanners, in this case, a Lexmark model 75 scanner. Your software may have more bells and whistles or fewer options to use — the basics will be the same, however, and you'll be able to perform the basic tasks — previewing and selecting the area to be scanned, and choosing the type of scan you want to do.

Figure 4-7: The interface design may be different for each manufacturer's scanner, but the tools and options are very similar.

Of course, you'll probably also be able to make adjustments to the image quality, right through the scanning software—making the image lighter or darker, increasing or decreasing the contrast, and so on. While this is possible, however, it's not advisable. Scan the image "as is" and make your adjustments through Elements—the tools in Elements are far more sensitive and intuitive than those that come with your scanner's software, and you'll be much happier with the results.

Tip

One of the simplest ways to assure a high quality scan is to keep the scanner's glass plate clean. Use the pre-moistened wipes that you buy for cleaning your monitor, or use a light spray of glass cleaner (spray on a rag/paper towel, not directly onto the glass) to get rid of fingerprints, smudges, dust, correction fluid (from edited documents, placed on the plate before the correction fluid dried), or any other kind of dirt that could adversely affect your scan.

Preparing with a Preview

The first step in the scanning process—after your scanning software is open, of course—is to preview the image or item you've placed on the scanner's glass plate (also known as the "bed"). This allows you to choose a portion of the image to scan, or to eliminate all the whitespace around a small photo—rather than scanning the underside of the scanner's lid. If you arranged several photos on the scanner, you can select them one at a time for scanning, previewing between each scan and selecting a different image each time. As shown in Figure 4-8, after you've done the preview, the process of selecting the area to be scanned is quite simple—it's just a matter of resizing a selection rectangle to encompass the desired section of your image.

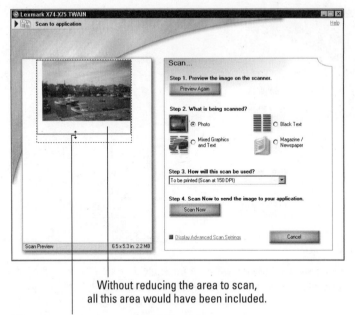

Without reducing the area to scan,
all this area would have been included.

When your mouse turns to a two-headed
arrow, drag to resize the selection box.

Figure 4-8: Preview and then select the area to scan.

Fine-Tuning the Scan

After the preview is completed and you selected the portion of your image to scan, you're ready to make some final adjustments before the actual scan occurs. First, you want to tell your scanning software what kind of scan you want to do — a color scan, or a black and white scan. I recommend color, even for black and white photos, so that you have as much color info (shades of gray, levels of black and white) as possible to work with. There's more information to come on this topic, later in the chapter.

The next thing you want to do is set the scan's resolution (Figure 4-9 shows the settings for my scanner). The resolution you choose determines how much information is gathered (in the form of image detail) when the scan is performed. A high-resolution scan (300 dpi to 9600 dpi, the top end depending on your scanner's capability) will create a large file (in terms of size in bytes), but will give you more details with which to work as you edit the image — retouching scratches and tears, blotting out blemishes, rearranging content, and so on.

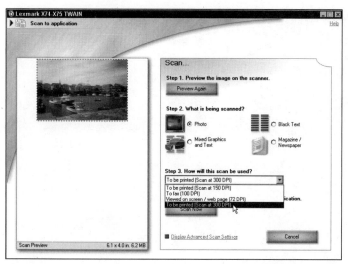

Figure 4-9: Set your scan's resolution — a low number for a quick, low-quality scan, or a higher number for a more detailed, clean scan.

I recommend at least a 300 dpi scan, even for images that will end up on the Web (where a dpi of 72 is preferable) or in a low-end printing situation, such as on a simple printed flyer. After scanning at the high resolution and editing the image, you can always reduce the resolution using Elements' image resizing tools, or if the image is Web-bound, using Elements' Save for Web dialog box. Both of these tools are covered later in this book.

As I stated earlier, your scanning software may also offer quality adjustment tools, such as those shown for my scanner in Figure 4-10. You can tinker with these if you want, but I recommend scanning on the default settings for light levels, contrast, sharpness, and so on, and then using Elements' tools to make adjustments after the image is scanned an in its own image window within the Elements workspace.

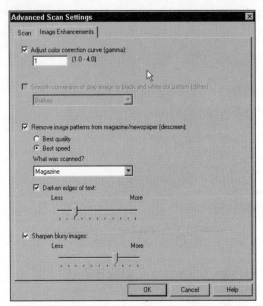

Figure 4-10: You can make your image brighter or crisper through the scanning software, but you will probably prefer Elements' tools for the same adjustments.

Tip   Another reason to let Elements be your tool for adjusting image quality is that if you make adjustments with the scanning software, you may lose valuable image content. For example, if you increase contrast, small details in the image — patterns in fabric, textured surfaces, facial details, and so forth may be lost to the increase in difference between lights and darks in the image.

Scanning the Designated Area

As soon as your settings — selected area to scan, the type of scan (color or black and white), and scan resolution are established, you can click the Scan or Scan Now button. The scanner makes one pass along the glass plate, gathering all the information about your image, based on the scan type and quality settings you put in place. After the scan is complete, the scanned portion of the image appears in a new image window, as shown in Figure 4-11.

Elements applies the name "Untitled-1" (and numbers
subsequent scans consecutively) to your scanned image.

Color photos are scanned
in RGB mode (see title bar).

Spots on the camera's lens made it to the
print, and are now part of the scan, too.

Figure 4-11: The scan is complete, and you have a new image window with
your scanned content to prove it.

Tip

A scan done at a high resolution (300 dpi or higher) will take a while to complete.
A low-resolution scan will go quickly, and if you've only ever done 72, 100, or 150
dpi scans before, you may be impatient with the scanner's performance when it's
scanning at 300, 600, 1200, or higher. Be patient, though, and don't cancel out of
the job. You'll end up with a big file (several megabytes, most probably), but you'll
be glad you have all the detail that such a high-resolution scan gives you.

As soon as the image window appears, saving the image is a good idea. Give it a
name, choose a place to store it, and then set about editing, resizing, or printing —
whatever you have in mind for the image. You should continue to save as you work,
so that you don't lose any time or risk having to repeat your efforts should you run
into any computer problems.

Specialized Scanning

Using the techniques described in the previous section, wherein you learned to initiate the scan, preview the content of the scanner's glass plate, and then select the area to be scanned, you're ready to do just about any type of scan. The only thing left is to inform your scanning software just what it's supposed to capture when it performs the scan: text, which would become a document (and not be involved with Elements at all); color, for color photos and other types of original artwork; or black and white, for line drawings, images from newspapers, old photos, or even new photos that were taken with black and white film.

Scanning in Color and Black and White

It will come as no surprise to you that scanning in color requires a color scanner. A further non-surprise will be the fact that you'd be hard-pressed to find a scanner in the stores or online that doesn't do a color scan. So, there's nothing standing in your way, and that includes cost—color scanners are quite inexpensive these days, many costing less than $150.

Of course, when scanning a color image, you're going to end up with a color image that has many of the same problems that the original had, and potentially some new problems, depending on the quality of the scanner and your scanner's settings. When it comes to problems borne out of the original, if that original was over-exposed or too dark, blurry, faded, torn, or oddly colored, those problems will follow the image from printed original to scanned electronic version. The advice given earlier to scan at a high resolution (to give you more image detail to work with in fixing problems) will help you resolve these issues after the image is scanned.

Color scanners can also be used to scan in black and white, of course, but you may not use that setting as often as you'd think. For example, black and white photos aren't really black and white—they're actually made up of many shades of gray (and lots of other colors, too), and will be seen as grayscale images after scanned into Photoshop Elements. The downside of scanning in black and white to get grayscale is that you'll have limited editing capability when trying to restore or retouch a grayscale image. You won't have as much color information built into the image pixels, and this can limit the effectiveness of some of Elements' tools.

When I scan black and white photos, I typically scan them in a color mode, using the scanning software's "best" or "high" quality, which translates to a resolution (dpi) of at least 300. This has several results, all of which are beneficial:

✦ The color information allows you to make more interesting use of Elements tools for lightening, darkening, and saturating the image.

✦ The grays are warmer, and the image has more visual depth and clarity, as shown in Figure 4-12. The image on the left was scanned in black and white, and the one on the right, the same image, was scanned in color. Even with black and white reproduction in the book, you can see the greater depth in the second image, and the greater degree of detail that's survived the scan.

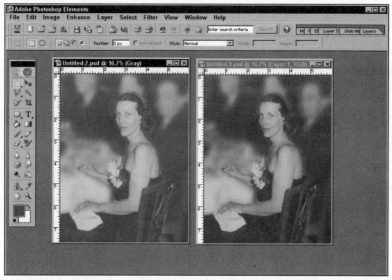

Figure 4-12: A black and white scan can give you a flat, lifeless image, and you may have trouble adding the depth and interest you want. Scanning in color gives the image more visual depth.

✦ The image is automatically set to RGB (Red, Green, and Blue) mode in Elements, which will make it easier on you if the image will ever be used on the Web.

✦ If I want to colorize the image later, applying a single-color screen or actually giving the image the "Ted Turner treatment," the image is already in RGB mode and that makes available many of the image adjustment commands and tools that would be dimmed if the image were in grayscale.

Tip

If you want to scan a drawing or a hand-written letter, scan it as you would a photo—in color if there is any color in the image, or if you want to get the deepest and most varied shades of gray in a black and white drawing. If the drawing is very simple and cartoon-like with very little shading or solid color fills, you can use the black and white mode for scanning, which will give you crisp blacks and whites.

Scanning Damaged or Low-quality Images

As I stated earlier, whatever's wrong with the original will become part of the scanned image. This is because the scanning process picks up everything—scratches, tears, scuffs, spots, and stains, just as it picks up the actual image content.

The good news is, however, that as you'll discover in Chapters 6 and 7, Elements provides significant tools for dealing with the problems your photos had to begin with, and those that are made part of the electronic image through the scanning process. You can eliminate some of the problems, however, saving yourself a lot of editing time later:

✦ If the edges of your photo are torn, cut, or ripped away completely, scan an area that includes some space all the way around the image. This technique will give you more room to work with if you want to create a new clean edge for the image or place the image in an Elements-generated frame.

✦ If there are raised scratches or tears in the image, try to press the raised edges down by rubbing over them with the back of a plastic spoon or something similarly rounded and smooth. This will eliminate some of the 3-D effects.

✦ If something's stuck to the surface of your photo, try to gently lift it off, if possible. However, if it's not going to come away without taking your photo's coating with it, don't lift it, just leave it alone and you can get rid of it later with Photoshop Element's Clone Stamp (to replace the damaged area with something from elsewhere in the image) or simply paint it out with a Brush or Pencil tool.

✦ If someone taped a torn image in the past, that tape may have turned yellow by now, or if it was clear, matte-finish tape, the matte finish may be hiding details on the image beneath it. Try to get rid of the tape if you can, but don't force it or you could damage the photo even more. You can always replace the tape-covered content, or counteract the effects of old, yellowed tape with various color adjustment tools.

Tip

Damaged photos really need to be scanned at a high resolution, no matter how low-end your eventual use for the images might be. The more resolution you grab when you scan, the more detail you have to work with in copying content from one place in the image to another (to mask a tear or to create missing content where something's been torn away completely), and the more color information you'll have to use in getting rid of discoloration or stains.

Capturing a Photo with a Digital Camera

If you've installed the software that came with your digital camera, just like a scanner, Photoshop Elements will detect the device and offer it as a choice from the File⇨Import menu. You can then plug your camera into the computer, select File⇨Import⇨Image from Digital Camera (the wording of the submenu command will vary by your camera's manufacturer and model number). After this is chosen, your digital camera's software opens, and you can browse the images stored in your camera.

You can also open your digital camera software independently, offload the images stored in the camera to your hard drive, and then open them using Photoshop Elements' File⇨Open command. You should have choices through your digital camera software for selecting a file format for the saved images, and in most cases, JPG is the default. This is based on the assumption that most digital images will end up on the Web or being shared via e-mail, and JPG is a good format for photos that have to look good but take up very little drive/disk space.

Whether you capture the image and bring it right into Elements through the Import command or open images you already offloaded from the camera, the next steps are up to you and are based on the quality of the images and what you want to do with them — if they're headed for the Web, clean them up (using tools covered in Chapters 6 and 7) and then use the File⇨Save for Web command, covered in detail in Chapter 18. If the image will be printed, again, use Elements' editing and retouching tools to make any required improvements, and then use the Print command to generate the printed copy of your image. You can find more about printing in Chapter 17, including printing on various types of paper, with various quality settings, and making the most of your printer's Properties' tools.

Performing a Basic Save

The first thing you want to do after capturing an image with your scanner or digital camera is save the image. This gets rid of any temporary, usually number-based name that the scanner or camera software will have applied to the image and allows you to apply a relevant name and choose a good place to store the image on your computer.

Saving an Image for the First Time

The first time you save an image, you can use any of the following commands:

✦ File⇨Save

✦ File⇨Save As

✦ Ctrl + S

All three of these techniques open the Save As dialog box, shown in Figure 4-13. Through the dialog box, you can name your file, choose a format to save it in (PSD is recommended until you're finished editing the image, at which point you can optimize it for the Web and save in a Web-safe format,) or you can pick a format for a third-party's preference or needs, such as TIF or BMP.

Figure 4-13: Give your file a name and choose the format that suits your needs best.

In addition to naming your file and choosing a format, you can choose where to save the file — using the Save In drop-down list, or the list of icons on the left side of the dialog box (Desktop and My Documents being popular choices). It's a good idea to avoid scattering your images all over your computer — try to keep just one folder for images, and break that folder into subfolders as a way of categorizing your images. This makes it easier to use features in other programs, such as the Microsoft Office Clip Organizer, which looks in specific places for specific types of images — you'll save time if the images you created or tinkered with in Elements are all in one place.

To create a new folder for the image being saved, click the Create New Folder button on the top-right side of the Save As dialog box. A new folder (called "New Folder" appears in the file list within the dialog box, and you can rename the folder as desired. As shown in Figure 4-14, the new folder's generic name is highlighted and contained within a box, indicating that you're able to rename the folder. If you press Enter before naming the folder, you'll have to right-click the New Folder and choose Rename from the shortcut menu.

Figure 4-14: Create a new folder to store your new image, as needed.

Saving New Versions of an Existing Image

After you save your image, you may want to save different versions of it — before editing, after editing, with different effects applied, with the edges cropped away, with people or objects removed, and so on. To create these multiple versions of a single image, all you have to do is use the File⇨Save As command and give the file a new name. When you do this, the open version of the file is closed, with the previous name intact, and the file unchanged since your last save (prior to the Save As save through which you changed the name). The new version is now the open version, and you can continue to edit it as desired. This process can be repeated as many times as you want versions of the file.

✦   ✦   ✦

Selecting and Masking Content for Editing

✦ ✦ ✦ ✦

In This Chapter

Identifying Elements' selection tools and their options

Making geometric and free-form selections

Making selections based on colors in the image

Changing an existing selection

Using selections as the basis for new layers

Duplicating selections

Using Elements' masking tools to protect parts of the image from editing

✦ ✦ ✦ ✦

If you've ever used a word processor, you know the importance of making a selection. Without selecting text, your software won't know which text you want to copy, format, or delete.

Mastering Elements' Selection Tools

The same is true for Elements, in which the process of selecting portions of your image allows you to control which part of the picture is copied, deleted, or retouched in some way. You can apply various Elements' features to the entire image, not making any prior selection at all, but for most retouching, restoring, and other forms of editing, you'll want to focus attention on a particular area.

Elements offers four different tools for making selections in your document, and two of them have alternative versions, expanding your total number of selection tools to seven:

✦ Rectangular Marquee tool

✦ Elliptical Marquee tool

✦ Lasso tool

✦ Polygonal Lasso tool

✦ Magnetic Lasso tool

✦ Magic Wand tool

✦ Selection Brush tool

You can activate any of these tools simply by clicking on them in the toolbox, shown in Figure 5-1, where each of the tools is identified as well. After selected, each tool has a set of its own options, which appear on the option bar, shown in Figure 5-2.

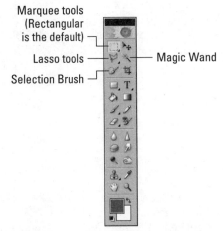

Marquee tools
(Rectangular
is the default)

Lasso tools ——— Magic Wand

Selection Brush

Figure 5-1: Click on any of the four selection tools or choose from the tool variations by clicking the triangle in the buttons' lower-right corner.

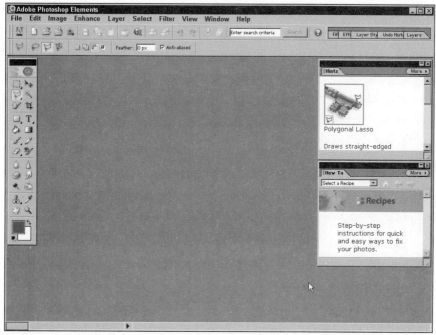

Figure 5-2: The Polygonal Lasso's options enable you to gain greater control over the tool.

Selecting Geometric Shapes

The aforementioned Marquee tools are the primary selection tools for selecting square or round shapes within your image. While the Polygonal Lasso allows you to select polygonal areas within your image, these are more free-form shapes, simply having straight sides.

To use the Marquee tools (Rectangular and Elliptical), simply click on the tool, and move your mouse onto the image. Being sure that you have the correct layer of your image selected, click and drag to draw the geometric-shaped selection. As shown in Figure 5-3, dragging diagonally away from your starting point allows you to control the size and proportions of your selection.

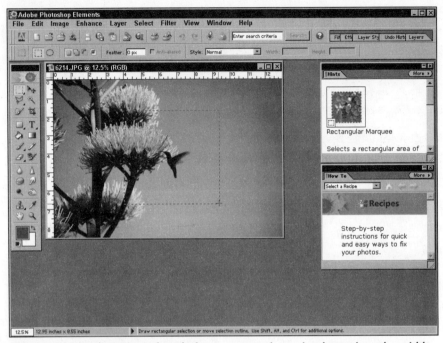

Figure 5-3: The distance and angle from your starting point determines the width, height, and overall size of your selection.

Tip

Find out more about layers — how to create them, how to use them — in Chapter 10.

You have some options for controlling the Marquee tools as you drag to make your selections:

✦ Hold down the Shift key as you drag to maintain equal height and width in your selection. This creates square selections with the Rectangular Marquee, and circular selections with the Elliptical Marquee.

✦ Hold down the Alt key to drag and have the selection grow in two directions at once — left to right, or top to bottom.

Tip

Why is it important that you have a particular layer selected before selecting with the Marquee tools (or any other selection tools)? Because if your image has more than one layer, you need to activate the layer that holds the content you want to select and edit. Always check the Layers palette before making a selection, and as needed, click on the appropriate layer for the selection you're about to make.

Selecting Free-Form Areas

The ability to draw a free-form selection within your image is essential to many types of editing. While the geometric selection tools are easy and quick to use, they can be a bit restricting if the area you want to edit, retouch, cut, or copy is not a rectangle or ellipse. What if you want to select someone's face to brighten or darken it or apply some color correction? If you were to select an oval with the Elliptical Marquee, encompassing the face, you would also get areas around the face, too, and the resulting edits and retouching would affect areas that you didn't want to change.

The Lasso tool provides the majority of your free-form selection capabilities — you can also use the Selection Brush (covered in the next section of this chapter), but for now, check out the three Lasso tools:

✦ The Lasso tool works by allowing you to draw free-form selections, anywhere on the image, in any active layer or within linked layers (more about linking layers can be found in Chapter 10), as shown in Figure 5-4.

Figure 5-4: Click and drag to draw a completely free-form selection.

✦ The Polygonal Lasso enables you to draw free-form selections with straight sides. The number and length of the sides is entirely up to you. As shown in Figure 5-5, your selections can mimic actual polygons (a large sunburst shape, in this case), which enables you to apply filters, special effects, color retouching tools, or even a solid color to the selection, for interesting effect.

✦ The Magnetic Lasso's free-form selections are free-form in that they follow existing shapes' edges within your image. As shown in Figure 5-6, the Magnetic Lasso follows an edge, and sticks to it, based on the pixels' color and light levels. This makes it possible to follow the edge of a face, a tree, along a roadway, or across the back of a sofa, and make sure your selection encompasses only the parts you want.

Closing Your Free-form Selections

When using any of the Lasso tools, you can close your selection (ending the selection process) when you come back to your starting point. For more elaborate selections, such as the one shown in Figure 5-7, you may forget where you started, but that doesn't matter—Photoshop Elements will tell you when you've come back to the starting point by placing a small circle next to the tool's cursor (your mouse pointer). When you see that circle, if you're ready to end the selection, just click.

Using the Dodge tool has brightened the selection.

Figure 5-5: Select a shape and then apply an effect to the selected area.

Figure 5-6: The Magnetic Lasso sticks to your image edges.

Figure 5-7: The little circle on your mouse pointer tells you you've come back to your starting point and can now close the selection.

If you don't want to end at your beginning, double-click and the endpoint (created by your position when you double-click) will throw out a line back to the starting point, and the selection will close, as shown in Figure 5-8.

Starting point

Where I decided to stop my selection

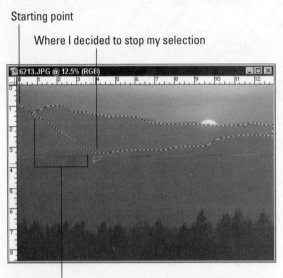

Figure 5-8: Force a selection closure by double-clicking to create a connection between your starting point and wherever your pointer is when you want to close the selection.

By double-clicking to force an end to the selection, I created this span of the selection's border.

Adding to, Subtracting from, and Combining Selections

As you make selections with the Marquee and Lasso tools, you have the ability to make multiple selections that may or may not be contiguous. This means you can create a selection that's a circle and a square (shown in Figure 5-9) or a combination of shapes where the selections have overlapped, as shown in Figure 5-10.

To augment, reduce, or combine your selections, use the buttons on the tools'
options bar, shown in Figure 5-11. The first button is for making selections that
encompass one area, drawn in a single click-and-drag step. The latter three buttons
(identified individually in the Figure) allow you to add to, subtract from, or create
selections from overlapping multiple selections.

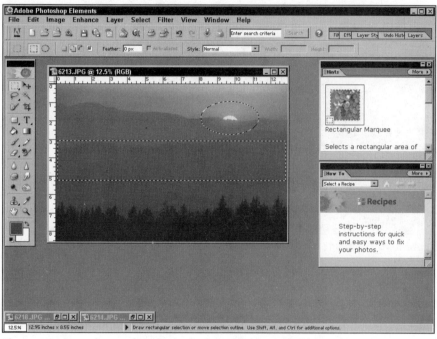

Figure 5-9: Two shapes that don't touch can be one selection.

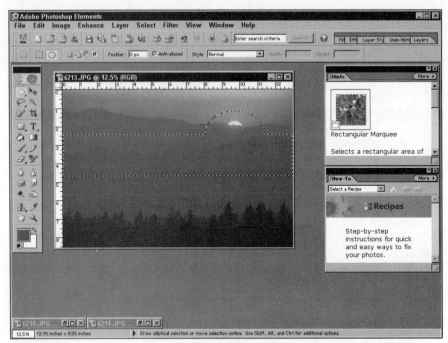

Figure 5-10: Combine a circle and a square to create an entirely new shape for your selection.

Figure 5-11: These four buttons control your ability to make multiple selections and determine how those selected areas interact.

You can also combine selection types when using these selection control tools, creating selections that have both geometric and free-form areas. For example, you can start with a Marquee, and then with the Add to Selection button in use, switch selection tools and add a free-form Lasso selection. Figure 5-12 shows just such a selection, which you could use to select both straight-sided areas and areas that don't lend themselves to the use of such a rigid selection tool. You can use this technique with the Subtract from Selection and Intersect with Selection tools as well.

Because the areas overlap, a single selection appears.

This area selected with the Rectangular Marquee.

This area selected with the Lasso.

Figure 5-12: Add to your selection and combine the selection tools and their effects.

Painting a Selection

The Selection Brush tool is unique to Photoshop Elements — it's not found in Photoshop, at least as of version 7 — and it's a very handy tool for making free-form selections. The tool is also easy to use, because it employs skills you already have if you've done any drawing or painting with Photoshop Elements or any other graphics or illustration application — you're simply painting your selection onto the image, creating a selection in the path of your paintbrush.

As shown in Figure 5-13, the Selection Brush options bar offers tools for choosing the style of brush (soft or hard edges, texture), the size of the brush, a Mode (Selection or Mask), and a Hardness level, which is set to 0 percent by default. You can use these options to customize the brush, which in turn customizes your selection. You can use a very small brush to make fine selections, a textured brush to create a selection that matches the texture of the image within it, or a very big, soft brush to make a selection with gentle edges that encompasses a large portion of the image.

Figure 5-13: Customize the Selection Brush to meet the exact needs of the selection you want to make.

As you drag to paint the selection, you can create a loop, shown in Figure 5-14, or you can paint within a looped area to "fill in" the selection partially or completely (see Figure 5-15).

Figure 5-14: Paint around an area to select what will become a border, filled with color or to which an effect is applied.

Tip   After you started painting your selection, you can stop and start again somewhere else in the image, and even change the brush settings, resulting in different selection effects in different areas of your selection.

Figure 5-15: Fill in a selected area you encompassed with the Selection Brush.

Selecting by Sampling

Sampling is a sort of appraisal that Elements performs on a single pixel or group of pixels, and depending on the tool in use at the time, Elements might establish a new Foreground color based on a sampled pixel, or it might select all the pixels that are the same color as the pixel sampled. When it comes to the Magic Wand tool, sampling (your clicking on a spot in your image) tells Elements to select all the similar pixels on the active layer, within the limitations set by the Magic Wand's options bar (shown in Figure 5-16).

Figure 5-16: Tell the Magic Wand how you'd like it to perform.

Depending on your options bar settings, you can select very few pixels, each of them nearly identical to the sampled pixel, or a lot of pixels, many of which won't bear a striking resemblance to the color or light levels of the sampled pixel with which you started. You can also choose whether the pixels selected must be Contiguous, meaning that they have to be touching the sampled pixel or one of the pixels that was touching the sampled pixel and that met the Magic Wand's requirements for matching the sampled pixel. This threshold for matching the sampled pixel is set through the Tolerance option, which is set at 50 by default. A Magic Wand-created selection appears in Figure 5-17.

Figure 5-17: Select all the pixels of the same shade of gray (or shade of any color) with the Magic Wand tool.

Your other Magic Wand options:

✦ **Anti-aliased.** If this is on, your selection will have smooth edges, despite any disparity between pixels along the selection's edge. You may not achieve a completely smooth edge, however, if your image has a lot of contrast.

✦ **Use All Layers.** This one's fairly self-explanatory. If you turn this option on (it's off by default), then no matter which layer is active or whether or not you have linked layers, the sampled pixel will be compared to all the pixels on all the layers. Those pixels on all layers meeting your Tolerance setting will be selected.

Modifying Selections

After you make a selection, you may decide that it's too small, too big, includes something you didn't want, or leaves out something you did want included in the selection. What to do? You can modify your selection in one of three ways:

✦ Return to the selection tool/s that can give you the selection you want, and with the Add to Selection or Subtract From Selection option turned on, augment or reduce your selection.

✦ Use the Selection Brush to change the shape and scope of an existing selection.

✦ Choose Select⇨Modify, and from the submenu (shown in Figure 5-18), choose what you want to do to your selection. A different dialog box appears for each of the submenu commands, each enabling you to tweak your selection.

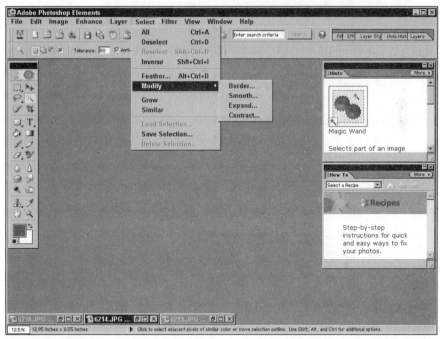

Figure 5-18: Add a border to your selection, smooth its edges, or make it bigger or smaller.

If you go with the Select⇨Modify technique, your submenu choices allow you to change the nature or size of your selection:

✦ **Border** allows you to turn a selection that's a closed shape into a selection that's more like a frame. In Figure 5-19, you can see the Border dialog box, and behind it, a rectangular selection (made with the Rectangular Marquee) that's been turned into a 20-pixel border selection and filled with color.

Figure 5-19: Turn your selection from a closed shape to a frame-like border.

✦ **Smooth** opens the Smooth Selection dialog box, shown in Figure 5-20. You can set a new pixel radius for your selection, which will soften the edges of a Rectangular Marquee or Polygonal Lasso-created selection, softening sharp corners. You can use the Smooth command on any type of selection, but its impact is more directly felt when it's applied to selections with straight sides and sharp corners.

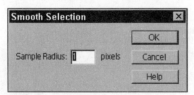

Figure 5-20: Soften the edges of your rectangular or polygonal selections.

✦ **Expand** and **Contract** work very similarly (the Expand dialog box is shown in Figure 5-21) and do just what their names imply. The Expand command enables you to increase the overall size of your selection by a number of pixels you establish, and the Contract command enables you to reduce the selection's overall size.

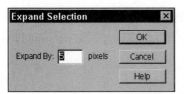

Figure 5-21: Make your selection bigger or smaller.

Creating Layers from Selections

Layers, which Chapter 10 covers in detail, are one of the cornerstones of Elements' power and flexibility. The ability to put portions of an image on separate layers enables you to apply various retouching and special effects tools to certain parts of the image with no fear of accidentally affecting other areas, to hide portions of an image, and to share content between images. You can take your selections and build new layers from them, breaking your image into separate layers (although the image will continue to look like one cohesive photo or drawing), creating duplicates of existing content that you can maintain as duplicates. You can also go back and remove the selected area so that the new selection-based layer is the only representation of that selected content.

To create a layer from a selection, follow these steps:

STEPS: Creating a New Layer from a Selection

1. Make the selection, using any selection tool that meets your needs for this particular selection.

2. Choose Layer⇨New⇨Layer via Cut if you want to remove the selection and have the new layer be the only form in which the content continues to exist, or choose Layer⇨New⇨Layer via Copy if you want to keep both the selection and the new layer created from it.

3. Observe the Layers palette, where the new layer appears (see Figure 5-22).

4. Rename the layer as needed, giving it a name that identifies the content or its purpose within the image.

If you want to make multiple layers from a single selection, choose Edit⇨Copy and then use Edit⇨Paste to create a new layer from the copied selection. You can then repeat the Paste command for as many times as you want a new layer for your selection, or use the Layers palette to copy the first pasted layer. Figure 5-23 shows a layer being dragged to the Create a New Layer button in the Layers palette, which creates a duplicate of the dragged layer.

Figure 5-22: Cutting or copying the selected content can create your new layer.

The selected layer

Create New Layer button

Figure 5-23: Create duplicate layers by dragging an existing layer to the Create New Layer button.

Cutting, Copying, and Deleting Selections

In addition to creating layers from selections via a cut or copy, you can use the Copy command to take content from one image and share it with another or use the Cut command to get rid of image content in its original location and move it to another image. Of course it's also easy to get rid of a selected area entirely, deleting it from the image to be replaced by content from elsewhere (selected and moved from another layer or another image) or by original artwork.

Sharing and Moving Selections between Images

To share and move content between images, you need to do three preparatory functions: Open both the source image and the target image (where the selected content will end up), and make the selection in the original image. After these actions are done, you're ready to share or move the content, as follows:

STEPS: Sharing Content between Images

1. With your selection made in the original image, choose Edit⇨Copy.

2. Switch to the target image, using the Window menu to select it and make it the active file.

3. Choose Edit⇨Paste. A new layer appears in the Layers palette for the target image, and the selected and copied content appears in the image. Figure 5-24 shows both a source (original) and target image, and the content copied into the target image.

To move your content from one image to another — in which case the content does not remain in the original source image — follow these steps:

STEPS: Moving Content between Images

1. Assuming your selection within the source image is made, choose Edit⇨Cut. The selected content disappears, as shown in Figure 5-25.

2. Using the Window menu, switch to the target image.

3. Choose Edit⇨Paste, and a new layer is created in the source image, and you can see the cut content appear in its new location.

As soon as the shared or moved content appears in the target image, you can move it with the Move tool, or resize the content by dragging the layer's handles (see Figure 5-26). You can also rearrange the content stacking order within the image by dragging the layer up and down in the Layers palette. In addition, you can apply any of Elements' retouching and special effects tools to the shared or moved content.

Figure 5-24: Create a new composite image by copying content from one image into another.

Figure 5-25: The Cut command removes the selection from the original.

Dragging by a corner handle allows you to control the ratio
of width to height as you resize the selection.

Figure 5-26: Make the content of the moved layer bigger or smaller by
dragging its corner handles.

Getting Rid of Selected Content

Deleting selected content is alarmingly easy — perhaps too easy. Luckily, you can
Undo your deletion (Edit ⇨ Undo) if you realize it was a mistake, or use the History
palette to go back in time to just before the deletion was made.

To delete part of your image, go to the layer that contains the unwanted portion,
and use the selection tool of your choice to select that content. When you're sure
you have only the unwanted portion selected, press the Delete button on your keyboard. Voila! The content is gone, and you can replace it with content from another
image or you can fill in the "hole" left from your deletion with a solid color, pattern,
or a fill created by applying one of Elements' special effects filters to that color or
pattern.

Note   If the content you deleted was on an upper layer and there's content beneath that
layer, that content will show through the layer and fill in the hole left from the
deletion. This may or may not solve your problem of having content removed from
the upper layer.

Tip   You find coverage of using fills — colors, patterns, and so forth — in Chapter 12.
Coverage of special effects and filters is found in Chapter 13, and you can learn
more about the History palette's use in Chapter 2.

Masking Areas of an Image

When comparing the concept of a selection to that of a mask, think of the preparation you'd do before painting a room. You mask off the woodwork, the trim around the windows, any area that you don't want to paint. By masking portions of your image, you're protecting them from any edits — retouching, filters, special effects, deletion — and you're allowing those same edits to apply to any area outside the mask.

Creating a Mask

Your primary tool for masking a portion of your image is the Selection Brush. Through its options bar (see Figure 5-27), you can use the Mode setting to switch from Selection mode to Mask mode and then paint the mask onto your image.

Choose the shape and texture of your brush.

Switch to mask mode.   Set the overlay opacity.

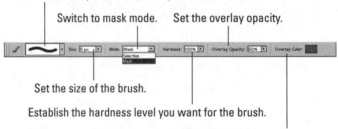

Set the size of the brush.

Establish the hardness level you want for the brush.

Choose a new Overlay Color if red won't stand out.

Figure 5-27: Establish how your Selection Brush looks and works as you use it to create a mask.

To paint the mask, follow this procedure:

STEPS: Painting a Mask to Protect Part of Your Image

1. Turn on the Selection Brush tool.

2. Using the tool's options bar, switch to Mask Mode.

3. Choose a brush preset, set the size, and hardness level.

4. Change the Overlay Opacity to a lower setting if you'll be painting an intricate mask and need to be able to see fine details within your image.

5. Zoom in as needed, so that you can see the details of the image. You can use the Ctrl + + shortcut or use the Zoom percentage box in the lower-left of the workspace.

6. Select a mask color — choosing one that will be visible on top of the image. The default is red, but if your image has a lot of bright red in it, you might want to pick another color, as shown in Figure 5-28.

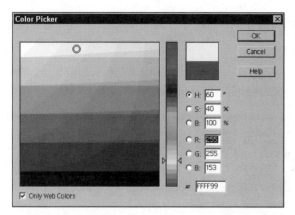

Figure 5-28: Use the resulting Color Picker to select a different color for your mask overlay.

Tip

The mask overlay never prints or displays outside of mask mode, so you just want to pick a color that stands out on the image at hand. If your image is black and white (Grayscale), you can pick any color that appeals to you, or simply leave the Overlay Color set to the default red.

7. Click and drag the brush and see a colored wash appear over the face of the image, in the path that you painted. Figure 5-29 shows a mask being painted on an image.

The painted area is the mask.   These areas of the image are not masked.

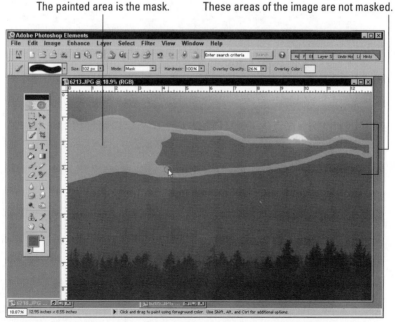

Figure 5-29: Mask any portion of your image by painting with the Selection Brush set to Mask mode.

8. After you finish painting the mask, click the Move tool to leave mask-creation mode and see that a selection is created — selecting all but the masked area, as shown in Figure 5-30.

The masked area is not included in the selection.

These areas are affected by whatever editing is performed next.

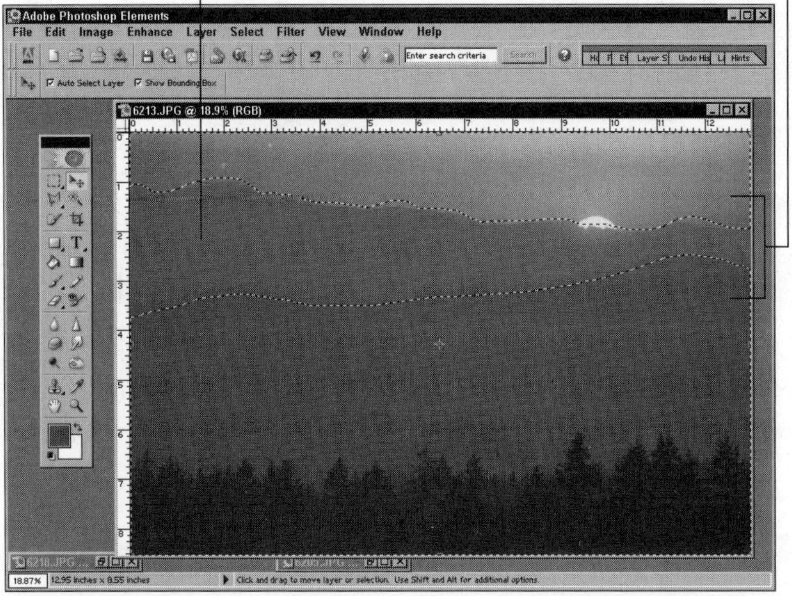

Figure 5-30: Your mask is turned to a selection, where all but your masked area is selected.

Saving a Mask Selection

As soon as your mask is made and converted to a selection, you can proceed to perform whatever editing or retouching you want to do, knowing that your masked area won't be affected by it. Figure 5-31 shows an image that is edited by using one of Elements' filters, and only the masked portion is unaffected.

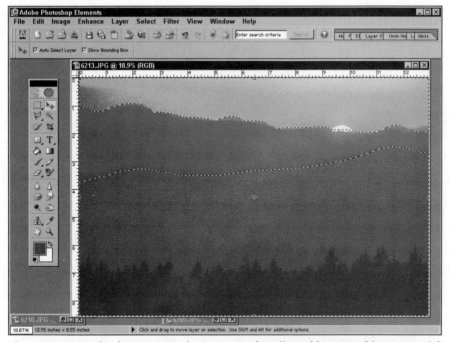

Figure 5-31: Mask whatever you don't want to be affected by retouching or special effects tools.

Note You can edit the mask-made selection by using other selection tools — Marquee, Lasso, or the Selection Brush set to Selection mode — and add to or subtract from the selection. All you need to remember is that the area you masked is not included in the selection as it is, so be careful that any changes to the selection made after the fact don't alter that portion of the selection and change your masking effect.

After creating one mask to control the effects of any retouching or special effects tools, you can deselect and create a new mask as needed, protecting another area of the image from further changes. You can save your selections, too — using the Select⇨Save Selection command. This opens the Save Selection dialog box, shown in Figure 5-32, through which you can give your selection a name and thus be able to use it again in the same image. You can save as many selections as you want.

Figure 5-32: The name you give your selection should be one that reminds you later what the selection is for—what it selects or protects, and when you'd want to use it.

To use a saved selection, choose Select➪Load Selection. The Load Selection dialog box appears (it looks just like the Save Selection dialog box), and from within it, you can choose the saved selection you want to load. To delete a saved selection, choose Select➪Delete Selection and choose the selection you want to delete from the Selection drop-down list.

Note   You can save any selection—not just those made through masking with the Selection Brush. For example, if you created an intricate selection shape with the Polygonal Lasso tool and want to be able to select that shape again without having to redraw it, save that selection, give it an illustrative name, and you'll always have it for future use. The only caveat? Saved selections are only available within the image that was active when the selection was saved.

✦   ✦   ✦

Photographic Housekeeping

✦   ✦   ✦   ✦

In This Chapter

Making images look better overall

Repairing damaged photos

Covering unwanted content

Getting rid of "red eye"

✦   ✦   ✦   ✦

Whether your photo was scanned or captured with a digital camera, it can and probably will contain something you want to get rid of, something you want to enhance, or something you want to move. The problems and issues of image quality that you'll want to resolve can include blurriness, damage from age or improper storage of your prints — or simply not liking what's included in the picture.

Enhancing the Quality of Photographs

Whatever the source or nature of the problem, Elements has the tools to enhance details you may have thought were lost, repair tears, scratches, and stains, and that allow you to rearrange your images, getting rid of content you don't like, moving content you do like, and helping you to create an image that's exactly what you want.

Adjusting Sharpness and Blur

One of the most common problems a photo can have is being too blurry — in one particular spot within the photo or across the entire image. Elements has tools that enable you to focus on specific areas or to enhance detail over the whole picture, so you're covered either way. The tools you use are:

- ✦ The Blur tool
- ✦ The Sharpen tool
- ✦ The Unsharp Mask
- ✦ The Blur filters
- ✦ The Sharpen filters

You may wonder why if I'm talking about getting rid of unwanted blurriness that I say you'll be using the Blur tools and filters. The answer is that sometimes in order to draw attention to something that's not terribly eye-catching, you have to take attention away from something else. As shown in Figure 6-1, the woman in the center of the image doesn't have a lot of fine detail — her image is soft, without any sharp edges or crisp details. Rather than attempt to add sharpness to her portion of the image, which would be aesthetically unpleasant, I blurred the rest of the image, making her stand out.

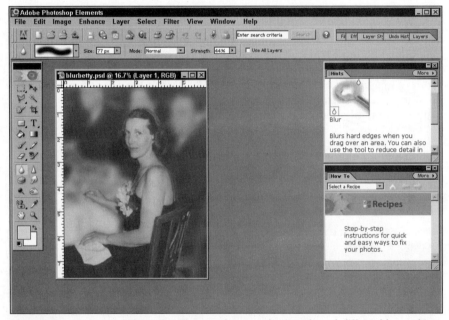

Figure 6-1: Draw attention to an image element that's soft and diffused by making everything else even more diffused.

Tip

You'll find that there are often several ways to solve a photographic problem — some that are "textbook" — using tools exactly as they were intended to be used — and others that employ tools and techniques that you may never have thought of. Throughout this chapter and the next one (on color and light), you'll learn the pre-scribed techniques to solve photographic problems, along with some of the more unexpected or unique solutions that I've discovered in my years restoring photos.

Using the Sharpen Tool

The obvious choice to deal with aforementioned blurriness would be the Sharpen tool, right? Well, yes, in most cases. How to use other tools comes later, but for now, focus on this obvious choice. The Sharpen tool, shown selected and in use in Figure 6-2, works by increasing the light and color differences between adjacent pixels. This heightened difference can bring out distinctions and edges, sharpening the detail in an image — if it's done subtly, and only where it's needed.

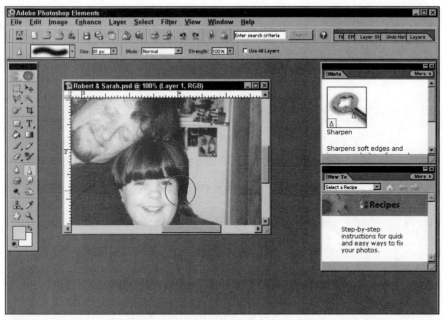

Figure 6-2: Sharpening here and there to bring out small details is an effective way to make subtle use of the Sharpen tool.

Like any Elements tool in the toolbox, you activate the tool by clicking on it. At that point, you can use it to apply sharpening effects to whatever portion of the image you want. Simply click on the tool and then drag it over or click on the area you want to sharpen.

To control the effects of the Sharpen tool, use its options bar, shown in Figure 6-3. You can adjust the size of the brush, choose a Mode for the brush (dictating the effect that the brush has, and on what aspects of the sharpened pixels), and set the Strength of the Sharpen tool. The higher the Strength setting, the more dramatic the sharpening effects.

Figure 6-3: Set your Sharpen tool's options to make sure the sharpening effect you get is the one you want.

You can also turn on the Use All Layers option, which enables you to sharpen all the content in your mouse's path, on all the layers of the image, all at once. This can be a convenience, or it can be a problem, if you have content on a layer that you don't want to affect. This option is off by default.

What if you go too far, as shown in Figure 6-4? Sometimes you can sharpen some-thing so much that it loses its detail to the heightened disparity between the adja-cent pixels. You can use the Undo History tab and go back a few steps to before the sharpening had a negative impact, or use the Undo command (Ctrl + Z) until the unwanted effects are reversed.

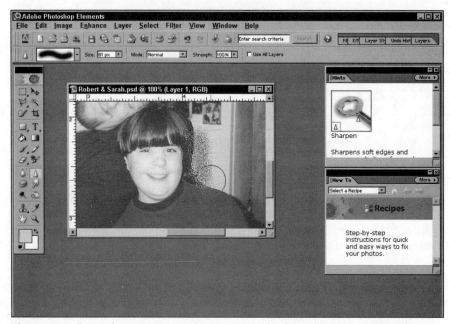

Figure 6-4: If you sharpen too much, you can go backward in time with Undo.

Using the Blur Tool

Used to create the opposite effect, the Blur tool functions in the exact same way as the Sharpen tool — click on the tool to activate it and then drag over or click on the area to be made softer by blurring. The effect of blurring is achieved by making pix-els in the area you click or drag on more similar — reducing the difference between adjacent pixels' color and light levels, so that the pixels seem to blend together more. Figure 6-5 shows blurring in effect, as the user "scrubs" over an area within the image.

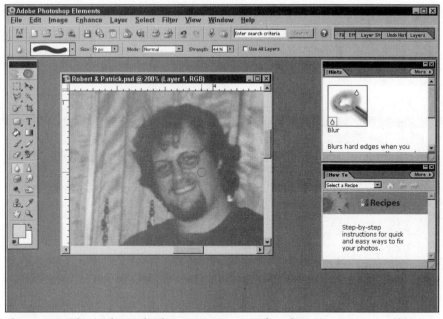

Figure 6-5: Blur in the path of your mouse to apply softness to a very specific area of the image.

The Blur tool's options bar is nearly identical to the Sharpen tool's options bar as well (see Figure 6-6). You can set the size of the brush and pick a preset for it, set the Mode, and determine the strength of the blurring effect. Set to 50 percent by default (as is the Sharpen tool), you can increase or decrease the Strength to control the amount of blurring you achieve.

Figure 6-6: Set the brush, Mode, and Strength settings for the Blur tool.

Tip

Sometimes starting out at a low Strength is a good idea. Apply that low strength effect repeatedly until you get the effect for which you're looking. This can easier to control than setting a high strength and finding yourself with too much blurring or too much sharpening right off the bat.

Using Filters to Enhance Detail

While Chapter 13 covers Elements' Filters and special Effects in detail, I can't in good conscience discuss improving overall image quality without discussing several of Elements' restorative filters — especially those found in the Blur and Sharpen categories with the Filters submenu (see Figure 6-7).

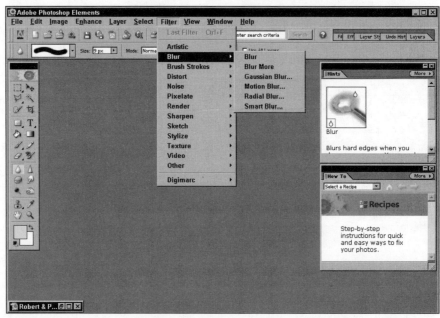

Figure 6-7: Of the many Filters menu categories, Blur and Sharpen are two that can help you make your image look better, rather than applying special or distorting effects.

Filters work by altering the color and light in various pixels in an image. New pixels can be added, existing pixels removed, and/or the remaining pixels altered so as to create the appearance of a particular pattern, special lighting effect, or even the look of painting or sketching with artists' medium.

The Blur and Sharpen filters do what the Blur and Sharpen tools do, altering the appearance of adjacent pixels so that they either stand out against one another (sharpening) or blend smoothing into each other (blurring). The reason to offer both the Blur and Sharpen tools as well as filters that do much the same thing is to enable you to make sweeping changes to the entire image, uniformly (or to selections within the image) using the filters, while also enabling you to make fine adjustments with your mouse, using the Blur and Sharpen tools.

Creating a Uniform, Soft Blur

When you open the Filter menu and then look at the Blur submenu, you notice six different Blur filters:

✦ Blur

✦ Blur More

✦ Gaussian Blur

✦ Motion Blur

✦ Radial Blur

✦ Smart Blur

These six Blur filters offer everything from very subtle effects to dramatic ones, as shown in Figure 6-8, which employs the Blur, Gaussian Blur, and Radial Blur filters in three separate sections of the photo. Of course, when used restoratively or to retouch a photo to help draw out one part (by blurring everything else), these blurring filters are part of an overall plan for the photo's improvement. Here, they're simply being demonstrated within one photo to help you see what they can do.

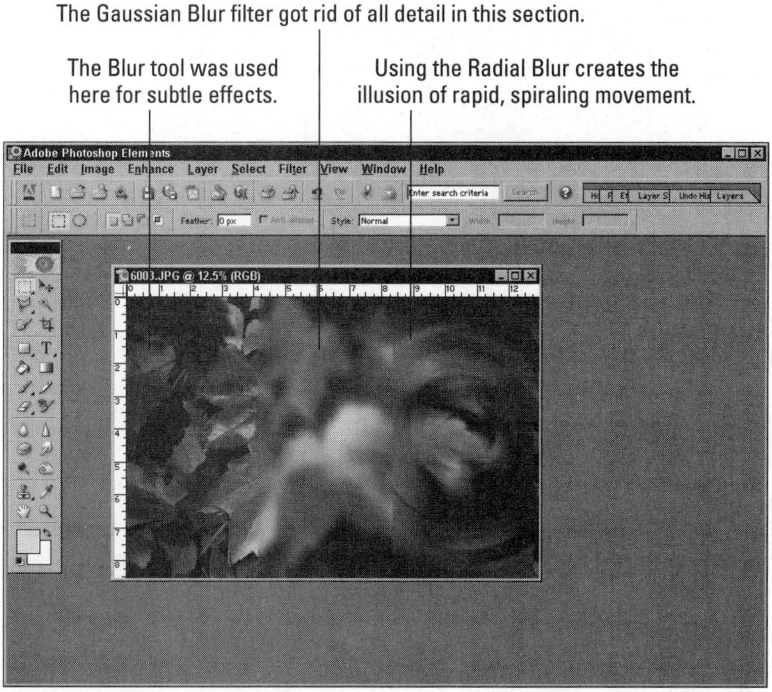

The Gaussian Blur filter got rid of all detail in this section.

The Blur tool was used here for subtle effects.

Using the Radial Blur creates the illusion of rapid, spiraling movement.

Figure 6-8: Blur something softly, blur something more dramatically, or apply a blur that makes things appear to be spinning.

Working with Motion and Radial Blurs

When you want to make one or more parts of a photo stand out, you can sharpen them, brighten them (Chapter 7 discusses use of lighting), or you can make everything else fade through the loss of some or all detail. You've seen how a simple blur can rob some parts of an image of their sharpness, resulting in the remaining parts standing out, but that's not the extent of your blurring options. In addition to an allover, gentle blur, you can go more dramatic and distort image content at the same time that you're blurring it. This is achieved with the Motion and Radial Blur filters, found in the Filter➪Blur submenu. As shown in Figures 6-9 and 6-10, you can create really interesting effects through the illusion of blurring movement.

Figure 6-9: The Radial Blur can make you dizzy!

To apply either of these blur effects, follow this simple procedure:

STEPS: Applying a Motion or Radial Blur

1. Select the portion of the image that should not be blurred — you can use whichever of Elements' selection tools is appropriate for the area to be selected. If the area has very detailed edges, zoom in so that you can see the edges clearly and use a tool that you find to be manageable for small and fine areas, as shown in Figure 6-11.

2. Choose Select➪Inverse so that everything but your selection is now selected and is now blurred — your original selection won't be blurred because it's now not part of the selection.

Figure 6-10: As everything else is whipping past, the static portion of the image holds center stage.

Figure 6-11: To control the exact areas to be blurred and not blurred, make a detailed selection of the area to be left alone.

3. Choose Filter⇨Blur⇨Motion Blur or Radial Blur. A dialog box opens for either of these filters, as shown in Figure 6-12 and 6-13.

Figure 6-12: The Motion Blur's dialog box allows you to determine how fast the items in motion should appear to be going.

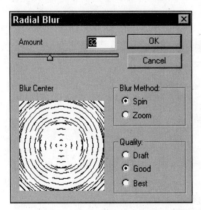

Figure 6-13: The Radial Blur dialog box offers options a Spin or Zoom blur, plus the ability to choose the center of the radial blur effect.

4. For either of the Blurs, adjust the settings as desired, using the Preview box in the Motion Blur dialog box or the image window itself for the Radial Blur.

5. When you like what you see (in either the Preview box or in the image window), click OK to apply the filter.

Tip

The Amount slider in the Radial Blur dialog box enables you to choose the intensity of the blur. The Quality options pertain to the detail within the spin or zoom — how accurately the blur effect will represent the actual blur that would occur if the image content were actually spinning or zooming. Good is the default.

Increasing Overall Sharpness

When blurring content to make other content stand out isn't an option or doesn't give you the results you hoped for, you can try sharpening the image overall (or a portion of the image overall). To do so, you can use the Sharpen filter, found within the Filter⇨Sharpen submenu. This filter does what the Sharpen tool does, but it does it uniformly over the entire image or within a selected portion of the image. This filter has no dialog box, so the degree of sharpening can't be controlled directly. The results are subtle, however, so that you may not even notice the effect. This is a good thing, because you can use the Ctrl + F shortcut to repeat the last-used filter to apply the Sharpen filter again and repeat this until you can see the sharpening take effect and like what it does to the image.

Tip If you used the Sharpen filter (and used it again, with Ctrl + F) and still don't see much of a difference, try the Sharpen More command, also found within the Filter⇨Sharpen submenu. The results will be more intense, and you may find you only need to use it once to get a significant amount of sharpening to occur.

Sharpening Edges

A filter that focuses on the edges of your image is also found in the Filter⇨Sharpen submenu. This is another filter that does not offer a dialog box, so you can't control its effects, but again, the results are subtle, and you may find that one or two applications of the filter is enough to give you the edge-honing effects you need.

The Sharpen Edges filter works by finding the edges of shapes within your image — places where areas of one color meet another, indicating an edge — and increasing the differences between the adjacent pixels on one side of the edge versus the other. As shown in Figure 6-14, the Sharpen Edges filter makes the edges within an image more distinct.

Using the Unsharp Mask

You can find a more sophisticated sharpening tool within the Unsharp Mask dialog box, accessed by choosing Filter⇨Sharpen⇨Unsharp Mask. In the dialog box (shown in Figure 6-15), you can establish the amount of sharpening applied to groups of pixels (the Radius setting establishes how big the groupings are) and how much of a difference to create (using the Threshold setting). The Amount setting determines the degree of overall sharpening achieved.

Figure 6-14: Heighten the differences between pixels along edges within your image to make details stand out.

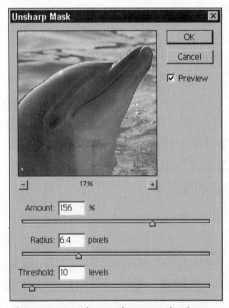

Figure 6-15: Choose how much of an effect the Unsharp Mask has by controlling its scope and intensity.

Certain situations really benefit from the use of the Unsharp Mask. Photos that have been colorized — black and white images that had color washes applied to areas within the image — can look a bit flat, especially if the colors have been applied in one step to large areas of the image. Other photos may have an overall softness that you want to maintain, but you feel that a little sharpness might help. Rather than apply the Sharpen filter or use the Sharpen tool, the Unsharp Mask applies sharpening in small areas, and only where the pixels meet the criteria you set in the dialog box — for current differences in color and light levels, and for how many pixels are compared simultaneously. By sharpening just a few of the pixels in an image, you get a subtle sharpening effect, but it's not so uniform as to detract from any smoothness or softness (or even existing textures) that you want to maintain. Figure 6-16 shows two images — the one on the left is before the application of the Unsharp Mask, the one on the right is after.

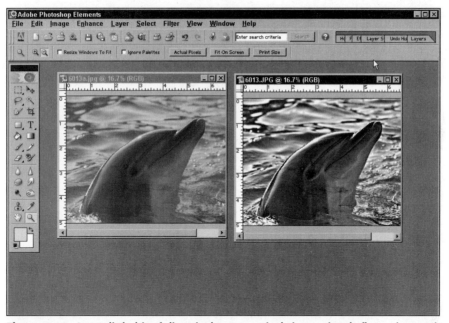

Figure 6-16: Just a little bit of diversity between pixels in previously flat, uninteresting areas of the image is achieved through the use of the Unsharp Mask.

Tip

Learn more about the Unsharp Mask filter and all the other Filters and Effects that Elements has to offer in Chapter 13.

Repairing the Signs of Wear, Tear, and Age

Photos that are stored improperly — loosely stacked in drawers or boxes, exposed to temperature extremes, humidity, excessive dryness, being handled a lot — these photos end up with folds and surface cracking, scratches, rips, tears, spots, and stains. Many times, a photo can end up so damaged that you can't make out the details anymore, or perhaps entire sections of the image are completely destroyed. Luckily, there aren't too many photo problems of this nature that Elements can't solve.

You can repair scratches and tears, you can smooth over a cracked edge, you can restore missing content (using other content from the same or another image), you can bring out details lost to scuffmarks, and you can wash away stains and spots in a variety of ways. Using Elements' restorative tools — the Clone Stamp, the Brush, the Smudge tool, the Sponge, the Dodge and Burn tools, and combinations thereof, you can fix just about anything that's happened to your photos.

Tip   In Chapter 7, you can read all about how light and color can be adjusted to improve image quality and to restore faded and discolored photos to a like-new appearance. This chapter deals primarily with the effects of physical damage and ways to repair and replace what's been damaged.

Getting Rid of Scratches, Scuffs, and Tears

Small damage — scratches, dulling scuffmarks, small tears along edges or even right down the middle of the image — can all be repaired with a few of Elements' more powerful tools:

✦ The Dust & Scratches filter, which gets rid of dulling scratches and scuffmarks

✦ The Clone Stamp, used to copy undamaged content from right next to a damaged spot, making the fold, scratch, or tear disappear

✦ The Smudge tool, used to blend away small blemishes – tiny scratches, spots, holes from a thumbtack, and so forth

✦ The Dodge tool, which lightens dark spots and shadows, bringing out details lost to fading and stains

✦ The Burn tool, which darkens any selected area within the image, handy for scuffmarks and some types of stains

Working with the Dust & Scratches Filter

If your photo has a dull, scuffed look, or has a lot of small scratches and "dings" in its surface, you'll probably find the Dust & Scratches filter (found in the Filter⇨ Noise submenu) to be quite helpful. The filter works by looking for adjacent pixels with a great degree of difference in light and color levels, and it reduces the differences, smoothing out the photo (or a selected portion thereof). This filter won't work on big scratches or tears, but if you have allover "noise" in the form of tiny marks and a dusty look, it can be just what you need.

To use the Dust & Scratches filter, follow these steps:

STEPS: Removing Small Scuffmarks and Dirt with the Dust & Scratches Filter

1. As needed, select the portion of the photo that you want to fix. If you don't make a selection, the entire photo is filtered.

2. Choose Filter➪Noise, and from the submenu, choose Dust & Scratches. The Dust & Scratches dialog box opens, as shown in Figure 6-17.

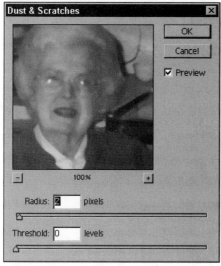

Figure 6-17: The Dust & Scratches filter removes "noise" created by scuffs, small scratches, dust, and general wear and tear.

3. Adjust the Radius for the filter, as needed. The Radius setting determines the size of groups of pixels that are compared to each other, looking for the disparity in pixel quality that would indicate the presence of unwanted scratches and scuffmarks.

4. Adjust the Threshold setting, which determines how much disparity Elements should look for before adjusting pixels within the specified radius.

5. Observe the Preview window to see if what you're looking for is what's happening when the filter is applied.

6. After making further adjustments to the two fields (Radius and Threshold) to make the Preview acceptable, click OK to apply the filter and view the impact on your entire image or the portion you selected. Figures 6-18 and 6-19 show a fairly scuffed image before and after the use of the Dust & Scratches filter.

Figure 6-18: Before the filter is applied, this image looks very dirty and worn.

Figure 6-19: After applying the filter, the image is smoother looking with many of the small scratches being eliminated or reduced in terms of their visibility.

Tip

You can use your mouse within the Preview window to pull the portion of the image that you want to observe into view. Your mouse pointer looks like the Hand tool, which allows you to pan around the image and drag it within the confines of the Preview box.

Cloning Undamaged Content to Cover Folds, Tears, and Scratches

If you find that the Dust & Scratches filter makes the image look too smooth or blurry, perhaps you need to take a different approach. Instead of a filter, which applies a uniform effect to a selection or over the entire image, you might do better with a tool that works in isolated areas, such as the Clone Stamp. Using such a tool generally gives you more control and allows you to make sure the effects appear only where you want them to, by replacing scratches, scuffs, and even more dramatic forms of damage with pristine content from nearby in the image.

The Clone Stamp is a unique tool in that it copies (clones) content from one spot, sampling a spot within your image (that you designate by clicking) for color, light, and content. That sampled content is then placed wherever you click next. Figure 6-20 shows an image in need of such an approach, and Figure 6-21 shows the results — a folded corner, a tear, and some scratches have all been eliminated by the use of the Clone Stamp.

Figure 6-20: Before the Clone Stamp is used, this photo has several minor problems, adding up to a very tattered-looking image.

Figure 6-21: After the Clone Stamp, the fold, tear, and scratches are gone, replaced by nearby undamaged content.

To use the Clone Stamp, follow this very simple procedure:

STEPS: Clone Stamping to Remove Scratches, Tears, and Other Damage

1. Activate the layer on which the damage appears. If your photo was scanned and you haven't created any other layers, the Background layer should be active.

2. Click on the Clone Stamp tool and observe its options bar, shown in Figure 6-22.

Figure 6-22: The Clone Stamp's options enable you to determine how much is cloned with each click of your mouse and how the cloned content looks in its new home.

3. As needed, change the brush preset and Size to accommodate the size of the marks and damage you're going to fix. For example, if you're repairing a scratch that's about two pixels wide, set the brush Size to four pixels so that you're cloning an area that's larger than the damage but not so much bigger that the replacement of damaged area with cloned, undamaged area is obvious.

4. Adjust the Mode setting as needed. The default, Normal, is best for most jobs of this nature, but you can experiment with other modes to see if they solve your problem more effectively.

Tip   You can find a list of Elements' Modes and their uses in Table 7.1, at the end of Chapter 7.

5. Using the Opacity drop-down list, increase or decrease this setting to determine whether or not the cloned content will be at all transparent. The default setting is 100 percent, based on the assumption that you'll want to completely cover the area on which the cloned content will be placed.

6. Use the Aligned option if you want to use the Clone Stamp repeatedly and have Elements re-sample a new spot in the image for each click of the tool. With the Aligned option on, a new sampling will be performed, the same distance from your mouse's current position as was established when the first sample was taken.

7. If your image has multiple layers and the problems exist in some degree over all of them, turn on the Use All Layers option.

8. Next, you're ready to sample a spot within your image, cloning it for use in covering the damaged areas, one by one. To do this, press the Alt key and hold it.

9. With the Alt key held down, click on the spot you want to use as the cover-up for your damage. Figure 6-23 shows an area being cloned — note the crosshair in a circle, the circle being the size of the brush you selected.

Figure 6-23: Sample an undamaged area and make that your cloned content.

10. Release the Alt key and click your mouse on top of the damaged area — a spot the size of your selected brush Size fills with the cloned content, masking the problems underneath. Figure 6-24 shows the cloned content partially covering a scratch.

Figure 6-24: Place the cloned content on top of the damaged area.

11. Continue cloning and stamping (Steps 8 through 10) until all of your damaged areas are covered up. Be sure to clone from areas that contain similar content to that which you're covering up — cloning from very close to the damaged area is usually your best bet.

Tip   Avoid dragging to deposit your cloned content. This usually results in an inadvertent and undesirable pattern. It's far more effective to clone a spot, stamp that over part of the damaged area, re-clone and then stamp again, until you've got a cover-up that looks very natural.

Eliminating Spots and Stains

Yellowed tape from when a photo was attached to a page in an album, a coffee-cup ring on the edge of the picture, ink or crayon from a child who thought they could improve on the photo — these are the source of just some of the spots and stains that may have caused you to write off a particular photo as beyond repair. In most cases, you can fix spots and stains of this type, and you can find yourself with a photo that looks like nothing ever happened to it.

One of the tools you can use has already been covered—the Clone Stamp. You can use it to clone a bit of the unstained area near where the stain or spot is, and stamp it over the stained/spotted area. The procedure is identical to that which you'd use to cover up a scratch or tear. The tools specific to spots and stains that we haven't discussed yet include:

✦ The **Smudge tool,** for tiny spots, used to blend the properly colored pixels nearby with the spot, a lot like using makeup to cover a blemish on your face.

✦ The **Dodge tool** lightens areas on the image and can be used to get rid of a dark stain or smudge on a photo.

✦ The **Burn** gives you the exact opposite effect—instead of lightening the image, it darkens it. It can be useful to eliminate the effects of matte-finish tape (that you couldn't peel off the picture before scanning), or where the image has been lightened by some liquid spilled on the image.

✦ The **Sponge tool** can be used to soak colors out of an image, getting rid of a stain or a spot that has applied color to the image. The tool can be used in two modes—Saturate and Desaturate, the latter being the one that removes color. If your staining substance has leeched the color out of your photo, you can use the Sponge tool (set to Saturate) to bring the color back.

Tip All this talk of color may lead you to think this is the only coverage that color may get in this book. Not so! Chapter 7 discusses all sorts of color application and adjustment tools, used for both creative and restorative purposes.

Smudging out Flaws and Marks

The Smudge tool is useful for very tiny spots and stains—much like those seen in Figure 6-25. Of course, you can use it, too, for getting rid of actual blemishes (tiny marks) that are part of the image itself, such as freckles or small scars on a face, tiny imperfections on furniture, a dot on the picture that came from dirt on the camera's lens, and so on.

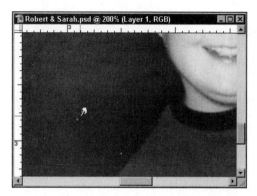

Figure 6-25: If your image has tiny spots such as these, you can use the Smudge tool to get rid of them.

For getting rid of small spots that were applied to the printed image (or to get rid of the aforementioned imperfections in the photo's subjects), follow these steps:

STEPS: Smudging Out Small Spots, Stains, and Image Imperfections

1. Be sure you activate the layer that contains the spot, stain, or other imperfection.

2. Click on the Smudge tool to activate it.

3. Observe the Smudge tool's options bar, shown in Figure 6-26. From this bar, you can control how intense the Smudge tool's effects are by adjusting the size and strength of the tool.

Figure 6-26: Adjust the size and intensity of your smudges.

4. You see some familiar options on the options bar, and you can adjust them as needed:

   • Choose a brush preset so that the shape and style of the "fingertip" with which you're smudging is appropriate for the image and the portions you're retouching.

   • Change the size of the brush so that you're smudging just the area that contains the blemish. The smallest brush size you can work with is best, as shown in Figure 6-27.

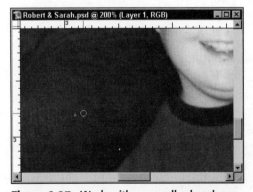

Figure 6-27: Work with as small a brush as you can so that your smudging is subtle and the "trail" of your smudge is not visible to the naked eye.

- Choose a Mode for the tool, if you want to apply light, shadow, color, or other special painting effects at the same time you're smudging the image.

- Change the strength (set to 50 percent by default) so that you're either smudging very little or a lot. Obviously, the higher the number in this field, the more dramatic your smudging effects. Figure 6-28 shows smudging done at 30 percent and then some done at 90 percent.

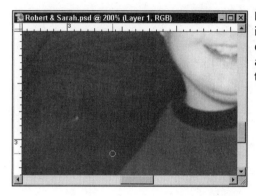

Figure 6-28: Smudge Strength is important to the overall effectiveness of the tool — a little may be too little, and a lot may be way too much. Find the appropriate middle ground.

5. After setting the Smudge tool's options to suit your needs, move your mouse onto the image and drag, moving a very small distance, smudging pixels from an unstained/unspotted area onto the area that contains the imperfection you want to smooth away.

6. Repeat Step 5, smudging in tiny amounts, until the blemish in question is gone.

Tip If the Smudge tool fails for any reason — you can see the smudges and the attempted repair is too obvious or there aren't enough clean pixels to use to cover the spot because the spot's too big, you'll want to switch to the Clone Stamp. Don't forget to Undo your attempts at Smudging first, though, so you have a pristine environment from which to clone clean content to cover the spot or stain.

Using the Dodge, Burn, and Sponge Tools

The Dodge, Burn, and Sponge tools change the appearance of the pixels within the spotted or stained area, rather than replacing or covering them. By adding or removing light and/or color, you can lessen the impact of a minor stain, such as from liquid spilled on the photo or fading due to prolonged exposure to sunlight. Each of the tools has its own set of options, which you can use to customize the tool's operation. If you find that these tools don't work well enough — perhaps the stain is too dark to wash it out or fade it with the Dodge or Sponge tools, or maybe there's nothing to be gained by darkening part of the image — you can revert to the old restorative standby, the Clone Stamp. For large stains, however, such as the one shown in Figure 6-29, you'll be better off trying to clean up the stain rather than covering it up — it simply takes up too much room on the image to easily (or perhaps even successfully) cover it up.

Figure 6-29: A large, generalized stain is probably best cleaned up with the Dodge or Sponge tools.

To look at each tool and discuss the way it functions, I start with the Dodge and Burn tools. These tools sort of work as a pair — they do opposite but related tasks. The Dodge tool lightens, and the Burn tool darkens. Their options bars (shown in Figures 6-30 and 6-31) are quite similar.

Figure 6-30: The Dodge tool lightens shadows by default and relies on a low Exposure for a subtle effect.

Figure 6-31: The Burn tool deepens highlights by default and also relies on a low Exposure setting for subtle results.

To use the Dodge or Burn tools, follow these steps:

STEPS: Lightening or Darkening Image Content to Get Rid of a Stain

1. Make sure you're on the layer that contains the stain or spot.

2. Click to activate the tool you want to use—Dodge for lightening, Burn for darkening.

3. Observe the tool's options bar. Your main options to adjust are the brush preset, Size, and the Exposure setting. The latter setting should only be adjusted after you use the default setting and determine if you need more light or dark to achieve the desired effect.

4. Try to use a brush Size that's the size of the stain (if it's a small stain) or that will require just a few contiguous clicks to apply the tool to the entire stain. Using a small brush repeatedly over a large area risks the creation of a pattern, wherein the path of the tool can be seen in the photo (see Figure 6-32). Better to lighten or darken a few pixels beyond the edges of the stain (a risk in using a very large brush Size) than to have visible circles of light or dark.

Figure 6-32: Clicking over and over within the stain with a small brush creates an undesirable pattern.

5. Click on the spot or stain and watch the effect be applied. If you're using the Dodge tool, the area where you clicked should become lighter, and the opposite will occur if you're using the Burn tool. Figure 6-33 shows a lightened area after a few contiguous clicks with the Dodge tool.

Figure 6-33: Just a few clicks and the stain is so light it can barely be seen.

6. You can drag over a large area, or click repeatedly, moving the mouse between clicks so as not to over-lighten or over-darken any one particular area of the image. Continue doing this, and stopping to make options adjustments as needed, until the desired degree of dodging or burning has taken place.

Tip   You can use the Burn tool to darken the areas around a stain that has simply darkened the image. By darkening the surrounding pixels, the dark stain is less visible. You only want to do this for very slight stains, not for deep, detail hiding stains — otherwise, you'll be hiding the content in the surrounding areas, too.

The Sponge tool is like another pair of tools — because it works in two Modes (Saturate and Desaturate), you really get two tools in one. You'll probably work in Desaturate mode most often when getting rid of stains, but there are cases where Saturate mode can help a stain blend in with the rest of the image. To use the Sponge tool, follow these steps:

STEPS: Sponging Away Color from a Large Stain or Spot

1. Activate the layer that contains the spot or stain you want to "wash" out with the Sponge.

2. Click on the Sponge tool to activate it. The options bar appears, as shown in Figure 6-34.

Figure 6-34: Choose which Mode the Sponge will work in—Saturate or Desaturate.

> **Note**
>
> Why didn't I suggest that you select the stain? Because to do so can create a sharp edge around the stain, where the color has been removed (or augmented). Better to adjust some of the stain's untouched surrounding pixels than to restrict the Sponge tool's effect to a clearly defined area. Adding a Feather around the selection can mitigate the edge effect, however, so if you want to select the stain first, set the Feather to 3–5 pixels so that you have a slightly softened edge on your selection.

3. Switch to the Mode you want to use—Desaturate to remove color or Saturate to add more of the existing colors.

4. Choose a brush size that's either the same size as the stain itself, or if that's not possible, choose one that's large enough so that just a few contiguous clicks will allow you to Sponge the entire stain without leaving a pattern behind.

5. Adjust the brush preset to a shape and texture that works within your image. For example, a soft-edged brush helps eliminate obvious circles of color fading (Desaturate mode) or the increase in the intensity of color (Saturate mode).

6. Adjust the Flow of the Sponge, which determines the rate of saturation change (adding or removing). The default is 100 percent, which means it will either wash out all color or add 100 percent of the existing color, doubling it.

7. Begin using the tool by clicking once on the stain or dragging over it, if you have a large stain and a brush that's about half the size of the stain itself. Figure 6-35 shows the removal of a colored stain, and although the figure is in black and white, you can see that part of the stain is gone, its color sipped right up by the Sponge.

Figure 6-35: Soak up the color of the stain, leaving the intact image behind.

8. Observe the effects, and if necessary, repeat Step 7, clicking or dragging again to further remove or add color.

Tip   If you need to remove a specific color and leave other colors behind within the stained area, consider the Color Variations command (choose Enhance⇨Adjust Color⇨Color Variations), which Chapter 7 covers in detail. The Color Variations command allows you to increase and decrease the presence of specific colors (Red, Green, or Blue) within a selected area of the image.

Replacing and Editing Content

Some photos were not well composed from the beginning—maybe someone in a group photo is too close to the edge of the image or there's a lamp right behind their head, looking like some sort of hat. Perhaps you took an outdoor photo, and something undesirable is in the photo—phone or electric lines in what should be a rustic setting, a car in front of an historic building. Whether there's a person or object you want to move or get rid of, Elements provides two sets of tools/techniques to help you, one of which you've seen before:

✦ The Clone Stamp can help stamp out phone lines, muddy puddles, the front bumper of a car that sneaked into the edge of your photo—any small problem that you want to eradicate by using existing content.

✦ The Edit⇨Cut command (Ctrl + X) allows you to remove content from its current position and move it to another spot in the same image. After it's cut, the content can be pasted (choose Edit⇨Paste, or Ctrl + V) and then repositioned on the new layer that is automatically created when the Paste command is executed.

How do you know which tool or technique to use? The size of the problem is your best guide. If it's something small — a beer can on an otherwise impeccably set formal dining table, a bit of graffiti on a sign or wall — something relatively small in relation to the entire image, use the Clone Stamp. If the problem is that someone or something is in the wrong place (or you don't want them in the photo at all), use the Edit⇨Cut command. Of course, if you're getting rid of the person or thing completely, you can select them and press Delete — no need to keep a duplicate around for pasting later!

Because I already covered the Clone Stamp for use in getting rid of scratches and tears, it doesn't really require further coverage here — the same technique works for getting rid of image content as you'd employ for getting rid of signs of wear and tear. If, for example, you were trying to get rid of a phone line running across what should be a pristine expanse of sky, just Clone the clear sky along the phone line and stamp that onto the line itself. If the sky has blue and clouds, keep re-sampling so that you're applying what's actually behind the phone line — be it cloud or blue sky. Figure 6-36 shows a phone line being eradicated by the Clone Stamp — a crisp, gray New England sky is being cloned and stamped over the line.

Figure 6-36: Progress isn't always a good thing. A phone line looks somewhat anachronistic in front of this old building, so away it goes.

Selecting, Moving, and Removing Content

So now you're left with cutting content that's not wanted in its current position, so that you can use it elsewhere — moving that lamp behind someone's head, relocating shrubbery, moving a person within a group photo. Any sort of similar adjustment can be made with the Edit⇨Cut command, and you can then reposition the cut content by using the following procedure:

STEPS: Cutting a Selection to Relocate Image Content

1. Be sure you're on the layer that contains the content you want to cut.

2. Using the selection tool of your choice, select the content you want to cut and then reposition.

3. If you simply want to get rid of the selection and not move it at all, press Delete after selecting the unwanted content. If, on the other hand, you want to move what's selected, press Ctrl + X or choose Edit⇨Cut. In either case — a deletion or a Cut, the content you selected is now gone from the image, leaving a hole behind, as shown in Figure 6-37.

Figure 6-37: Gone, but not forgotten, the hole must be filled — but you get to that later.

4. To reposition the cut content, press Ctrl + V or choose Edit⇨Paste. A new layer is automatically created, as shown in Figure 6-38.

Figure 6-38: The pasted content appears right on top of the spot from where it was cut.

If you paste the cut content more than once, the subsequent pastes place the new layer's content in the middle of the image, rather than on top of the spot from where the content was cut.

5. Using the Move tool, reposition the new layer's content, as shown in Figure 6-39.

If you want to resize the pasted content, use the handles that appear when you're using the Move tool on the new, active layer. You can also rotate the content, by pointing to a corner handle and moving slightly away from the handle so that a curved, 2-headed handle appears. Drag either clockwise or counter-clockwise to rotate the selection.

Figure 6-39: Point in the middle of the content, rather than on a handle and drag to reposition the layer.

Covering Up Unwanted Content and Filling In Holes

After you delete or cut content from one spot and in the case of cutting it, move it to another spot, you're probably left with a hole—the place where the cut content used to be. You can fill that space with content from the surrounding area of the image—extending whatever was behind the missing content, adding a new background, or cropping away the part of the image that's missing, assuming it's along the edge of the image and not in the middle. There are many options, and Elements has several tools to assist you:

✦ Use the Clone Stamp to fill in where the missing content used to be. If there was a wall behind the person or thing you cut or deleted, extend that wall to fill in the hole. If the item you cut or deleted was in front of another person, find some object for that person to "hold" to cover up the hole. It takes creativity, and sometimes a vivid imagination, but you'll come up with something.

✦ Use the Edit⇨Copy command and grab content from the same or another image for pasting into the hole. If you cut a car from along the curb in front of your house, copy some shrubbery or nice green grass from elsewhere and paste it in where the car was. Of course, don't forget to extend the curb, which can be done by choosing Edit⇨Copy (and then choose Edit⇨Paste to add the copied curb) or with the Clone Stamp.

Just like pasting cut content creates a new layer, pasting copied content will do the same thing. To move or resize the new layer, click on it and then use the Move tool to reposition the pasted content and as needed, use the side and corner handles to resize and/or rotate the content into place.

✦ Drag a layer from another image into your current image and position that new content over the hole. If you have an image with selections from within it on separate layers, open both images and drag the desired content layer from the source image's Layers palette and drop it into the image window where you have a hole to fill. Then, use the Move tool to resize and/or move the content to fill in the hole. Figure 6-40 shows a layer in transit from one image to another.

Figure 6-40: Borrow content from another image by dragging a layer from that image to the one you're working on.

Creating a Patterned Background with the Pattern Stamp

So you have a hole to fill or a background to extend, and you don't want to use existing content to do it. Maybe there isn't any content in the existing image that will serve your needs, and you don't have any images that have anything you could borrow in them. What to do? Fill the space you need to fill with a pattern, courtesy of the oft-used Clone Stamp. Instead of using it exactly as you have throughout this chapter, however, you can use the Clone Stamp's "alter ego," the Pattern Stamp, to fill in holes in images, create a new background, or fill any selected area. To use the Pattern Stamp, follow these steps:

STEPS: Filling in Spaces with the Pattern Stamp

1. Click on the Clone Stamp tool and then click the Pattern Stamp button on the options bar, shown in Figure 6-41.

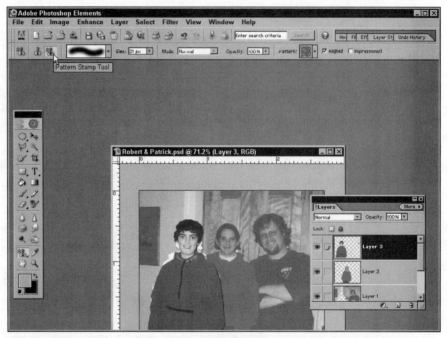

Figure 6-41: Switch from the standard Clone Stamp to the creativity-inspiring Pattern Stamp.

2. Observe the addition of a button on the options bar — accompanied by a drop-down list, this new option is called Pattern. After you click that drop-down list, you'll see the same set of presets you saw in Chapter 2, where you discovered how to create fill patterns of your own and save them as presets.

3. Click the Pattern drop-down list and choose one of the presets. If you want to have more of a selection, click the options menu button (right-pointing triangle on the right side of the palette, shown in Figure 6-42) and choose another group of Pattern presets.

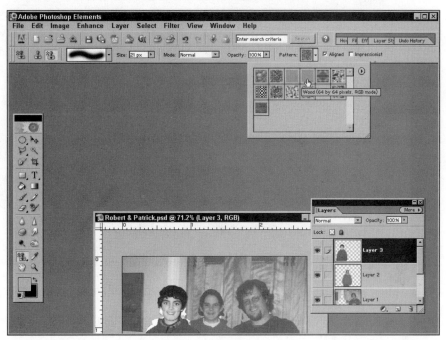

Figure 6-42: No sense restricting yourself to the small set of default patterns — open a new set of presets and pick one that's appropriate for your image.

4. After selecting a pattern to use with the Pattern Stamp, make sure that you're on the appropriate layer within your image or create a layer for the pattern fill you're about to stamp into place.

Tip Read more about creating and using layers in Chapter 10.

5. Click on the image to apply the Pattern Stamp's designated pattern, the Size of the brush (and the shape and style of the brush preset you chose, also on the options bar) dictating the way the pattern is applied. Figure 6-43 shows a pattern applied to part of an image background.

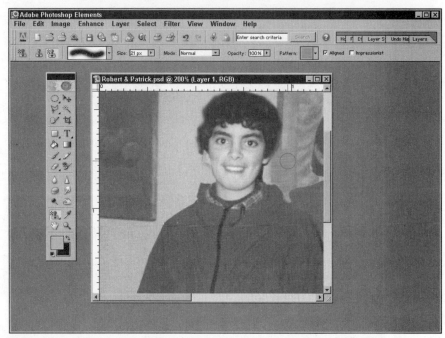

Figure 6-43: Click over and over until you've filled the desired area with your selected pattern.

Tip   You can also drag with the Pattern Stamp, drawing a line that's filled with the selected pattern. The brush Size you set for the Pattern Stamp determines the line's thickness.

Eliminating Red Eye Automatically

"Red Eye" is a very common problem in photos that contain people (especially children, who often get right in front of the camera) and animals. It can ruin a nice portrait, make an otherwise professional-looking photo look painfully amateurish, and otherwise annoy you as you realize that no matter what's going on in the photo you've taken, nobody notices anything other than the demonic glow in the subject's eyes. Figure 6-44 shows just such a problem, in an otherwise charming amateur photo.

Figure 6-44: Look into my eyes — I dare you to notice anything else!

So what can you do? One of the tools that Elements has that the original Photoshop application does not, is the Red Eye Brush. Prior to this tool's addition to the Elements' toolbox (and for all Photoshop users, through the current version), you could only get rid of red eye by painting out the glow with the paintbrush, finding the right iris color by sampling the non-glowing portions of the eye and filling in the iris with that. The pupil would be recreated with black, although that black had to be tinkered with in terms of opacity and potentially, a light source, so as to not look fake. I cover this manual method later, because sometimes it's still the best way to get rid of red eye. For now, though, check out the Red Eye Brush, the tool intended to simplify our lives and exorcise the demonic glow from our images.

First, to use the Red Eye Brush, follow these steps to customize the tool's effects and apply them to the glowing eyes in question.

STEPS: Using the Red Eye Brush

1. Check to see that the layer containing the eyes is the active layer.

2. Click the Red Eye Brush tool to activate it and make any desired adjustments to the following options, as shown in Figure 6-45.

Figure 6-45: Set up the way you want the Red Eye Brush to work.

- **Brush presets.** Choose the style brush you want to use. A solid brush is preferable. If your image is slightly blurry, you might want to choose one with soft edges.

- **Brush size.** Pick one that matches the diameter of the pupil you are fixing. If you can't find an exact match, go with one slightly smaller than the pupil, to avoid an obvious edge against the color of the iris.

- **Sampling method.** The default is First Click, and the alternative is Current Color, meaning that whatever color is currently showing in the Current color box is used as the bad pupil color, and any pupil in that shade is replaced with the Replacement color.

- **Tolerance.** This sets the threshold for spotting the sampled color within the pupil when you click to apply the Red Eye Brush tool. A higher number raises the bar and applies the Replacement color more liberally. A lower number lowers the threshold, and more of the pupil is recolored, even the parts that aren't actually glowing.

- Note that the other options (Current, Replacement, and the Default Colors option button) come into play later as you're using the brush.

3. Set your Current color, being the color of the glowing portion of the pupil. You may prefer to set this yourself, using the First Click sampling option. With this Sampling mode in place, click once on the portion of the pupil that's glowing.

4. Set the Replacement color. If you click the displayed color, you open the Color Picker from which you can choose the color the pupil should be.

Tip   If you click the Default Colors button, the Current color becomes red, and the Replacement color is set to black.

5. Click on the pupil to apply the Replacement color. The glow is removed in favor of the color you selected. If the pupil is larger than your brush or not shaped like your brush tip, you may have to drag to apply the Replacement color to the entire glowing area.

6. If both eyes are visible and glowing (they usually are), you can repeat this process for the second eye.

Tip   You may want to choose a different size brush and a slightly different Replacement color for the second eye, especially if the subject's head is at an angle — chances are, the light didn't hit both eyes the same way, and an identical pupil in different sized and colored eyes will look false.

Manual Options for Red Eye Removal

While my earlier description of the manual red eye removal process may have sounded very complex, it really isn't — you're simply using a handful of Elements' tools to make additions to and adjustments within your image. But why even think about a manual method if the Red Eye Brush exists? Because sometimes the Red Eye Brush creates fake-looking results, or the eye and its particular glow cannot be effectively removed with the tool. In these cases, you want to get rid of the red eye manually, relying on the Paintbrush, Eyedropper, and perhaps even the Clone Stamp tools to replace the red, glowing pupil with a properly-colored iris and dark, realistic pupil.

To rid your image of red eye manually, follow these steps:

STEPS: Removing Red Eye Manually

1. Using the Eyedropper tool to select a Foreground color from the very edge of the glowing pupil, establish the color that you want to paint over the glowing portion of the eye, as shown in Figure 6-46.

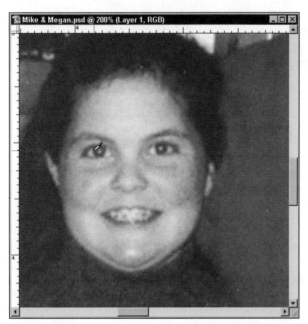

Figure 6-46: Sample a color to replace the glow in your subject's eyes.

2. Next, use the Brush tool (sized to match the pupil) to paint out the glow. You can do this with a single click, or if the pupils are oblong, two clicks or a short drag with the brush. Figure 6-47 shows a single click ridding this eye of any glow, replacing the red eye with a nice, dark pupil within a properly colored iris.

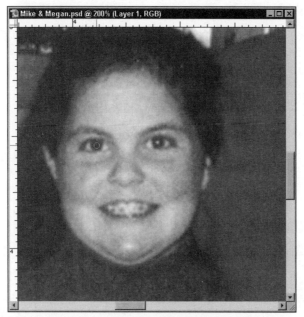

Figure 6-47: If your brush is sized right, a single click and you fill in the pupil with the right color.

Tip   Be careful to use a brush that's slightly smaller than the brush so you don't end up with a crisp edge — it looks funny against the iris, and consider reducing your brush Opacity setting so that your color isn't too dense.

3. As needed, you can add a light or white sparkle on the pupil with a small-sized paintbrush for a shiny-eyed effect — just take note of where any light spots are on the iris, which will indicate where reflected light is already appearing, as shown in Figure 6-48.

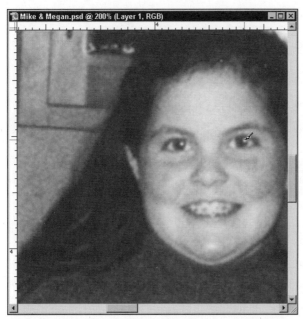

Figure 6-48: Should there be a dot of light on the eye for shine? Add one quickly and subtly with a tiny brush.

Tip

When applying a fake sparkle to your subjects' eyes, make the sparkle is very small and subtle—and don't drag the mouse. Any attempt to "draw" the shine on will look just that—drawn. Instead, click once or twice to create a very tiny, crystalline spot of reflected light.

Note

When manually removing red eye, working with your zoom set to a very high magnification is good—get right in there and work as close to the eyes as you can. You may find, however, that working at that close a zoom, you can't tell if your results are very natural looking. When you zoom out, which you can do intermittently during the red eye removal process, you can see how the image will look when printed or viewed in actual size on-screen.

✦　　✦　　✦

Mastering Color and Light

Elements' Set Foreground and Set Background color tools (shown in Figure 7-1) open the Color Picker when you click on them. The resulting dialog box, presumably set to the Adobe version (rather than the Windows version, as discussed in Chapter 3) shown in Figure 7-2, enables you to select any of millions of colors for your painting or filling pleasure.

◆　◆　◆　◆

In This Chapter

Choosing colors to use for painting and filling

Sampling colors from within your image

Using color effects

Changing color values

Using and understanding your brush-based tools' Mode settings

◆　◆　◆　◆

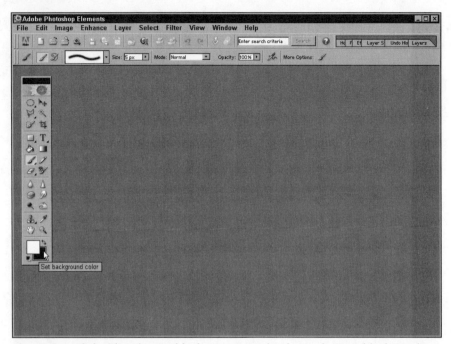

Figure 7-1: Click either the top block (Foreground Color) or bottom block (Background Color) to open the Color Picker.

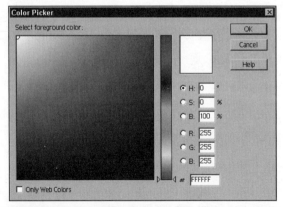

Figure 7-2: The Adobe Color Picker allows you to choose a color by eye or by values.

Selecting Foreground and Background Colors

The colors you choose for the foreground and background colors are entirely at your discretion — you can select colors that are already in your image or select colors that will complement the existing colors.

If your image is bound for the Web, you can use the Only Web Colors option, which changes the appearance of the Color Picker somewhat — breaking the previously smooth spectrum of colors into blocks of color (see Figure 7-3), each considered "Web safe."

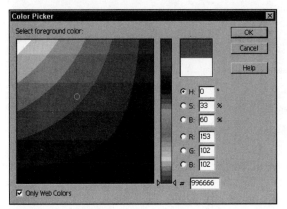

Figure 7-3: The Web-safe Color Picker offers only colors that are acceptable to browser software, which faithfully displays online.

Restoring Default Colors

As stated, the opening the Color Picker is easy — just click on either the Set Foreground Color button or the Set Background Color button. After you select a color from the resulting Color Picker, that color is displayed on the face of the button you just used.

If you want to return to the defaults (black and white, respectively), click the Default Foreground and Background Colors button, shown with its tool tip displayed in Figure 7-4. This replaces whatever colors you may have selected or sampled earlier and set as your fore or background colors, and you can fill a background with white, or paint, draw, or fill shapes or selections with black.

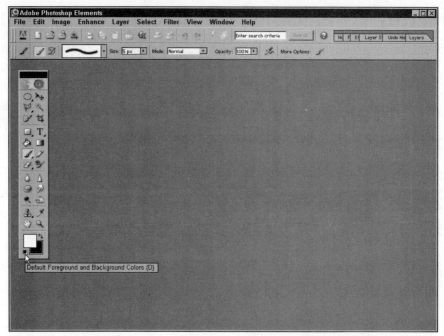

Figure 7-4: Going back to the default black and white colors is easy.

Swapping Foreground and Background Colors

No matter which colors are currently selected for your fore and background colors, you can easily switch them — swapping the foreground for the background, and the background for the foreground color. To do this, just click the little curved arrow to the right of the Set buttons, as shown in Figure 7-5. The display within the Toolbox immediately changes to reflect the swap.

Note

Aside from using the Switch button to swap an erroneously set foreground or background color (the right color, applied to the wrong button), you may want to swap the colors as a way of utilizing the same set of colors but in different ways. For example, the color set as your foreground color is the default color for text when you click the Type tool. After typing some text in that color, you may want to use the previously established background color for new text, so that all of your type either matches the color you are using for painting and filling, or for backgrounds.

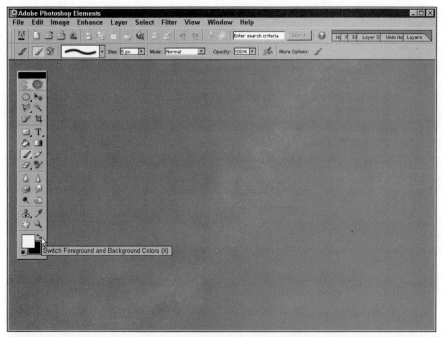

Figure 7-5: Did you set a color as the background when you meant it to be the foreground color? Easily fixed — just swap them!

Sampling Colors from Existing Content

You may have noticed that while the Color Picker dialog box is open, your mouse pointer turns to an eyedropper whenever you move your mouse outside of the dialog box. The mouse pointer is a circle when you're on top of the color palette within the Picker, it's an arrow when it's on top of the spectrum and over any of the fields or options in the dialog box, but if you point outside of the box, you're in sampling mode. *Sampling* means making a selection based on existing content — sipping up color that's already in the image (or, for that matter, anywhere in the workspace) with the eyedropper, and then using that color as either the fore or background color — depending on which Set button you clicked to open the Color Picker in the first place. You can sample in three modes — a single pixel, or in squares of 3x3 (9) or 5x5 (25) pixels at a time.

As shown in Figure 7-6, you can sample a color within the open image, an image behind the active one (if the appropriate portion of the image is visible), or from any portion of the workspace, including buttons, toolbars, menus, of even your Windows or Mac desktop, if it's visible behind the Photoshop Elements workspace.

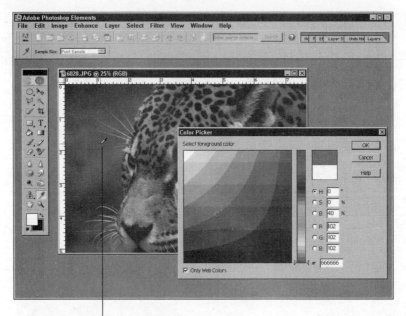

Mouse pointer is an eyedropper.

Figure 7-6: Sample an existing color so that you know the color you choose works visually within the image.

After you click on a color with the eyedropper, its statistics show in the Color Picker — the RGB and HSB levels, the color number (a hexadecimal number if you're in Only Web Colors mode) — and you can then click OK to accept the sampled color as your new Foreground or Background color.

Note   What do RGB and HSB stand for? RGB stands for Red, Green, and Blue, the three colors used to create other colors. HSB stands for Hue, Saturation, and Brightness, the color and light levels that make colors unique. White, for example, has no H (hue) and no S (saturation, or level of color), but has 100 percent B (brightness). Black has no B (brightness), no S (saturation), and no H (hue). The RGB levels for white are 255 (the most you can have) for all three (R, G, and B), as white is the presence of all color — 100 percent of all available color is required to "make" white. To create black, you need no color at all — so black's RGB levels are all 0. Experiment with selecting different colors within the Color Picker and observing their HSB and RGB levels. At some point, especially for a project that will be printed, you may be given specs for colors that have specific HSB and RGB levels, so you'll want to know how to read and set them manually (by typing in the fields).

Applying Special Color and Light Effects

So you've set new colors and painted with them or applied them to selections or shapes, or maybe to your background layer. Or maybe you haven't done anything to your image in terms of color, and it is only a background layer with the scanned content of your photo in place. At this point, you may want to tinker with the colors in your image, brightening or dulling them, intensifying or fading them, removing an unwanted color, or adding more of a desired color. Elements provides all the tools you need to make both manual adjustments to the levels of color and light in your image, as well as several handy automatic tools that make fine adjustments to your image without any input required from you — rather intuitive and effective tools, as you'll see as you move forward.

Making Color Corrections

Photos can have weird or otherwise unpleasant colors in them for a variety of reasons or from to a variety of causes. When photos age, especially those taken in the 1970s and earlier, their colors can shift, leaving you with greenish or yellowish images. Photos exposed to sunlight (framed and placed in or across from a sunny window, for example) can fade or see certain colors wash out and other colors intensify or change. Photos that have been exposed to certain chemicals may also change, whether those chemicals were in the form of a gas or actually spilled on the photo. Improper development techniques can also give you a funky-colored photo, as can too much or too little flash.

Whatever the cause of your photo's color problems, you can correct them with a series of manual and automatic color correction tools. You find most of them in the Enhance menu, shown in Figure 7-7 — you find the rest in any brush or fill tool's Mode drop-down list (each mode discussed later in this chapter in Table 7.1), or through the use of Adjustment Layers, also discussed later in this chapter.

For now, look at the abundance of tools for color correction — those listed here are found in the main Enhance menu and within the Enhance⇨Adjust Color submenu, as indicated:

✦ Auto Color Correction

✦ Adjust Color⇨Color Cast

✦ Adjust Color⇨Hue/Saturation

✦ Adjust Color⇨Remove Color

✦ Adjust Color⇨Replace Color

✦ Adjust Color⇨Color Variations

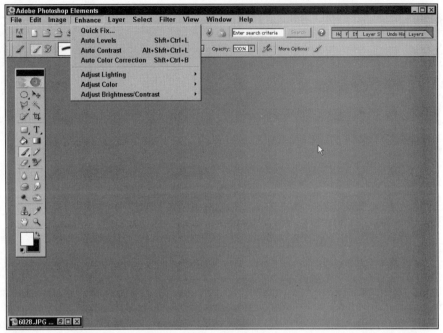

Figure 7-7: The Enhance menu contains an Adjust Color submenu with virtually all the color correction tools you'd ever need.

It's important to note that all of these tools can be used to adjust some or all of your image — to restrict the changes to only part of your image, use the selection tool of your choice before invoking the command. Or to allow the changes to apply to all of your image, make sure nothing is selected (Ctrl + D) before opening the Enhance menu in the first place. If you're selecting a portion of the image to be adjusted, be sure that if your image has more than one layer and that the appropriate layer is active as well.

Correcting a Color Cast

First, to be clear what a color cast is — it's not a single funny color in the image, but rather an overall color that's predominant in most or all of an image. It is usually either green or red, making any people in the image look either nauseated or angry. You may also see yellow casts that simply make the image look dirty or faded. To get rid of such a cast, choose Enhance⇨Adjust Color⇨Color Cast. In the resulting dialog box (see Figure 7-8), you use an eyedropper (your mouse automatically becomes a sampling tool if you point outside the dialog box) to sample the colors that should become gray, white, or black.

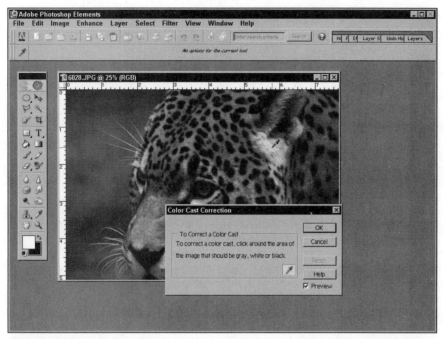

Figure 7-8: Sample the offending colors in your image to replace them with their opposite in the color wheel.

Tip   What's this *color wheel* to which I refer? Check the Color Section of this book for a color wheel that shows primary, secondary, and tertiary colors, how they relate to one another, how to select complementary colors, and how colors are mixed to create other colors. Understanding the color wheel can help a lot of Elements' color-adjustment tools and their behind-the-scenes functionality make more sense to you.

How does replacing certain colors with gray, white, or black solve the problem of a color cast? By clicking on certain pixels, you're telling Elements which color you want to eradicate in favor of neutrals — gray, white, black — and the image colors are adjusted to the opposite color to that which you sampled. For example, if you click on a blue pixel, the overall cast turns yellow or orange, depending on the shade of blue sampled. If you click on a reddish pixel, the image turns aqua or greenish-blue. Clicking on a white, gray, or black pixel causes no color change.

You can sample more than one pixel, watching your image change with each successive sampling (the dialog box is on top of, but not obscuring your entire image, presumably). If you get an undesirable result at any point, click the Reset button, and the image goes back to its state prior to your opening the Color Cast Correction dialog box. When you like what you see, click OK to apply it to your image. To bail out of the process entirely without making any changes at all, click Cancel. Of course, be sure the Preview check box is on—otherwise you won't see the changes take place in your image as you sample colors within it.

Adjusting Hue and Saturation

You've seen these terms before—Hue and Saturation—in our discussion of the Color Picker and the various color values/levels that can be observed and set there. Hue is the color itself—whatever it is, and Saturation is the amount of that color. When you open the Hue/Saturation dialog box (choose Enhance⇨Adjust Color⇨ Hue/Saturation), you are also given the ability to adjust the Lightness (amount of white) included in the colors of your image. Figure 7-9 shows the Hue/Saturation dialog box, with its three sliders (one each for the Hue, Saturation, and Lightness levels).

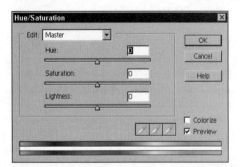

Figure 7-9: Adjust the color, amount of color, and lightness of that color in your image.

You'll also notice three eyedropper buttons, which are dimmed when the dialog box first opens—one is plain, and the other two have a plus sign (+) and a minus sign (–) next to them, respectively. These droppers come to life (as does the spectrum on the color bar, below the sliders) when you switch the Edit drop-down list from Master (the default, representing the entire image, all colors included) to one of the colors listed in that drop-down list, shown in Figure 7-10.

When and if you do make a selection—say Reds—from the drop-down list, you can use the eyedroppers to select pixels that represent the Hue and Saturation levels you want to set—you see that the color bar (located underneath the three sliders) changes to indicate the range of colors represented by the pixel you've sampled. As you click around on the image, depending on which pixel you've sampled, you also see the Edit drop-down list color change — from Blues to Reds, or to Magentas — to whatever color group your sampled pixel falls within.

Figure 7-10: Adjust the Hue and Saturation of specific colors within your image by making a choice from the Edit drop-down list.

To use the dialog box, you can play with the droppers and deal only with certain colors in your image, or you can adjust the Hue, Saturation, and Brightness of all the colors at once (leaving the Edit field set to Master). If you opt to use the latter technique, you'll get fast results, and you can tinker with the simple sliders to get them. If you opt for the more specific approach of using the droppers to sample, add, or remove color, you'll have more to tinker with, but will require more time and tinkering to get the results you desire.

Tip What's the Colorize option do? If your image is in Grayscale mode (black and white), you can convert to RGB mode (using the Image⇨Mode command) and then use this option within the Hue/Saturation dialog box to apply the currently-selected Foreground Color (as long as it's something other than black or white) to the image. You can then use the Hue slider to pick a new color or choose a slightly different shade of the current color. You're essentially creating what's known as a *duotone*, which is any image that's comprised of two colors, one being black.

Removing Colors

The Remove Color command, found in the Enhance⇨Adjust Color submenu, doesn't open a dialog box, and therefore doesn't ask for or allow any input from you. The command essentially converts a color image to grayscale (but it doesn't change its mode) by changing all colors in the image to equal Red, Green, and Blue levels, relative to their current color. As shown in Figure 7-11, after a photo has had its color removed, if we refer to the Info palette and sample any pixel, note that all three color levels — Red, Green, and Blue, are equal.

Figure 7-11: Leave your image in RGB mode, but remove all color by equalizing the colors within the image, turning them all to shades of gray.

Replacing Colors

This command, also found in the Enhance➪Adjust color submenu, does offer a dialog box and does offer you the ability to provide input in terms of which colors you want to replace, and which colors will replace them. You can achieve subtle effects that improve an image by removing unwanted colors (a more focused approach than the Color Cast Correction method), or you can achieve very dramatic or esoteric results by replacing colors with unexpected alternatives. For example, in a photo of boats in a harbor (see Figure 7-12, where a photo is visible behind the Replace Color dialog box), you could make the color of the water green instead of blue, or make the sky red.

To determine which colors change within your image, use your mouse to click within the image, and watch the thumbnail, which shows the image in one of two states — showing just the selected pixels (based on sampling you do with the eyedropper, as soon as the dialog box is open) or showing the image itself, in full color, as it is. It's usually best to leave this set to Selection, so that you can see which pixels will be altered and which ones will not.

With the Preview option on so you can see your changes as they apply to the actual image (and not just the thumbnail), click on a representative pixel within the image — say the blue in the sky, or the color of a house, or a flower in a garden or fabric pattern. The thumbnail, if set to Selection, then changes, as shown in Figure 7-13, to show only the pixels that match the one you sampled. To increase or decrease the number of pixels deemed "matching," use the Fuzziness slider — a lower setting creates less tolerance and requires a closer match, and a higher number includes more pixels and considers them matches.

You can augment or reduce the selection with the plus (+) and minus (–) eye droppers, telling Elements to add or remove pixels from the selection — just click within the image with the appropriate dropper and watch the Selection change accordingly.

After you make the desired selection, use the Hue, Saturation, and Lightness sliders to change the color of the selected pixels, making the aforementioned subtle changes or completely altering the reality of the image with unexpected color choices. After you click OK, the image changes to match what you saw in the Preview, and only the Undo command or the Undo History palette can restore the image to its pre-Replace Color state.

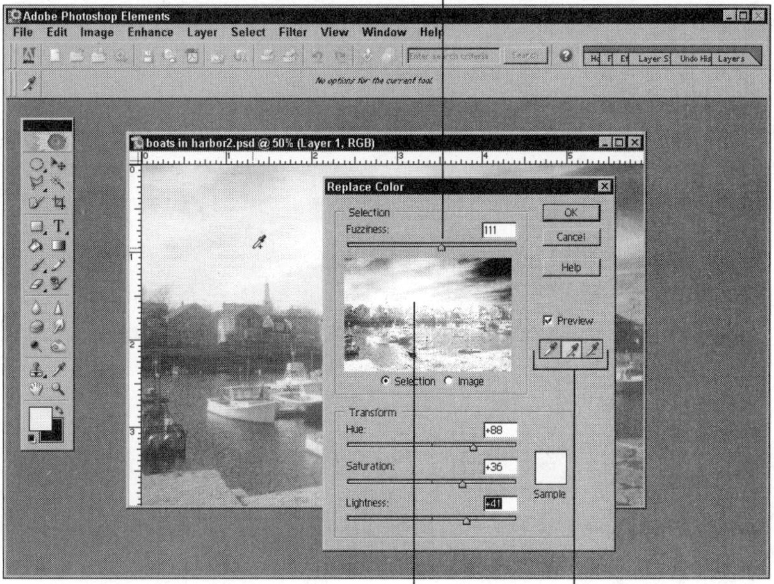

Use the Fuzziness slider to allow more or fewer pixels
to meet your sampled pixels' selection criteria.

Use these eyedroppers to select, add to a
selection, or remove pixels from a selection.

The thumbnail, set to Selection, shows the pixels that change after you
make your Hue, Saturation, and Lighness adjustments.

Figure 7-12: Make specific replacements for particular colors within your image.

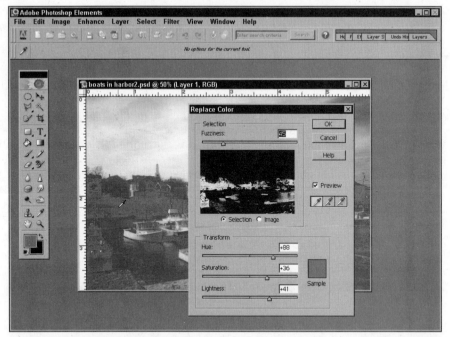

Figure 7-13: Clicking elsewhere in the image changes the selection, as shown in the dialog box thumbnail box.

Using the Color Variations Window

Now this tool is very useful — it enables you to make a variety of changes to the quality of your entire image or just part of it by using simple thumbnail examples to guide you, as shown in Figure 7-14. To open this window, choose Enhance⇨Adjust Color⇨Color Variations.

To use the Color Variations window for color correction, follow these steps:

STEPS: Using Color Variations to Adjust a Photo's Color Levels and Quality

1. Make any selection within your image (including selecting the appropriate layer, if you have more than one to choose from) if you want to restrict the Color Variations effects to a portion of your image. If you want to apply the changes to the entire image, be sure nothing is selected by pressing Ctrl + D.

2. Using the default Midtones setting in the Select area (section #1) section of the window, look at the Before and After thumbnails to decide what changes are required.

3. Click the buttons (they look like tiny thumbnail images) in section #3 to make color changes to your image.

4. Continue to click the Increase and Decrease buttons as needed until you like the After image.

5. If you decide you don't like your changes, click Undo to go back one step or Reset to go back to the original Before state in the After view.

6. As soon as you like the changes you made, click OK to apply them.

Of course, you can change the selection in section #1 of the window, altering the Shadows, Highlights, or Saturation of the image. If you pick Saturation, you have just two options, represented by two buttons in section #3, as shown in Figure 7-15.

The After image shows the effects
of your choices within the window.

Add or remove Red, Green, or Blue levels.

The Before image is how your
image looked before opening
the Color Variations window.

Click Reset Image to revert to
the Before state and start over.

Undo and Redo enable
you to go back and forth
between adjustments.

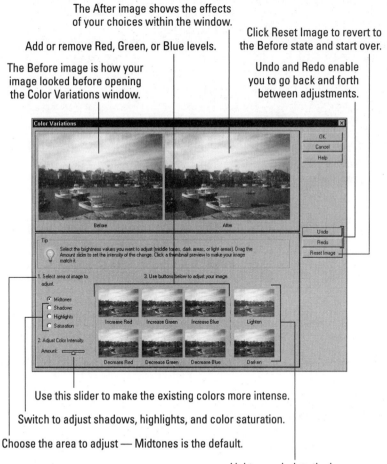

Use this slider to make the existing colors more intense.

Switch to adjust shadows, highlights, and color saturation.

Choose the area to adjust — Midtones is the default.

Lighten or darken the image.

Figure 7-14: Add more Red, Green, or Blue or adjust the lighting or color intensity instead.

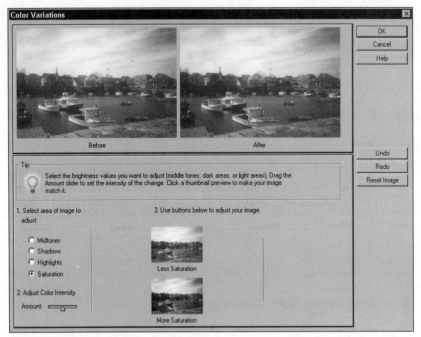

Figure 7-15: Choose between Less Saturation or More Saturation to change the overall intensity of your image colors.

If you use the Adjust Color Intensity slider (which you would understandably think might do the same thing as making changes to Saturation), you can adjust the amount of color added or taken away while in Midtones, Shadows, or Highlights mode — it makes the Increase Red, for example, *really* increase the amount of red if you previously dragged the slider to the right. If you drag the slider to the left, all the Increase and Decrease changes (for all three colors) will be more subtle.

Tip   Using the Lighten and Darken thumbnail buttons does not adjust color, they just make whatever colors the image has in it darker or lighter. You can use these buttons in conjunction with the Increase and Decrease color buttons, in which case the color adjustments are made lighter or darker, too.

Correcting Light Levels

The amount of light in an image affects two elements — detail within the image and color quality. If there's too much light, details (and colors) can be washed out, and conversely, if there's too little light, shadows can engulf and obscure details and make colors look muddy or dense. Elements offers two tools within the Enhance menu's Adjust Lighting submenu to help fix lighting problems, and then there are automatic tools that adjust lighting overall. I get to these later. For now, the two tools you can use to adjust light sources and problems are:

✦ Adjust Lighting➪Adjust Backlighting

✦ Adjust Lighting➪Fill Flash

These tools enable you to change the appearance of light as captured by your camera, and where light in the room or in the outdoor setting was coming from and how it affected your image. You may not love the results of either tool, depending on the degree of lighting problems you have, and where they are in the image. For example, if you have a big backlighting problem, the Adjust Backlighting tool may not give you the results you want (no big shadows cast by the photo's subject, as shown in Figure 7-16), and you may have more luck literally getting rid of the shadows with the Clone Stamp.

Figure 7-16: Dark, distinct shadows next to and behind subjects indicate a problem with backlighting.

Adjusting Backlighting

To use the Adjust Backlighting command, select the portion and/or layer of your image that's got the lighting problem, or if it's uniform over the entire image, select nothing. Then, choose Enhance➪Adjust Lighting➪Adjust Backlighting. In the resulting dialog box (see Figure 7-17), you can use the Darker slider to add or subtract light from the image, reducing the amount of shadow overall. To some users, it simply looks as though the image is being faded, and you may therefore want to deal with the individual shadows with other tools, as described in Chapter 6.

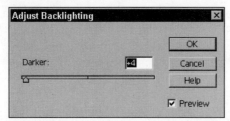

Figure 7-17: Drag the slider and look at your image to see if this feature is solving your backlighting problem.

If you do like the results, click OK to apply them. If not, click Cancel. Be sure the Preview option is on so that you can see your changes in the image window before committing to them. Of course, if you click OK and then change your mind, you can choose Edit⇨Undo, Ctrl + Z, or use the Undo History palette to go back to the image state before the Adjust Backlighting command was issued.

Using the Fill Flash

The Fill Flash command, also found in the Adjust Lighting submenu, gives you two sliders — one to adjust the amount of light within your selection (or absent a selection, across the entire image) and another one to adjust saturation, as shown in Figure 7-18. Why both? Because in adding light, you can see colors fade, and you can counteract that by increasing saturation.

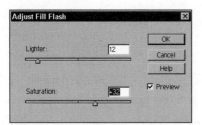

Figure 7-18: Add more light to your image with the Adjust Fill Flash dialog box.

Tip   Be careful that in adjusting Saturation through this dialog box that certain colors don't become unnaturally bright or vivid. You may want to use other tools instead of making Saturation adjustments here, such as the Hue/Saturation dialog box, where you can adjust certain colors, or the Color Variations window, which enables you to add and subtract specific colors in varying intensities.

Using Auto Color Correction

Talk about quick and easy! This command, found in the main Enhance menu, makes color adjustments without any input from you. It works by locating the midtones, highlights, and shadows within your image (based on light levels) and then neutralizes the midtones and reduces the disparity between shadows and highlights. You may not like the results and find that it makes your image too dark or too light, or that it makes your colors too dull or too bright—the results really depend on the colors and light levels found in the original image. If you don't like the results of this command, use any of the aforementioned Undo procedures to go back in time to before Auto Color Correction was applied. If, on the other hand, you like the results (as will often be the case), you'll have saved yourself a lot of work and manual adjustments.

Working with Brightness and Contrast

The Brightness/Contrast dialog box (shown in Figure 7-19) offers two sliders—appropriately, one adjusts the brightness, and the other adjusts contrast. As you see as you drag the sliders while viewing one of your images, dragging to the right on either slider increases the brightness and contrast, respectively. If you drag to the left, you reduce brightness and contrast.

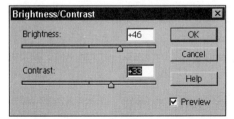

Figure 7-19: The Brightness/Contrast dialog box offers you the ability to control two related aspects of the image in one place.

What do the Brightness levels do to your image? If it's an outdoor image and you increase the brightness, it makes it look as though there was a lot more sun that day than there really was or than your camera managed to capture. If you decrease the brightness in that same image, you can achieve the look of a cloudy, overcast day. For indoor photos, adding brightness makes the room look well lit—as though more outdoor and artificial light was spilling in, and spilling uniformly. Reducing brightness dims the photo, as though the room was lacking lamps and no outdoor light was available. Figures 7-20 and 7-21 show a photo before and after adding brightness—even in this black and white representation of a color photo, you can see the increased appearance of sunshine in this already bright outdoor image.

Figure 7-20: Before adding Brightness, this image was bright, but it didn't pop.

Figure 7-21: After adding just a small amount of Brightness, the added "sunlight" augments the highlights on the water and pulls detail out of the shadows.

Adjusting the Contrast slider requires very slight adjustments in order to have constructive, rather than destructive results. As shown in Figure 7-22, adding too much contrast makes the image look too stark, and details are lost to the heightened shadows and highlights. In Figure 7-23, reducing contrast is shown to make the image dull and lifeless—nothing stands out, even things that should, such as bright lights and deep shadows under and between solid objects.

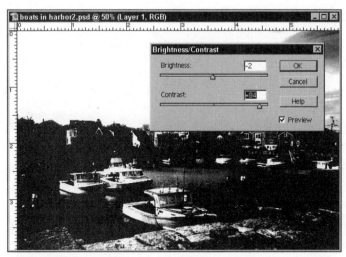

Figure 7-22: Too much contrast can ruin an image by making everything either too bright or too dark, with nothing in the middle.

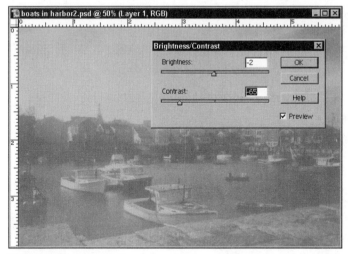

Figure 7-23: A reduction in contrast can make the image dull if you're not careful.

Now don't think that the Contrast slider can't do some good. If you have an image with brights that are just too distinct — a glare on a forehead, a shine on a chrome bumper, a bright white building that's blinding in contrast to the rest of the image — toning those contrasts down can be a good thing. The key is in making small adjustments and going for subtle results.

Tip

If you restrict the results of the Brightness/Contrast dialog box to a specific area of your image, be careful that your selection and the resulting adjustments don't stand out as unnatural—leaving a clear delineation between what was adjusted and what wasn't. You can avoid stark, obvious edges by adding a Feather to your selection or conversely, selecting very specifically, with the Magnetic Lasso or the Magic Wand, so that only the very pixels you want to adjust are changed, with no obvious line created.

Using the Auto Contrast Command

If you liked the manual adjustments you could make through the Brightness/Contrast dialog box, you may love the automatic results that you get with the Auto Contrast command. Offering no dialog box, the command, found in the Enhance menu, requires no input from you, other than to have made a selection within the image before issuing the command, thus controlling the portion of the image to which the automatic contrast adjustments are made. Figure 7-24 shows an image wherein a section of the image (for demonstration purposes) has been adjusted.

Figure 7-24: The highlights are much brighter, and the shadows are much deeper after using Auto Contrast.

The Auto Contrast feature works by adjusting the contrast and combination of colors in your image overall. Elements looks for the lightest pixel in the image, and also for the darkest pixel, and converts them, respectively, to white and black. Then, the rest of the pixels (which now fall between these two extremes) are adjusted, resulting in brighter highlights and deeper, more distinct shadows. Midtones are not drastically (and often not even noticeably) changed.

Using the Levels Command

Found in the Enhance⇨Adjust Brightness/Contrast submenu, the Levels command uses a *histogram* to allow you to adjust the shadows, highlights, and midtones within your image, adjusting the overall tonal range within the image. A histogram is a visual representation of levels — as shown in Figure 7-25, the light and dark levels appear as peaks and valleys within the Levels dialog box, and by dragging the triangles on the slider beneath this display, you can adjust the intensity of those peaks and valleys, and therefore adjust the intensity of the lights and darks within your image.

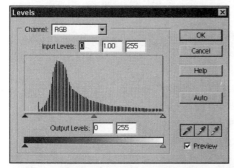

Figure 7-25: See the values within your image displayed through a histogram's peaks and valleys.

To use the dialog box, follow these steps:

STEPS: Using the Levels Command to Adjust Shadows and Highlights

1. If you want to restrict the effects of the Levels command to a portion of your image, select that area and/or layer before opening the Levels dialog box. If you want the effects to apply to the entire image, make sure nothing is selected by pressing Ctrl + D.

2. Leave the Channel set to RGB so that all levels of all three colors are affected. If you want, however, you can choose just the Red, Blue, or Green channel from the Channel drop-down list. If you do so, only the highlights and shadows within that channel will be adjusted.

3. As desired, adjust the Input Levels for the Highlights (first of the three fields), Midtones, and/or Shadows. You can do this manually, typing new numbers in the three boxes, or you can drag the sliders shown in Figure 7-26.

4. Adjust the Output levels if you want to restrict the range (and therefore the potential intensity) of your highlights and shadows.

Drag this triangle to set the midpoint for midtones.

Drag this triangle to adjust the intensity of the shadows within the image.

Drag this triangle to adjust the intensity of the highlights within the image.

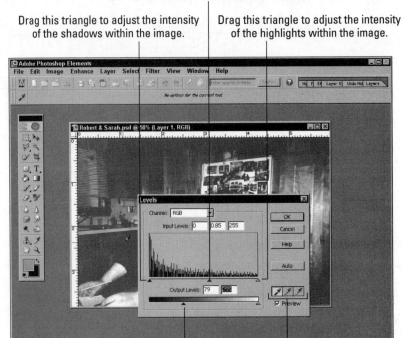

Establish the range within which the highlights and shadows can be adjusted with the Output Levels sliders and triangles.

Use the three eyedroppers to select the Black Point, Gray Point, and White Point, which establishes the darkest shadow, middle point for midtones, and brightest highlight.

Figure 7-26: Adjust the amount of highlights, midtones, and shadows in your image.

5. If you want to set the Black Point, Gray Point, and White Point (darkest, middle, and brightest pixels), use the three eyedroppers located above the Preview check box. This lets you tell Elements where the two extremes and their midpoint are, rather than letting Elements decide on its own.

6. After adjusting the Levels in your image using one or more of the tools available in the dialog box, click OK when you're happy with the results within your image.

Tip

If you find that you don't like having so many adjustments available (and some people find the abundance of options within the Levels dialog box to be confusing), you can click the Auto button to achieve the same results you'd get by issuing the Auto Levels command, which adjusts the highlights and shadows automatically.

Making Overall Adjustments Automatically

You saw Auto Contrast at work and experienced the quick, nearly automatic results of the Color Variations window. Consider these two automatic enhancements, however—Quick Fix and Auto Levels. These two commands, one with a dialog box and one without, allow you to make sweeping changes quickly, adjusting the overall quality of your command with very few decisions required from you, and very little clicking with your mouse.

Working with Quick Fix

The Quick Fix command is rightfully first in line in the Enhance menu. This command is really one-stop-shopping for remedying a vast assortment of problems with any photo you scanned or captured with a digital camera. The window, shown in Figure 7-27, will remind you a great deal of the Color Variations window—it has the same Before and After thumbnails, and similar options in three sections of the window:

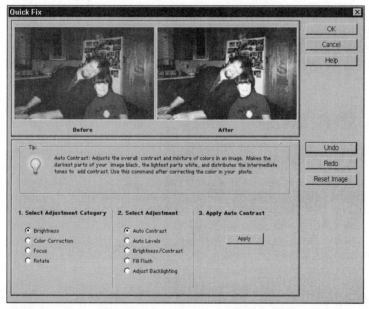

Figure 7-27: The Quick Fix window offers several different aspects of your image to fix and then provides automatic tools for making the requisite changes.

✦ Select an Adjustment Category (choose what aspect of the image to adjust).

✦ Select an Adjustment (what do you want to do to the category you selected).

✦ Apply, where the blank represents the application of some change —
Brightness/Contrast if you chose Brightness from the first section of the
dialog box or Auto Color Correction if you chose Color Correction.

You can, of course, make multiple changes, choosing two or more categories (one
at a time), selecting an adjustment to be made and then applying the changes.
When you like what you see in the After thumbnail, click OK to apply the changes
you made. Of course, the Reset Image button puts everything back to its original
state, and you can start over, tinkering with different categories and adjustments.

Using Auto Levels

The manual adjustments you can make with the Levels command can be made
automatically with the Enhance⇨Auto Levels command, wherein Elements finds the
darkest and lightest pixels in the image and then redistributes the rest of the midtones pixels' levels to fall evenly within the range created by the lightest and darkest pixels.

There is no dialog box with this command — you just choose it from the Enhance
menu, and Elements goes to work on your image. The command works best on
images without grave problems — images that just need a small nudge in terms of
contrast, brightness, and overall distribution of color. If your image has serious
problems in any of those areas, I'd suggest using multiple manual tools to fix the
problems, rather than relying on any automatic (dialog box-less) command.

Using Adjustment Layers to Improve an Image

Many of the same adjustments you can make with the Enhance menu's commands
(and Adjust Lighting and Adjust Color submenus' commands) can be applied
through the use of what is known as an *adjustment layer*. Adjustment layers are an
interesting and often very effective way of applying a color or lighting change,
because the changes are on a separate layer, and the image itself is unchanged —
the existing layer/s are not affected, but are seen through the overlay of a filter that
applies color and lighting changes.

To create an adjustment layer, you must first display the Layers palette, which you
can do by clicking its tab in the docking well or by choosing Windows⇨Layers. I
usually move the Layers palette off the docking well for any extended use, just so it
doesn't roll back up to the palette the minute I click off of it. With the palette displayed, click the Create New Fill or Adjustment Layer button (shown in Figure 7-28)
and note the menu that appears.

Figure 7-28: See some familiar commands? You can create layers that apply the same changes you've applied through the Enhance menu, but apply them via a new layer.

Tip   Read a thorough discussion of the Layers palette and the role layers play in your images in Chapter 10.

Assuming you know which adjustment you want to make—applying the Levels command, Brightness/Contrast, or Hue/Saturation—makes that selection from the menu and then use the same dialog box you'd work with if you'd selected the command from within the Enhance menu. When you click OK to apply your changes, a new layer appears, one that you can hide or display, which hides or displays the changes created through the dialog box you used.

Tip   The Create New Fill or Adjustment Layer button's menu also offers Gradient Map, Invert, Threshold, and Posterize commands, which you read more about later in this chapter. These commands apply special color effects, more so than providing restorative or corrective effects, but they can still be even more effective in a layer, just as the corrective effects that we've discussed thus far can.

Working with Modes

When you work with any of Elements' brush-based tools—the paint Brush, Pencil, Eraser, Dodge tool, Burn tool, Smudge tool, and the Clone Stamp, a Mode options appears in the options bar, as shown in Figure 7-29, which depicts the Brush tool's options bar and list of Mode choices. These modes allow you to accomplish more than one task at a time with the tool in use—instead, for example, of simply applying a color with the paintbrush, or just darkening part of the image (with the Burn tool), you can also apply other color and lighting effects.

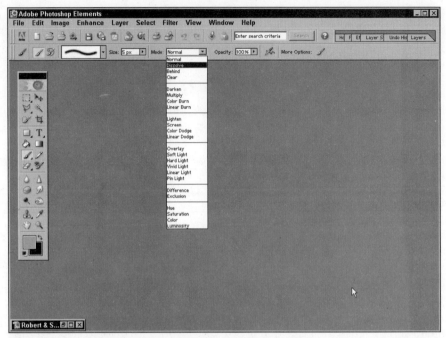

Figure 7-29: Brush on a color and a color or lighting effect at the same time with the brush-based tools' Mode options.

Of course, each of the brush-based tools has its own subset of these modes — some of modes in the full list (available only with the Brush tool) aren't appropriate for certain other tools, as the tools' function and one or more of the modes might be contradictory. For example, the Dodge tool wouldn't really be a good choice for applying the Color Burn mode, because burning darkens while the Dodge tool lightens.

You learn which tool offers which modes as you spend more time with Elements, of course. In the meantime, to help you familiarize yourself with the entire list of Mode choices, check out Table 7-1, which includes each of the modes available with the Brush and a description of the effect/purpose for each of them.

Tip

Even though it's not brush-based, the Paint Bucket tool also has a Mode list in its options bar.

Table 7-1
Brush and Brush-based Tool Modes

Mode	Effect/Purpose
Normal	This mode paints each painted pixel to make it the *result color* (the color you chose for the Foreground color on the Color Picker).
Dissolve	This works the same as Normal mode, except that the paint is applied as though the color were dissolving on the painted surface.
Behind	This mode paints the transparent areas of a layer only and is obviously only applicable on layers with Lock Transparency turned off. You read more about locking transparency in Chapter 10, which covers layers in detail.
Clear	The Clear mode makes each pixel you paint transparent, or clear, which gives this mode its name. You can use Clear mode on tools other than the Brush, such as the Paint Bucket tool, and the Pencil. Like Behind mode, Lock Transparency must be off in order to use this mode.
Darken	This mode refers to the color information in each color channel (Red, Green, or Blue) and selects the darker color when comparing the *base color* (the original color in the image) and *blending color* (the color you're applying with the active tool). Pixels that are lighter than the blend color are replaced, and the pixels that are darker than the blend color are left as is. You use Darken when you want to apply a light color and darken a base color that's already darker than the color with which you're painting.
Multiply	Use this mode to create a darker color by multiplying the base color by the blend color, based on the color information in each channel. When you use Multiply mode and paint with colors other than white you create increasingly darker colors as you paint over and over in the same spots — much like applying layers of translucent color and overlapping the same or different colors — the more you paint or draw in the same spot, the darker your colors become.
Color Burn	This mode darkens the active layer (wherever you paint on it) by increasing the contrast between base and blend colors. You can use this blending mode to get a starker, high contrast effect.
Linear Burn	This mode works much like Color Burn, but it uses the color information in each color channel to reduce the brightness levels of the base color.

Continued

Table 7-1 *(continued)*

Mode	Effect/Purpose
Lighten	If your base color is lighter than your blend color, the base color is chosen as the result color, and vice versa — if the blend color is lighter, that becomes the result. If there are pixels in the painted area that are darker than the blend color, they're changed to the result color, and pixels that are lighter than the blend color don't change at all. You can use this mode to achieve an eraser-like effect — wiping out darker colors in favor of a lighter one. If you paint with a color that's already in the image, that color is unaffected by the new paint, but whatever's darker is replaced with white, and transparent areas are filled with the painting color.
Screen	Unlike Multiply, which creates darker colors where painting overlaps, the effect of Screen mode is a lighter color. Screening with black doesn't change the color, and screening with white gives you white. For a good visual analogy, imagine aiming dueling overhead projectors (with color slides on them) at the same spot on the wall. Unlike overlapping slides on the same projector, which would produce darker colors where they overlap, the two projected images would appear lighter at their common target.
Color Dodge	For an extreme brightening effect, use Color Dodge mode. This mode takes the color information in each channel and then brightens the base color (and thus the result color) by decreasing the contrast. If you paint with white or very light colors, you increase the effect.
Linear Dodge	The results of this mode are very similar to Color Dodge, but instead of reducing contrast to achieve added brightness, the brightness level is directly increased.
Overlay	This mode works like Multiply or Screen in that overlapping colors maintain highlights and shadows. The base color is mixed with the blend color to give you a result color that has the same light or dark quality of the base color.
Soft Light	Imagine shining a soft, white light on something — the shadows and highlights are increased by the light source, but the effects are subtle. Changes to color in this mode are based on the blend color, and the lightness or darkness of that color determines the lightening effect — if the blend color is lighter than 50 percent gray, this mode produces an effect similar to the Dodge tool. If the blend color is darker than 50 percent gray, the Burn tool's effect is mimicked.
Hard Light	Having the opposite effect of the Soft Light mode, Hard Light creates a harsh, bare-bulb lighting effect on your image. The blend color is used as in the case of Soft Light, but the effects are much harder and not subtle in the least.

Mode	Effect/Purpose
Vivid Light	This mode will lighten (dodge) or darken (burn) as you paint by adjusting the contrast in relation to the blend color. When the blend color is lighter than 50 percent gray, the Vivid Light mode lightens the image by reducing contrast. Conversely, if the blend color is darker than 50 percent gray, a darkening effect will be applied by increasing the contrast.
Linear Light	The same way Vivid Light bases contrast adjustments on the blend color, Linear Light mode adjusts brightness based on the blend color. A blend color that's lighter than 50 percent gray results in a lighter effect, achieved by increasing the brightness level. If the blend color is darker than 50 percent gray, brightness will be decreased, resulting in a darker effect.
Pin Light	In Pin Light mode, if your blend color is lighter than 50 percent gray, any pixels darker than your blend color are replaced with the result color. If there are pixels lighter than the blend color in the path of your paintbrush, they are not changed. On the other hand, if your blend color is darker than 50 percent gray, any pixels lighter than your blend color are replaced, and if there are pixels darker than the blend color in the path of your paintbrush, those don't change, either.
Difference	Use this blending mode to inverts lower layers based on the levels of brightness in the layer on which you're painting. This mode takes the color information in each channel and takes the blend color from the base color or the base color from the blend color — it all depends whether or not the base is brighter than the blending color, or vice versa. The results can be quite dramatic, resulting in a sort of color-negative effect.
Exclusion	This mode has virtually the same effect as Difference mode, with lower contrast levels.
Hue	Working with the HSB color model (Hue, Saturation, and Brightness), this blending mode gives you a result color that has the luminosity and saturation of the base color and the hue of the blend color.
Saturation	Again using the HSB mode, this mode gives you a result color with the luminosity and hue of the base color and the saturation of the blend color.
Color	Yet another combination of the HSB color model's components, this blending mode gives you a result color with the brightness of the base color and the hue and saturation of the blend color. You'll find this mode works well when you're changing the tint of a color image or when you're adding color to a monochrome image.
Luminosity	This mode gives you a result color with the hue and saturation of the base color and the luminosity of the blend color.

Note Did some of these Mode options seem like more than you'd ever want or need to do to your images? You're not alone. These modes sort of "came with" Elements as it was developed as a less powerful version of Photoshop. Photoshop's average user *would* have use for most of these modes, but the average Elements user might not. You can experiment with the modes you aren't sure of and see their effects take place. In some cases, simply seeing how they work can give you ideas for how and when to make use of them, opening creative doors that might have remained closed otherwise. As with all applications, the best way to master Elements it to experiment and to put the product and your own skills through their paces!

Using Special Color Effects

Not to be confused with Elements' Effects tab, these commands, found in the Image menu (in the Adjustments submenu, shown in Figure 7-30), create interesting and sometimes unexpected color effects in your images. The commands' names are not necessarily obvious in terms of preparing you for what the commands will do, and because they're not purely restorative or used for standard retouching tasks, I've chosen to cover them as a group, not mixing them in with color and lighting-related commands discussed earlier in this chapter.

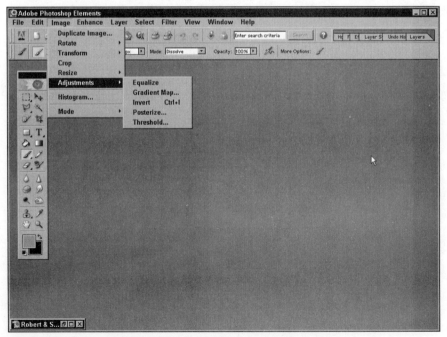

Figure 7-30: Access some special color and lighting adjustment and effects tools through the Image⇨Adjustments submenu.

Note All but the Equalize and Invert commands in this submenu offer a dialog box for you to use in customizing the commands' effects. For the two that do not use a dialog box, the effects are automatic, and the effects are dependent on the color and light within your image to begin with. Of course, even the commands that provide a dialog box are dependent on your image content, but with the ability to customize a commands' effects, you can create subtle or quite dramatic results, all through the options in the various dialog boxes.

Equalizing an Image

This first command in the Adjustments submenu evens out the brightness levels of all the pixels in your entire image. It does this by finding the lightest and darkest pixels and then evenly distributing the rest of the pixels to fall within the range set by those two extremes. This may sound a lot like the Auto Levels command, but it's different in that it also changes the brightest and darkest pixels' values. The lightest is changed to white, and the darkest to black, allowing the rest of the pixels a full range of values. The Auto Level command doesn't change the two extremes (brightest and darkest), so the rest of the image pixels have a more narrow range within which to be distributed.

If your image is just about "there" in terms of the brightness and contrast being right for the setting — indoors, outdoors — and for the overall quality of the image, the Equalize command will have very subtle, and perhaps unnoticeable effects. If, on the other hand, your image has very little difference between its lightest and darkest pixels, the changing of those pixels to white and black (respectively) will have a dramatic effect on the rest of the pixels in the image. Figure 7-31 shows an image that's very faded and dim — so there aren't any bright whites or deep blacks. In Figure 7-32, after the Equalize command is applied, the image comes to life, with extremes of light and dark and more realistic spectrum of color and light levels in between.

Working with Gradient Maps

The Gradient Map command applies any one of a number of gradient presets (the ones you'd apply by using the Gradient fill tool in the toolbox, used to fill shapes and layers with a range of colors) and turns your image into a grayscale image that utilizes the selected gradient effect. As shown in Figure 7-33, you can apply multi-color gradients, or simple gradients that go from one color to another, with variations of the starting and ending colors in between. This can have a very interesting effect on a color photo, and can bring an image that's already in grayscale to life by applying color in an unexpected way.

Figure 7-31: Got a dim photo with no extremes of bright and dark? Equalize.

Figure 7-32: After Equalize is applied, the colors and light levels pop.

To use this command, simply choose Image⇨Adjustments⇨Gradient Map and choose a gradient preset. After you choose a gradient, the dialog box expands (see Figure 7-34), enabling you to choose where the gradient colors kick in the spectrum of colors, from highlights to midtones to shadows. You can tinker with these added settings until you like what you see (your results are previewed in the image window, also seen in Figure 7-34), and as soon as you click OK, the gradient is applied to your image.

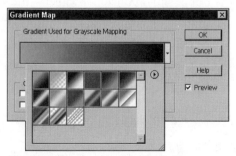

Figure 7-33: The gradient map (the range of colors from starting color to ending color) is applied to your image, recoloring the image pixels according to the map's "coordinates."

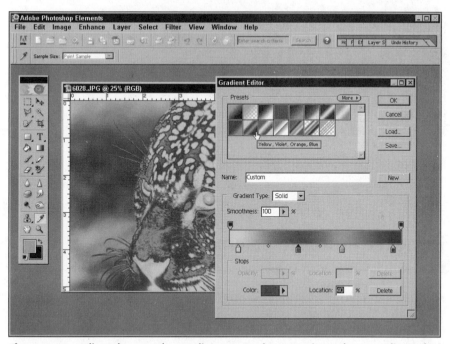

Figure 7-34: Adjust the way the gradient moves from starting color to ending color by working with this expanded version of the Gradient Map dialog box.

Inverting Colors

This command, which does not provide a dialog box, is very simple in its effects. It swaps all the colors in your image for their opposite on the color wheel — turning your image into a color negative of the original. Of course, if your image were in grayscale, you get the black and white negative when using the Invert command. Figure 7-35 shows an image before the Invert command with a rectangular section that's been inverted.

This selected area within the image was inverted and now looks like a negative.

Figure 7-35: A regular color photo with a selection made and inverted

Tip   You can find the color wheel and its uses in selecting and understanding colors in the Color Section of this book.

Using the Posterize Command

If you want to flatten your image colors, reducing the entire image to a range of just a few colors, the Posterize command makes that possible. It's an interesting, artistic effect, rather than one that improves the quality or detail in an image. Actually, even with a high number of color levels — 20 or more — the image is stripped of much of its detail simply by the reduction in the number of pixel values available to the image.

How does this command work? If you apply two levels to your image, the image will consist of two colors — black and white. Adding more levels — three, four, five, or six — adds that many colors. You can have as many as 255 levels in the image, but choosing a number that high won't make much change in your image — you get the most interesting effects by applying 10 or fewer levels, as shown in Figure 7-36, which shows both the Posterize dialog box and the effects the current setting has on the image.

Figure 7-36: Reduce the number of colors in your image and create flat areas of simple color.

Setting Thresholds

Like the Posterize command, which reduces an image to a number of colors you specify (by entering a number of levels), the Threshold command turns any color or grayscale image into a true black and white image — with just those two colors, and no shades of gray in between. Through the Threshold dialog box, shown in Figure 7-37, you can adjust the levels of light and dark, establishing the amount of white and black in the image.

To use this command, choose Image⇨Adjustments⇨Threshold, and then drag the slider triangles (below the histogram) until you like the results, which you can see taking place in your image window. You can also type new numbers into the Threshold Level field, but you'll probably prefer using the slider, as it allows you to adjust the image effects "by eye."

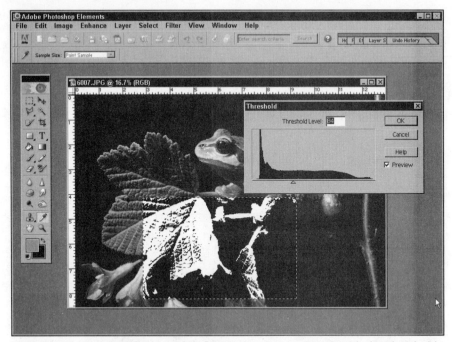

Figure 7-37: Find the lightest and darkest points in your image with the Threshold command.

Tip   Not sure why you'd use this command? Well, you can use it for artistic reasons, if you simply like the way the image looks after you apply the command. The other use is in establishing (and displaying, clearly) the lightest and darkest spots in your image.

✦   ✦   ✦

Changing Image Size

In This Chapter

Changing image size

Adding to the size of your canvas

Cropping images

Using Elements' Transformation tools

Image size can be a confusing concept. Some people confuse it, understandably, with *file size*, which is the actual amount of space the image file takes up on a disk — typically in kilobytes for small, Web-bound images, or megabytes for images in typical formats for print media.

Resizing Your Image

Image size, on the other hand, is the physical dimensions of your image, which includes three types of measurement:

+ **Pixel dimensions,** which is the dimensions (width and height) in pixels.

+ **Document size,** which is the physical size of the image when printed — typically measured in inches, but can be measured in pixels or any of Elements' other measurement options: as a percentage, in centimeters, millimeters, picas, or points.

+ **Resolution,** which is the pixels per inch (ppi) of the image, and which affects the file size (the higher the resolution, the larger the file size) and the amount of information included in the file. As stated in our chapter on scanning (see Chapter 4), it's always best to scan at a high resolution so that you have more detail to work with in restoring and retouching the image. Starting a new image at a high resolution achieves the same goal.

Tip

To create a new image and adjust its resolution, choose File➪New, and in the resulting dialog box, use the Resolution field and enter a new number in the first field, and choose the measurement method (it's pixels, by default) with which you want to work.

Adjusting Pixel Dimensions and Depth

To change the size of an existing image, choose Image⮞Resize⮞Image Size. In the resulting dialog box (shown in Figure 8-1), you can adjust both the Pixel Dimensions and the Document Size. You can also apply two controls — Constrain Proportions, which means that if you adjust the width, for example, the height will adjust proportionately, and Resample Image. This second control determines the *interpolation method* (the way new pixels will be added) that will be used when your image size is increased:

✦ **Bicubic:** This is the default, and it's the most precise and therefore preferred method. The results are the smoothest in terms of the tones within the image, especially important in photographs.

✦ **Nearest Neighbor:** This is the fastest method, but isn't as precise as the other choices. You can end up with choppy, jagged edges within your image, and these can become exaggerated when and if you resize again or use the Transform commands to resize layers within your image.

✦ **Bilinear:** This method falls between Bicubic and Nearest Neighbor in terms of speed and quality. If you used Bicubic and find that it takes too long, or if you used Nearest Neighbor and are dissatisfied with the image quality, give this method a try.

The file size estimate, based on all of the sizing options, appears here.

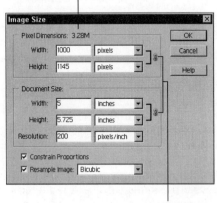

These chains appear when the Constrain Proportions option is on.

Figure 8-1: Enter new pixel and/or document dimensions for your image.

Note If your computer is taking too long to resize images, you may want to consider increasing the memory in your computer. This can be done at home for most computers, after ordering the right memory for your particular computer, and following the instructions that come with it. The minimum recommended amount of RAM memory in a computer running Photoshop or Photoshop Elements is 256MB, but 512MB or more will give you even better results. Memory is fairly inexpensive these days, so you might consider an upgrade.

The Pixel Dimensions setting, as well as the Resolution setting (found in the Document Size section of the dialog box) enable you to leave the print size of the image alone while changing the size of the image as it will appear when viewed online (in pixels) and to make the image larger or smaller in terms of file size. The Resolution directly affects file size, and the higher the resolution, the more pixels are used to make up the image, therefore the more information stored in the image.

Changing the Image Print Size

Whether or not you change the pixel dimensions and resolution, you may want to keep the Document Size the same, to meet your needs for when the image is printed. For example, even after reducing the image resolution to 100 pixels (down from 300), you may want the image to remain at 5 × 7 inches, to match a frame size or the size of a piece of stationery on which the image will be printed.

You can use the Image Size dialog box to put the Document Size back to the desired dimensions after reducing resolution (or pixel dimensions), or you can print it before making these adjustments in the first place. One reason to print before reducing resolution is that after you decrease the pixel depth (another way to refer to resolution), you may find that the image doesn't look as sharp or clean if you enlarge its print or Document Size. As shown in Figure 8-2, an image that's been reduced to 72 ppi doesn't look very clear after being enlarged from 2.5" × 3.5" up to 5" × 7". There are jagged edges in the image, and the image looks choppy all over — despite the aforementioned use of Bicubic as the resampling method, which should give us the best, cleanest results when enlarging an image.

Note Why reduce the pixel dimensions and resolution of an image? Because it enables you to prepare to use an image online (which also requires the Save for Web command, covered in Chapter 18), and it can allow you to store images and make more efficient use of your hard drive space. If you know you'll need to print again, don't reduce the image size, because you'll also risk losing image quality and limiting the ability to resize the image without losing clean edges and crisp delineations between components of the image. If storage space on your hard drive is at a premium, consider storing large images on removable media (CDs, zip disks) or invest in an extra, external hard drive.

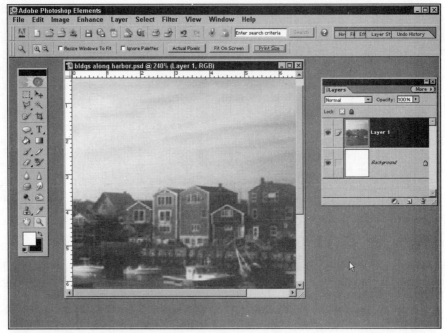

Figure 8-2: Resizing a low-resolution image can be risky — better to print it at the size you need it before reducing its pixel depth.

Changing the Canvas Size

The *canvas* for your image is the workspace around your image. Typically, the canvas size and the image size are the same in terms of their width and height, and there is no workspace beyond the edges of the image itself — the image and the canvas are essentially one element.

When you add canvas on one edge or around multiple edges of your image, however, you're adding workspace that bumps out around the image, as shown in Figure 8-3. You can add canvas on one, two, three, or all four sides of the image, using the Image⇨Resize⇨Canvas Size command.

Increasing or Decreasing Canvas Size

As shown in the Canvas Size dialog box (see Figure 8-4), you can choose what size the new canvas will be, adding to or taking away from the current workspace. You can also choose an Anchor, which dictates where the new canvas is added.

The canvas, on all sides of the image
bldgs along harbor.psd @ 36.3% (Background, RGB)

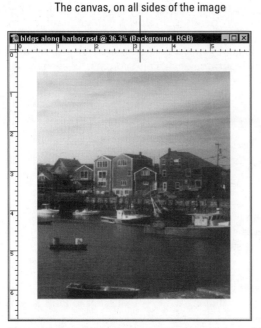

Figure 8-3: Add workspace on any or all four sides of the image.

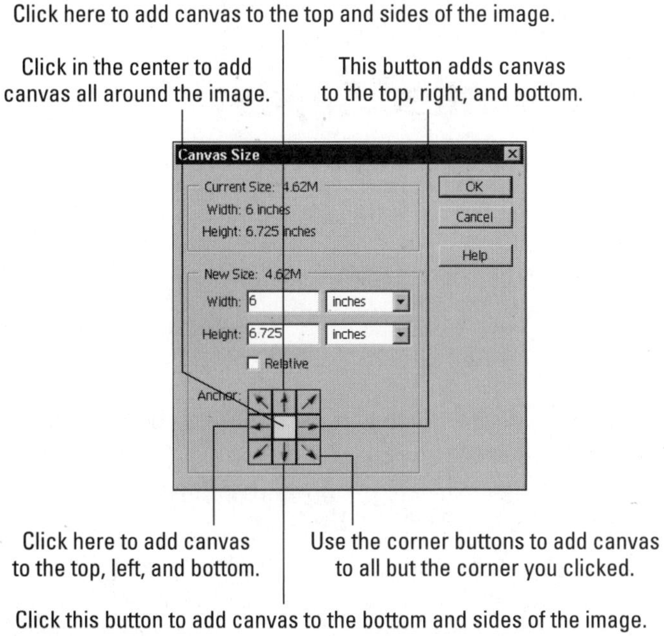
Click here to add canvas to the top and sides of the image.
Click in the center to add canvas all around the image.
This button adds canvas to the top, right, and bottom.
Canvas Size
Current Size: 4.62M
Width: 6 inches
Height: 6.725 inches
New Size: 4.62M
Width: 6
inches
Height: 6.725
inches
Relative
Anchor:
OK
Cancel
Help
Click here to add canvas to the top, left, and bottom.
Use the corner buttons to add canvas to all but the corner you clicked.
Click this button to add canvas to the bottom and sides of the image.

Figure 8-4: View the current canvas size and choose how much to add or remove.

After you add to the canvas size, your file size (shown next to the words "New Size" in the Canvas Size dialog box), grows, depending on how much you add. Taking away canvas size has two results—a prompt that indicates that the canvas will be smaller than the image (if this is the case), and a reduction in both workspace and file size. The prompt that appears if your image size and canvas size were the same in at least one direction (width or height) appears in Figure 8-5.

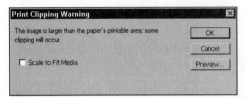

Figure 8-5: Warning! If your canvas and image size are currently the same, reducing canvas size will cause part of your image to be clipped away.

Tip

The term *clipping* refers to clipping away, or chopping off part of the image. You'll also see error prompts that refer to clipping when you attempt to print an image that's larger than the paper size currently set for your output. In the case of printing, the clipping only occurs in the printed output, and the image is unaffected. When clipping occurs due to a reduction in canvas size, the portion/s outside the edges of the image are literally removed.

Cropping Away Unwanted Edges

Cropping, such as the aforementioned clipping that occurs when you reduce canvas size, removes part of the image. When you crop, however, you're purposely removing edges of the image—on one or more sides of the image, presumably to improve the image by removing unnecessary or unattractive borders. As shown in Figure 8-6, cropping can reduce the image to just what's key—extraneous content on the periphery of the photo's composition is removed.

You can crop your image in one of two ways:

✦ Use the Crop tool to indicate the portion of the image you want to retain and then get rid of what's not selected.

✦ Use the Rectangular Marquee to select the portion of the image you want to keep and get rid of everything outside that selection.

Figure 8-6: Needless stuff around the edges of your image? Crop it away.

The method you choose depends on which technique you feel most comfortable with, as they really both give you the same end result. If you prefer the latter, selection-tool-based technique however, bear in mind that only the Rectangular Marquee can be used to set up a manual crop—oval or lasso-based selections can't be cropped.

Note

Cropping isn't just for getting rid of edges. You can also crop down to a very small portion of an image, some central figure or object, creating the appearance of a detailed study or portrait of that person or thing. Cropping is most often used to get rid of tattered photo borders or unnecessary content along the edges, but you can use it to refocus the subject of the image and then resize the remaining image content as desired.

Cropping with the Crop Tool

Of course, the logical choice for cropping your Elements images is the Crop tool, found in the toolbox and shown active in Figure 8-7, which also shows the tool's options bar.

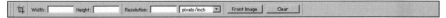

Figure 8-7: Crop to a specific area by using your mouse and/or the Crop tool's options for width, height, and resolution of the crop.

To use the crop tool, follow these steps:

STEPS: Cropping Image Edges with the Crop Tool

1. With the image open that you want to crop, click the Crop tool to activate it.

2. As needed, enter Width and Height measurements in the fields in the tool's options bar.

3. If you want to set a new resolution for the cropped image (what's left after cropping), enter it in the Resolution field and choose pixels per inch or pixels per centimeter as your units in the field to the right.

4. Click the Front Image button if you want to use the values for width, height, and resolution from the currently active image.

5. If you want to get rid of any custom settings you put in place for width, height, or resolution, click the Clear button.

6. To indicate where the image cropping should occur, click and drag to draw a rectangle that encompasses the portion of the image that should remain after the cropping has occurred, as shown in Figure 8-8.

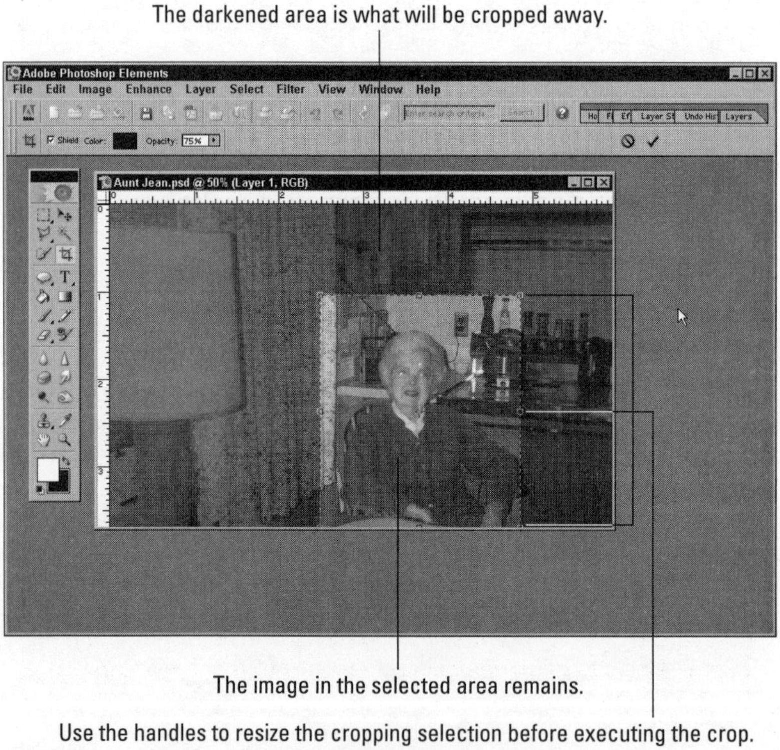

The darkened area is what will be cropped away.

The image in the selected area remains.

Use the handles to resize the cropping selection before executing the crop.

Figure 8-8: Tell Elements what you want to have left after the cropping is performed.

Tip

Want to start over? Press Esc and the current Crop tool selection disappears and you can re-drag to select the area to remain after cropping the image.

7. After the selection is made, the options bar changes, as shown in Figure 8-9. Use these options to turn off the Shield (the darkening of the portions that will be cropped away) or to change the shield's color. If you want to make the shield more or less opaque, use that field by dragging the Opacity slider that appears when you click the triangle on the right side of the option.

Figure 8-9: Customize how the cropping setup looks within the image window.

8. When you like what you see in terms of the selection in the image and the options bar settings (in both versions of the Crop tool's options), press Enter to execute the crop, which appears, completed, in Figure 8-10.

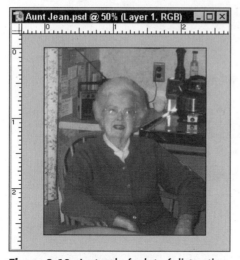

Figure 8-10: Instead of a lot of distracting content around the subject, the image is now a nice informal portrait.

Note

In addition to resizing the selection-to-be-cropped, you can rotate it by pointing to a corner handle and looking for the two-headed arrow that's bent in the middle. After rotating the image, press Enter to complete the crop, and the image content will be rotated to match your adjustment made with the mouse.

Cropping Manually

Very similar procedurally to cropping with the Crop tool, the manual method offers fewer options for establishing the crop, but it's fast and easy, which may be two attributes you find appealing! To crop your image manually, follow these steps:

STEPS: Cropping an Image Manually

1. Open the image that you want to crop.

2. Activate the Rectangular Marquee tool.

3. Select the portion of the image that should remain after cropping — you're essentially selecting the image you want from within the image you have, as shown in Figure 8-11.

Figure 8-11: Your cropping can take place anywhere in the image — just select what should remain, and you're ready to go.

4. Choose Image⇨Crop. The portions of the image outside of the rectangular selection are removed.

Tip   Given the destructive nature of the Crop tool and the manual cropping method — they both remove part of your image — it's important to remember that you can use Edit⇨Undo if you change you mind or use the Undo History palette to go back in time to just before you decided to crop your image.

Transforming Your Image and Layers

Photoshop Elements' Transform command, found in the Image menu, provides a submenu (shown in Figure 8-12) through which you can make manual, mouse-based transformations — skewing, distorting, rotating, and also resizing your image and/or the layers within it. Note that none of the commands have dialog boxes (you don't see an ellipse after the command names), so selecting any one of the commands will simply put your mouse in the mode to make the selected change, and you'll drag the handles on the layer/s to apply the chosen transformation. Figure 8-13 shows a selected layer being rotated.

Tip　What's the difference between Free Transform and the Skew, Distort, and Perspective commands? They all use the mouse and the layer's handles, so why not just use Free Transform for any kind of transformation? You can resize and rotate the image with the Free Transform command, but the remaining three types of transformations must be performed with the specific Skew, Distort, and Perspective commands.

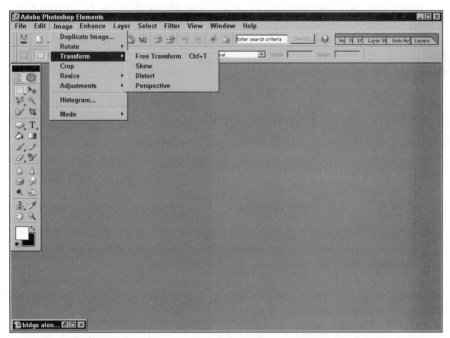

Figure 8-12: Transform your image in four different ways with the Image⇨Transform submenu's commands.

The bent 2-headed arrow indicates you're in rotate mode.

Corner handles allow you to rotate an image.

Figure 8-13: Watch the mouse and use the handles around the selected layer and then make your changes.

Rotating Layer Content

Rotating layers enables you to create special effects with composite photos, turning specific portions of the photo's content (assuming the content is on its own layer) and leaving other portions of the photo un-rotated. You can also use rotation to spin a rectangle drawn with the Shape tool (creating a Shape layer), or any other shape that could be effectively rotated. Rotating a circle, for example, wouldn't change the appearance of the circle, unless it had a gradient fill that you wanted to see from another direction. Rotating polygons, however, as shown in Figure 8-14, can provide interesting changes, making shapes look entirely different, simply by changing their degree of rotation.

While in Free Transform mode, you can rotate your layer by following these steps:

STEPS: Rotating an Image Layer

1. Using the Layers palette, click on the layer that you want to transform. This makes it your active layer.

2. Choose Image⇨Transform⇨Free Transform to display the layer's handles — one in each corner and in the middle of each of the sides.

3. Point to a corner or side handle, just outside the selected layer's content, as shown in Figure 8-15.

A selection within the photo is placed on its own layer.

That layer is rotated, leaving the
background to show behind it.

A shape (cut-out rectangle) is
placed on top and rotated, too.

Figure 8-14: Rotate any polygon to change its
appearance and therefore its effect within the image.

4. When your mouse pointer turns to a bent two-headed arrow, you can drag clockwise or counter-clockwise to rotate your layer. The rotation displays in real time — there is no ghost or outline of the layer.

5. As soon as you achieve the desired rotation, release the mouse and press Enter to confirm your transformation.

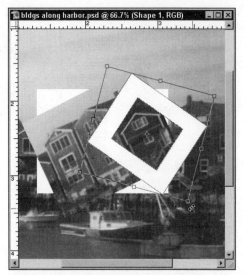

Figure 8-15: Don't drag *by* the handle, drag *near* it to activate the rotation mode.

You can also rotate your object using the options bar that appears when you choose Free Transform from the Image⇨Transform submenu. Through this options bar (shown in Figure 8-16), you can enter a specific angle of rotation, and also change the layer's Width and Height as desired.

Figure 8-16: Enter the exact angle of rotation you want, rather than rotating "by eye."

Note   When you activate the Move tool and follow Steps 3, 4, and 5 from the previous procedure, you can rotate any shape or layer just as you would if you used the Image⇨Transform⇨Free Transform command. The options bar with Width, Height, and rotation fields in it appears as soon as you begin to drag on any handle or drag to rotate the shape.

Tip   Press and hold the Shift key as you rotate your layer and you can more easily stop at 15 degree increments. This makes it possible to quickly achieve a 45 degree angle of rotation, or to rotate your layer exactly 90 degrees.

Resizing Your Layers

You can resize any layer by clicking on the layer with the Move tool and then using the side or corner handles. Your other options are:

✦ Use the options bar that appears as soon as you activate the Move tool and drag from any handle on the selected layer — enter new Width and Height settings into the fields and press Enter to confirm and apply them.

✦ Click on the layer to activate it and choose Image⇨Transform⇨Free Transform, and use the handles to resize the layer — the side handles make it wider or narrower, the top and bottom handles change its height, and the corner handles can be used to adjust both width and height at the same time, as shown in Figure 8-17.

Figure 8-17: Adjust width and height simultaneously from a corner handle.

Tip   Press and hold the Shift key as you resize from a corner handle, and you retain your current *aspect ratio*, or width-to-height proportions. Be sure to release the mouse before releasing the Shift key, however, so that your controlled ratio is maintained. If you release the key first, your layer's size will revert to what it would have been had you not used the Shift key at all while resizing.

Note   You can place a see-through shape on top of an image, resize and reposition as desired, and turn the shape into a frame overlay to draw attention to part of the image. You could follow that by cropping to just outside the frame, and then erasing anything outside the frame. After that, apply a texture or pattern fill to the shape used to create the frame. Find out more about erasing in Chapter 9 and about applying fills in Chapter 12.

Skewing Image Content

The term *skewing* isn't exactly self-explanatory, is it? It sounds more destructive or distorting than it really is. To skew a layer is to take it from a rectangular area and turn it into a parallelogram, as shown in Figure 8-18, where a photo is being transformed with the Skew command.

For non-rectangular shapes and layer content, skewing stretches the sides of the shape to tilt it to the left or right, or from the top or bottom. A layer containing one of the boats from the harbor picture is skewed in Figure 8-19 (the background, containing the rest of the photo, has been hidden to make it easier to see the skewing effect).

Of course, the Skew command (choose Image⊅Transform⊅Skew) works just like the Rotate command, or the resizing you do through the Free Transform command. Activate the layer in question and then issue the command, after which you can use your mouse to drag from top, bottom, left, or right sides. The skew pointer, seen in Figures 8-17, 8-18, and 8-19 looks like a two-headed arrow, and points in the direction you're about to skew — horizontally or vertically.

On the Options bar, note that you can switch between Rotate, Scale, and Skew mode.

Figure 8-18: Turn 90-degree angles into both acute and obtuse angles on two or more corners of your layer.

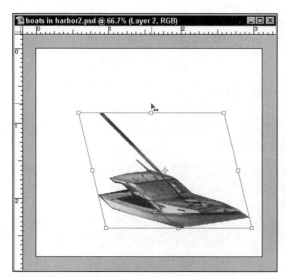

Figure 8-19: Skewing need not be restricted to rectangular or linear content and shapes.

Tip   The box and handles that appear around a layer or shape that you're about to transform is called a *bounding box*. The name reminds us that the box shows the layer or shape's current boundary and then allows us to change the shape or size of that box, and therefore change the shape or size of the content within it.

Distorting the Image

Going a bit further than skewing, the Distort command doesn't retain any parallel sides unless you use it very carefully and drag equal amounts from opposite handles. Used as intended, the Distort command enables you to lengthen or shorten image sides, distorting photographic content as it is stretched and/or squeezed to fit within a no-longer rectangular shape. Of course, you can also Distort shape layers — hearts, circles, rectangles, check marks, starbursts, and so on. Figure 8-20 shows a distorted photo layer, and Figure 8-21 shows a shape layer (a left-pointing block arrow) being distorted.

Figure 8-20: You can use the Distort command to achieve the look of an exaggerated perspective by dragging one or more handles, one at a time.

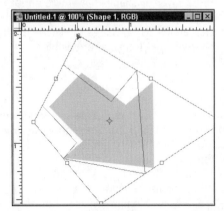

Figure 8-21: Stretch a shape into a new vision by distorting it.

Changing Image Perspective

The Distort command took you close to making true perspective changes in an image, but it doesn't provide the precision you need. The Image⇨Transform⇨ Perspective command works by your dragging one or more corner handles to change the perspective of the content within the selected layer. As shown in Figure 8-22, you can change the perspective on a building by placing it on its own layer and then using the Perspective command.

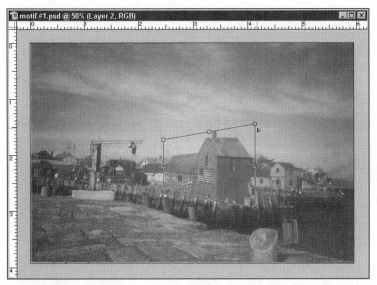

Figure 8-22: Change the perception of the viewer's position relative to the object in a photo.

You can also apply the Perspective command to shape layers, applying it most effectively to rectangular or highly linear shapes, as shown in Figure 8-23, where a check mark in a box now looks like it's turned and facing to the left, rather than sitting squarely on a line parallel to the bottom of the image and facing the viewer directly.

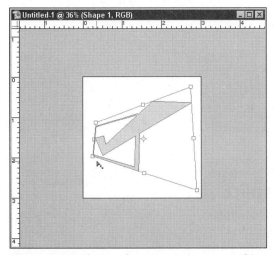

Figure 8-23: Change the perspective on anything — even a shape in two dimensions.

To use the command, just grab a corner handle and drag—typically starting with one corner and then moving to another corner to achieve the desired perspective. As shown in Figure 8-24, you can also use a side handle to change the vertical angle of the layer or shape to which you're applying the Perspective command.

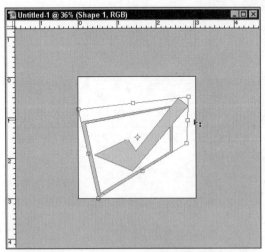

Figure 8-24: After having adjusted the perspective from a corner handle, change the vertical angle of the layer's content by using a side handle.

Tip   Read more about drawing shapes and creating shape layers in Chapter 11.

✦   ✦   ✦

Creating Your Own Works of Art

Chapter 9
Drawing and Painting
with Elements

Chapter 10
Using Layers to
Control Image
Content

Chapter 11
Using the Shape Tools

Chapter 12
Applying Fills
and Styles

Chapter 13
Using Filters
and Special Effects

Drawing and Painting with Elements

◆ ◆ ◆ ◆

In This Chapter

Customizing and
painting with the
paintbrush

Working with brush-
based tools

Drawing with the
pencil

Drawing and editing
with the Erasers

◆ ◆ ◆ ◆

You'd be hard pressed to find a more powerful tool than the brush in the Photoshop Elements toolbox. You use the brush for applying color to everything from an individual pixel to a selection or shape.

Working with the Paintbrush

The brush (usually referred to as the paintbrush) is one of the most customizable tools available, with not only an options bar, but a set of More Options that enables you to change the shape and behavior of the brush as well. As shown in Figure 9-1, I can't imagine anything more that you'd want to do to customize a paintbrush than can be found between the Brush tool's options bar and the More Options dialog box.

The Brush tool options bar with its standard set of five options.

The More Options button opens this additional set of options.

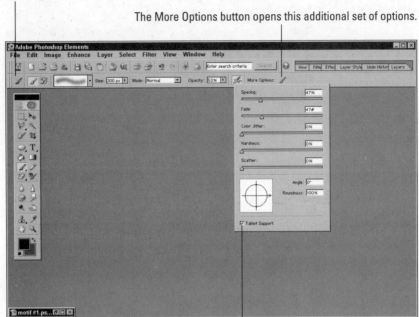

If you use a tablet and pen device, make sure this is on so that you can get full support.

Figure 9-1: Much more than brush size and opacity, the More Options dialog box lets you change the angle, shape, and quality of your brush strokes.

Of course, Elements has several similar tools that are considered "brush-based" in that they work like a paintbrush and have very similar options on their options bars. You read about these tools' common features and uses throughout this chapter, but for now, I focus on the Brush and its capabilities.

Selecting the Brush Size and Preset Options

After you activate the Brush, its options bar appears (see Figure 9-2, with the available Brush presets displayed), and you can begin setting up the brush for whatever work you have in mind. If you're about to paint over something or add some original artwork or retouching content to your image, you may have one set of options in mind. If you're about to paint to fill in a shape or fill a free-form area with a solid color, you'll want a different options set.

Figure 9-5: A more roundabout way to choose a preset group, the Load dialog box lists the same preset groups, with the same names, but they appear as files instead.

Note Why would you use the Load Brushes method to display a list of presets? Because you can append a set of presets to the one that's already displayed rather than replacing them. When you make a choice from the drop-down list at the top of the presets list, the one you choose replaces the set that's displayed. Using the Load Brushes command is more flexible, assuming that you want to add to the list of available brushes.

Working with Brush Modes

Brush Mode settings let you determine what, beyond applying color, will be accomplished with the Brush tool. Some modes add light or increase color saturation, others take away color and add shadow. Some modes affect the way the base color (existing color) is affected by the blending color (the color you're painting with) and how the result color (the color you get by mixing base and blend colors) will appear. You find dramatic effects amongst the modes, as well as effects that are so subtle that you can hardly see what effect they have. Some modes are very specific to certain situations, and you may never or rarely have need for them. In any case, Table 9-1 describes each of the Brush tool's modes and how they work.

Note Chapter 7 discusses Modes so that whichever tool you're using that has a Mode option on its options bar, you'll understand your choices. The Brush tool utilizes all of the available Mode options, whereas some tools only offer a subset of this master list, shown in Table 9-1. You find the same information in Chapter 7, but for your convenience and to enable you to apply these concepts to painting, they also appear here in Chapter 9.

Table 9-1
Mode Options

Mode	Effect/Purpose
Normal	This mode paints each painted pixel to make it the *result color* (the color you chose for the Foreground color on the Color Picker).
Dissolve	This works the same as Normal mode, except that the paint is applied as though the color were dissolving on the painted surface.
Behind	This mode paints the transparent areas of a layer only and is obviously only applicable on layers with Lock Transparency turned off. You read more about locking transparency in Chapter 10, which covers layers in detail.
Clear	The Clear mode makes each pixel you paint transparent, or clear, which gives this mode its name. You can use Clear mode on tools other than the Brush, such as the Paint Bucket tool, and the Pencil. Like Behind mode, Lock Transparency must be off in order to use this mode.
Darken	This mode refers to the color information in each color channel (Red, Green, or Blue) and selects the darker color when comparing the *base color* (the original color in the image) and *blending color* (the color you're applying with the active tool). Pixels that are lighter than the blend color are replaced, and the pixels that are darker than the blend color are left as is. You use Darken when you want to apply a light color and darken a base color that's already darker than the color with which you're painting.
Multiply	Use this mode to create a darker color by multiplying the base color by the blend color, based on the color information in each channel. When you use Multiply mode and paint with colors other than white, you create increasingly darker colors as you paint over and over in the same spots — much like applying layers of translucent color and overlapping the same or different colors — the more you paint or draw in the same spot, the darker your colors become.
Color Burn	This mode darkens the active layer (wherever you paint on it) by increasing the contrast between base and blend colors. You can use this blending mode to get a starker, high contrast effect.
Linear Burn	This mode works much like Color Burn, but it uses the color information in each color channel to reduce the brightness levels of the base color.
Lighten	If your base color is lighter than your blend color, the base color is chosen as the result color, and vice versa — if the blend color is lighter, that becomes the result. If there are pixels in the painted area that are darker than the blend color, they change to the result color, and pixels that are lighter than the blend color don't change at all. You can use this mode to achieve an eraser-like effect — wiping out darker colors in favor of a lighter one. If you paint with a color that's already in the image, that color is unaffected by the new paint, but whatever's darker is replaced with white, and transparent areas are filled with the painting color.

Mode	Effect/Purpose
Screen	Unlike Multiply, which creates darker colors where painting overlaps, the effect of Screen mode is a lighter color. Screening with black doesn't change the color, and screening with white gives you white. For a good visual analogy, imagine aiming dueling overhead projectors (with color slides on them) at the same spot on the wall. Unlike overlapping slides on the same projector, which would produce darker colors where they overlap, the two projected images would appear lighter at their common target.
Color Dodge	For an extreme brightening effect, use Color Dodge mode. This mode takes the color information in each channel and then brightens the base color (and thus the result color) by decreasing the contrast. If you paint with white or very light colors, you increase the effect.
Linear Dodge	The results of this mode are very similar to Color Dodge, but instead of reducing contrast to achieve added brightness, the brightness level is directly increased.
Overlay	This mode works like Multiply or Screen in that overlapping colors maintain highlights and shadows. The base color is mixed with the blend color to give you a result color that has the same light or dark quality of the base color.
Soft Light	Imagine shining a soft, white light on something—the shadows and highlights are increased by the light source, but the effects are subtle. Changes to color in this mode are based on the blend color, and the lightness or darkness of that color determines the lightening effect—if the blend color is lighter than 50 percent gray, this mode produces an effect similar to the Dodge tool. If the blend color is darker than 50 percent gray, the Burn tool's effect is mimicked.
Hard Light	Having the opposite effect of the Soft Light mode, Hard Light creates a harsh, bare-bulb lighting effect on your image. The blend color is used as in the case of Soft Light, but the effects are much harder and not subtle in the least.
Vivid Light	This mode lightens (dodge) or darkens (burn) as you paint by adjusting the contrast in relation to the blend color. When the blend color is lighter than 50 percent gray, the Vivid Light mode will lighten the image by reducing contrast. Conversely, if the blend color is darker than 50 percent gray, a darkening effect will be applied, by increasing the contrast.
Linear Light	The same way Vivid Light bases contrast adjustments on the blend color, Linear Light mode adjusts brightness based on the blend color. A blend color that's lighter than 50 percent gray results in a lighter effect, achieved by increasing the brightness level. If the blend color is darker than 50 percent gray, brightness will be decreased, resulting in a darker effect.

Continued

	Table 9-1 *(continued)*
Mode	**Effect/Purpose**
Pin Light	In Pin Light mode, if your blend color is lighter than 50 percent gray, any pixels darker than your blend color are replaced with the result color. If there are pixels lighter than the blend color in the path of your paintbrush, they are not changed. On the other hand, if your blend color is darker than 50 percent gray, any pixels lighter than your blend color are replaced, and if there are pixels darker than the blend color in the path of your paintbrush, those don't change, either.
Difference	Use this blending mode to invert lower layers based on the levels of brightness in the layer on which you're painting. This mode takes the color information in each channel and takes the blend color from the base color or the base color from the blend color—it all depends whether or not the base is brighter than the blending color, or vice versa. The results can be quite dramatic, resulting in a sort of color-negative effect.
Exclusion	This mode has virtually the same effect as Difference mode, with lower contrast levels.
Hue	Working with the HSB color model (Hue, Saturation, and Brightness), this blending mode gives you a result color that has the luminosity and saturation of the base color and the hue of the blend color.
Saturation	Again using the HSB mode, this mode gives you a result color with the luminosity and hue of the base color and the saturation of the blend color.
Color	Yet another combination of the HSB color model's components, this blending mode gives you a result color with the brightness of the base color and the hue and saturation of the blend color. You find this mode works well when you're changing the tint of a color image or when you're adding color to a monochrome image.
Luminosity	This mode gives you a result color with the hue and saturation of the base color and the luminosity of the blend color.

Setting Brush Opacity

The Opacity of your brush determines whether or not you'll be able to see facets through it (if there's content under the path of your brush, on the same or an underlying layer) and how dense the color will be. For example, as shown in Figure 9-6, a painted line that appears above another layer allows that layer's content to remain visible, thanks to reduced opacity.

To adjust opacity, simply use the Opacity slider, shown in Figure 9-7. The higher the number, the more opaque the color will be, 100% being the highest setting possible. If you set your opacity to 10% or less, you may not be able to detect the paint at all, unless you're using a dark color on a light background, or vice versa. Figure 9-8 shows a 15% opacity stripe of navy blue painted across a white field.

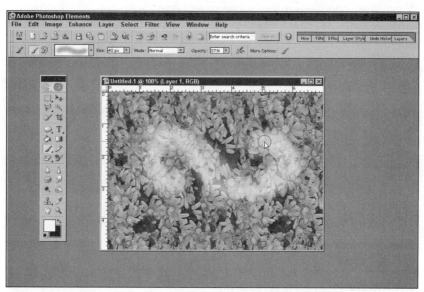

Figure 9-6: Both subtle and see-through — often a benefit when painting over existing content.

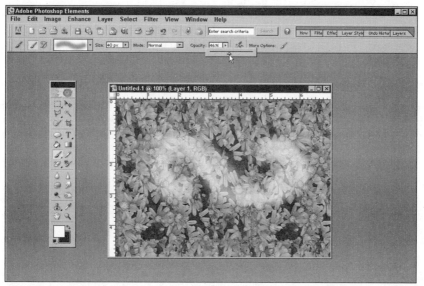

Figure 9-7: Drag the slider or enter a new number to set your Opacity percentage.

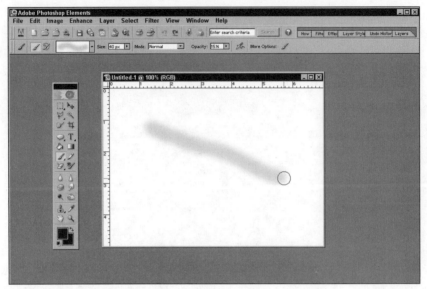

Figure 9-8: A very low opacity creates a nearly invisible effect.

Working in Airbrush Mode

When working with the Brush tool, you may want to soften your brush edges, and not necessarily by switching to one of the brush presets that seems to offer that sort of soft look. What's the difference? When you're in Airbrush mode, you literally get the look of having painted with an airbrush. Lingering over a particular spot thickens the paint and can result in what looks like a drop or puddle of paint forming (see Figure 9-9). The edges of the paint are also somewhat thicker, yet the edges of the painted area (and of each stroke) are soft, diffused by the way the "airbrush" applies paint — by spraying it on in a fine mist.

To work in Airbrush mode, simply click the picture of the airbrush on the Brush or brush-based tool's options bar (see Figure 9-10). The button remains in use until you turn it off, so be careful to turn it off (by re-clicking the button) if you're going on to paint an area where an airbrushed look would not be appropriate.

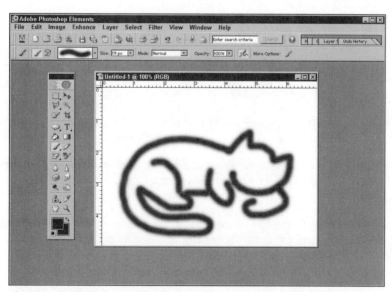

Figure 9-9: Make your paint look as though it was applied with an airbrush — sprayed on the image.

Figure 9-10: One click and it's on, another and it's off. Airbrush mode can be used for however long you need it.

Accessing More Options for Your Brush

At the far end of the Brush tool's options bar, you see the words "More Options," followed by a paint brush icon (see Figure 9-11). If you click the brush, a set of additional options (also shown in Figure 9-11) appears. Through these options, you can really change everything about your brush — the angle of the nib (brush tip), the amount of jitter and spacing within the strokes, you can add a Fade (so the brush stroke fades out), and turn on Tablet support if you're using such a device. Between this dialog box and the options bar itself, you have total control over your brushes.

Given that some of the settings' names aren't terribly intuitive or self-explanatory—Jitter or Spacing, for example—you can use the preset sample (on the options bar) to see how your changes made in the More Options dialog box will affect the strokes you paint with the brush you're about to use. As shown in Figure 9-12, after increasing the Spacing option and adding Fade and Scatter, the once solid brush stroke is now very choppy. The strokes (before More Options and after) applied to the image are also shown in this figure.

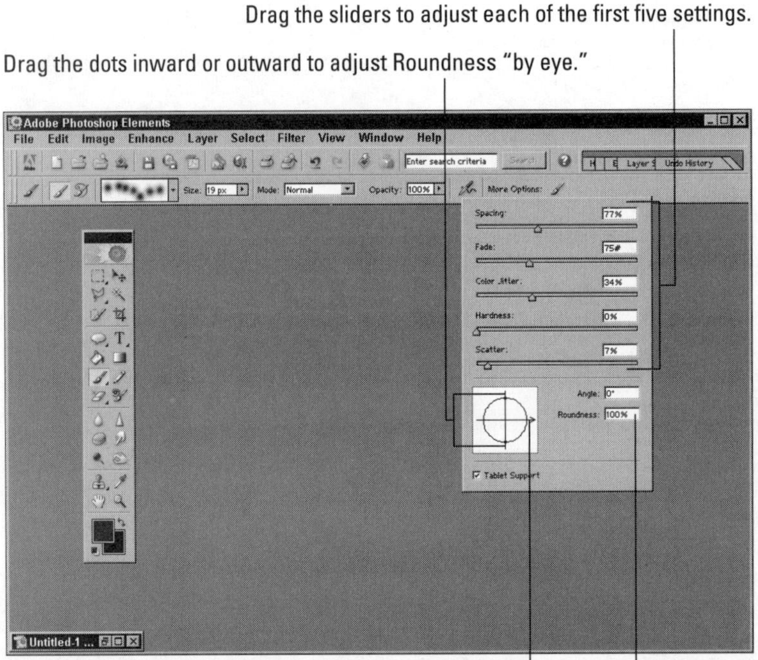
Drag the sliders to adjust each of the first five settings.
Drag the dots inward or outward to adjust Roundness "by eye."
Adobe Photoshop Elements
File Edit Image Enhance Layer Select Filter View Window Help
More Options:
Spacing: 77%
Fade: 75#
Color Jitter: 34%
Hardness: 0%
Scatter: 7%
Angle: 0°
Roundness: 100%
Tablet Support
Untitled-1 ...
You can drag the arrow in this sample or enter a new number for the Angle.
Type a new Roundness percentage.

Figure 9-11: More options? I'll say – you have several more options for your brush, including brush shape and angle.

The Spacing and Scatter settings made
this a brush that paints a series of dots.

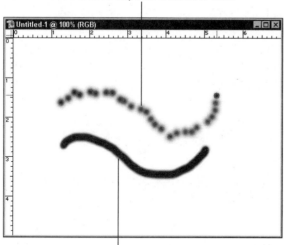

The brush before any More Options settings were adjusted

Figure 9-12: Get a preview of the impact of your More
Options settings through the Options bar. Or, just paint
a stroke to see how it affects the brush you're using.

Tip

Hate the way your brush works now that you adjusted the More Options settings?
Just use Edit⇨Undo (Ctrl + Z) or go to the Undo History palette and go back in
time to before you edited the brush.

Designing Custom Brushes

While it may seem as though there could never be a need for more brush presets —
Elements comes with so many — you may want to tweak an existing preset for some
specific need, or you may want to create a new one outright. By tweaking an existing preset, you can make the brush more textured, or change the default pixel size
of the brush. In creating a new preset outright, you may create a texture that's not
currently represented, even within the extensive set of presets that appear by
default or that you can load and use as needed.

To customize an existing brush preset, follow these steps:

STEPS: Customizing an Existing Brush Preset

1. Select the brush preset that is the closest match to your needs — select it
   from the list of presets while the Brush tool is active.

2. Use the options bar to make changes to brush size, Opacity, use of the Airbrush mode, and the list of Modes.

3. Use the More Options dialog box as needed, adjusting Spacing, Fade, Jitter, Harness, Scatter, and/or brush Angle and Roundness.

4. When the brush you see in the preset field (on the options bar) is what you need (you may want to test it with a few strokes of the Brush tool), click the options menu button in the preset drop-down list (see Figure 9-13), and choose New Brush from the menu.

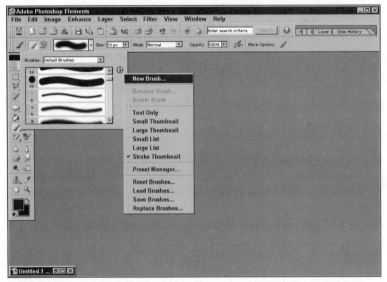

Figure 9-13: Customize the brush preset and then give it a name of its own.

5. In the resulting New Brush dialog box, give your brush a name — preferably a name that explains its quality or its intended use — and click OK.

6. Proceed to use your customized preset, renaming it as desired, using the options menu's Rename Brush command (while the customized preset is selected).

A completely new brush preset can also be created, using part of an existing image, as shown in Figure 9-14. Here, a small square is selected within an image, a spot with a particularly interesting texture, and this selection is used to create a new brush.

Figure 9-14: Base a new brush on an existing one to create a brush that meets specific needs.

After you make the selection that will serve as the basis or sample for the new brush, follow the steps below to further customize and name your new brush.

STEPS: Creating Your Own Brush Preset

1. With a selection made within your image, choose Edit⇨Define Brush. The Brush Name dialog box appears, as shown in Figure 9-15.

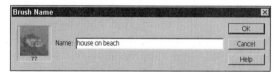

Figure 9-15: Defining a new brush simply requires naming a selection within your image that serves as the brush size and texture.

2. Type a name for the brush in the Name box, giving the brush a name that illustrates a typical use for the brush, or that describes the way the brush strokes will look.

3. Click OK to create the brush preset based on your selection.

4. To use the new brush, select it from the list of presets (it should be selected immediately after creating it) and use the Brush tool to paint with it. Figure 9-16 shows the new brush, called "Granite Blocks" applied to an image.

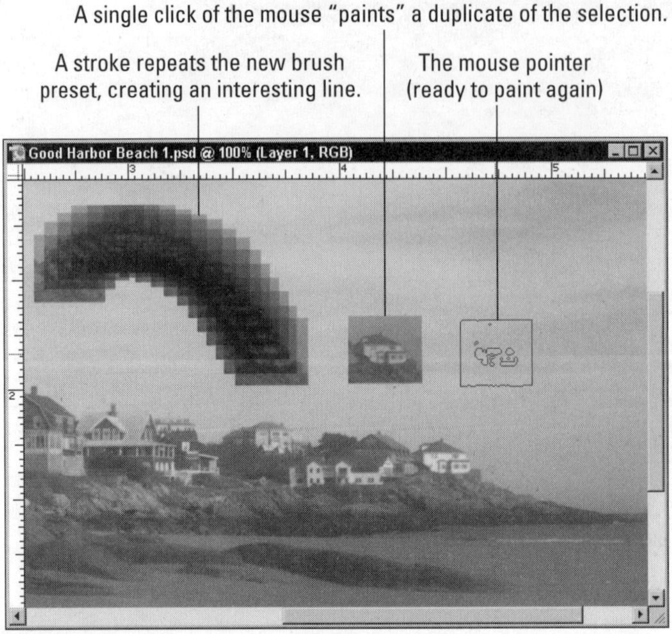
A single click of the mouse "paints" a duplicate of the selection.
A stroke repeats the new brush preset, creating an interesting line.
The mouse pointer (ready to paint again)
Good Harbor Beach 1.psd @ 100% (Layer 1, RGB)

Figure 9-16: Test your new brush – if you don't like the results, use your Brush options to customize it further.

Tip

While the new brush preset is active, you can use the options bar and More Options dialog box to customize the preset and then save it by choosing New Brush from the options menu. You can give it the same name as the one you created originally, or add a "B" or "#2" after the main name to indicate that this is a second version of that custom brush.

Painting Tips

The following are some tips for using the Brush tool to draw and paint selections, shapes, and areas with color.

✦ **Don't do it all at once.** If you're drawing (painting) something freehand, such as the shape shown in Figure 9-17, don't try to draw it all in one go — you'll find that if you do and make a mistake, Undo will wipe out your entire effort, not just the last bit in which you made the mistake. Instead, draw/paint in shorter sections, stopping at logical points where a corner or break in the line works with what you're drawing. That way, if you do make a mistake and use Undo, only the last section will be lost.

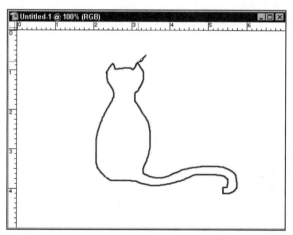

Figure 9-17: Create your drawing in sections so that you have distinct stages through which to go back with Undo History, as needed.

✦ **Painting Straight Lines.** Press the Shift key before dragging your brush to paint a straight line. To paint a second straight line, release the Shift key and click once with the brush tool and then use the Shift key again to paint the second straight line as you drag. Why click between uses of the Shift key? Because if you go right into the second line without letting up the Shift key or without clicking to break the painting into two separate activities, your two lines will be connected — by a diagonal line, as shown in Figure 9-18.

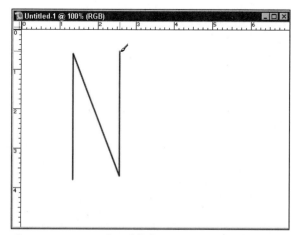

Figure 9-18: Use the Shift key to paint straight lines. This also works with the Pencil tool.

✦ **Don't resist change.** When drawing or painting on an image or creating an image through what you're drawing, don't try to do it all with one set of brush options. Very few items you draw—even a cartoon or simple line drawing—consists of the same kind of lines with the same textures, shapes, and thicknesses (see Figure 9-19). Don't hesitate to stop and start again with a brush that's more conducive to the portion of the image you're drawing at the time.

Use wider brushes at varying opacities
for the appearance of a pattern.

Switch to a thinner brush
for these fine details.

Use a very big, slightly opaque brush
for filling in spaces with soft color.

Figure 9-19: Drawing a person, place, or thing? Rarely will one set of brush settings do for the entire drawing.

Tip   When drawing very small, detailed items, don't forget to Zoom in. You'll find that it's much easier to create tiny elements of a drawing when you're as close to them as possible (without losing visual context).

Using the Impressionist Brush

This variation of the Brush tool does just what the name implies—it enables you to paint over an image and apply an impressionist style to the image, as shown in Figure 9-20. This can be applied to some or all of a photo or other type of image, and you can adjust the settings of the Impressionist Brush to give you a variety of effects.

This area has been painted with the Impressionist Brush.

Figure 9-20: Take a clean, crisp photo and turn some or all of it into an impressionist painting.

To use the Impressionist Brush, follow these steps:

STEPS: Using the Impressionist Brush Tool to Change the Appearance of a Photo

1. Click on the Brush tool, and either activate the Impressionist Brush by clicking the triangle in the lower-left of the Brush tool's button or use the options bar and click the Impressionist Brush button there.

2. Observe the Impressionist Brush options bar (see Figure 9-21). There are slight differences from the Brush tool's options, which you find in the shorter list of brush Mode options (click the Mode list to see a reduced set of modes from which to choose).

Figure 9-21: The Impressionist Brush options bar looks nearly identical to the Brush tool's version.

3. Click the More Options button to open a small dialog box of additional Impressionist Brush options, shown in Figure 9-22.

Figure 9-22: A small set of very powerful options enables you to determine the style and scope of the Impressionist Brush and its effect on your image.

- **Style:** This option, set to Tight, Short by default, has nine additional choices, from Tight Long to Dab to Loose Curl. These options determine the nature of the impressionist strokes that are applied to the image.

- **Area:** This determines the size of the brush strokes, as in how many pixels are affected by each stroke. The default is 50 pixels.

- **Tolerance:** This option establishes how close to the pixel you click (when you begin painting with the Impressionist Brush) the surrounding pixels must be (in terms of color values) in order to be affected by the brush. If you have the Tolerance set to a low number, the surrounding pixels must be much closer to the original pixel's values. If you set Tolerance to a high number (more than 50), a wider range of pixels are affected by your painting.

4. Make whatever changes you want to the Impressionist Brush — through the main options bar and through the More Options dialog box as well.

5. Paint with the Impressionist Brush, applying its effects to as much or as little of the image as you desire.

Note   Your painting method — long, continuous strokes, short, quick strokes, or a more dabbing effect affect the Impressionist style. You can combine your own stroke methods with different Style settings (from the More Options dialog box) to achieve a variety of unique effects.

Drawing with the Pencil Tool

Just as an artist would need both paintbrushes *and* pencils to create their artwork on canvas and paper, so does an Elements user need them both when creating electronic artwork for use online or on paper. The paintbrush (Brush) tool enables you to apply color creatively, using a variety of brushes — fat, soft brushes, thin, crisp brushes, and even brushes that work more like rubber stamps — applying flowers and leaves and other natural images in a stroke of the Brush. With all that creativity and flexibility, however, is a lack of real precision, an inability to draw sharp, clean lines and execute the kind of precise lines that one gets from a nice, sharp pencil. Or a slightly soft drawing pencil. Or a textured chunk of charcoal. You get the idea — you need to apply color in flowing strokes as well as in tidy lines, and that's where the Pencil tool comes in, as shown in Figure 9-23.

A softer line, drawn with the Soft Round, 13 pixel Pencil

A plain, thin line drawn with a
Hard Round, 1 pixel Pencil

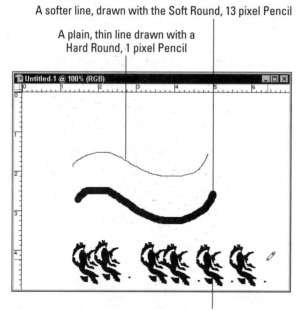

When the Pencil is used with the Scattered Roses preset,
only the shadows of the roses appear, creating a textured line.

Figure 9-23: The Pencil isn't just thin lines, but a series of "brush" presets that allow both crisp and soft, clean lines and textures to be drawn.

Choosing a Pencil Preset and Size

When you activate the Pencil tool, the options bar (shown in Figure 9-24) offers settings that look very much like the Brush options — a choice of brush presets, a Size slider, a Mode drop-down list, and an Opacity slider. In addition, there's an Auto Erase option, which is on by default. Auto Erase applies the current background color over any pixels that contain the current foreground color.

Figure 9-24: The Pencil options bar looks a lot like the Brush options bar.

Note   You may notice no More Options button on the Pencil options bar. This is because the pencil's point size and shape are determined solely by the preset chosen—just like a real pencil—other than sharpening it or buying a pencil that has a certain shape to begin with, there's a lot less you can do to alter a pencil's output.

Tip   While there is no More Options button, there is a full set of Mode options available for the Pencil, and you can refer to Table 9-1, found earlier in this chapter, for a definition of each of the Mode choices and how each one would affect an image.

The preset (still called Brushes, as shown in Figure 9-25) list offers the same presets you saw for the Brush tool. The presets, however, look different—the soft and detailed presets that could be applied by the Brush are now hard-edged, crisp, and in the case of the Special presets (roses, leaves, and so forth), the Pencil creates only the shadows or crisp edges of those shapes.

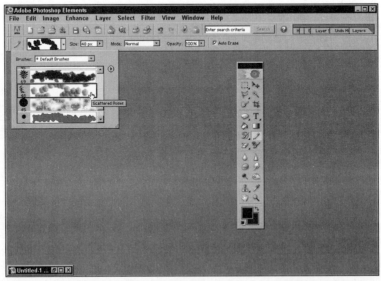

Figure 9-25: Same presets, but the Pencil gives you a different take on all but the simplest.

After choosing a preset, choose a Size, which determines the thickness of the pencil "point." Just as in the case of the Brush, you aren't restricted to the pixel dimensions of a selected preset—just use the Size slider to augment or reduce the Pencil size for any given preset. Figure 9-26 shows the same preset at a series of increasing Size settings. Given the texture of the preset and the nature of the Pencil tool, more detail is visible as the Size is increased.

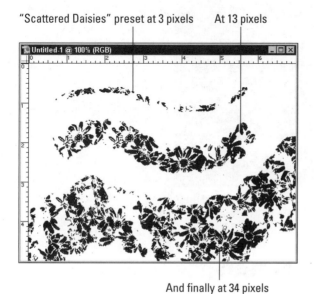

"Scattered Daisies" preset at 3 pixels   At 13 pixels

And finally at 34 pixels

Figure 9-26: Not a subtle tool, a detailed preset only reveals its detail when the Pencil is set to a large Size.

Tip Just as you can create new brushes for use with the Brush tool, you can use customized and user-created Brush presets for the Pencil, too. You can also use the Define Brush command (found in the Edit menu) to turn a selection from within an image into a Brush to use as a Pencil preset.

Using Auto Erase

When you first read what the Auto Erase option does, you may ask yourself, "Why would I ever use *that?*" Well, you may never have need of it, or you might think it's the most convenient option invented. It works by painting the currently selected background color over any pixels containing pixels that are painted the currently selected foreground color. As you're painting, if you come upon pixels that aren't the foreground color, the background color won't be applied to them, so it's a one-for-one effect—you're essentially swapping foreground for background, but by drawing, not by re-applying a fill color. Figure 9-27, using black and white as the background and foreground colors respectively, shows the use of the Auto Erase feature—the zebra stripes within the selected area that are white are being turned black as the Pencil is applied to them.

Figure 9-27: Apply the Background color to any Foreground colored-pixels with the Pencil's Auto Erase feature.

Working with the Erasers

Erasers do more than remove image content. The three forms of the Eraser tool— the standard Eraser, the Background Eraser, and the Magic Eraser—can all be used creatively as well as restoratively or destructively. Some examples:

✦ You can erase existing color to "draw" a clear path through a pattern or solid color.

✦ You can erase the background in favor of a more interesting backdrop for your image.

✦ You can quickly rid a photo or other image of any particular color through the Magic Eraser's ability to sample and then remove (as you drag with your mouse) the color from pixels that match the sampled spot on your image.

When you click on the Eraser tool and hold the mouse button down (or if you click the triangle in the lower-right of the button), you'll see your three Eraser alternatives, as shown in Figure 9-28.

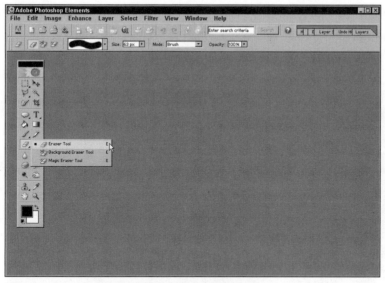

Figure 9-28: Choose from three Eraser variations.

Using the Standard Eraser

The standard Eraser works quite simply—you activate it by clicking on it from within the Toolbox (or press its shortcut key E). After it's active, follow these basic steps to erase some or all of the content on any layer in your image:

STEPS: Erasing Image Content

1. With the Eraser active, observe its options bar, shown in Figure 9-29.

Choose from the three different Erasers with these three buttons.

Figure 9-29: The standard Eraser has a simple set of options.

2. Choose a Mode for the Eraser—Brush, Pencil, or Block.

3. If you choose Brush or Pencil for the Mode, go back to the brush presets drop-down list and choose one of the presets for the Eraser. Note that if you choose Block, the presets drop-down list is unavailable.

4. Set a Size for the Eraser.

5. Choose an Opacity for the Eraser — the higher the number you set, the more of the content you'll erase. If you set it to a lower number, you erase some of the content, but leave a percentage of it behind, as shown in Figure 9-30, where the Eraser opacity is set to 50%.

Figure 9-30: Skim just some of the content off the top with a lower Opacity setting.

6. Choose a Layer (from within the Layers palette) and begin erasing content on that layer, as desired.

Tip   If you want to erase content from multiple layers at the same time, you can merge those layers (see Chapter 10 for information on how to Merge your layers).

Working with the Background Eraser Tool

Not to be confused with an eraser that can intuitively erase just your Background layer, the Background Eraser samples the color at the center of the eraser's brush (pencil or block) and erases only the pixels that match it. How might you use this tool? Imagine you want to get rid of some sky along a tree line, but don't want to lose any of the trees — by using the Background Eraser and clicking to begin the erasure on the sky, you can erase just the sky and leave the skyline, all without making a selection or masking the skyline ahead of time. In Figure 9-31, you see sky erased, leaving trees and buildings intact.

To use the Background Eraser tool, click it within the toolbox. If the standard Eraser is the active tool (it's the default Eraser, or it may have been the last version of the erasers you used), you can use the options bar to choose a different Eraser tool — click the second button, with the scissors in the button (see Figure 9-29).

Figure 9-31: The Background Eraser doesn't erase the background layer — it erases what you consider the background in your image.

After becoming active, the Background Eraser's options appear on the options bar, as shown in Figure 9-32. Instead of choosing a preset or a Mode, you're choosing a size and setting the Limits for the tool. You're also setting a Tolerance, which determines how the tool works within the Limits you set.

Figure 9-32: Set up the Background Eraser to do exactly what you need it to do.

To master the Background Eraser, try these steps:

STEPS: Erasing Background Content with the Background Eraser:

1. After setting a Size for the Background Eraser (based on the amount of content you want to erase), click the Limits drop-down list and choose either Contiguous or Discontiguous. What do these two options mean?

   - **Contiguous** erases only the pixels that match the sampled pixel (also known as the *hotspot*) and that are connected to the sampled pixel or a pixel connected to it.

   - **Discontiguous** erases any sampled color, no matter where it appears in the image, as long as it's under your Background Eraser as you drag over the image.

2. Move to the Tolerance field and drag its slider. A low Tolerance (it's set to 50 percent by default) erases only those pixels that are a very close match to the hotspot or originally sampled pixels. If you set the Tolerance to a high number, you expand the range of pixels considered a close match—lowering the standards, essentially, as the Background Eraser does its work on your image.

3. Activate the layer on which you want to make your erasure and begin using the Background Eraser. Note that the pointer is a circle (indicating brush size) with a crosshair in the middle (see Figure 9-33). The center of the crosshair is the hotspot, the pixel to which the pixels you move across are compared and erased, based on your Limits and Tolerance settings.

Figure 9-33: Click on the "hotspot" and then begin erasing the pixels that match it.

When you use the Background or Magic erasers on what is actually your Background layer, that layer is converted to a regular layer. If you don't want that to happen, just use the Eraser tool, perhaps with a selection made beforehand to achieve the exclusion of certain pixels (as the Background and Magic erasers would automatically).

Yes, "Discontiguous" isn't really a word, but you get the idea. Noncontiguous would have been the correct term, but Photoshop is the industry standard for photo retouching (and by association and similarity, so is Elements), so who wants to argue with them about a single word on the options bar?

Erasing Specific Colors with the Magic Eraser

Magic is quite a term or any tool. It implies that the tool has some special skills of its own, that it can read your mind (or acts as though it can), or that it works independently, performing some exciting task. Is this term an overstatement for the Magic Eraser? Perhaps — but not if you want to erase only the pixels that match a single pixel you click. This may sound a lot like the Background Eraser, but there's a crucial difference — instead of your dragging over the adjacent pixels, the Magic Eraser erases all of the matching pixels, no matter where they are in the image. With no dragging required, all you need is a click or two, and whole portions of your image can be removed fully or partially (depending on how you set up the tool). To see the tool in use, see Figure 9-34.

Figure 9-34: Want to get rid of that sky again? Or all the ugly green wallpaper behind your group photo's subjects? The Magic Eraser can handle it for you.

To use the Magic Eraser, follow this simple procedure:

STEPS: Erasing Specific Colors with the Magic Eraser

1. Activate the Magic Eraser from the toolbox or by clicking the third eraser button on the options bar. As soon as the Magic Eraser is activated, a new options bar appears, as shown in Figure 9-35.

Figure 9-35: Set up your Magic Eraser to perform the tricks you want.

2. Establish a Tolerance setting, using the slider or by entering a number manually. Just like the Tolerance setting on the Background Eraser, this option controls how close a match pixels must be to the sampled pixel in order to be erased. A low Tolerance reduces the number that match by requiring that the pixels be very similar to the original pixel, whereas a high Tolerance allows more pixels to be erased, considering those that are not quite the same color to be seen as close enough.

3. If you want the edges of the areas you erase to be smooth, turn on the Anti-aliased option.

4. Use the Contiguous option (it's on by default) if you want the pixels erased to have to be touching the original pixel and/or those that were touching it and that were already erased.

5. Turn the Use All Layers option on if you want to erase content on all the layers of your image.

6. Set your Opacity, reducing it if you want to leave a bit of the erased areas behind, or increasing it (100% is the highest setting) if you want to totally eradicate the matching pixels.

7. Click on the image, choosing a spot where the pixel you're clicking on is the color that you want to get rid of throughout your image.

✦   ✦   ✦

Using Layers to Control Image Content

In This Chapter

Working with the Layers palette

Making new layers from scratch or based on existing layers

Giving your layers relevant names

Removing unwanted layers

Hiding and displaying layers

Sharing layers between images

Without the ability to place portions of your image on separate layers, your editing capabilities within Elements are extremely limited. You couldn't easily isolate parts of the image to edit them or preserve them from editing, you couldn't hide parts of the image while editing or printing other parts, and you couldn't take advantage of several editing techniques that rely on duplicate layers of the same content. You also wouldn't have the ability to create adjustment layers, which you read about in Chapter 8.

Mastering the Layers Palette

Through the list of what you couldn't do without layers, you now have an idea of what layers can do for you. Layers are created, named, rearranged, hidden, displayed, duplicated, and deleted via the Layers palette, shown in Figure 10-1. As this Figure shows, the Layers palette contains a list of all the layers in your active image, and displays the status of each layer — hidden or displayed, what opacity level's been set for the layer, the layer's name, and what kind of layer it is — text, shape, or image content.

The type of layer is indicated here.

Lock a layer to control changes.

The layer's name appears here.

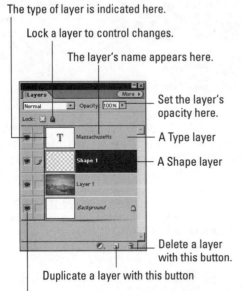

Set the layer's opacity here.

A Type layer

A Shape layer

Delete a layer with this button.

Duplicate a layer with this button

An eye in this box indicates the layer is visible.

Figure 10-1: Keep track of your image components through the Layers palette.

Creating a New Layer

When it comes to building layers, you have several choices, and your preferred technique will most probably be dictated by the situation and/or the image in question. Some ways to create a new layer:

✦ You can create layers from existing content, cutting or copying selections and then turning the cut or copied content into a new layer.

✦ You can create a new, blank layer and then populate it with content and/or color.

✦ You can copy content from another image and paste it into the active image, creating a new layer.

✦ You can use the Type or Shape tools to add a layer automatically.

As you can see from this list, the situation you're in — wanting to add content from another image, needing some text for your picture, wanting to take existing content and place it on its own layer — forces you into one of the methods available for creating new layers. After the layer's been created, you can rename it, rearrange it (change its stacking order amongst the other layers), hide it, duplicate it, or delete it. You can perform all these actions from within the Layers palette, making it a very powerful palette within the Elements application.

Creating a New, Blank Layer

The most direct way to create a new layer is to choose Layer⇨New⇨Layer. You can also click the More button on the Layers palette and choose New Layer from the resulting menu (see Figure 10-2). Either way, the New Layer dialog box appears, asking you to name your new layer, replacing the generic Layer # name that's applied by default. Through this dialog box, shown in Figure 10-3, you're also able to decide whether or not to link (group) this new layer with the previous layer (the layer just beneath it in the Layers palette), to set a Mode for the layer, and to set the layer's Opacity.

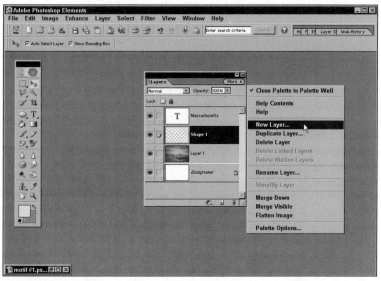

Figure 10-2: The More menu offers a variety of Layer-related tasks, including the creation of a new, blank layer.

Of course, the Mode and Opacity settings can be established later, and in many cases you won't know what you want to do with the layer right away. All you may know is that you want to keep some new (yet to be created) content separate from the rest of the image, and you may not have any other plans for that content yet. If this is the case, just name the layer (choose something short and relevant) and click OK. As soon as you do, the layer appears in the Layers palette, and you can proceed to do whatever you want to do with the new layer.

Figure 10-3: You can do much more than just name your new layer in the New Layer dialog box.

Note   There's that word Mode again, and yes, if you click the Mode drop-down list (either in the New Layer dialog box or on the Layers palette itself), you see the same list of Modes we talked about with regard to the Brush tool in Chapter 9 and in Chapter 7's discussions on color and light. You can refer to those chapters, each of which contains a table of all the Mode options in the Mode drop-down list. The table lists each Mode and discusses its purpose and potential uses within your image.

Creating a Layer from Existing Content

So you have an image and you want to isolate part of it — some of the existing content needs to be on its own in a layer so that it can be treated separately or preserved from any kind of editing. You may also want it on its own layer so that it can be moved, rotated, resized, or in some other way transformed. Whatever your motive, placing existing content on its own layer is easy by choosing the Edit⇨Cut or Edit⇨Copy commands, and then using commands within the Layer menu, as shown in the following steps:

STEPS: Cutting or Copying Content to a New Layer

1. Using the selection tool of your choice — the Lasso, Marquee, Wand, or Selection Brush — select the portion of your image that you want to place on its own layer.

2. If you want to remove the selection from the image and have it only exist in the new layer (that you've yet to create at this point), choose Edit⇨Cut or press Ctrl + X. If you want to have both the selection and the new layer with the same content in it, choose Edit⇨Copy.

3. With the cut or copied content on the clipboard, go to the Layer menu and choose New⇨Layer Via Cut or New⇨Layer Via Copy (depending on whether you cut or copied the content in Step 2). The New submenu is shown in Figure 10-4.

A new layer appears, with a generic "Layer" name, as shown in Figure 10-5, where a portion of the main image is now seen on its own layer and also remains in the layer that contains the entire image.

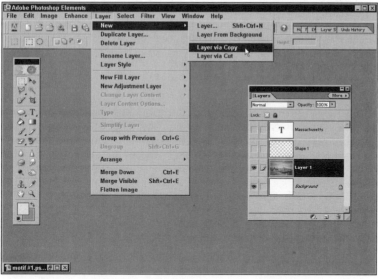

Figure 10-4: See the many ways to create a new layer in the Layer⇨New submenu.

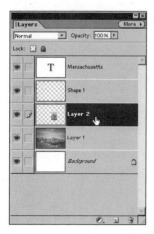

Figure 10-5: A new layer is created from cut or copied content.

Of course, you can repeat Step 3 as many times as you want layers with the cut or copied content. Why would you create more than one layer from some cut or copied content? Imagine that you're copying some flowers from one part of the image to cover up a muddy lawn or some other undesirable content elsewhere in the image. Creating more than one layer with those flowers would enable you to place the layers in various spots on the image, covering up whatever you don't want to see. Of course, you can also use the Duplicate Layer feature, discussed later in this chapter, to create multiple identical layers.

Note   You can also skip the Image⇨New⇨Layer Via Cut (or Copy) command and just choose Edit⇨Paste to create a new layer from cut or copied content. This procedure can also be used to copy content from another image into your active image. I discuss other methods of sharing content between images (and keeping the shared content on separate layers) later in this chapter.

Creating a Type or Shape Layer

The very act of typing text with the Type tool or drawing a shape with the Shape tool creates a new layer. In the latter case, you do have options for adding shapes to existing layers, but the default is to create a Shape layer whenever a shape is drawn on an image. Figure 10-6 shows an image photographic content, type, and a shape, each existing on its own layer.

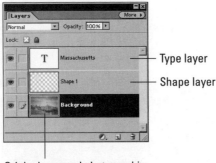

— Type layer

— Shape layer

Original scanned photographic
content on its own layer

Figure 10-6: Type and Shape content automatically appear on their own layers.

A T icon designates a Type layer, and a gray box with the shape you drew represented within the box indicates the Shape layer. Type layers are named by default with the text that was typed on the layer. Shape layers are called Shape, followed by a number indicating the order in which the Shape layer was created — if it's your first Shape layer within a particular image, it is named Shape 1 by default.

Tip   After you finish typing and click the Move tool to reposition your text, the Type layer's name appears (and is based on the text you've typed). Until you leave the Type tool for another tool, the layer's name will be Layer #, where the # (pound sign) indicates the layer's rank amongst any other Type layers in the image.

When you're using the Shape tool, note that on the options bar (see Figure 10-7), you have a series of five buttons, identified in the Figure. Each one is an option for how the shape you're about to draw will become part of the image. The first button (Create New Shape Layer) is on by default and assumes you want the shape you draw to be on its own layer, and on a Shape layer at that. Shape layers get slightly different treatment overall, in terms of what you can and can't do to them, which you read in Chapter 11.

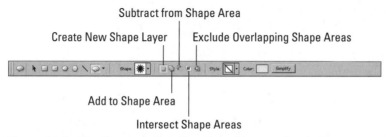

Figure 10-7: The Shape tool's options bar gives you the choice as to whether or not the shape you're drawing will be on its own layer or part of an existing layer.

 Tip   Read more about using Type in Chapter 14, and all about creating shapes (and working with Shape layers) in Chapter 11.

Hiding and Displaying Layers

One of the handiest aspects of being able to keep content on individual layers is the fact that you can hide and display layers at will. You can hide them to keep them from getting in your way as you lay out or edit other parts of the image, you can hide them so that their content won't print, or you can hide them so that you can have two versions of the same image — one with one or more layers hidden, and another where the layer/s are visible. Figure 10-8 shows an image with some of its content hidden and the Layers palette with one eye icon missing.

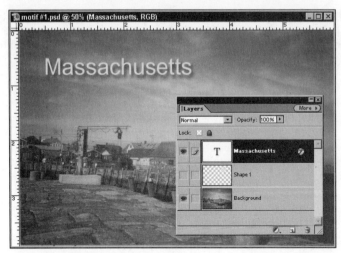

Figure 10-8: Hide some of your image by hiding the layer/s that contain it.

To hide a layer, simply click the eye icon, which removes the eye and hides the content of that layer. To redisplay a hidden layer, click the box where the eye icon used to be, and both the eye and the layer's content reappear. Some details to remember about hiding layers:

✦ If you hide a layer and then go back and click on it later to make it the active layer, it is automatically redisplayed.

✦ If two or more of your layers are linked (more about how to link them later in this chapter), you can hide one of the linked layers without hiding the other layers to which the hidden layer is linked.

✦ If a layer is hidden, it won't print.

✦ You can rename a hidden layer without redisplaying it.

✦ You can change layer properties without redisplaying the layer.

✦ You can't merge linked layers if one or more of the linked layers is hidden.

✦ If you flatten an image while one or more layers are hidden, you will be asked (prior to the Layer⇨Flatten Image being executed) if you want to discard the hidden layers. If you choose to discard them, the layers are gone for good (unless you Undo the Flatten command).

Duplicating a Layer

Making a duplicate of an existing layer couldn't be simpler. The process requires just two factors — you knowing which layer it is that you want to duplicate and a functioning mouse or other pointing device:

STEPS: Duplicating a Layer

1. Click on the layer you want to duplicate, which makes it the active layer.

2. Drag the selected layer to the Create New Layer button at the bottom of the Layers palette (this process is shown in progress in Figure 10-9).

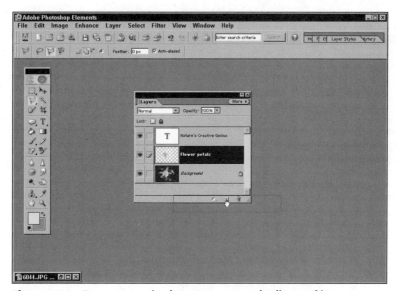

Figure 10-9: Drag your active layer to create a duplicate of it.

3. A duplicate layer is created, as shown in Figure 10-10, with the word "Copy" in the name, along with the name of the layer you copied. You can repeat Steps 1 and 2 for any additional layers you want to duplicate, or just Step 2 if you want more duplicates of the currently active layer.

Another way to duplicate a layer is right-click it and choose Duplicate Layer from the shortcut menu. When you employ this method, however, an extra step is involved — a Duplicate Layer dialog box appears, asking you to name the duplicate layer and to choose the document to which the duplicate should be added (see Figure 10-11).

Figure 10-10: After duplicated, a layer's clones are labeled as copies.

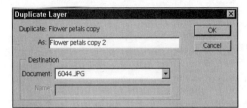

Figure 10-11: Duplicate a layer AND choose its destination.

This last feature of the dialog box opens up an important new capability for users who want to not only duplicate layers but have the duplicate end up in another image. Unlike the dragging method described in the previous procedure, where your duplicate layer lives in your active image, you can click the Document drop-down list (in the Destination section of the dialog box) to see a list of all the open images. Choose the one you want to send the duplicate layer to, and then click OK to create the duplicate in the selected image.

Of course, this method requires that you have that target image open at the same time that you have open the image that contains the layer you want to duplicate. Not a big deal, but it's a step that you're likely to forget until you go to choose the Destination, click the Document drop-down list, and see that your target image is not listed because it's not open. This is yet another example of how planning and preparation can save you a lot of time and aggravation as you go about retouching, editing, and creating images with Elements!

Tip   For more methods that enable you to share layers between images, see the section entitled "Moving Layers between Files," which you find later in this chapter.

Changing Layer Properties

If you double-click a regular layer (by "regular" I mean not a Type or Shape layer), the Layer Properties dialog box appears, through which you can rename the layer (see Figure 10-12). Of course, you can more easily do this by double-clicking the layer's existing name, at which point the current name becomes selected (see Figure 10-13), and you can type a replacement name.

Figure 10-12: Double-click here to open the Layer Properties dialog box.

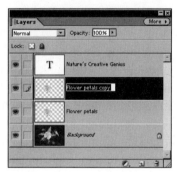

Figure 10-13: Double-click the existing name and type a new one.

If you double-click a Type layer, the text on that layer is selected, as shown in Figure 10-14. You can read more about type — adding it to an image, editing it, formatting it, and so on, in Chapters 14 and 15. After the text is selected, you can replace it by typing new text, or you can use the type formatting tools to change the appearance of the selected text. If you double-click a Shape layer, the Color Picker opens, as Elements assumes that you want to change the color of the shape on that layer.

Tip   You can right-click any layer and choose from the layer-appropriate options in the resulting shortcut menus. All three types — regular, Type, and Shape — offer Rename, Duplicate, and Delete Layer commands, but the Type and Shape layers offers the Simplify Layer command, which prepares the content on that layer for editing and retouching that cannot normally be performed on type or shapes. After simplified, type and shapes can be edited with filters and effects, and can be filled with color or patterns, just as you would content on any layer containing original art or photographic content.

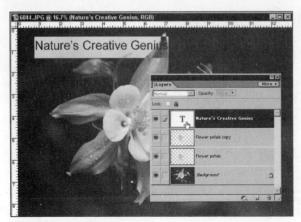

Figure 10-14: Double-clicking a Type layer selects all the text on that layer.

Rearranging Layers

The order that your layers appear in the Layers Palette determines their stacking order within the image. This means that a layer at the top of the list is literally on top of the layer below it in the list, and that layer is on top of the layer below it, and so on. The placement of a given layer in this stack can be a problem if the content of an upper layer obscures content on a lower layer.

Noting how layer order is determined is important. A layer is placed in the stack in the order in which you create the layers and based on which layer is active when the new layer is created. Typically, if you have a layer selected and then use the Layer⇨New⇨Layer command, the new layer appears just above the active layer, and then this new layer becomes the active layer. The same holds true for Shape and Type layers — they appear just above the layer that was active before the Shape was drawn or the text typed.

To rearrange layers, follow these steps:

STEPS: Rearranging Layers in the Layers Palette

1. Click on the layer you want to move up or down in the list of layers.

2. Drag the layer up or down, whichever direction is desired, watching the thick horizontal line that follows it (see Figure 10-15).

3. When the horizontal line is between the layers that should be above and below the layer you want to move, release the mouse.

Basic Elements

While Elements considers all colors to be made up of Red, Green, and Blue (the RGB color model), the original color wheel shows us how the colors that we see are created.

Primary Colors

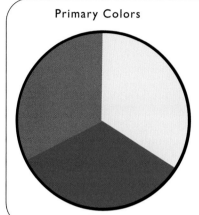

Color 1:

The three primary colors — red, blue, and yellow — cannot be made by mixing any other colors.

Primary & Secondary Colors

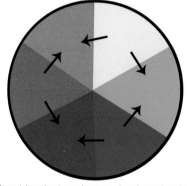

Color 2:

Mix two primary colors and get the three secondary colors, making six colors in the wheel.

Arrows indicate the primary color mixtures that make secondary colors

Primary, Secondary, and Tertiary Colors

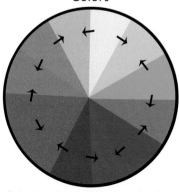

Color 3:

Mixing a primary and a secondary color creates a tertiary (third-level) color. Now there are 12 colors in the wheel.

Mixing primary and secondary colors creates tertiary colors

Color 4:

A black-and-white photo can be dramatic and visually interesting simply through its lack of color.

Color 5:

If you think the photo needs some color, use Elements' Color Variations tool to add color to selected areas. You can also use the Hue/Saturation dialog box to add color to an image that's gone from Grayscale mode to RGB. Finally, the Unsharp Mask filter helps make edges stand out and gets rid of color flatness.

Color 6:

Half the image is in the original colors, the second half turned to a duotone image. The color is stripped away by switching to Grayscale mode, and then back in RGB mode a single color is added.

Rustic Portraits

Color 7:
Create the illusion of a vintage photo by applying a sepia tone to an entire grayscale (turned RGB) image — you can do this with a very see-through layer filled with sepia color. To complete the vintage portrait feeling, create a frame and apply the look of textured paper to it with the Texturizer filter.

Correcting Color and Light

Color 8:

This photo looks awful with a greenish cast that may have been caused by improper development technique or the film fading in sunlight.

Color 9:

The greenish cast is gone, and the photo looks refreshed. Using Color Variations to remove a color cast is one way to do this, and another way is to use the Enhance⇨Adjust Color⇨Color Cast dialog box.

Color 10:

The selected portion of this image shows how the whole image used to look — dark and dreary, with details lost to shadow. After applying light through the Dodge tool and by adjusting Brightness & Contrast, details emerge from the darkness.

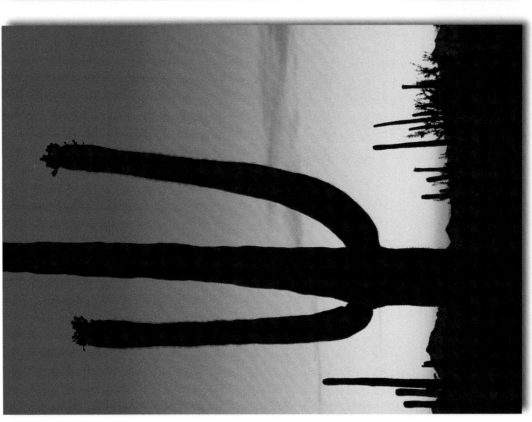

Color 11:

The left half of the image has been left as it was originally. Using the Lens Flare and Lighting Effects filters has relit the right side. The picture now has the look of a camera's flash sparking on a single spot in the image and the addition of a soft spotlight within the image.

Restoring and Retouching

Color 12:

So many problems, most caused by time and improper storage methods. The picture has scratches, fading, wrinkled corners, and a small tear. Can this image be saved?

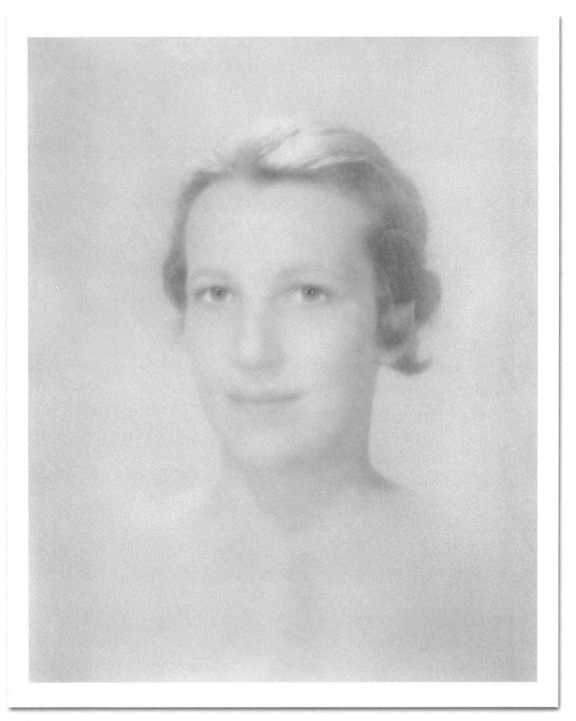

Color 13:

Certainly it can. The image is repaired, the tear mended, the scratches smoothed over, and the faded areas brought back to life. The Clone Stamp, Blur tool, and the Sponge have been utilized.

Using Artistic Filters

Color 14:

Turn a so-so photo into something that looks like an artist, using oil paints, painted it. Now this is suitable for framing!

Color 15:

Convert any photo — this one happens to be in black and white — to a sketch. This can make any photo seem more personal, as though it were drawn by hand.

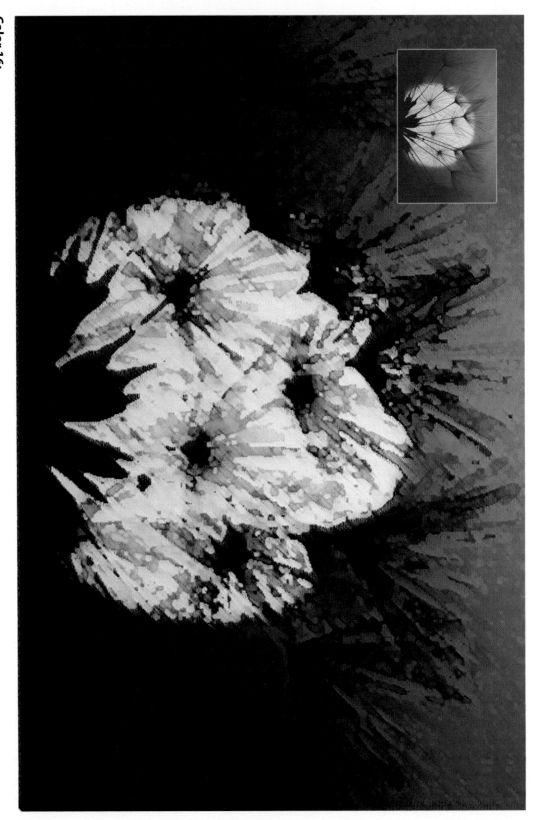

Color 17:

Converting image modes is often a good idea before applying a filter. In this case, a color photo was turned to grayscale to enable the Ink Outlines filter to do its job well.

Distorting and Destructive Filters

Color 18:
Create a monstrous alien from a simple human face (see inset for the "before" look) with the Liquify filter's various tools that enlarge, condense, stretch, and twist image content.

Color 19:

Water's the theme here, so the Ocean Ripple filter is applied, and then using the Brush tool and the Glass filter creates a watery frame. Also, using the Layer Styles palette's bevel options creates a 3D frame.

Color 20:

The Twirl and ZigZag filters create interesting effects when applied to selections within the image.

Glass, Tiles, and Textures

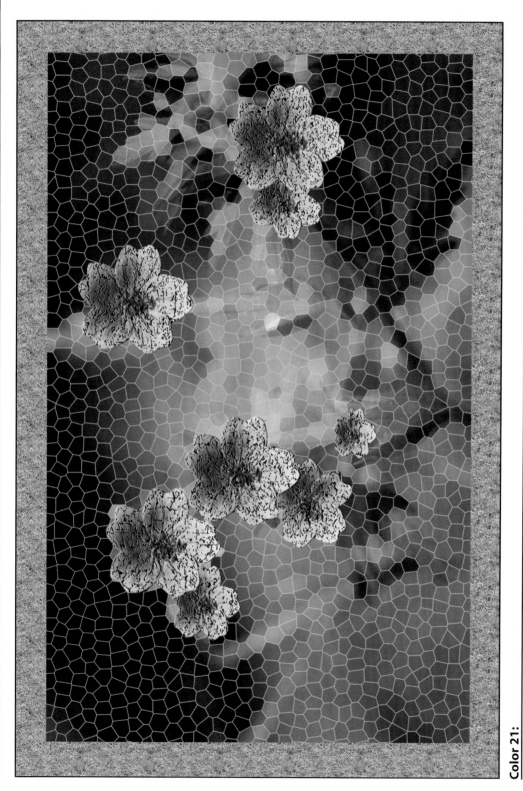

Color 21:

Applying two filters can give you results you'd never get any other way. Here, the Craquelure and Stained Glass filters create a very interesting look when applied to a section of a photo.

Color 22:

Applying fabric textures (through the Texturizer filter) to flat areas within an image brings the image to life, giving it more detail and helping to make individual areas stand out.

Composite Images

Color 23:
Using the PhotoMerge feature, you can combine unrelated images as well as create a panoramic image from several side-by-side shots. Here, three images with no connection to each other are grouped, and a new image is created from them.

Color 24:

Don't like the way a group was grouped? Rearrange them using selection tools and the Move tool. After everyone is in new locations, you can add shadows behind people (with the Burn tool) and add new light sources to make everyone look like they're where they should be.

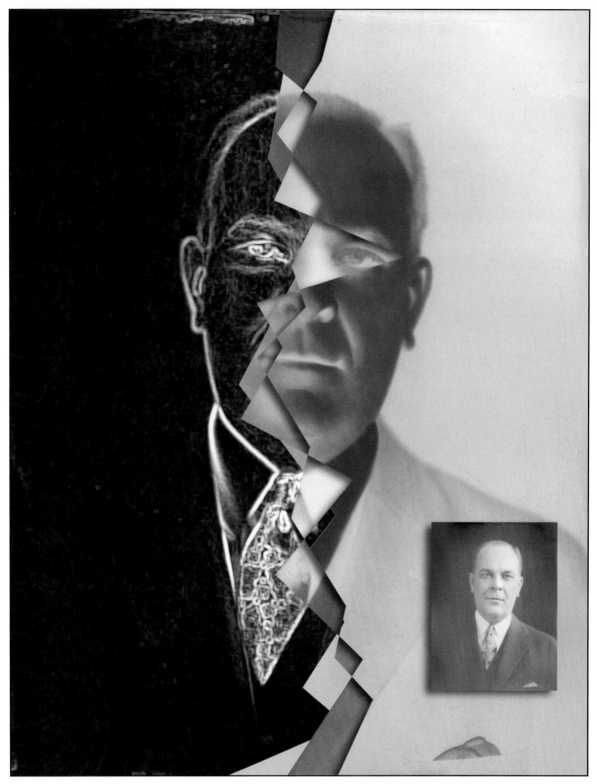

Color 25:

Combining two versions of the same image creates an interesting portrait. To create this look, save two versions of the same photo (each treated differently), select the two halves (one half from each image), and put them together in a new image.

Web Work

Color 26:

Create navigation buttons that catch the eye and load quickly. Here, simple colors and solid shapes mean we can save the image as a GIF and end up with a clean graphic that can be repeated on all the site's pages to give the site consistency and easy navigation.

Color 27:

Rather than boring names that link to e-mail addresses and phone numbers, why not use pictures of your staff? It can make for a personal feel for your Web site, especially if you're designing for a small organization or a small department within a large company.

Color 28:
Type that's applied as a mask can be turned into a selection and deleted, allowing a lower level to show through the "holes" cut by the deleted text.

T POWER
corruption
R lies greed
U question authority.
T
H

?. P O W E?R

Color 29:

Text doesn't have to be simple or boring. Use the characters and words like shapes and graphic content, creating a mood or a feeling that goes beyond what the text literally says.

Original Artwork

Color 30:

Don't have any photos taken in space? Create your own world in the cosmos, using the Shape, Brush, Pencil, and Paint Bucket tools.

Color 31:

Like any artwork, the content doesn't have to be representational or realistic. Go abstract and create a totally unique image with shapes and lines drawn by hand and then turned into a painting through the use of Artistic filters.

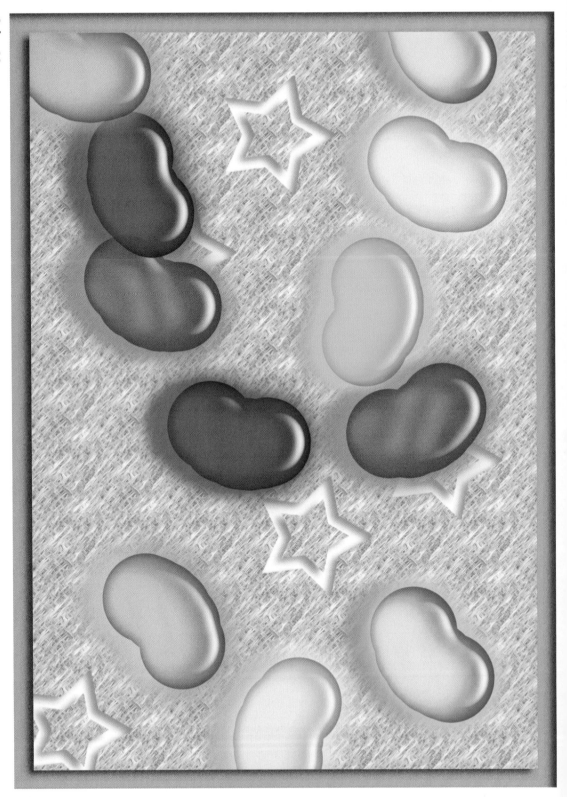

Color 32:

A pile of jellybeans invites a nibble. Using the Lasso tool to create a bean-shaped selection (which was saved for reuse), the Layer Styles's glass buttons style is applied in various colors. Use of shadows also makes the jellybeans look 3D, within themselves and as they relate visually to each other.

Color 33:
Here's looking at you. This eye was drawn using the Brush, Shape, and selection tools, along with solid color and hand-painted fills and lines. You can make a version that's closed and use the two versions in a single image (placed on separate layers) to create a winking animation. See the Save for Web dialog box for the tools you need.

Color 34:
Here's a unique creature, drawn from scratch using Brush tools, pattern fills, filters, and Layer Styles.

Tip

If you're not sure which layer is obscuring your other layer/s content, try hiding various layers (one at a time) to see which one, when hidden, reveals the previously obscured content.

Figure 10-15: Drag your layer up or down to change its stacking order in the image.

Deleting a Layer

Sometimes hiding a layer isn't enough. You not only don't want to see the layer on-screen or when you print the image, you don't want the layer to be part of the image at all. When a layer has outlived its usefulness, you have a few options to get rid of it:

✦ Right-click the layer and choose Delete Layer from the shortcut menu.

✦ Drag the layer to the garbage can icon at the foot of the Layers palette (see a layer being thrown out in Figure 10-16) and release the mouse when this Delete Layer button highlights.

✦ Select the layer, press Ctrl + A to select all of it's content and use the Edit⇨Cut command. This makes it possible to preserve the content of the layer and paste it into another image. You can then use either of the two previous deletion methods to get rid of the now empty layer in your active image.

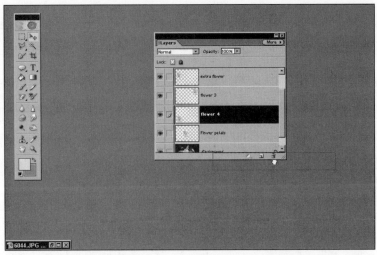

Figure 10-16: Don't want that layer anymore? Toss it in the garbage.

Tip

Regret that deletion? Choose Edit⇨Undo if it's one of the last few actions you did, or use the Undo History to go back to the state just prior to the point where you deleted the layer.

Moving Layers between Files

While many of your images will be entirely separate, unrelated works of art, some of them may have connections — similar content, the same client asked you to create or edit them, or something is in one that you can use in another. Imagine, for example, that you're creating a Web graphic with text on it — perhaps the name of the business and its phone number or address. If you're also making some printed materials for that same client and want that text in the print-bound image, you can avoid retyping (and the margin for errors that entails) by sharing the Type layer from the Web graphic with the image that you intend to print.

To share content between images, the content you intend to share must either be on its own layer or be part of a layer you identified. In the former case, you can drag the layer from the current image to the image where you want to use it, as shown in Figure 10-17 — all that's required is that both the source and target images be open at the same time. After the layer is dragged to the target image, you see it in the target image Layers palette with the same name it had in the source image.

Tip

The layer remains in the source image — don't worry that you're removing it from one image and adding it to another. This is sharing, not moving.

Figure 10-17: Drag a layer from one image to another.

If the content you want to share is on a layer with other content that you don't want to include in the target image, you'll want to select the desired content, and then choose the Edit⇨Copy command to place the content on the Clipboard. Then, you can go to the target image and choose the Edit⇨Paste command to place the copied content in the target image *and* create a new layer for the content at the same time.

Linking and Merging Layers

I discussed all the benefits of distinct layers in an image and keeping each separate element on a separate layer to give yourself as much editing freedom as possible. But what if all that distinction and separateness is a hindrance, rather than a help? If you rather that two or more of your layer were either connected or combined, Elements gives you commands to make it happen.

Linking and Unlinking Layers

Linked layers can be moved in tandem, and you can also transform, copy, paste, and merge linked layers simultaneously, saving time and effort, and also making sure that layers with related content are treated the same way at the same time. This sort of consistency can be a huge help when you're working on a complex project with a lot of layers in the image. To link two or more layers, follow these steps:

STEPS: Linking layers for Tandem Movement, Transformation, and Copying

1. Click on one of the layers to be linked.

2. Click in the column to the left o the layers you want to link to the active layer—a chain icon appears in the formerly empty box next to the now linked layers, as shown in Figure 10-18.

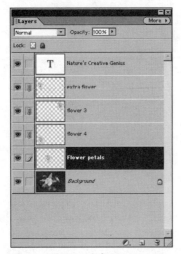

Figure 10-18: Link two or more layers by chaining them together.

3. Continue linking layers until you have the desired group created.

Unlinking layers is just as simple as linking them in the first place. Simply click the chain icons in all the layers in your current grouping and see the chains disappear. After they're all gone, so are the connections between the formerly linked layers.

Merging and Flattening Layers

After you painstakingly position two or more layers relative to each other and/or after you know that two or more of your layers are completed in terms of any editing or retouching that was required, you may want to merge those layers. Merging layers accomplishes two functions:

✦ Merged layers are permanently connected, taking linking to the next level. Merged layers reside on a single layer, which can be copied, pasted, transformed, duplicated, even deleted, and all the formerly distinct layers' content is uniformly affected by the action you take.

✦ Merging layers reduces files size. Every layer you add to an image increases its file size (because of the layer information that has to be stored as part of the file), so obviously, reducing the number of layers by merging two or more of them makes for a smaller file. This can be helpful if you're e-mailing the file to someone, storing it on a low-capacity disk, or if you're running short of hard drive space for images.

To merge two or more layers, link them first, and then choose Layer⊅Merge Linked. This merges the linked layers into one layer, with the name of the layer that was active at the time the Merge Linked command was issues.

If you want to merge all of your layers, you can choose Merge Visible from the Layer menu. This command merges all of the layers that aren't hidden at the time, which means that you can preserve the separation of an individual layer by hiding it before using this particular Merge command.

To seriously reduce file size and create one layer from all of your image layers, simply choose Flatten Image. There are some caveats to this seemingly swift and effective way to reduce file size, however:

✦ Hidden files are discarded when an image is flattened.

✦ All transparent areas are filled with white.

Because of these potential drawbacks to the flattening process, be sure you do all the editing you want to do before you issue the Layer⊅Flatten Image command. You can undo it, but not after saving and closing the image. Given the drawbacks, I'd go so far as to suggest never flattening an image unless a particular action you're taking absolutely requires it. I'd also go so far as to save an unflattened version of the image (see Chapter 16 for more information on saving versions) before flattening your layers.

Tip   Chapter 7 covers using layers to transform image content and retouching images. Discover how to resize, rotate, skew, and otherwise manipulate layer content as well as how to create adjustment layers to change the light, color, and overall quality of layer content.

✦   ✦   ✦

Using the Shape Tools

✦ ✦ ✦ ✦

In This Chapter

Drawing shapes

Using shape tool
options

Working with shape
layers

Using the Marquee
and Lasso tools to
create shapes

✦ ✦ ✦ ✦

Back before Photoshop Elements existed (and going back
to an earlier release of Elements' "parent," Photoshop),
you could only create shapes in an image by using one of
the selection tools and filling the selection with color or a
pattern. The advent of the Shape tool in both applications has
created a considerable amount of freedom for the artist, and
variety within the images created and enhanced with these
applications.

Using the Shape Tool

Elements' Shape tool works very simply — click it to activate
it and then observe the options bar, shown in Figure 11-1. As
soon as the options bar is visible, you can choose which type
of shape you want to draw (or you can display the Shape
tools' alternate buttons, shown in Figure 11-2), and after making that choice, select the fill and layer Style for the shape
you're about to draw. With those selections made, drawing
any shape is as simple as click and drag. It's important to
note, for clarity's sake, that the Shape tool appears as the
Rectangle tool (as seen in its screen tip) by default, and the
screen tip name changes depending on which of the shapes
you choose to draw — an Ellipse, a Rounded Rectangle, a
Polygon, a Line — so you won't see "Shape Tool" in the screen
tip specifically. To refer to all of the potential shapes in general, however, we refer to the Shape tool in this chapter.

Figure 11-1: The Shape tool's options enable you to choose the shape you'll draw, the fill color it will have, and to apply drop shadows, bevels, and other Style alternatives.

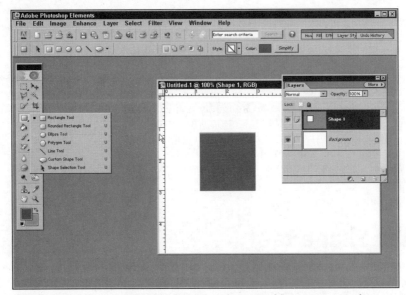

Figure 11-2: You can click and hold the Shape tool button to see alternate button faces if you'd prefer to choose your shape and activate the tool at the same time.

Tip   If you use one of the Shape tool alternatives this time, this button face will be the one you see throughout the current Elements session, and the next time you open the application. Most people, therefore, prefer choosing the Shape tool variant they want to use by making their selection from the options bar after the Shape tool (in any of its forms) is activated.

Drawing Simple Geometric Shapes

The Shape tool offers Rectangle, Rounded Rectangle, Ellipse, Polygon, Line, and Custom Shape variants, as shown in Figure 11-3, where each of these alternatives is identified.

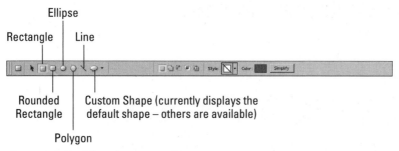

Figure 11-3: Pick a shape, any shape.

If you choose the Rectangle or Ellipse options, your options bar fields consist of the Shape Area buttons (also identified in Figure 11-3), and the Style and Color options. In the case of these simple shapes, drawing the shapes is equally basic:

STEPS: Drawing Rectangles and Ellipses

1. Click the Shape tool to activate it.

2. Using the options bar, click the Rectangle tool or the Ellipse tool.

3. Choose a Color to fill the shape after it's drawn. This opens the Color Picker. Pick a color and click OK to proceed.

4. As desired, click the Style drop-down list and choose a drop shadow or other style for the shape. Chapter 12 covers the full details on the use of layer Styles.

5. Click and drag on your image, where the shape should appear. The farther from your starting point you drag, the larger the shape will be. Figure 11-4 shows a shape in progress.

6. If you don't want your shape to appear on a colored background, click the Simplify button to make the shape appear on a transparent field. Figure 11-5 shows the Layers palette and a simplified shape layer (Shape 2) that shows the "checkerboard" representation of transparency. The other shape layer (Shape 1) still has a gray field, indicating a colored background remains on that layer.

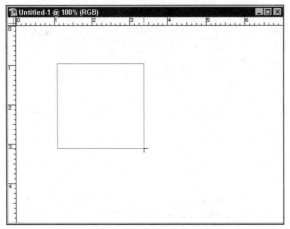

Figure 11-4: Drag diagonally from your starting click point to draw a shape the size and proportions you desire.

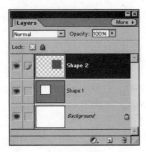

Figure 11-5: A background can interfere with the shape's role in the image — the Simplify button gets rid of the offending colored field in one click.

Tip   If you press and hold the Shift key as you drag (and release the mouse before the Shift key when the shape is complete), you'll draw a perfect square with the Rectangle tool or a perfect circle with the Ellipse tool.

If you decide to draw a slightly more complex variation of the Rectangle tool's output, you can choose the Rounded Rectangle tool instead. This works the same as the Rectangle shape tool, except for the presence of an additional field in the options bar, shown in Figure 11-6.

Figure 11-6: Use the Radius field to make a rectangle with rounded corners.

When drawing a Rounded Rectangle, you need to establish the Radius for the corners — the curve, or degree of rounding that will be applied. The default is 10 pixels, but you can increase or decrease that number as desired. Obviously, a higher Radius setting increases the curve and a lower number decreases it. If you increase the Radius to 100, you'll get what looks like an Ellipse — if you decrease it to one or zero, the rounding will be so slight (at one pixel) or nonexistent (at 0 pixels) that the resulting shape will look like a standard rectangle. Figure 11-7 shows a Rounded Rectangle with a 25 pixel Radius.

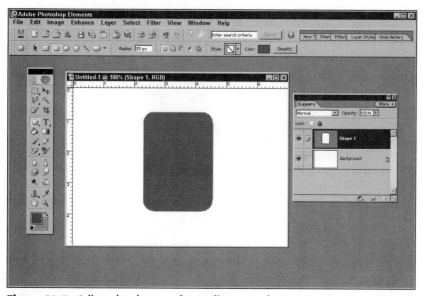

Figure 11-7: Adjust the degree of rounding to make a very soft or more angular rounded rectangle.

Drawing Polygons

If you need a more complex geometric shape, the Polygon shape tool is a good choice. You find some overlap with the Custom Shapes list of shapes, but if you want to draw a triangle, hexagon, octagon — any multi-sided shape — the Polygon tool makes it very simple:

STEPS: Drawing a Polygon

1. Click the Shape tool to activate it.

2. From the options bar, click the Polygon shape tool.

3. Note the change in the options bar, as shown in Figure 11-8. In place of the Radius option displayed for the Rounded Rectangle, the Polygon tool offers a Sides field.

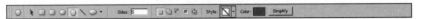

Figure 11-8: The Sides field enables you to determine which polygon you're going to draw — a triangle (three sides), a pentagon (five sides), and so on.

4. Enter the number of sides in your polygon — 3, 5, 6, 7, or more. I've left out 4 from the list, because a 4-sided polygon, of course, is a rectangle.

5. Choose Color to fill the shape, and as desired, select a Style.

6. Click and drag to draw the shape, as shown in Figure 11-9.

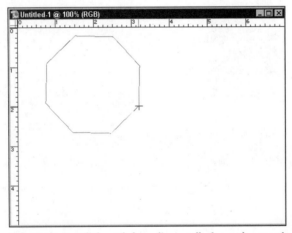

Figure 11-9: Click and drag diagonally from the starting point to control the size and proportions of your polygon.

7. To get rid of the shape's surrounding background, click the Simplify button.

Tip

After the polygon is drawn, you can rotate it by choosing the Image⇨Transform Shape⇨Free Transform Shape command. If you already made changes since drawing the shape, the Image⇨Transform⇨Free Transform command gives you the same options and enables you to spin the shape to any angle you desire.

Drawing Custom Shapes

Just as the Rounded Rectangle and Polygon shape tools give you more options to accommodate the needs of their particular shapes, the Custom Shape tool offers you a list of shapes and the ability to view other groups of shapes. The default shapes, as shown in Figure 11-10, run the gamut from standard geometric shapes (stars, arrows) to more complex shapes that contain both straight-sided parts and round areas, such as cherries, a heart, a cloud, or an animal footprint.

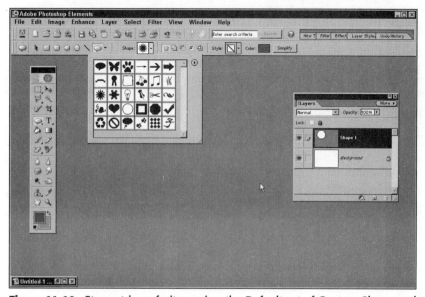

Figure 11-10: Stars, stripes, fruit, music — the Default set of Custom Shape tool choices is fairly extensive in its own right.

To display the available custom shapes, click the Custom Shape tool on the Shape tool's options bar and then click the drop-down arrow to see the available shapes. A default set of 30 shapes appears, along with an options menu button, through which you can choose from 14 alternative shape groups, plus All Elements Shapes (to see all the groups' shapes at once) or Default. Figure 11-11 shows the display after you choose All Elements Shapes — it's a considerable list, and is only partially visible in the figure. To see all 400+ shapes, just scroll through the list.

Note
The shapes that appear when you choose All Elements Shapes appear in the groups you have seen individually if you chose them individually from the options menu. All the Asian characters are together, all the cartoon bubbles are together, all the travel-related symbols are together, and so on. If you're not sure what a given shape is, just point to it and view the screen tip that displays its name, often accompanied by a number if there's more than one similar shape.

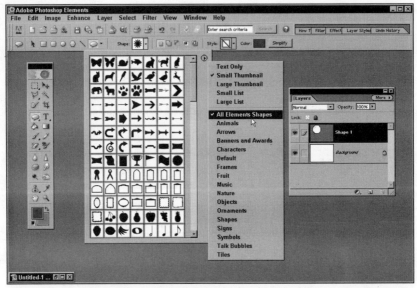

Figure 11-11: Making the Default set look silly, the All Elements Shapes selection from the options menu displays more than 400 shapes for you to choose.

After you choose the shape you want to draw, just draw it — click and drag to draw the shape, using the angle from which you drag away from the starting click point to determine the shape's size and proportions. The options bar's other fields — Color and Style — work just as they do for the other Shape tool alternatives.

Drawing Lines

You thought you learned about drawing lines in Chapter 8, where you read how to use the Brush and Pencil tools (along with the Shift key) to create lines at 45- and 90-degree angles, right? Well, while those tools and that technique work fine for many lines you want to create, the Shape tool's Line tool gives you a lot more flexibility and power. As shown in Figure 11-12, you can choose the Weight (in pixels), Color, and through your click and drag technique (and the use of the Shift key or not), you can draw a line of any thickness, color, or angle.

Tip   Even though it may look choppy on-screen, a line at an angle other than 45 to 90 degrees prints as a straight line.

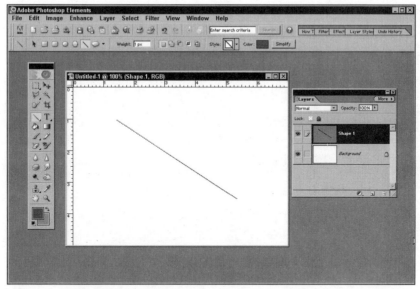

Figure 11-12: Control the thickness and color of the straight line you need.

Working with Shape Layers

All these shapes you draw — rectangles, ellipses, polygons, custom shapes, lines — each one creates a new layer in your image, a Shape layer with special needs and capabilities. As shown in Figure 11-13, each shape you draw creates its own Shape layer, each displaying the shape you drew, in the location you drew it, accompanied by a number indicating the order in which the shapes were drawn.

When drawing shapes and lines with the Shape tool, you can use the Add to, Subtract from, Intersect Shape Areas, and Exclude Overlapping Shape Areas options to create new shapes and draw more than one shape on an individual shape layer (these buttons are identified in Figure 11-14). Working much the way the same tools work with the selection tools (Marquee, Lasso, Magic Wand), you can add a shape, subtract from an existing shape or create a new shape by combining or excluding parts of two overlapping shapes. Figure 11-15 shows a rectangle losing a circular center section through the use of the Subtract from Shape Area tool — the Ellipse tool is activated after the rectangle is drawn, and the circular shape is therefore removed from the center of the rectangle. Figure 11-16 shows a very unique shape created by adding shapes to an original shape, and then using the Intersect option to remove part of the combined shapes.

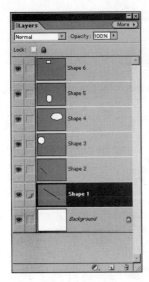

Figure 11-13: Each shape drawn with the Shape tool creates a Shape layer.

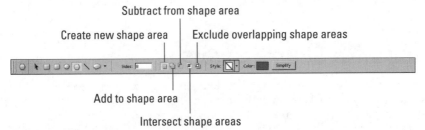

Figure 11-14: Choose how to change an existing shape or add more shapes to an existing shape layer.

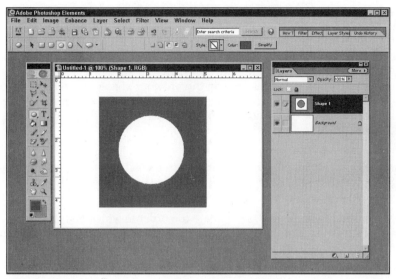

Figure 11-15: Cut away from a shape with another shape — all on the same Shape layer.

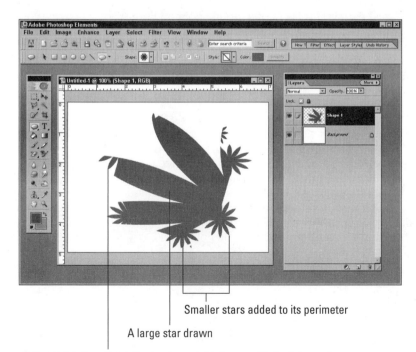

Smaller stars added to its perimeter

A large star drawn

A star larger than the entire image canvas drawn with the Intersect option turned on, reducing the image to only what overlapped

Figure 11-16: Get creative and build your own new shapes by combining several rather basic shapes into one.

So what are these special needs and capabilities I mentioned? Shape layers have some unique characteristics:

✦ Each Shape layer can only contain the shape drawn on it. After you start a new shape (without using the Add, Subtract, Intersect, or Exclude options, which would keep the next shape on the previous shape's layer), the shape layer you just created (by drawing the previous shape) becomes unchangeable in terms of the shape content. You can transform a shape, but you can't add a new shape to an existing shape layer.

✦ Shape layers can be simplified after the fact. Right-click an existing Shape layer and choose Simplify from the shortcut menu. The layer becomes transparent (except for the shape), and the outline (that appeared by virtue of the Shape layer's background) disappears).

✦ Shape layers are numbered, to indicate the order in which shapes were drawn. Unless you simplify layers (to get rid of their backgrounds), you can't see shapes beneath other shapes (each on their own layers).

Creating Shapes with the Selection Tools

As I mentioned earlier in this chapter, at one point in Photoshop's history, you could only draw shapes by filling selections with color or patterns and by manually placing the selections on their own layers. Of course, the Shape tool has eliminated this as the primary technique for shape-creation, but it by no means eliminates the use for it. As shown in Figure 11-17, some interesting shapes are quickly created with the Lasso tool.

As soon as you make the selection, you can use the Paint Bucket or Gradient fill tools to fill the selection with a solid color, a pattern (one of the Paint Bucket's options), or a gradient involving two or more colors. Before making the selection (or immediately afterward, but before filling the selection), you can choose the Layer⇨New⇨Layer command to build a new layer to house the shape-to-be. On the other hand, and this makes the selection-to-shape technique somewhat more flexible than the Shape tool, you can incorporate the selection (and later the shape) into an existing layer (even the original Background layer) within the image. Figure 11-18 shows the complex shape created with the Polygonal Lasso tool, now filled with a 3-color gradient.

These crossovers create isolated closed shapes, which can be filled.

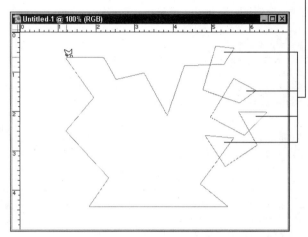

Figure 11-17: Create a selection in the shape of anything—something representational or totally abstract—and then fill it to make it a shape.

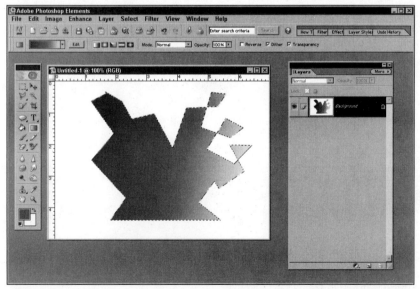

Figure 11-18: The shape is created when the selection is filled—without a fill, it's just a selection.

Tip   Read all about fills — solid colors, patterns, and gradients — in Chapter 12.

Manipulating Shapes

After you draw a shape, you can use a variety of transformation techniques to change the rotation and size of the shape, or you can skew, distort, or change the shapes perspective. You may want a taller star, a chunkier arrow, a rectangle that leans to one side, or to create a shadow (with a second shape) beneath an existing shape, as shown in Figure 11-19. You can achieve these effects through the Image⇨ Transform command and its submenu commands.

Stretch a shape to make it taller or wider.

Skew a shape to make it lean to one side.

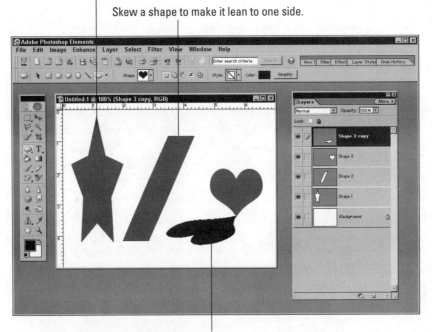

Place a duplicate shape on a new layer and then alter its perspective to create a shadow for the previous shape.

Figure 11-19: Transform your shapes, and even create special effects, such as a customized shadow in perfect perspective.

Transforming Shapes

The Transform Shape command (found in the Image menu) is only available while a shape is new — before you go on to create another shape (on another Shape layer) or to create other image content — type, painted lines and areas, and so on. While the command is available, you can rotate, resize, skew, and adjust the perspective of the active shape, simply by dragging the handles on the shape. Figure 11-20 shows a polygon being rotated to a more pleasing angle.

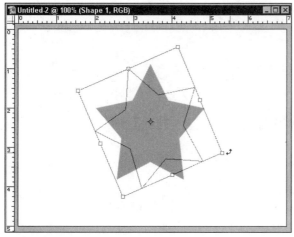

Figure 11-20: Your polygon can stand on a different corner if you rotate it ever so slightly.

You can also resize a shape, dragging its top/bottom, side, or corner handles. If you go on to another layer or to another task within your image, the Transform Shape command goes away, replaced by the Transform command. From here, you can choose Free Transform, or any of the other Transform submenu commands and use them just as you would on any other sort of layer content.

Another way to control and manipulate your shapes is through the options drop-down list (the Polygons' resulting dialog box appears in Figure 11-21 and the Custom Shape's in Figure 11-22). To display these additional settings for a shape tool, click the tool, and then go to the drop-down list just to the right of the Custom Shape tool. Click the drop-down arrow, and view the dialog box — one for each of the shape tools, offering options appropriate for that tool.

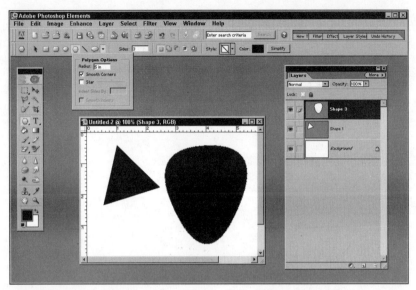

Figure 11-21: Control the radius curve and the indent of the sides on a Polygon-created star.

Each click creates a new shape layer.

After you choose a fixed size, just click to create the shape.

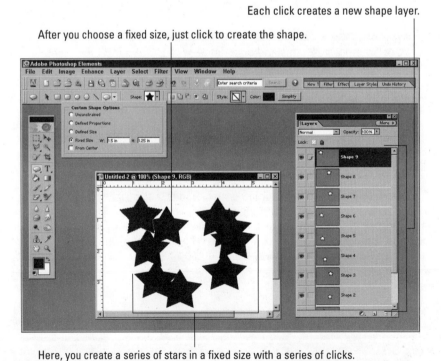

Here, you create a series of stars in a fixed size with a series of clicks.

Figure 11-22: Basic shapes have basic options—size and proportions.

Moving Shapes

Moving a shape requires moving a shape layer (unless you created the shape by filling a selection). To do so, choose one of these techniques:

✦ Click on the desired layer in the Layers palette and when handles appear around the shape, point to the shape itself and drag.

✦ Click on the Move tool and then click on the shape you want to move. The shape's Shape layer is automatically selected and you can drag to any position within the image.

✦ Go to the Shape tool in the toolbox, and display the alternate buttons — from them, choose Shape Selection tool and use it to click on and select a particular shape (and thus its layer).

✦ Select the Shape layer as desired (with the Move tool and a click, or through the Layers palette) and then use the arrow keys to *nudge* the shape up, down, left, or right.

As shown in Figure 11-23, dragging a shape to a new position is easy. As soon as you let go, however, you find out if your shape is obscured by another shape layer that hasn't been simplified (made transparent, except for the shape), or by other layers in the image containing photographic content, type, or the work of the paintbrush or pencil.

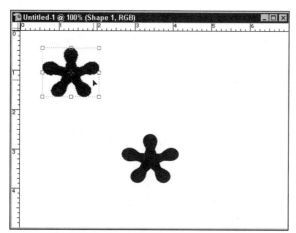

Figure 11-23: Move your shape by dragging the entire Shape layer.

If you find that something is obscuring your shape, drag its layer up in the Layers palette — move it above the obscuring content. You can also simplify the offending layer (so that only the shape on the layer is capable of obscuring underlying layer content) by right-clicking the layer and choosing Simplify Layer from the shortcut menu (see Figure 11-24).

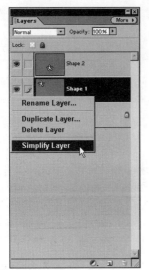

Figure 11-24: Rearrange your layers or make the layers transparent to solve overlapping problems.

✦   ✦   ✦

Applying Fills and Styles

✦ ✦ ✦ ✦

In This Chapter

Using the Paint Bucket to create solid fills

Filling shapes and areas with a pattern

Applying and creating gradient fills

Controlling fill quality

Creating shadows and other 3D effects with Layer Styles

✦ ✦ ✦ ✦

You can fill any area — a group of like-colored pixels within a layer, a selection, an entire layer — with solid color. The process is extremely simple, requiring only that you activate the Paint Bucket tool and choose a Foreground color (if the current one is not the one you want).

Filling Selections and Layers with the Paint Bucket

As shown in Figure 12-1, the Paint Bucket's options bar is filled with fields that enable you to customize the tool's functioning, but you needn't reset anything — just pick a foreground color and click inside the selection or layer you want to fill.

Figure 12-1: As simple as pouring paint from a bucket — the Paint Bucket tool makes applying a solid color quick and easy.

If you do want to tweak the way the Paint Bucket works, your options include:

✦ Choosing to fill with a Pattern instead

✦ Selecting a painting Mode, the list being identical to the Brush tool's Mode selection

✦ Setting an Opacity level

✦ Setting a Tolerance level, which determines the degree of similarity between adjacent pixels that you want to fill with color

✦ Turning Anti-aliasing on or off, controlling the softness of the edges of your fill

✦ To fill only Contiguous pixels with color

✦ To have the fill color apply to All Layers at once, despite one layer being active at the time the Paint Bucket tool is used

The defaults for these settings — Foreground for the Fill, Normal for the Mode, 100% for the Opacity, 32 for Tolerance, and Anti-Aliasing and Contiguous in the ON position — works well for most situations. You can change the way your fill color affects the existing color and light levels in your image with different Mode choices (see Chapters 7 and 10 for a list of the Modes and their results), and adjusting Opacity and Tolerance will determine how much of an impact your fill has on the image overall. The best way, as usual, to get the best results is to experiment. You can always Undo and start over.

Tip

Remember that you can select a new Foreground color by choosing a new color from within the Color Picker, or you can click with the eyedropper (activated when the Color Picker is open) to sample a color. You can sample color on your workspace, within the image window, or even on the Desktop (if it's visible beyond the perimeter of the workspace) and make that color your new Foreground color. This latter capability makes it possible to quickly select a color that's already in your image, making your fill a good match for the existing color scheme.

Applying a Pattern Fill

If you chose Pattern from the Fill option, the Pattern field becomes available (see Figure 12-2) and you can click the drop-down list to choose a pattern with which to fill your layer or selection. The rest of the options on the options bar remain the same if you switch to a Pattern fill.

The Pattern option and associated drop-down list give you a series of patterns from which to choose — ranging from somewhat psychedelic to very textured and natural looking. To apply one, simply click it in the drop-down list box and then use the Paint Bucket as you would if you were applying a solid color — click within the selection or on a spot in a layer where you want to add the pattern. Figure 12-3 shows a pattern applied within a layer, filling contiguous pixels.

You aren't stuck with the somewhat limited selection of patterns, however, as you can switch to one of seven alternate groups of patterns, located in the options menu (see Figure 12-4). To switch to another group of patterns, follow this simple procedure.

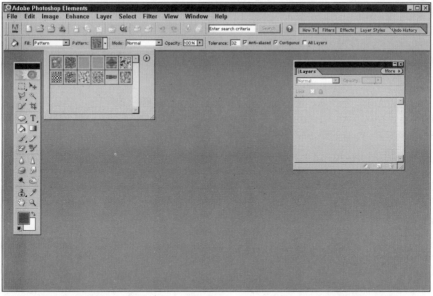

Figure 12-2: Fill your selection or layer with a pattern instead of a solid color.

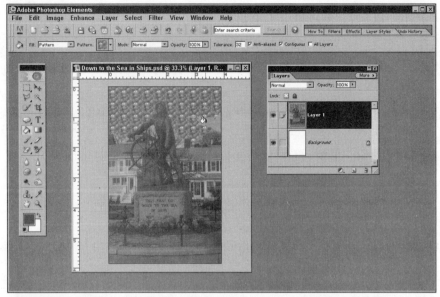

Figure 12-3: Click to apply the selected pattern in your selection or layer.

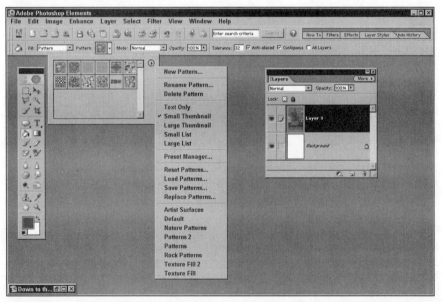

Figure 12-4: Seven different sets of patterns (plus the Default group) give you many patterns from which to choose.

STEPS: Choosing a Different Set of Patterns

1. Turn on the Paint Bucket tool by clicking it in the toolbox.

2. Using the options bar, change the Fill method from Foreground to Pattern.

3. Click the Pattern option drop-down list, displaying the current (most probably Default) set of patterns.

4. Click the options menu button to display a menu of pattern-related menu commands and choices.

5. Choose a group of patterns — Artist Surfaces, Patterns, Rock Patterns, to name just three of the seven available.

6. With your new pattern group selected, click the desired pattern from that group by clicking on its sample in the Pattern drop-down list box.

If you choose Load Patterns from the options menu, a Load Patterns dialog box opens (see Figure 12-5), from which you can choose from the same set of pattern groups found in the options menu, but each one appears as a file instead of a menu selection. The one you choose is added to the current group of patterns, instead of replacing the current set as occurs when you choose a pattern group outright from the options menu. This works much like the Load Brushes command discussed in Chapter 9.

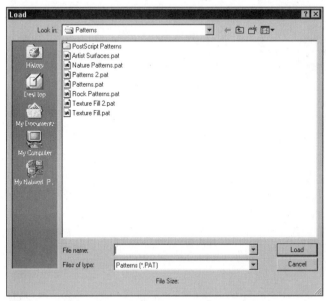

Figure 12-5: Append a group of patterns to the existing group rather than replacing it.

Tip

Don't forget the other Pattern commands in the options menu. You can Reset, Save, and Replace your pattern groups in addition to loading a group to append to the current one. These command names are fairly self-explanatory, but realize that Reset puts the Default set back in use, and Replace removes the Default set (from the drop-down list box, not from your computer) and puts a group you choose in its place. You use the Save command when you create your own custom group of patterns (those you made, those you've renamed, and groups that have had some of the patterns deleted), and you save them with a name of your own choosing.

Creating Your Own Patterns

Just as you can create your own brush presets by selecting a portion of your image and making it a brush, you can also select a portion of your image and make it a new pattern. Figure 12-6 shows a small block selected in a photo — the content of the selection becomes a pattern that can be used to fill a selection or content within any layer in your image.

Figure 12-6: Turn a rectangular selection into a new pattern that you can apply to the same or another image.

To create your own pattern, follow these steps:

STEPS: Creating a Custom Pattern from an Image Selection

1. Using the Rectangular Marquee selection tool, select a rectangular section of the image. Be sure you're on the layer that contains the actual content you want to use as the pattern.

2. Choose Edit➪Define Pattern. The Pattern Name dialog box appears, with your selection displayed in a thumbnail, and a Name field awaiting the name for your new pattern, as shown in Figure 12-7.

3. Type a name for the pattern to replace the generic Pattern 1 that is assigned by default. Choose a name that either describes the content of the pattern ("satin fabric" or "sea foam" rather than "my pattern") or how it would be used.

4. Click OK. Your pattern joins the currently selected group of patterns and can be used in the open or any other image. Figure 12-8 shows our new pattern in use, creating an original fill for a selection within an image.

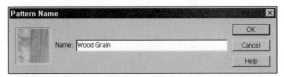

Figure 12-7: Create and name your own special pattern.

Figure 12-8: The wood grain behind the man is now a pattern and therefore easily applied to create an entirely wood grain background behind him.

Tip

A fun way to use this feature is to select someone's face and create a pattern from it. You can then use their face as a background or to fill an area, perhaps a frame around the person's portrait, or in some original artwork depicting or inspired by that person. This is especially popular with kids. Making a pattern out of words or single characters is also effective.

After you create a pattern, you can use the Pattern option menu to rename it or delete it if you no longer need it. This applies to patterns that "came with" Elements, but it's not a good idea to delete the default or installed patterns — you're likely to want them at some time in the future, and nothing is served by deleting them — these patterns don't take up room, and an extra pattern you have no use for doesn't interfere with using the ones you like. Deletions should be reserved for patterns you created, typically because you want to re-create it to achieve a slightly (or entirely) different look to the pattern. To delete and rename patterns, simply right-click the one in question and choose the appropriate command from the resulting shortcut menu, shown in Figure 12-9.

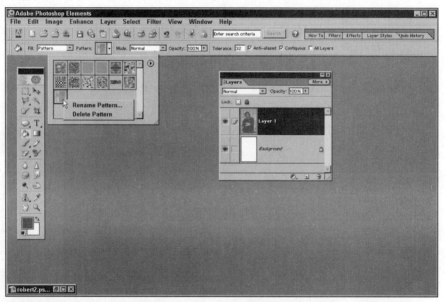

Figure 12-9: Replace or delete any pattern with a right-click.

Working with Gradient Fills

A gradient is a fill that starts out as one color and slowly changes to another. Two-color gradients go from your current Foreground color to your Background color, and gradient presets incorporate two, three, or even four colors, as shown in Figure 12-10, which depicts a simple two-color gradient in one selection and some more complex gradients that utilize more than two colors to achieve their effects.

You can apply a gradient through the Gradient tool, shown, with its options bar activated, in Figure 12-11. In addition to applying color, you can choose from a series of gradient presets, select the shape and direction of your gradient, and apply a Mode to the gradient. The gradient can affect existing content's light and color values, and you can set the Opacity of the gradient fill. The remaining three options enable you to control the appearance of the gradient:

✦ **Reverse:** This option flips the gradient preset 180 degrees. If, for example, you choose a simple two-color gradient that went from Foreground to Background color, the Reverse option makes the gradient start with the Background color and end with the Foreground color.

✦ **Dither:** This option is on by default and determines the smooth transition between colors in the gradient.

✦ **Transparency:** This option is also on by default and allows the gradient to include transparency — perhaps taking no color to a color or vice versa. When there's a transparent portion of the gradient, whatever's on the layer beneath it can be seen through the gradient, enabling you to achieve some very interesting effects, as shown in Figure 12-11.

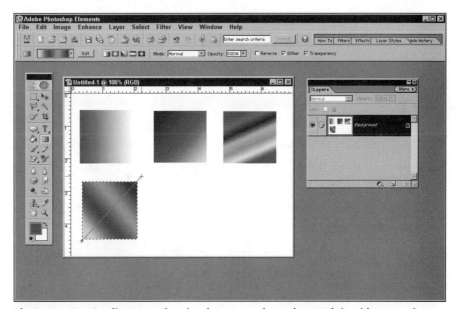

Figure 12-10: Gradients can be simple or complex — the result in either case is a smooth transition from one color to the next across the span of a selection or layer.

Figure 12-11: Sometimes what you can't see is as interesting as what you can. With a gradient that includes transparency, you get both.

Choosing Gradient Colors

If you opt to use the simple Foreground-to-Background gradient (the first one in the array of Default presets, shown in Figure 12-12), you need to establish the two colors involved by using the Color Picker to establish the desired Foreground and Background colors. Nothing is unique about the process — you click the Foreground color box to open the Color Picker, and then pick a color. Repeat that with the Background color box and you have your two gradient colors.

Selecting a Gradient Preset

As soon as you activate the Gradient tool, you're able to choose the kind of gradient you'll apply. The first option on the options bar is a series of presets — you can choose from 15 default presets or click the options menu button to display any one of eight additional preset groups (see Figure 12-13).

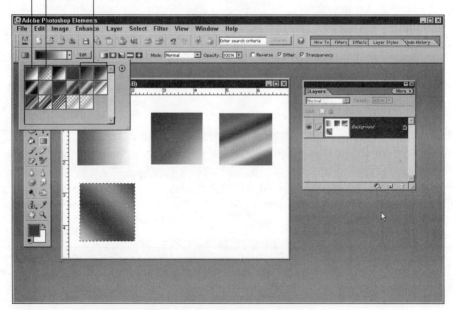

This gradient uses your Foreground and Background colors as the starting and ending colors for your gradient.

This second gradient looks similar, but finishes in transparency.

These gradients employ multiple colors, unrelated to your current Foreground and Background color choices.

Figure 12-12: Pick your starting and ending gradient colors for a simple two-color gradient.

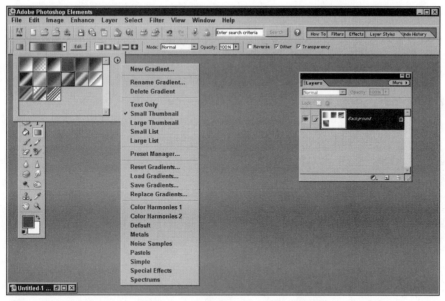

Figure 12-13: Choose a different set of presets, such as Metals or Pastels, for interesting gradient effects not available in the default group.

Just like Paint Bucket and Brush presets, you can use the Reset, Load, Save, and Replace Gradients commands to control the display of presets within the first drop-down list in the Gradient tool's options bar. If you choose a gradient preset group from the list in the options menu, it will replace the set that's currently displayed. If you use the Load Gradients command, you can choose a gradient group from the Load Gradient dialog box and the one you choose will be appended to whichever preset group is currently displayed.

Applying Directional and Shape Gradients

Another way you can control the appearance of your gradient, is to choose from the five different shape and directional gradient options (see them identified in Figure 12-14). From a simple linear gradient (from one color to another in a straight line) to a gradient that makes your shape look spherical or conical, you can achieve a wide variety of effects simply by changing the shape and direction of the gradient you selected in the previous set of options. Figure 12-15 shows a series of shapes, each with a different shape/direction of gradient applied. Choosing one that matches the shape that it will be filling is a good idea—Radial or Angle for a circle or ellipse, Linear or Reflected for a square or rectangle, or Diamond for a polygon, to take advantage of the multiple sides of the shape.

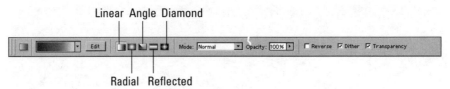

Figure 12-14: Get to know your shape and directional gradient options.

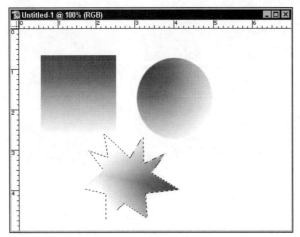

Figure 12-15: Choose the shape and direction of your gradient to match your selection.

When you apply the gradient tool, you drag across the shape/selection, and it's the direction and distance you drag that determines the overall appearance of the gradient. Using a simple two-color gradient to demonstrate, Figure 12-16 shows a variety of different application methods, each resulting in a very different effect on an identical shape.

Using the Gradient Editor

The Edit button on the Gradient tool's options bar opens a great dialog box for tweaking the way any gradient (from any of the preset groups) looks and works. As shown in Figure 12-17, you can click on any preset and then adjust the Gradient Type, the Smoothness, and change the Opacity setting for the transitional stops (where colors transition from one to the next) across the span of the gradient. You can save your settings as an entirely new gradient for future use, too.

Drag from left to right, covering the exact width
of the selection or shape to get this tidy effect.

Start outside the shape and end inside it.

Start inside the shape
and end outside it.

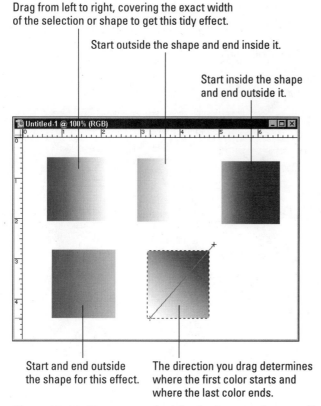

Start and end outside
the shape for this effect.

The direction you drag determines
where the first color starts and
where the last color ends.

Figure 12-16: Your mouse has the final say on the overall
appearance of your gradient.

After you create a new gradient (by tweaking an existing one, even beyond recognition), you can click the Save button to add it to the displayed presets group. The
Save dialog box opens (see Figure 12-18), through which you can name your new
group. Of course you probably don't want to create a whole new group with a new
name just to reflect the addition of one or two new gradients—rather, reserve the
Save command for when you create several new gradients, perhaps adding them to
the Default group, and then save that new group with a new name, leaving the original Default intact.

Pick a preset.

Click the options menu button
to access a preset from another group.

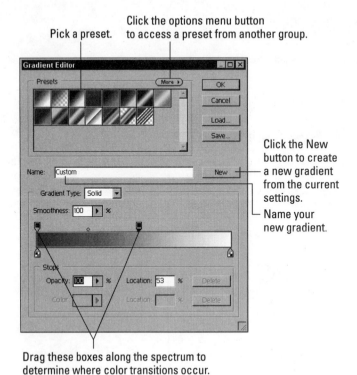

Click the New
button to create
a new gradient
from the current
settings.

Name your
new gradient.

Drag these boxes along the spectrum to
determine where color transitions occur.

Figure 12-17: Customize a gradient and then give it a name so you can use it again.

Figure 12-18: Create a new group of presets with a name
that reflects their purpose or anything they have in common.

Applying Layer Styles

The available Layer Styles are visible through the Layer Styles palette in the docking well, and they include 13 different categories of special effects that you can apply to the layers in your image (see Figure 12-19). If your image is a photo that's just been scanned and you haven't added any layers or pasted any content from another image (which would create a new layer), your image may consist solely of a Background layer and nothing else. If that's the case, the effects of the Layer Styles may be less than effective because they won't make any visual difference, or they'll completely cover up your photo. In the case of drop shadows and bevels, the fact that the photo fills the background will make it impossible to apply a shadow or beveled edge, and if you choose one of the special fills—Complex, Glass buttons, and so on—you'll find that the one you choose can obscure everything in the layer.

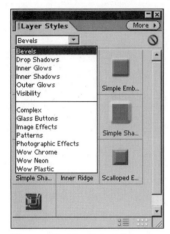

Figure 12-19: Select from several Layer Style categories.

To apply a Layer Style, click the Layer Styles palette tab to display the palette, and then use the drop-down list to choose the category of styles from which you want to choose. As soon as you choose a category and see a style you want to apply, you have two choices:

✦ Click the thumbnail to apply the style to the selection or active layer.

✦ Drag the thumbnail onto your image, dropping it on the content to which the style should apply.

Tip
To make it faster and easier to apply multiple Layer Styles, detach the palette from the docking well and drag it down onto the workspace for quick access. You can close it back to the palette after you finish applying styles.

Customizing Layer Styles

After you apply a style, you can tweak the way it looks. To do so, double-click the style layer in the Layers palette (see one highlighted in Figure 12-20), and then use the resulting dialog box (shown in Figure 12-21) to adjust the depth of the shadow, width of the glow, color of the outline, angle of the beveled edge, and so on. The dialog boxes are as numerous as the styles you can apply, but all rely on common tools — sliders, check boxes, and textboxes into which you can enter numbers, indicating the degree of rotation, width, height, or thickness of the style's components.

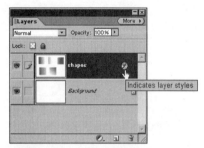

Figure 12-20: The little icon on the right side of the layer indicates that a style has been applied — double-click it to see tools for controlling the appearance of any styles in use on the active layer.

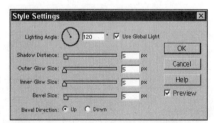

Figure 12-21: The Style Settings dialog box enables you to choose the direction of your shadow, the depth of your bevel, and the amount of glow applied.

Note   As you apply the Layer styles, you'll see a preview applied to a small, gray box within the palette. This technique makes it difficult to imagine how the styles will look when applied to a layer in your image, so you may end up applying them first, and then using Undo to start over. Unlike the Filters and Effects tabs (discussed in Chapter 13), which offer a fairly illustrative thumbnail, the Layer Styles tab is not terribly helpful.

Removing Layer Styles

You can change your mind and turn off a style that you applied by clicking the Clear Style button (see it highlighted in Figure 12-22), and the last style you applied disappears from the image.

Figure 12-22: Clear your last style with the Clear Style button.

If you already left the palette and want to get rid of a style without reopening the Layer Styles palette, you can:

✦ Choose Edit, Undo.

✦ Press Ctrl/Command + Z.

✦ Use the Undo History palette and go back in time to just before the Layer Style/s were applied.

Of course, you can redisplay the Layer Styles palette and click the Clear Style button to get rid of applied styles. You must go to the category of style you applied, and clear the style, and then proceed to switch to any other style categories you worked with and clear each one of the separately.

✦   ✦   ✦

Using Filters and Special Effects

◆ ◆ ◆ ◆

In This Chapter

Applying Filters and special Effects to photos and original artwork

Creating type effects

Customizing filters and effects

Creating frames for your Elements images

◆ ◆ ◆ ◆

Elements offers a very convenient set of palettes — Filters and Effects — and you find them in the docking well, in the upper-right corner of the workspace. The filters and effects are combinations of formats that you can apply to images of all kinds — photos, original artwork, or combinations thereof — and to text as well.

Viewing Your Filter and Effect Choices

Figure 13-1 shows the Effects palette and the group of thumbnails visible within the palette's current size — you can resize the palette as needed or change the way the thumbnails are displayed so that you can see more at one time. Figure 13-2 shows the Effects palette, dragged out onto the workspace, giving you easy, fast access to the available Effects without having to reselect the palette from the docking well each time you want to apply an effect.

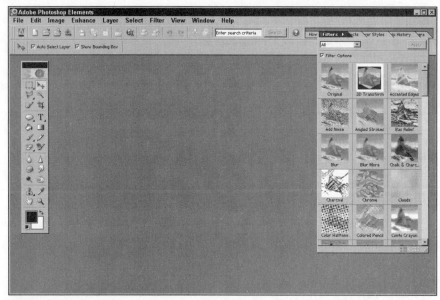

Figure 13-1: View Elements various Filters or Effects by displaying the palettes.

Click the X to close the pallette to the docking well.

Point to a corner and drag by the two-headed arrow to resize the pallette as needed.

Figure 13-2: Move the palettes out onto the workspace for convenience. If they're taking up too much room, resize or close them to the docking well.

Displaying Filters and Effects by Category

By default, both the Filters and Effects palettes display All of the available filters and effects at once. You may, however, want to reduce the displayed choices to just those in a particular group—grouped just as you see them in the Filters menu, shown in Figure 13-3. To display the palettes' offerings in smaller groups, use the drop-down list shown in Figure 13-4.

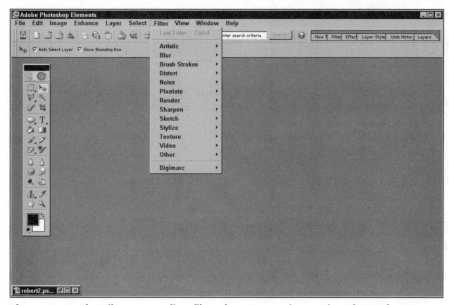

Figure 13-3: The Filters menu lists filters by category, in a series of 13 submenus.

Tip   Not all of the category/submenu names are completely illustrative of the types of filters and effects you find within them. For that reason, it's a good idea to poke around in all the categories and experiment a bit—you may be surprised what you find in a category that by name didn't seem too inviting. Reading this chapter in its entirety will help, too!

Viewing Filters and Effects as a List

To simplify the view of the Filters and Effects through the palettes, you can display them as a list rather than as a group of thumbnails. Of course this makes it hard to make a choice of filter or effect based solely on the names, but after you're familiar with some of the filters and effects and know which ones you like or that do particular jobs, you can choose them by name with no problem.

Displaying Effects and Filters as a list is simple—just click the List View button at the foot of either palette (see Figure 13-5). To go back to thumbnail view, click the Thumbnail View button to the right of the List View button.

Figure 13-4: Want just the Artistic or just the Texture filters? Choose the category you want from the drop-down list.

Of course you can also access the filters through the Filters menu—a list of sub-menus and filter commands that work like any other menu and submenus. No thumbnails are there, but virtually each filter requires the use of a dialog box, through which you can preview the effects of the filter and see if it's the one you want. You can also customize the way the filter works by tweaking various settings in these dialog boxes.

Tip   The filter dialog boxes are also going to open if you choose a filter from the palette. Unless the Filter Options check box is unchecked (it's checked by default), you'll get a dialog box for virtually every one of the filters in the Filters Palette. If the Filter Options check box is unchecked and you leave it that way, the filters you choose will be applied with no questions asked, using default settings.

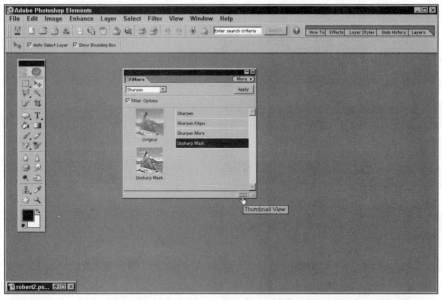

Figure 13-5: Pare down the palettes' content by viewing their content as a list.

Working with Filters and Effects

Applying filters and effects is easy—requiring only that you know which filter or effect you want to apply (or with which one you want to experiment) and making a selection within your image if you want to control where the filter or effect is applied. Follow these steps for seamless Filters and Effects application:

STEPS: Applying Filters and Effects

1. Open the image to which you want to apply the filter or effect.

2. Activate the layer that has the content you want to change through the use of a particular filter or effect.

3. As needed, make a selection within the layer to restrict the filter or effect's results to just one portion of the image, as shown in Figure 13-6.

4. Click on the filter or effect thumbnail that you want to apply (if you're in List View, click once on the filter or effect by name) and either drag the thumbnail onto the image window or click the Apply button in the palette. Figure 13-7 shows a thumbnail in transit.

Figure 13-6: Make a selection so that the
filter or effect doesn't affect your entire image.

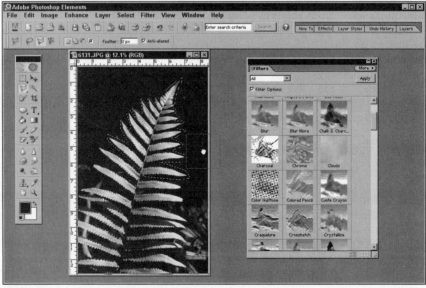

Figure 13-7: Drag a thumbnail onto the image you want to change via a filter or effect.

Applying Filters that Mimic Artistic Media

The Artistic filters, which should really also include the Brush Stroke and Sketch filters, turn images — photos, original line and shape creations — into what looks like artwork created with brushes, pencils, pens, and other artistic mediums. You can use them to add interest to an otherwise dull image, to create contrast within a single image (applying the artistic filter to just part of the image), or to hide scratches, scuff marks, and so forth that would be too time-consuming to eradicate with retouching tools.

Using Artistic Filters

The Artistic category filters include everything from pencils to painting, including some artistic "tools" you may not have thought of, such as Plastic Wrap and Neon Glow. If you ever studied art or taken an art class, most of the filter names will be clear and you'll have a good idea what effect the given filters will have. Here's a list of the filters you find in the Artistic category, many of them accompanied by a view of the filter's dialog box and a single image previewed — this should help you get an idea of what each filter does. (Those not pictured here are shown elsewhere in this section of the book):

✦ Colored Pencil (see Figure 13-8)

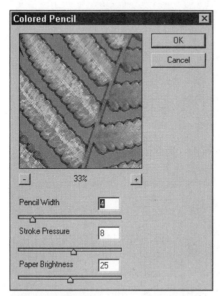

Figure 13-8: Like to draw but don't have the time or the tools? Use the Colored Pencil Filter.

✦ Cutout

✦ Dry Brush (see Figure 13-9)

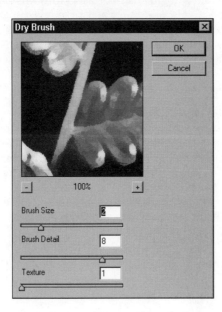

Figure 13-9: Get a soft, smooth painted look with the Dry Brush filter.

✦ Film Grain (see Figure 13-10)

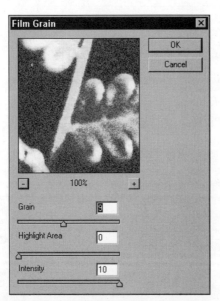

Figure 13-10: Great for black and white photos, this filter makes the image look like it was shot on old, grainy film.

✦ Fresco (see Figure 13-11)

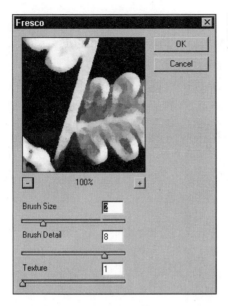

Figure 13-11: With the Fresco filter, your image looks like it was painted with bold, yet soft strokes on a plaster wall.

✦ Neon Glow (see Figure 13-12)

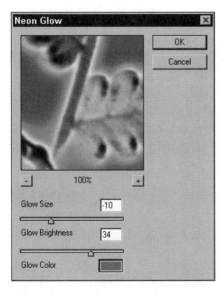

Figure 13-12: Depending on your settings, this filter can make your content unrecognizable, or it can make it look as though it's basking in the glow of a neon light, in a color you choose.

✦ Paint Daubs

✦ Palette Knife (see Figure 13-13)

✦ Plastic Wrap (see Figure 13-14)

✦ Poster Edges (see Figure 13-15)

✦ Rough Pastels (see Figure 13-16)

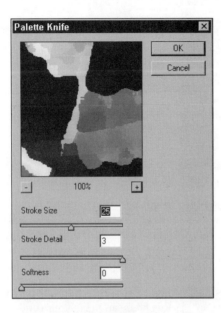

Figure 13-13: Achieve the bold, impressionistic effects of painting with a Palette Knife.

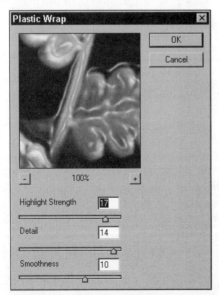

Figure 13-14: Not a typical artist's medium, this filter makes the content look as though it's shrink-wrapped.

Figure 13-15: Thick outlines and every little mark turned into a brush stroke or dab of color, this is a very heavy-handed filter that can give you dramatic results.

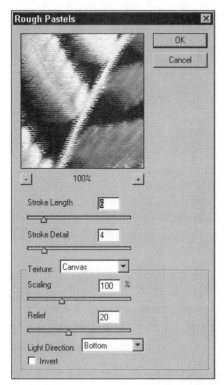

Figure 13-16: Your image is now painted on a textured paper and drawn with thick, pastel crayons, the thickness and roughness of which you can control.

✦ Smudge Stick (see Figure 13-17)

✦ Sponge (see Figure 13-18)

✦ Underpainting (see Figure 13-19)

✦ Watercolor

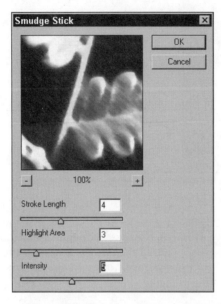

Figure 13-17: Softer than Rough Pastels, the Smudge Stick creates the look of soft, smudged pastel crayons or chalk.

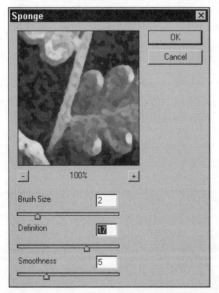

Figure 13-18: If you're a fan of sponge painting on walls for a "faux finish," you might like the Sponge filter's blobby effects.

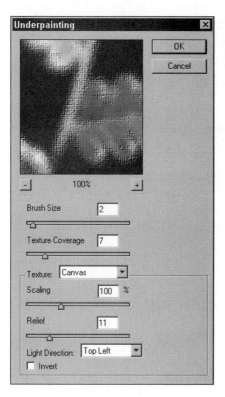

Figure 13-19: Used by classic artists to apply light beneath coats of paint, the Underpainting filter applies textured layers of paint from any of a number of Light Directions.

All of the Artistic filters require a dialog box (note the ellipsis after each command in the Filter⇨Artistic submenu) and the dialog boxes enable you to control how the filter is applied. You can choose the width, length, or strength of the brush or pencil strokes, the level of detail, and in some cases, establish the brightness or amount of shadow applied by the medium in question. Figure 13-20 shows the Paint Daubs dialog box, where you can set the size and sharpness of the brush, along with the type of brush used to apply the daubs of paint.

As you tweak the settings in the Artistic filter dialog boxes, you find that some of the settings can actually make your images (or the selected content within them) unrecognizable, as shown in Figure 13-21. Sometimes, the painting or drawing effects can obliterate details, which can be a good thing if you wanted a more abstract view of photographic content. It can be also be a bad thing if you still wanted to be able to recognize the content specifically. Most of the filters' settings enable you to leave some detail in place, by making specific adjustments to the filters' settings. Figure 13-22 shows the Watercolor filter dialog box — by making changes to the Brush Detail, Shadow Intensity, and Texture sliders, you can keep a good deal of detail in the image while still achieving the look of a watercolor painting.

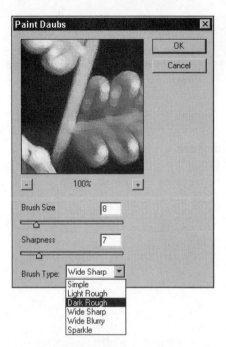

Figure 13-20: Even someone who's all thumbs with pencils and brushes can create a work of art with the Artistic filters.

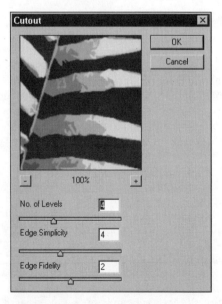

Figure 13-21: Identifying elements are lost through the use of the Cutout filter — the look of an image made of cut pieces of paper doesn't allow for much detail.

Using Brush Stroke Filters

Most of the Brush Stroke filters should have been included in the Artistic submenu, because many of them are just variations on the same kinds of media used in the

Artistic category. The Sketch category, however, does live up to its name, as it's more concerned with dry, drawing-based medium, such as charcoal or crayon. There are a few filters in this category that seem to defy their appearance in such a group—Photocopy and Torn Edges to name a few. The Sumi-E filter is a rather obscure one with effects that are rather similar to other filters, such as Dry Brush or Smudge Stick, as shown in Figure 13-23.

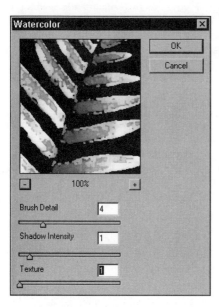

Figure 13-22: Keep the detail by tinkering with the sliders and reducing any extreme effects.

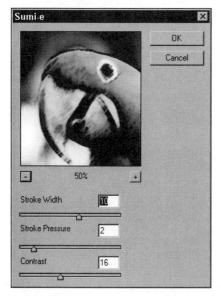

Figure 13-23: You may find some of the filter names confusing and not be able to detect a big difference between one and several others.

Here's a list of the Brush Strokes filters, most of which are accompanied by figures of their dialog boxes (with an image preview) to help you understand how they affect your images:

✦ Accented Edges (see Figure 13-24)

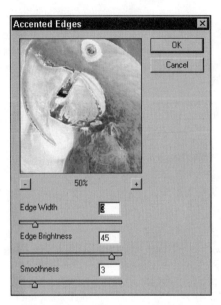

Figure 13-24: Looking a lot like a pastel drawing but with bright edges, this filter enables you to control the edge size and brightness as well as overall smoothness.

Tip   To Elements, an "edge" is anywhere that two areas of different color or light quality meet. The more different the areas, the more definite the edge will be when filters that focus on the edges — Accented Edges and Unsharp Mask, for example — are applied.

✦ Angled Strokes (see Figure 13-25)

✦ Crosshatch (see Figure 13-26)

✦ Dark Strokes (see Figure 13-27)

✦ Ink Outlines (see Figure 13-28)

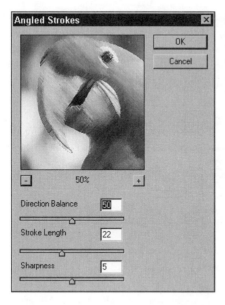

Figure 13-25: As though sketched with colored pencils, this filter applies strokes that all go in one direction. You can control the direction, length, and sharpness of the strokes.

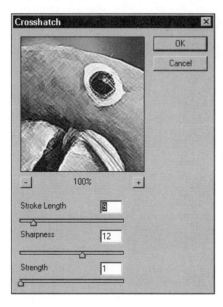

Figure 13-26: Going "Angled Strokes" one better, Crosshatch has strokes going in both directions. This allows for more detail to be maintained in the image.

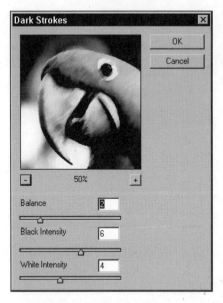

Figure 13-27: This filter focuses on the lights and darks in your image and turns dark colors into large, dark areas. You can adjust the intensity of black and white for a more balanced effect.

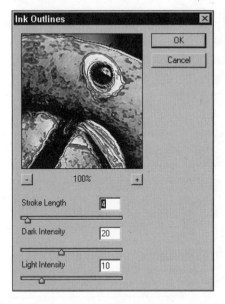

Figure 13-28: Again, edges are found and highlighted, this time with distinct outlines. Inner content is filled with a mottled, blotted ink effect.

✦ Spatter (see Figure 13-29)

✦ Sprayed Strokes (see Figure 13-30)

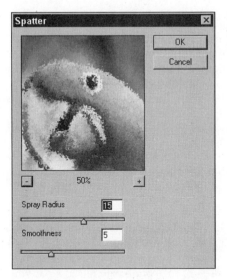

Figure 13-29: Control the intensity of this filter's spattered, spongy look with Spray Radius and Smoothness sliders.

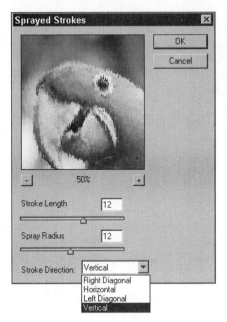

Figure 13-30: This filter looks a lot like Angled Strokes, but the strokes are applied with a spraying device rather than pencils or pastels. You can also control the direction of the strokes, as well as their length and radius.

✦ Sumi-e

Note

The term *radius* refers to the scope or area covered by a particular filter's effects. Many times, the number of pixels affected or compared (to determine where and when to apply a filter within an image/selection) is what the Radius setting controls.

Working with Sketch Filters

Again, here's a category that easily can be merged with the Artistic set of filters —
most of them are artistic media, such as Chalk and Charcoal, or Graphic Pen — and
a few show artistic ways to use unlikely tools to get interesting effects. Photocopy
and Torn Edges are examples. Most of the filters in this group give your image the
look of a drawing or sketch — which is why the set of filters was given this name,
presumably.

All of the filters in this group offer dialog boxes to help you tweak their results. The
following is a list of the filters, along with Figures of each filters' dialog box to help
you see how the filters work and what effects they have on a given image:

✦ Bas Relief (see Figure 13-31)

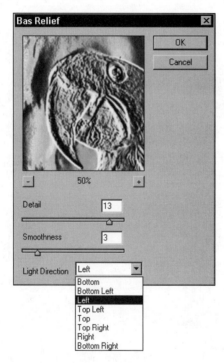

Figure 13-31: Art students recognize this
term — an image is represented by a
sculpture with raised areas where lighter
colors appear, depressions where darks
appear. Control the light source and levels
of detail and smoothness with the dialog
box sliders.

✦ Chalk & Charcoal (see Figure 13-32)

✦ Charcoal (see Figure 13-33)

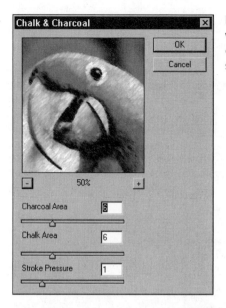

Figure 13-32: Combining colored chalk with black and white charcoal, this filter creates the look of a duotone with sketched appearance.

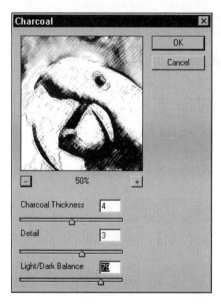

Figure 13-33: Not a big mystery here — the image looks like a single-colored charcoal pencil was used to sketch the image. You can control the detail, thickness of the charcoal, and the balance of light and dark.

✦ Chrome (see Figure 13-34)

✦ Conte Crayon (see Figure 13-35)

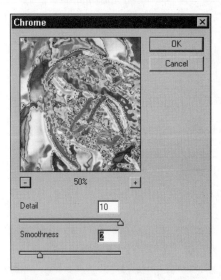

Figure 13-34: Sculpt your image in chrome, creating a metallic treatment for your image. You can control the detail and smoothness of the chrome to make sure essential identifying image details aren't lost.

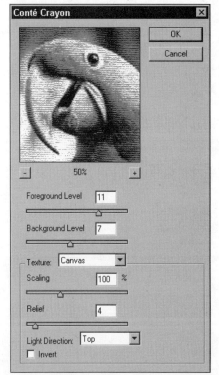

Figure 13-35: This sketched effect also enables you to control the texture of the "paper" on which the crayon is applied.

✦ Graphic Pen (see Figure 13-36)

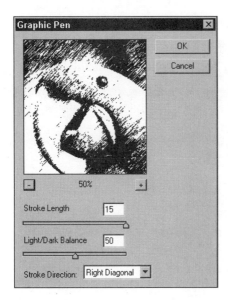

Figure 13-36: Sketching with a monotone pen gives you the same look as this filter creates. You can control the stroke length and direction, as well as the balance of light and dark.

✦ Halftone Pattern (see Figure 13-37)

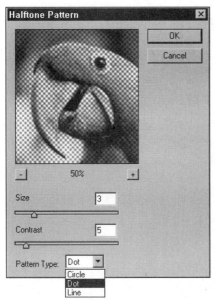

Figure 13-37: Like a halftone screen, this filter gives your image a patterned look, as though it was printed in the newspaper or painted in monotone by Lichtenstein.

✦ Note Paper (see Figure 13-38)

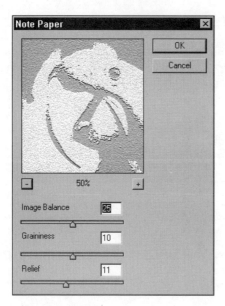

Figure 13-38: This filter looks like large areas of color are printed on thick, textured paper. The name "Note Paper" isn't terribly intuitive.

✦ Photocopy (see Figure 13-39)

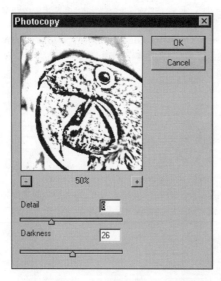

Figure 13-39: Need to make your image look like a photocopy? Here's your obvious choice. You can adjust detail and darkness to determine how many copies of copies were made to create the look of your image.

✦ Plaster (see Figure 13-40)

✦ Reticulation (see Figure 13-41)

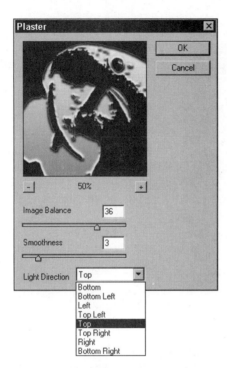

Figure 13-40: Rather than painting on plaster (a la the Fresco filter in the Artistic category), this creates the look of an image rendered in plaster, poured to sculpt lights and darks in a "solid" medium.

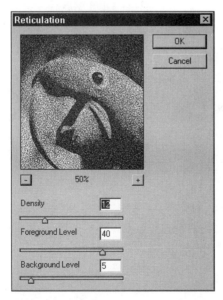

Figure 13-41: Lots and lots of dots are combined to recreate your image with this filter. You can control the density of the dots in both the foreground and background of the image.

✦ Stamp (see Figure 13-42)

✦ Torn Edges (see Figure 13-43)

✦ Water Paper (see Figure 13-44)

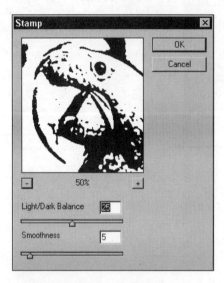

Figure 13-42: This filter makes your image look as though it was created with a rubber stamp. Not much detail is preserved here, but basic shapes are still recognizable.

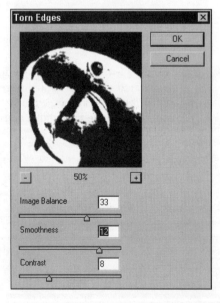

Figure 13-43: Make your image look as though it was created by pasting together lots of torn paper, torn in the shape of objects in your image. Control the smoothness and contrast between areas within the image.

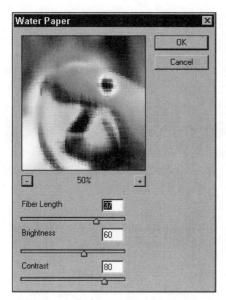

Figure 13-44: Imagine drawing or painting on textured paper to which water was applied, making the medium seep into the paper's nooks and crannies. That's the look this filter gives you, along with controls that determine the paper's texture (Fiber length), brightness, and contrast.

Tip You can achieve interesting effects by applying some of these filters to only part of your image — for example, applying Torn Edges to a particular person or object within the image gives the selected content the appearance of having been torn out of another photo and pasted into the current one.

Blurring and Sharpening effects

Performing both restorative/retouching roles and providing interesting special effects, the Blur and Sharpen filters remove and add detail by making pixels more similar (in the case of blurring) or more distinct (in the case of sharpening). These two categories really go hand in hand, because they're often used together — an image requiring blurring in one area and sharpening in another, or sharpening after blurring on the same selection, to create a specific look. Of course you also have the Blur and Sharpen tools on the toolbox, but those require "painting" the blur and sharpen effects with your mouse. The filters apply uniformly to an entire layer or selection within a layer, creating a much smoother and reliable result.

First, the Blur filters — these perform both restorative functions, hiding spots and scratches with an overall softening of detail, and they also can create special effects through the appearance of motion (the radial and motion blurs). The filters are listed here, with figures showing the controls or effects available (not all the filters have dialog boxes enabling you to control the filter's results):

✦ Blur (see Figure 13-45)

✦ Blur More (see Figure 13-46)

Figure 13-45: The right side of this image looks softer with the pixels made more similar to one another in terms of light and color levels.

Figure 13-46: If Blur doesn't give you enough softening, try Blur More.

Tip

When you apply a filter, the Filter menu's first command changes to the last filter you applied. Use the Ctrl + F shortcut to reapply the last filter, increasing the intensity of whatever effect was achieved by applying it the last time.

✦ Gaussian Blur (see Figure 13-47)

✦ Motion Blur (see Figure 13-48)

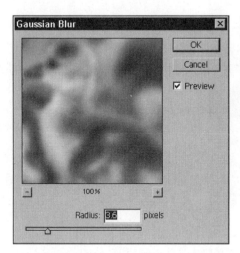

Figure 13-47: The Gaussian Blur filter creates an extreme, overall blur. Drag the Radius slider to determine how many adjacent pixels are compared and made more similar, achieving the blurred effect.

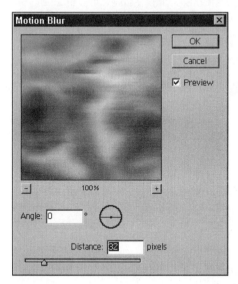

Figure 13-48: Going places? It looks like you are if you apply the Motion Blur to some or your entire image. Control the angle of the motion and determine the intensity by increasing the Distance setting.

✦ Radial Blur (see Figure 13-49)

Tip

The Radial Blur filter doesn't show a preview within the dialog box. To see the results, click OK and then click Undo if you don't like the results and want to start over.

✦ Smart Blur (see Figure 13-50)

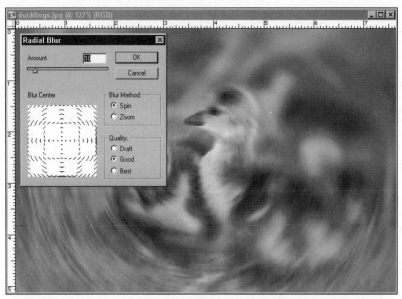

Figure 13-49: If you ever had the feeling that the room was spinning, you'll relive that experience with the Radial Blur filter. Make some or all of your image spin, choosing between Spin and Zoom blurring, and choosing the intensity of the spin/zoom with the Amount slider, and a Quality setting to control the level of detail included in the spun pixels.

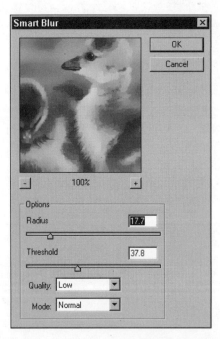

Figure 13-50: The Smart Blur is just that — an intelligent, controlled way to blur an image. You can drag the Radius slider to determine how many adjacent pixels are compared, the Threshold slider to determine the level of blurring, and set a Quality and Mode selection, too.

The Sharpen filters are used, just like the Sharpen tool, to make details stand out. All but one of the Sharpen filters work without a dialog box—therefore, only the Unsharp Mask filter in this category enables you to control the filter's results. In the following list, each filter is accompanied by an image that's had a Sharpen filter applied to half the image, creating a "before and after" effect for you to see how the filter works. For the Unsharp Mask filter, a view of the dialog box is provided.

✦ Sharpen (see Figure 13-51)

Figure 13-51: Increase the diversity between adjacent pixels with the Sharpen filter, here applied to the right side of the image.

✦ Sharpen Edges (see Figure 13-52)

✦ Sharpen More (see Figure 13-53)

Tip

Sharpen More, especially on top of one or more uses of the Sharpen filter, can give you unpleasant results—diversity becoming splotches and oddly-colored areas instead of the heightened detail for which you were hoping.

✦ Unsharp Mask (see Figure 13-54)

Figure 13-52: Draw attention to just the edges within an image by sharpening only the pixels along areas that are different in terms of color and light levels.

Figure 13-53: Did the Sharpen filter not give you enough sharpness, even on repeated uses? Try Sharpen More.

Figure 13-54: The one Sharpen filter with a dialog box, the Unsharp Mask gives you three sliders to control the amount of sharpening applied, the number of adjacent pixels compared at one time, and the intensity of the results.

Working with Filters that Distort Image Content

Unlike filters that restore image quality and make the image cleaner, softer, or more detailed, the Distort filters essentially destroy the original image, bending, pulling, squeezing, and otherwise manipulating it. All of the Distort filters have dialog boxes that let you control the degree of distortion, and the Liquify filter has its own window, complete with view options, a toolbar, and options for how the filter is applied. You also use your mouse to apply the different Liquify tools manually—stretching this, tucking in that, spinning here, twirling there.

Following is a list of the Distort filters, each accompanied by a view of the dialog box, showing the controls available and their impact on the image in question.

✦ Diffuse Glow (see Figure 13-55)

✦ Displace (see Figure 13-56)

✦ Glass (see Figure 13-57)

Figure 13-55: A gentle glow of soft, almost ethereal light bathes your subject with the Diffuse Glow filter. Adjust the level of grain, glow, and the number of pixels to be left unaffected, preserving detail.

Figure 13-56: As shown on the right side of the image, the Displace filter moves your content horizontally and/or vertically, by a percentage you choose.

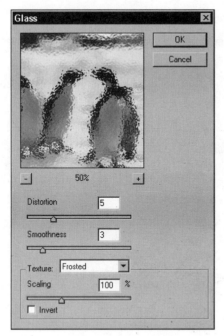

Figure 13-57: View your image through rippled glass and adjust the level of distortion, smoothness, and texture for a completely customized look.

✦ Liquify (see Figure 13-58)

Tip If you make a selection before opening the Liquify dialog box, you'll only be able to affect that portion of the image, despite being able to see all of the image through the window.

✦ Ocean Ripple (see Figure 13-59)

✦ Pinch (see Figure 13-60)

Pick a tool and then click and/or drag on parts of the image.

Use the Zoom and Pan tools to move around on the image.

Use the Revert button to start over.

Control the Zoom percentage here.

Adjust the size of your mouse pointer (brush).

Figure 13-58: The Liquify window gives you tools (down the left side) and settings (on the right) to stretch, pinch, expand, and collapse parts of your image, distorting their appearance with both subtle and dramatic results.

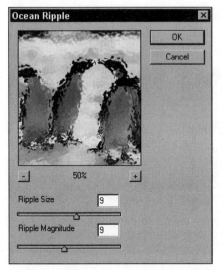

Figure 13-59: A lot like the Glass filter, but more organic looking, view your image as though through gently rippling, clear seawater. Adjust the ripples to control the level of distortion achieved.

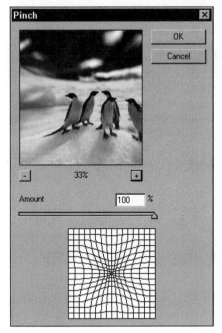

Figure 13-60: Squeeze your image (or portions thereof) into new shapes with the Pinch filter. You can adjust the Amount of pinch and view the effects both in the Preview window and on the grid.

✦ Polar Coordinates (see Figure 13-61)

✦ Ripple (see Figure 13-62)

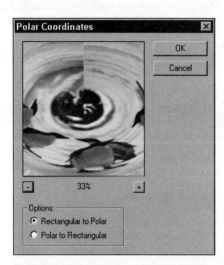

Figure 13-61: Twist your image inside out or outside in (using the Options) with the Polar Coordinates filter.

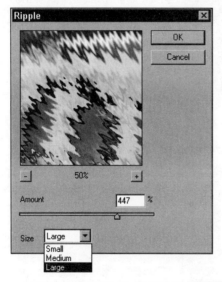

Figure 13-62: Perhaps redundant with the Glass and Ocean Ripple filters, the Ripple filter gives your image a gentle rippled effect. Adjust the amount of ripple and the size of the ripples for subtlety or dynamic effects.

✦ Shear (see Figure 13-63)

Drag the dot up or down on the line
to determine where the curve occurs.

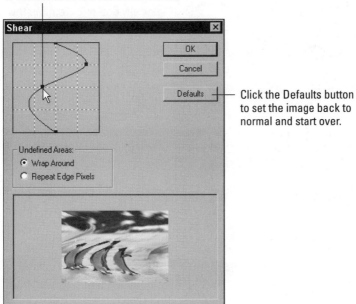

Click the Defaults button
to set the image back to
normal and start over.

Figure 13-63: Drag the line on the grid to stretch your image and
bend it in one direction or another.

Tip

Turn on the Repeat Edge pixels option to avoid repeating the main image outside
the sheared portion.

✦ Spherize (see Figure 13-64)

✦ Twirl (see Figure 13-65)

Figure 13-64: View your image through a round lens, making some or the entire image look like it's printed on a glass sphere. Drag the Amount slider to control how round you want the sphere to be and pick a Mode to determine the direction of the distortion.

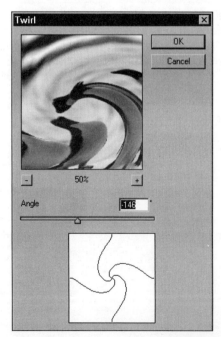

Figure 13-65: The Twirl filter lets you twist your image. Drag the Angle slider and view the four-section grid to choose the degree of twirling applied — from slight to severe.

✦ Wave (see Figure 13-66)

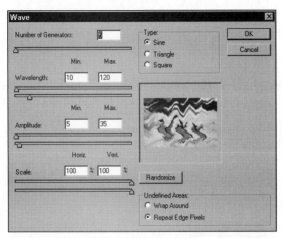

Figure 13-66: Like viewing your image through waves of heat pouring off a desert highway, the Wave filter offers seven sliders and two sets of options for determining the degree and shape of wave applied.

✦ ZigZag (see Figure 13-67)

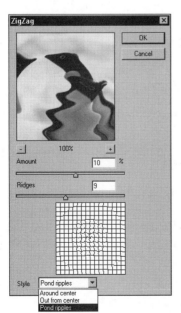

Figure 13-67: Again, you have an Amount slider and a grid to determine where the zig-zags appear. Drag the Ridges slider to determine the number of concentric circles used to create the zig-zag effect.

Note   Several of the Distort filters do the same function you can do in the Liquify window: Wave, Twirl, and Pinch, to name just a few. If you prefer an automated, uniform effect, use the individual filters. If you like the idea of manual control over where and how the distortion occurs, you'll prefer the Liquify filter and its tools.

Applying Noise Filters

The category name "Noise" implies that sounds are being added to your images, but the name actually refers to the sort of marks that appear on a photo, the sort of overall visual distractions known as *noise*. Scuff marks, tiny bits of dust ground into a photo's surface, overall graininess (from any number of causes), all this sort of damage comes under the definition of noise and is solved by the use of the Noise filters. Figure 13-68 shows a photo in need of some Noise attention.

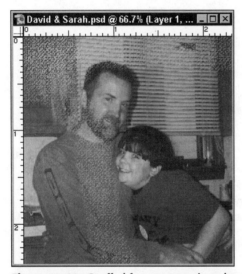

Figure 13-68: Scuffed from storage in a drawer, this photo has noise all over it, distracting us from its details, making the photo look older than it really is.

The filters range from those that eliminate some or all of the noise to those that make more noise, hopefully making the noise seem intentional and therefore artistically appealing. The following list includes the three Noise filters that offer dialog boxes and an example of a photo to which the Despeckle filter is applied. This filter has no dialog box, but the effects are obvious, applied by using defaults that the user needn't change:

✦ Add Noise (see Figure 13-69)

✦ Despeckle (see Figure 13-70)

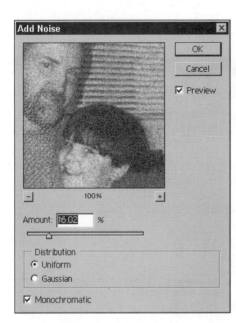

Figure 13-69: If you have some noise, sometimes adding more is better than trying to get rid of it. The Add Noise filter's dialog box enables you to add Uniform or Gaussian noise and to determine the amount of noise to add.

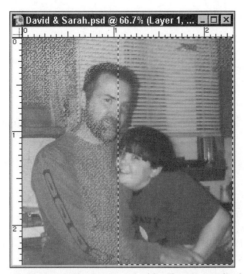

Figure 13-70: The Despeckle filter is applied to half of this image, and you can see that disparate pixels (the noise) are reduced in terms of their visibility by making them more closely match their neighbors.

Tip

Despeckling your photo can result in a loss of crispness, much like you'd see with a Blur filter. Use it with caution and try to apply it only to the most damaged areas rather than to the entire image all at once.

✦ Dust & Scratches (see Figure 13-71)

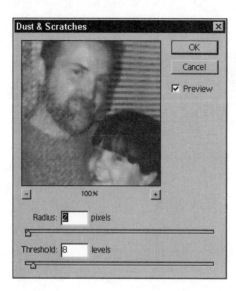

Figure 13-71: This filter makes all the pixels in the image more uniform, based on your use of the Radius and Threshold sliders, which control the number of simultaneously compared pixels and the tolerance for pixel similarity, respectively.

✦ Median (see Figure 13-72)

Figure 13-72: The Median filter really belongs in the Blur filter group because it creates a blurred effect, ranging from subtle (the Radius set to a single-digit number) to one that completely obliterates detail (a Radius set to anything over 50).

Applying the Pixelate Filters

The Pixelate group of filters gets its name from the sort of results that you see in your images — the pixels are either exaggerated or recolored in some dramatic way. Figure 13-73 shows the effects of the Fragment filter, one that operates through a set of defaults that you cannot change — there is no dialog box for the filter in question.

Figure 13-73: You automatically see double vision in an image after you apply the Fragment filter. The image is duplicated and offset to produce these results.

The remaining Pixelate filters appear in the following list, all applied to a single image so that you can more easily compare their effects. When no dialog box is available (Facet, for example), an image is shown, with half the image altered by the filter in question:

✦ Color Halftone (see Figure 13-74)

Tip

Setting the Maximum Radius field to four (the lowest setting you can enter) preserves a good deal of the image content, at least in terms of your being able to recognize shapes and objects. The Channel settings in the dialog box pertain to the color channels, CMYK (Cyan, Magenta, Yellow, and Black).

✦ Crystallize (see Figure 13-75)

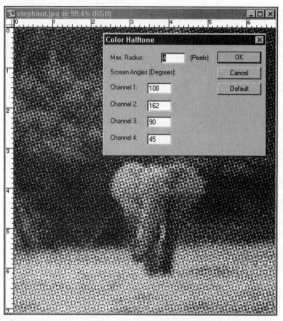

Figure 13-74: Wildly colored dots appear here, created by dividing the image into rectangles and replacing those rectangles with circles, based on the rectangle's brightness. Depending on your settings in the dialog box, the image either retains some detail and/or recognizability, or it looks like a color comic gone mad.

Figure 13-75: The Crystallize filter breaks the image into shards of color. You can adjust the size of the cells, increasing or decreasing the amount of detail preserved. The smaller the cells, the more fine detail you retain.

✦ Facet (see Figure 13-76)

Figure 13-76: Another filter that belongs in the Artistic category, the Facet filter makes the image look like an impressionist painting, with the image detail turned into blocks of solid color. There is no dialog box to control the size of the blocks.

✦ Fragment

✦ Mezzotint (see Figure 13-77)

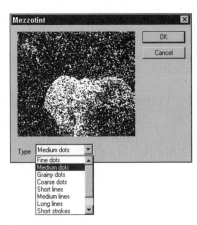

Figure 13-77: Use the Mezzotint filter when you want to create the look of a sort of psychedelic pointillist painting — using Fine Dots (the Type field's default) or any of seven other dots and strokes.

✦ Mosaic (see Figure 13-78)

✦ Pointillize (see Figure 13-79)

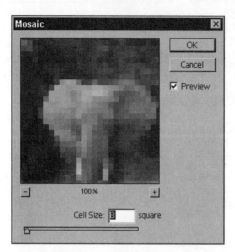

Figure 13-78: This filter turns your image into a series of color blocks, the size of which you control by dragging the Cell Size slider or entering a number into the field.

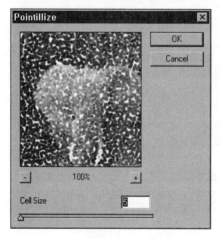

Figure 13-79: Now here's the real pointillist filter — Pointillize. This filter uses the current Background color to fill in the areas between the dots created from the image colors. The dialog box enables you to determine the dot size, which determines the size of the space between the dots as well — a large Cell Size gives you an interesting, but completely unrecognizable image.

Using the Render Filters

The majority of the Render filters create 3D effects — the illusion of three dimensions in some or your entire image. In addition, you find filters that create clouds, special lens and lighting effects, to produce any sort of camera flash and light that wasn't present at the time that your photo was taken or your image created.

In the following, you find a complete list of the Render filters along with images of their results on a single image. All but the two Clouds filters have dialog boxes, which let you control the filters' effects, and for those two, the final results of the filters, as applied with their defaults, are demonstrated:

✦ 3D Transform (see Figure 13-80)

Tip

Click the Options button to access options for controlling the resolution of the effects and the level of anti-aliasing applied. The defaults are Medium for resolution and Low for anti-aliasing — after you adjust the two fields to meet your needs, click OK to return to the main 3D Transform dialog box and complete your settings for the filter.

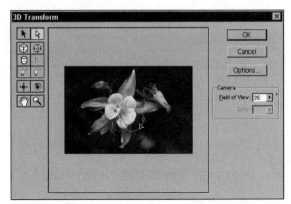

Figure 13-80: The 3D Transform dialog box offers a set of tools on the left and access to further options on the right. You can turn any image into one or more shapes based on three basic 3D shapes — a box, a sphere, and/or a cylinder.

✦ Clouds (see Figure 13-81)

Figure 13-81: No dialog box enables you to control this filter — it simply fills the active layer with a sky-full of clouds. Place this on its own layer (rather than obliterating existing content) and create a nice background for an outdoor image.

✦ Difference Clouds (see Figure 13-82)

✦ Lens Flare (see Figure 13-83)

Figure 13-82: This filter works by randomly applying color values in a cloud-like pattern. The color values are based on the current Foreground and Background colors. Try applying the filter several times for an interesting marble-like effect.

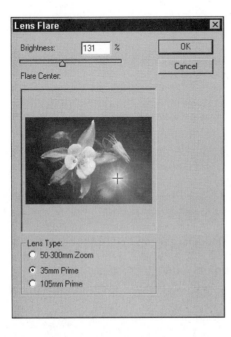

Figure 13-83: Wish there'd been a bright light aimed right at your camera lens when you took the photo? You can go back and create such an effect with this filter, choosing the position, brightness, and type of camera lens you'd like to simulate.

Tip

To reposition the flare, point to the crosshair in the preview of the image and drag the crosshair with your mouse. Then adjust the Brightness slider and experiment with different lens types to get just the look you're shooting for.

◆ Lighting Effects (see Figure 13-84)

Drag the dots to enlarge the pool of light.

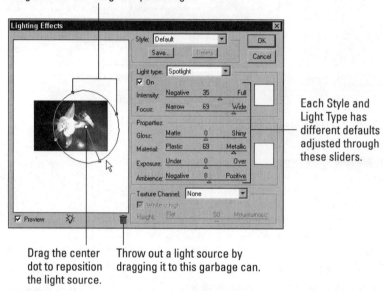

Each Style and Light Type has different defaults adjusted through these sliders.

Drag the center dot to reposition the light source.

Throw out a light source by dragging it to this garbage can.

Figure 13-84: This rather busy dialog box offers several options for creating anything from the look of a spotlight to the appearance of stage lighting with multiple light sources shining on the subject. Pick a Style and Light Type and then tweak the effects with any or all of the sliders.

Tip

See that little light bulb under the preview of your image? Drag that onto the image to create multiple light sources.

Tip

Don't have a photo or other image that's right for the texture you're looking for? Create one. Make sure the color mode is Grayscale and save the file in the native Photoshop format (PSD) so that it can be applied as a texture. Depending on the depth and diversity of color in the image, you can achieve subtle or dramatic textures.

Note

Why isn't this filter in the Texture filters category? Because the texture created by the image you select creates a 3D effect within the image, thus being more of a rendering effect than that of a simple texture being applied.

◆ Texture Fill (see Figure 13-85)

A PSD file has been applied as a texture in the main image window.

Select the image to be applied as a texture from this dialog box.

Figure 13-85: Choose any grayscale photo saved in the Photoshop format (PSD) and make it a texture for your image.

Using the Stylize Filters

The Stylize filters are hard to pin down in terms of finding one clear explanation for their use. The problem starts with the rather enigmatic name for the category and continues through the odd mix of filters, some of which appear to belong in other groups. Never mind, though, because you'll find all of the filters useful, in one way or another. They may not be filters you'll use often — such as the sharpen, blur, and artistic/sketch/brush strokes filters — but they have their uses.

Following is a list of the filters, along with examples of their use and/or dialog boxes that show how you can control the filters' effects.

✦ Diffuse (see Figure 13-86)

Note

You may not recognize the term *anisotropic*, or it may not be a term with which you're completely familiar. According to Merriam-Webster's dictionary, the definition is:

"exhibiting properties with different values when measured in different directions."

For our purposes in Photoshop Elements and within the context of the Diffuse filter, this means that the pixels are being rearranged uniformly, in all directions, creating an overall diffused look.

Figure 13-86: Lose the focus in your image by rearranging pixels based on which Mode you choose — Normal softens randomly, Darken Only and Lighten Only replace light pixels with dark and dark with light (respectively), and Anisotropic affects all pixels uniformly.

✦ Emboss (see Figure 13-87)

 Tip

You can also adjust the Angle by dragging the line within the circle to the right of the Angle field. Drag it clockwise or counter-clockwise and see the preview's angle change as you do so.

✦ Extrude (see Figure 13-88)

✦ Find Edges (see Figure 13-89)

 Tip

While the Find Edges filter has interesting prospects from a purely artisitic standpoint, you can also use it temporarily to help you select the borders within the image. Use the Selection Brush, for example, to follow the edges emphasized with the filter, save the selection and then undo the filter.

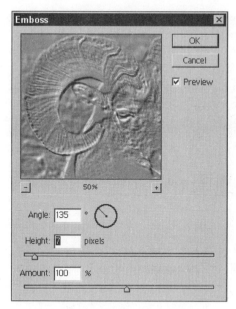

Figure 13-87: The Emboss filter creates a raised, stamped look in the image, changing all but the pixels along content edges to grayscale. Edges retain the color of the nearby pixels' original fill color. Adjust the height and amount of embossing by dragging the sliders and change the angle of the 3D look by entering a new number in the Angle field.

Figure 13-88: Choose Blocks or Pyramids for the extrusion effect and then enter new Size and Depth settings until you like what you see in the image. Here we see the dialog box and the Extrude filter already applied within the image window.

Figure 13-89: No dialog box required here — this filter finds the edges within the image and emphasizes them by making all the other pixels white. The color applied to the edges is drawn from the original color of adjacent pixels.

✦ Glowing Edges (see Figure 13-90)

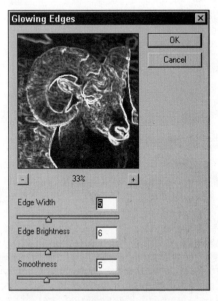

Figure 13-90: And you thought Find Edges drew attention to the borders within your image! Glowing Edges applies a neon glow to the edges within your image and turns the rest of the image black. Use the sliders to adjust the size and brightness of the glow.

✦ Solarize (see Figure 13-91)

✦ Tiles (see Figure 13-92)

Figure 13-91: This filter gives you the effect of exposing film to a tiny bit of light — giving you not quite a negative and not quite a positive image. There is no dialog box, so your results depend entirely on the internal defaults and the colors and light levels in your image.

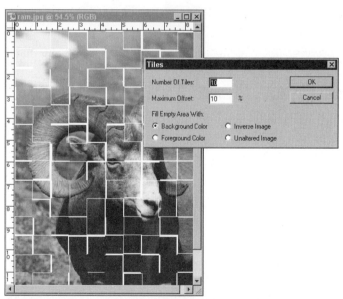

Figure 13-92: Another filter that relies on a dialog box but doesn't give you a preview, the Tiles filter lets you choose how many tiles your image is broken into, how much of an offset appears between tiles, and lets you choose what to do with the empty areas. In this image, Tiles is applied to the image, and the dialog box is also displayed.

Tip

Want to turn a photo into a puzzle? Apply the Tiles filter with a very small offset, print it on cardstock and then use a paper cutter to cut along the slim offset between tiles. You can give the photo as a gift or send it in lieu of a birthday or other greeting, a message having been either written on the back or incorporated into the image with Elements' Type tools.

✦ Trace Contour (see Figure 13-93)

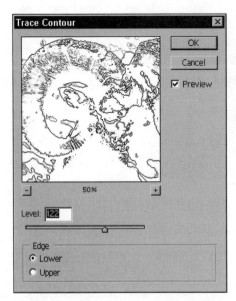

Figure 13-93: This filter may remind you of Find Edges, and with good reason — it does virtually the same function, but the edges and lines within your image are traced with a very fine line rather than a thick border. Adjust the Level slider to determine how many edges are found — just the major ones or every little edge within the image.

✦ Wind (see Figure 13-94)

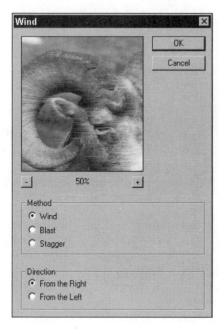

Figure 13-94: Choose between Wind, Blast, and Stagger as the Wind filter Method, and then pick the direction from which the wind is blowing. The filter is similar to the Motion Blur in terms of its results, except for the fact that the wind seems only to be blowing the edges of the image — like wind blowing sand and affecting only the high points first.

Working with Texture Filters

The filters in this category tell you about themselves through the use of the names of objects — Mosaic Tiles, Patchwork, Stained Glass — and one called Texturizer that enables you to create a customized texture and apply it to your image. The complete list of Texture filters, along with examples of their results and the dialog boxes that let you tweak them appears here:

✦ Craquelure (see Figure 13-95)

✦ Grain (see Figure 13-96)

Figure 13-95: The Craquelure filter can mimic the subtle crackling you'd see on an old piece of glazed ceramic, or it can look like deeply cracked leather or parched earth. Drag the Crack Spacing, Depth, and Brightness sliders to adjust the degree of crackling achieved.

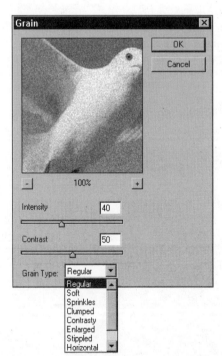

Figure 13-96: Pick from 10 different Grain Types and then adjust the Intensity and Contrast. The Grain filter gives you a textured look, applying colors to various pixels in the image, mimicking the grain Type you selected.

✦ Mosaic Tiles (see Figure 13-97)

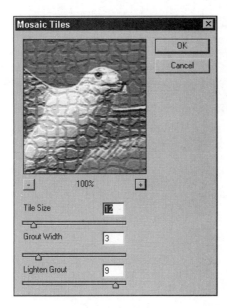

Figure 13-97: The name says it all — like a mosaic, created from many pieces of seemingly random pieces of tile, your image is displayed as a group of odd-shaped tiles. You can adjust the size of the tiles, the distance between them (Grout Width), and the color of the grout.

Tip

For a realistic mosaic look, go for a light colored grout — the lightest you can go is a setting of 10, which isn't as light as white grout, but it's better than having the grout follow the same colors as the adjoining tiles.

✦ Patchwork (see Figure 13-98)

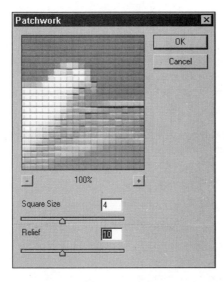

Figure 13-98: The name implies that the filter gives you the look of a Patchwork quit, but it's something of a misnomer. Unlike a fabric quilt, the color of portions of the image make the tiny blocks of color look raised (lighter areas look raised) and others look indented. It does look like the image is comprised of tiny textile blocks, however, the size and depth of which you can determine.

✦ Stained Glass (see Figure 13-99)

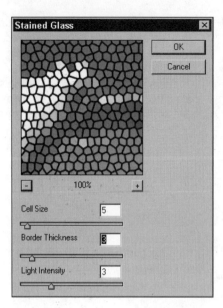

Figure 13-99: This filter is a real disappointment for most users, as instead of turning your image into glass-like shapes with lead lines between them, it creates a cartoon-ish, very unrealistic effect.

Tip   The smaller the cell size you establish, the more detail (or at least the ability to identify shapes or objects in the image) you retain within the image. Reducing border thickness is also helpful in this regard.

Note   If you use the Stained Glass filter all by itself — with no other filters or effects applied before or after it, the result will be less than desirable for most people. You find that the image doesn't look like glass panes separated by strips of lead — instead, it looks like a heavy-handed drawing of that effect. To improve the realistic quality of the Stained Glass filter, try using the Glass or Ripple filters (from the Distort category) first, and then apply Stained Glass. You'll find that many filters are enhanced by being combined with other filters — experiment with both similar and wildly diverse filter effects and see what happens!

✦ Texturizer (see Figure 13-100)

Tip   You can also apply a PSD file as a texture, clicking the Load Texture selection from the Texture drop-down list. An Open dialog box appears, from which you can select an image to serve as the texture. This works much like the Texture Fill filter, which you find in the Render category.

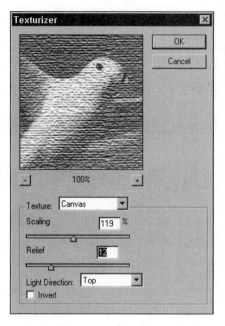

Figure 13-100: Here's a filter that truly belongs in this category — a filter that allows you to pick a texture from a selection of recognizable textures — Brick, Burlap, Canvas, or Sandstone.

Using Video and Other Filters

If your images will end up on TV, you may want to run them through the Video filters, which reduce the range of colors within the image to those that can be successfully displayed on TV. When you apply the De-Interlace filter, you'll probably not even be able to notice any difference in the image — as shown in Figure 13-101. The NTSC Colors filter applies the NTSC video format's color range to your image, making sure that all the colors in your image fit the standard.

The Other filter's category contains five filters, each of which enables you to control or create filter effects — making adjustments to color, changing the position of a portion of the image by a distance you specify, allowing you to control the *spread* and *choke* (printing terms for the way overlapping colors print), and creating definite color transitions within an image to emphasize edges.

✦ De-Interlace (see Figure 13-101)

✦ NTSC Colors (see Figure 13-102)

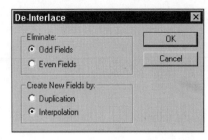

Figure 13-101: This Video category filter removes the lines that you can see on a still image taken from moving images (video). Also, you can choose how to remove those lines.

Tip

If you never use images captured from a video and/or never create images that will be incorporated into a video, you'll probably have no use for the Video category filters.

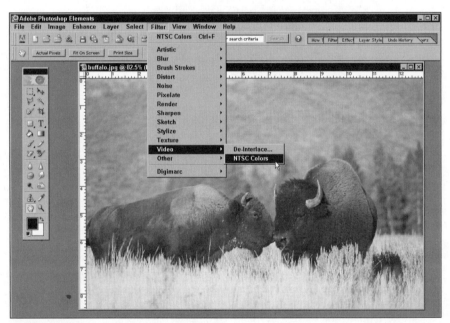

Figure 13-102: Use the NTSC Colors filter to make sure your image contains only the colors that can be effectively displayed within the NTSC video format.

✦ Custom (see Figure 13-103)

Tip

After you like what the Custom filter does (with numbers you choose in specific boxes within the dialog box), click the Save button to save the filter for future use. To use a saved Custom filter, click the Load button and choose your saved filter by name.

✦ High Pass (see Figure 13-104)

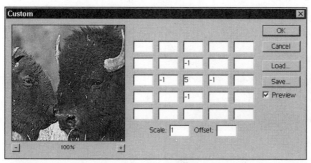

Figure 13-103: The first of the Other category filters, Custom enables you to create your own filter through the entry of numbers into an array of boxes, utilizing a mathematical operation called *convolution*. This recolors pixels based on the numbers you enter and on the color of the adjacent pixels.

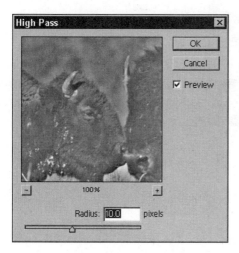

Figure 13-104: The High Pass filter, second in the Other category, highlights edge details within your image and dims the rest of the image. You may find this to be artistically interesting, or you can use it to help select only the edges of an image for some other kind of treatment.

When overlapping colors are printed, the printing devices (software, hardware) establish *choke* and *spread* settings to make sure the overlapping areas print properly — with no gaps or holes where content beneath other content is visible through the uppermost layer of content. The Maximum and Minimum filters control this, Maximum spreading out white or light areas and choking black or dark areas, and Minimum spreading out black areas and choking white areas. Figure 13-105 shows the Maximum dialog box, with the radius setting that establishes the number of pixels to compare when establishing the choke. Figure 13-106 shows the Minimum dialog box, which appears identical, except that it's used to establish the spread.

✦ Maximum (see Figure 13-105)

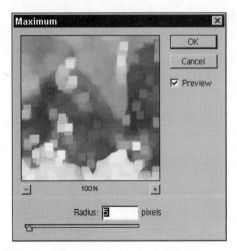

Figure 13-105: Lighten your image by spreading the white or light areas and choking dark or black areas.

✦ Minimum (see Figure 13-106)

✦ Offset (see Figure 13-107)

Figure 13-106: Darken your image by spreading black or dark areas and choking white or light areas.

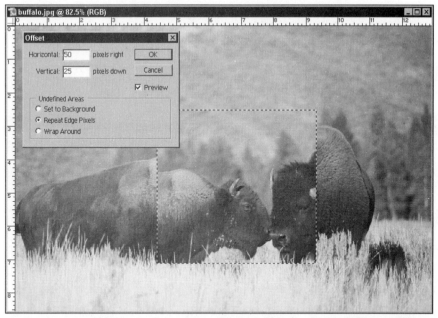

Figure 13-107: The Offset filter moves a selection within your image by a horizontal and vertical measurement you specify within the dialog box. You can also determine how the empty space created by the offset is handled — filling it with transparency, repeating the edge pixels, or wrapping the side and bottom pixels. Wrap Around is the default.

Tip   If you want to offset only part of the image, make a selection of that image before invoking the filter.

Applying Special Visual Effects

The Effects palette contains several features that look a lot like the Filters palette's offerings. As shown in Figure 13-108, the palette's thumbnails, at first glance, could be the same as the Filters thumbnails. So why have Effects as well as Filters? It's anyone's guess, but presumably to provide quick, easy, no-dialog- box-required tools for creating special effects for images and text. The Effects palette also offers tools for creating frames for your images, mimicking the mat that surrounds a photo when it's framed or to eliminate the need for a physical frame altogether. Figure 13-109 shows a "framed" photo, the frame created with Elements' Wood Frame effect.

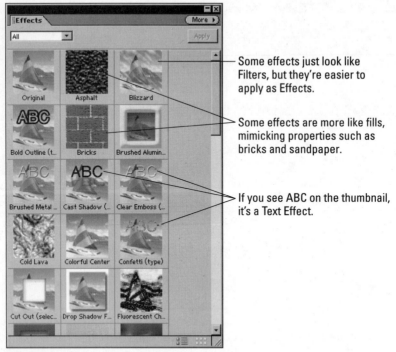

Some effects just look like Filters, but they're easier to apply as Effects.

Some effects are more like fills, mimicking properties such as bricks and sandpaper.

If you see ABC on the thumbnail, it's a Text Effect.

Figure 13-108: Select any effect from the Effects palette and apply it to the appropriate portion of your image.

Tip   Creating a frame in Elements also lets you place that sort of finishing touch on images bound for the Web — portraits, original artwork, and so on. You read about saving images in Web-safe formats in Chapter 18.

Elements' Effects palette offers effects that fall into four categories:

   ✦ Frames

   ✦ Image Effects

   ✦ Text Effects

   ✦ Textures

By default, the palette is set to All, which displays all of the effects, regardless of their category. If you switch to a particular category (using the drop-down list at the top of the palette, as shown in Figure 13-110), you will see only the Effects in that category. If you'd prefer to see the Effects as a list, click the List View button at the foot of the palette.

Figure 13-109: Create a "wooden" frame for your image and then place it between panes of glass.

Click the drop-down list to choose an Effects category.

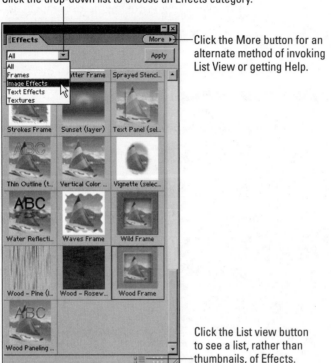

Click the More button for an
alternate method of invoking
List View or getting Help.

Click the List view button
to see a list, rather than
thumbnails, of Effects.

Figure 13-110: Choose which Effects to view and how to view them.

Applying effects

To apply an effect, be it to a layer or selection within the image, or to text only, all
you have to do is follow these simple steps—you get to use the Frames effects later:

STEPS: Applying Image and Text Effects

1. If you're applying the effect to only part of an image, select that part and/or
   activate the layer you want to be changed. For text effects, select the Text
   layer to which you want the Effect to apply.

2. Display the Effects palette and choose All to display all the Effects. You can
   also distill the list to a single category if you want, but be sure to choose the
   one that matches the part of your image that you're about to alter.

3. View the available Effects and click on the one you want to apply. Your
   choices for applying it to your selection/layer/text are:

✦ Click the Apply button.

✦ Drag the Effect thumbnail onto the image window (see this in progress in Figure 13-111).

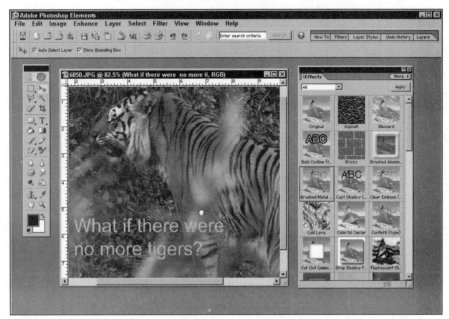

Figure 13-111: The little fist indicates you're carrying something from one place (the Effects palette) to another (the image window).

Tip   If you have nothing selected within the image, the effect will be applied to the entire image. Only making a selection first restricts the Image Effect to one particular area within a specific layer.

4. Choose your application method and use it to apply the desired Effect.

After you apply the Effect, you can get rid of it by using the Undo command (choose Edit ➪ Undo or press Ctrl + Z) or you can use the Undo History palette to go back to the step before you applied the Effect. If the effect created a layer (this happens when you choose an effect such as Brick or Asphalt, something that covers the image entirely, as shown in Figure 13-112), you can drag the new layer to the garbage can in the Layers palette, or select the layer and press Delete.

It's important to note that when you apply an Effect to text, the layer containing the text is no longer a text layer. As shown in Figure 13-113, the type changed by using onc of the Text Effects is no longer on a type layer — it appears like any other layer you might have created for original, non-text content.

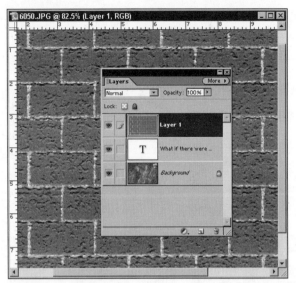

Figure 13-112: Applying the Brick effect created an entirely new layer, all filled with the look of a brick wall. Drag the layer to the garbage if you don't want it.

Figure 13-113: The act of applying an Effect to text changes the text to regular content — you can no longer edit the text in terms of its font, point size, or spelling.

Creating Specialized Frames

The Frames Effects are simple to apply, and they work much like the Text and Image Effects. All you have to do is click on the Frame Effect you want to use, and either drag it to the image or click the Apply button in the Effects palette. After you do this, you receive a prompt, as shown in Figure 13-114, asking if you want to flatten your layers. Your only choice is to OK this, so go ahead and flatten. If you decide after seeing the frame applied that you don't want it, you can use the Undo History palette to go back to before the flattening occurred, giving you access once again to your individual image layers.

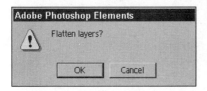

Figure 13-114: You need to flatten your image layers before you can add a frame to your image.

As soon as you OK the flattening process, you see a lot of work going on, all performed by Elements, with no further interaction required from you. You see square selections of various sizes appearing, the canvas size temporarily increases, you see colors and fills being applied, and then finally, after the frame effect you choose is ready, you see the image window return to the size it was when you first applied the effect, and the frame will be in place, encompassing your image.

So what's all that stuff going on? It's a series of steps being performed, one by one, all building toward the particular frame you chose. Several layers temporarily may be created, Effects applied to those layers, selections made and then deselected, each step performed automatically, in the right order for the frame you chose to be successfully built.

After applied, the frame can be transformed — resized, rotated, renamed (it's on its own layer, as shown in Figure 13-115) and even deleted if you decide you don't like it and want to start over.

Tip   If you're adding a frame to your image, you are either intending to print the image for display on paper or to display it online or on-screen. If you intend to print the image, see Chapter 17 for tips for successful printing on a variety of papers and printers, and if you're intending to display your image online, see Chapter 18.

The frame is on its own layer.

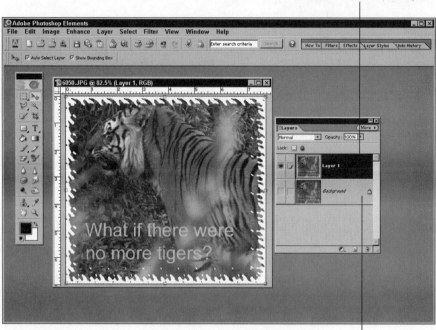

The rest of the image layers are flattened into a single layer.

Figure 13-115: Your frame is ready — after many steps and procedures, all performed automatically by Elements, based on the frame effect you chose.

✦   ✦   ✦

Working with Type

P A R T

IV

◆ ◆ ◆ ◆

Chapter 14
Adding Text to Images

Chapter 15
Applying Type Styles
and Effects

◆ ◆ ◆ ◆

Adding Text to Images

In This Chapter

Adding type to
an image

Applying character
and paragraph
formatting

Controlling type
quality

A *type layer* is created each time you use the Type tool, in either its default Horizontal Type tool mode, or as the Vertical Type tool — you get to use type masks later, and they're covered in depth in Chapter 15.

Creating a Type Layer

For the purposes of adding text to your image, however, simply click on the Horizontal or Vertical Type tool (see them displayed in Figure 14-1) to activate it and then click on the image to create a type layer. The layer is initially called Layer 1 (or whatever number is assigned based on the other layers you've created so far) and then changes its name when you type text onto the layer. The layer name becomes the first few words of the text you typed, as shown in Figure 14-2.

Elements knows that you have completed the type layer (for now, anyway) when you click on the Move tool or one of the selection tools, and the type layer is set up. If you click on the Move tool, the type tool acquires handles, as shown in Figure 14-3. You can resize the type layer as you would any other sort of layer — the text can be enlarged, reduced, or even stretched up or down. It remains editable text, even if you rotate it.

Tip If you want to enlarge or reduce your type size without losing current width-height proportions, hold the Shift key while you drag the type layer's handles. Release the mouse first, and then the Shift key, after you finished resizing.

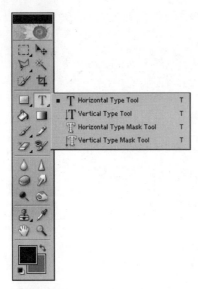

Figure 14-1: Choose from the two Type tools that add text to your image. The Type Mask tools perform a different role in your image editing process.

The text is truncated — the entire string of text is not displayed as the layer's name

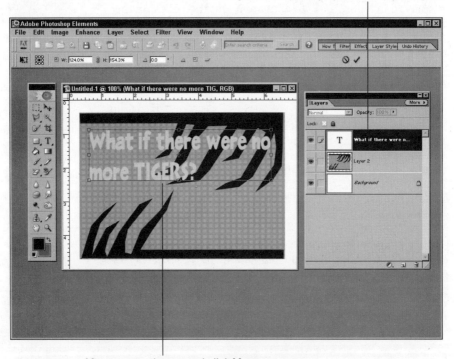

After you type the text and click Move or some other tool, your Type layer is officially named.

Figure 14-2: Type some text and create a Type layer.

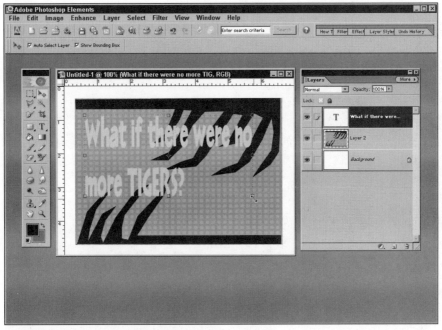

Figure 14-3: Use the handles to make your text taller, shorter, wider, or narrower — or point to a corner handle and rotate it.

Activating the Correct Type Tool

You have four Type tool variations from which to choose, and each one does a different job. Your options are:

✦ Horizontal Type Tool

✦ Vertical Type Tool

✦ Horizontal Type Mask Tool

✦ Vertical Type Mask Tool

The first two apply text to your image and enable you to format the text as you would in a word processor — changing its font, size, color, and alignment. The latter two create masks from the text you type, creating a selection within the image that's the shape of the text you typed. You can then fill the selection with a color or pattern or delete content within the selection. If you leave the type mask as a mask, you can use it to protect a portion of your image from any editing. In both cases (type tools and type mask tools), the horizontal or vertical aspect only determines the direction in which the type (or mask) runs. Figure 14-4 shows a vertical type mask that creates more of a border than text that's intended for reading.

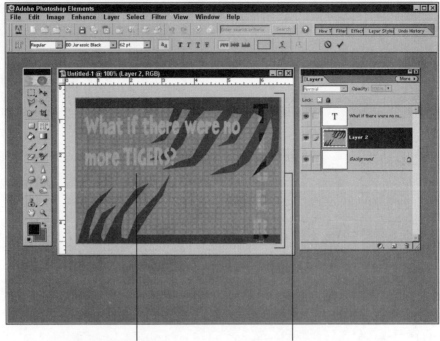

Although seen in gray here, a red wash appears over the image when you're using a Type mask.

Only the typed text is not part of the mask.

Figure 14-4: Create vertical type for a more interesting, yet less legible addition of text to your image.

Tip   Click on the Move tool to turn your mask into a selection and then fill the selection with color, a pattern, or some free-form painting effects of your own.

Typing Your Text

This might seem like a silly topic — of course you know how to type text, even if you only type with one or two fingers and go very slowly. Even such rudimentary typing skills should serve you well with Elements' Type tool, but there are a few details to remember:

✦ When typing, you need to tell Elements when to move down to the next line. Elements has no word-wrap, and you have no way to make Elements force a line break when some invisible right margin is reached. If you want the text to break and start on the next line, press Enter.

✦ Unlike Photoshop, which offers a helpful and powerful Character palette (and a Paragraph palette as well), Elements offers very few tools for formatting your text. There are no kerning or tracking tools, no way to adjust leading. You can adjust alignment (horizontal only), and you can change the font size of the text, which changes the spacing between lines. Beyond that, however, your formatting capabilities are very limited.

✦ Elements has no spell check, so type carefully. As discussed later in this chapter, you can use a word processor to check your text before you place it in the image, or you can copy your text to a word processor for checking, and then paste back the corrected text.

With these caveats in mind, you can begin typing. Just click on the Type tool to activate it and then click on the image, where you want the text to begin. You don't have to worry about finding the exact spot with your initial click, however, because you can always use the Move tool to reposition the text.

After you click and start typing, you can press Enter to start a new line, press Enter more than once if you want to visually separate paragraphs, and after you finish typing, click on the Move tool to indicate that you have completed the typing. Figure 14-5 shows text that's been typed and that is now selected and ready for any transformation (resizing, rotation) that you may have in mind.

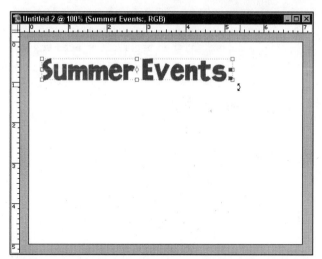

Figure 14-5: The Move tool is a natural post-typing choice — it selects your type layer and gives you handles for transforming your new text.

To begin typing again on an existing Type layer, double-click the T icon (also called the *layer thumbnail)* on the type layer in question, and see that all the text is highlighted (see Figure 14-6). You can now take your mouse and click within the text to position the cursor (to begin inserting text amongst existing characters) or you can double-click an individual word or click and drag through some of the text for replacement. Figure 14-7 shows text being replaced — the selected word is replaced by the very next word that this user types.

Figure 14-6: Select all of your type layer's text and then begin editing or adding text as needed.

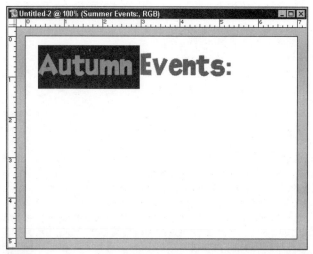

Figure 14-7: Editing existing text is relatively simple, based on your selection within the existing text.

Choosing the Right Font, Size, and Color

These basic formatting decisions can be made before you type the text, or afterwards, after you see the text in place. Making font, size, and color choices (along with alignment and special formatting selections, such as underline, italic, or boldface) are often made both before *and* after the type layer is created. Typically, you know what font you want or have to use, based on other fonts already in use within the image or within documents where the image will be used. You may know the preferred font size ahead of time, too. Color may also be an obvious choice, based on existing colors within the image. Figure 14-8 shows the Type tool's options bar and a set of options in place for text about to be typed.

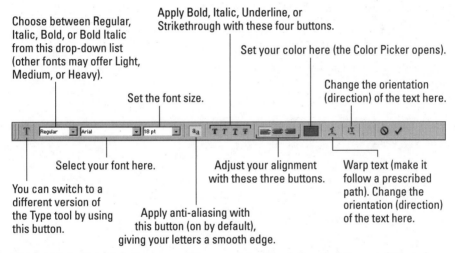

Choose between Regular, Italic, Bold, or Bold Italic from this drop-down list (other fonts may offer Light, Medium, or Heavy).

Apply Bold, Italic, Underline, or Strikethrough with these four buttons.

Set your color here (the Color Picker opens).

Change the orientation (direction) of the text here.

Set the font size.

Select your font here.

Adjust your alignment with these three buttons.

Warp text (make it follow a prescribed path). Change the orientation (direction) of the text here.

You can switch to a different version of the Type tool by using this button.

Apply anti-aliasing with this button (on by default), giving your letters a smooth edge.

Figure 14-8: Establish the type settings you're sure of ahead of time and/or make changes later on.

Note   What is anti-aliasing? It's a process by which the edges of text are smoothed by the addition of pixels along the otherwise choppy edges of the characters. Typically seen on letters' curves, the choppy edges are filled in and made smooth. This sounds like a completely positive feature, and most of the time it is — on the other hand, if your text is bound for the Web, you might choose NOT to use anti-aliasing, because it (A) can increase file size because of the added pixels, and (B) it can cause unwanted colors to appear along the edges of text. In general, anti-aliasing is a good thing, though, and it can make your text appear cleaner and crisper.

After the text is typed, however, you can tweak these choices, going for a slightly darker or lighter color, a different font size, or even a different font. Your other choices — for using underline, italic, bold, or to choose a different alignment for the text — are usually made after the text is typed, because sometimes you really need to see the text in place in order to make these choices.

Tip

Not sure which font you want to use? Select the text and then select the displayed font by name in the options bar (click once on the displayed font name). Then, use your up and down arrows to move through your font list, one at a time, and see your selected text displayed in each font. After you find one you like, press Enter to confirm it.

Selecting and Reformatting Text on the Type Layer

Assuming you have typed your text and now see the need to change something about its appearance, you need to select some or all of the text in order to make that happen. To do so, follow these steps:

STEPS: Selecting Existing Text on a Type Layer

1. Make sure the Layers palette is displayed and find the type layer containing the text you want to reformat.

2. Double-click the T icon for that type layer. All of the text in the layer is selected, as shown in Figure 14-9.

Figure 14-9: Select the Type layer and select all the type in it.

3. To make a formatting change to all of the text in the layer, simply use the Type tool's options bar to make changes to the font, size, color — any aspect of the appearance of the selected type. Note that having double-clicked the T icon on a type layer automatically selects the Type tool in the toolbox, which displays the Type tool's options.

4. If you want to reformat just some of the text — say to italicize a single word, or to make a phrase within a sentence stand out in bold or with a different color or font, click within the selected text (your mouse pointer looks like an I-beam (see Figure 14-10), and a cursor blinks within your text.

Figure 14-10: Click to position your cursor within the text as a preparation for a more focused selection.

5. Use your mouse to drag through the text you want to select from within the type layer. You can also double-click to select a single word (double-click on that word) or click in front of the desired word or phrase and then use the Shift and right mouse buttons to select text one character at a time. Figure 14-11 shows a single word selected and reformatted with a different font.

6. With the desired text selected, use the Type tool's options bar to change any aspect of the text's appearance.

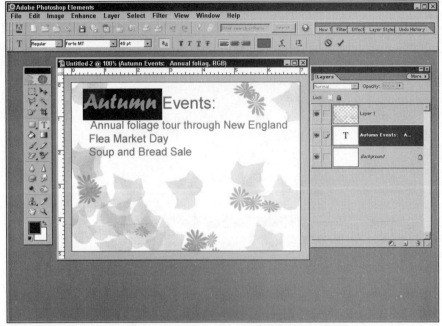

Figure 14-11: Double-click to select a single word within the text.

Warping Text

The Create Warped Text tool appears on the Type tool's options bar, and when clicked, opens a dialog box through which you can choose how to warp your text. *Warping* text means to change its shape — to make the text follow a path and/or adhere to a prescribed shape, as shown in Figure 14-12.

Through the Warp Text dialog box (see Figure 14-13), you can choose from 15 different shapes (plus None, to get rid of a previously-applied warp effect), all found in the Style drop-down list. It's helpful that you can see the Warp in effect within the image window (see Figure 14-14) while the Warp Text dialog box is still open. To get the whole preview, simply drag the dialog box aside (by its title bar) so that it doesn't obscure any of the text.

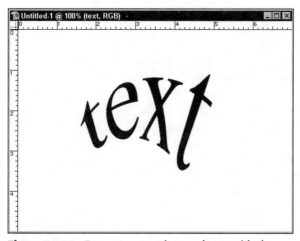

Figure 14-12: Force your text into a shape with the Warp Text option.

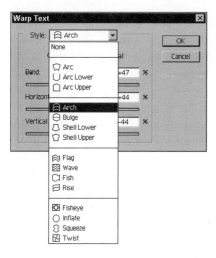

Figure 14-13: Pick a shape, any shape, for the Style of your warp.

Figure 14-14: No need to guess how the Style and settings you choose will affect your text—you get a preview in the image window.

After you make a Style selection, you can use the Bend, Horizontal Distortion, and Vertical Distortion sliders (as well as the Horizontal and Vertical radio buttons) to fine-tune the warp effect you chose. These options work as follows:

✦ **Bend** determines the direction (depending on the direction in which you drag the slider) of the warp. If, for example, you choose the Arc Style, dragging the Bend slider to the right will create a very sharp, deep arc, with the high point at the top, as shown in Figure 14-15. If you drag to the left, the arc runs in the other direction, with its peak at the bottom (see Figure 14-16).

✦ **Horizontal Distortion** enables you to determine the way the warp affects the text left to right. By dragging the slider to the right, the shape is more dramatic on the right end of the text (see Figure 14-17). If you drag to the left, the distortion is more dramatic at that end of the text. Placing the slider in the middle creates an even amount of warp over the entire length of the text.

Figure 14-15: Drag the Bend slider to the right to change the direction of the warp.

Figure 14-16: Drag to the left to change the direction again.

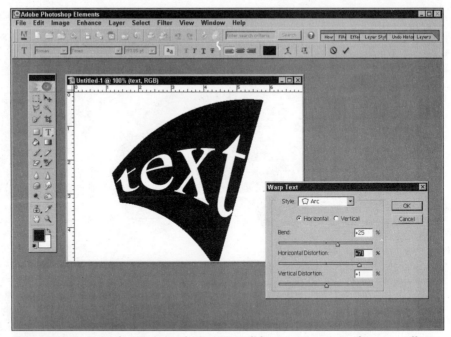

Figure 14-17: Drag the Horizontal Distortion slider to concentrate the warp effect at one end (left or right) of the text.

✦ **Vertical Distortion** determines how much of the warp effect appears at the top of the text or at the bottom. Dragging to the right concentrates the warp at the bottom of the text, and dragging to the left concentrates the warp at the top of the text. Figures 14-18 and 14-19 show the two opposite effects that can be achieved with the Vertical Distortion slider when applied to the Flag warp.

✦ The **Horizontal** and **Vertical** radio buttons enable you to choose the way the Style is applied to the text. Using the Flag warp again as an example, if you choose Vertical, the flag is waving from top to bottom, as shown in Figure 14-20. If you choose Horizontal, the flag waves from left to right.

Of course, the effects aren't permanent until you click the OK button in the Warp Text dialog box. And even then, they're not really permanent. You can always use Undo (Ctrl + Z) or use the Undo History palette to go back to your pre-warped state.

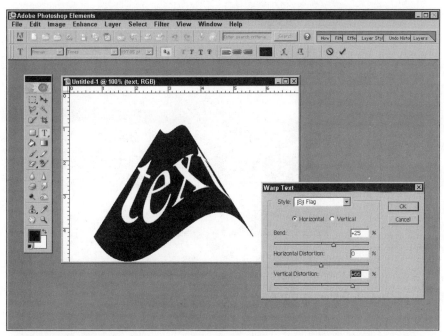

Figure 14-18: Your flag flares out at the bottom if you drag the Vertical Distortion slider to the right.

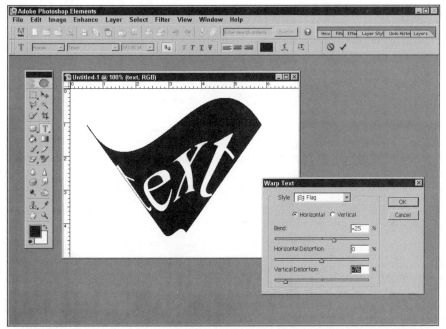

Figure 14-19: Now the flag flares at the top, as the slider's been dragged to the left.

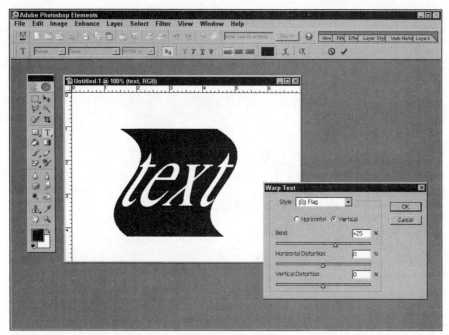

Figure 14-20: Choose the orientation for your chosen warp Style by selecting either Horizontal or Vertical.

Changing Text Orientation

So you typed your text with the Horizontal Type tool, and now you want it to run vertically. Rather than delete the text, switch to the Vertical Type tool and retype the text, use the Change the Text Orientation button, found at the far right end of the Type tool's options bar. As shown in Figure 14-21, text that was typed horizontally can become a vertical strip of text with a single click of the button.

To set the text back to the former orientation, simply click the button again. This may result in the text moving, starting higher or lower on the image than you originally had it, but you can use the Move tool to put it back where it was. If that's not easy enough — perhaps the text is now outside of the image window — use the Undo History palette to go back to the state prior to your having changed the text's orientation in the first place.

Why does the text move? If you switch, for example, from horizontal to vertical orientation, the text starts out higher on the image so that the entire string of text is visible (or as much of it as possible) within the image. If you then go back to horizontal orientation, the text appears where it started when it was vertical text.

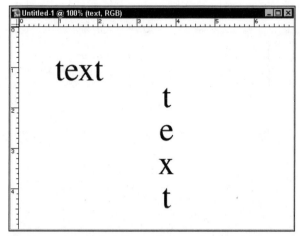

Figure 14-21: Switch from Horizontal to Vertical text, or vice versa.

Editing Paragraph Content

What if your text *looks* fine, but you realize now that you want to change what it says? You can use the same selection techniques described in the previous section — double-click the Type layer to select all of its content, or double-click a single word (with the Type tool activated), or use the Shift and arrow keys to select text character-by-character. After the offending text is selected, simply type replacement text or press Delete if you want to get rid of it entirely and have nothing you want to appear in its place.

You can also break a single paragraph into two by positioning your cursor within the text, as shown in Figure 14-22, and pressing the Enter key. This works just as it would in a word processor — it forces the text down to a new line. You may end up with more text on the next line than you wanted, and subsequent uses of the Enter key may be required to keep your paragraph within the shape you wanted it.

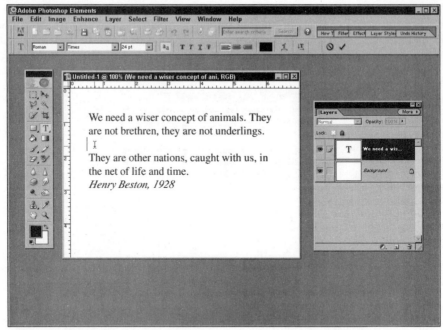

Figure 14-22: Break your paragraph into two or more paragraphs with artful use of the Enter key.

Checking Your Text for Spelling Errors

Photoshop Elements does not have spell-checking capabilities. Therefore, sending any paragraph text (more than a line or two that you can proof by eye) through a word processor to check the spelling and grammar is a good idea. Simply copy your text content to the Clipboard by selecting it (drag through it with your mouse or double-click the T icon on the Type layer in question, as shown in Figure 14-23) and press Ctrl + C. Then go into your favorite word processor and use Ctrl + V to paste the text. You can then use the word processor's spell-checking tools to verify the spelling of your text. If the word processor also has grammar checking tools, use those, too.

After you put your text through the spell-check process, copy it from within the word processor (only if any errors were found), and then paste it back into your Elements image. You can replace your text by selecting it and then pasting—the pasted text replaces what you had to begin with (only the selected portion, however). You can also paste to a new Type layer and then delete the layer with errors in it.

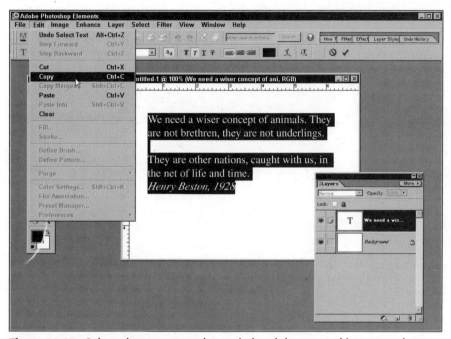

Figure 14-23: Selected text can now be copied and then pasted into a word processor for spell checking.

Tip

If you have a big paragraph of text, why not type it in a word processor and then paste it into a text layer in Elements? You can check the spelling ahead of time, and then paste the text as soon as you click the Type tool to begin building the content of a new or existing type layer. The pasted text will take on the formatting that's in effect at the time—whatever font, size, color, and so on that you see on the Type tool's options bar at the time. You can't carry formatting from the word processor, so don't bother formatting the text until it's been pasted into the Elements image.

✦　　✦　　✦

Applying Type Styles and Effects

In This Chapter

Understanding the
Layer Styles palette

Creating 3D illusions
with Shadows and
Bevels

Applying Special
Layer Styles

Whether applied to type or to shapes and layers (as discussed in Chapter 12), Layer Styles are a great ally for the user in search of a quick, simple tool to add real visual interest to an image. For the purposes of this chapter, you work exclusively with type and the way layer styles can enhance it.

Working with Layer Styles

Using the Layer Styles palette (shown in Figure 15-1, along with an image window with some simple text in it), you can choose from several different style categories, and apply one, two, or many styles at once. You can apply Layer Styles to an entire type layer (every word in the layer) or if you want the illusion of having applied it to just some of your text on a given layer, break the text up into multiple layers and arrange them to look like they're one contiguous string or paragraph of text. Figure 15-2 shows a paragraph with the first letter (on its own layer) formatted using layer styles, creating an interesting, eye-grabbing start to the text.

If your image is bound for the Web, adding visual interest to text is paramount. People don't like to read, and if faced with more than a few words, many people will simply skim the text for "the highlights" or skip over the text entirely. By adding some visual interest through layer styles, you can attract attention to your text and make sure it's read. You can find out all about the creation of Web graphics with Elements in Chapter 18.

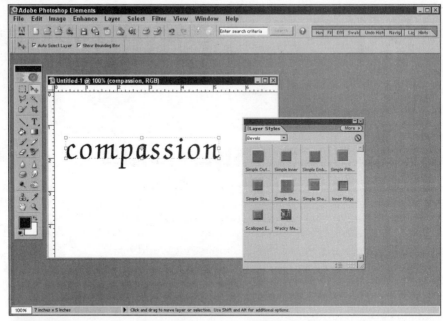

Figure 15-1: The Layer Styles palette offers 14 different style categories from which to choose.

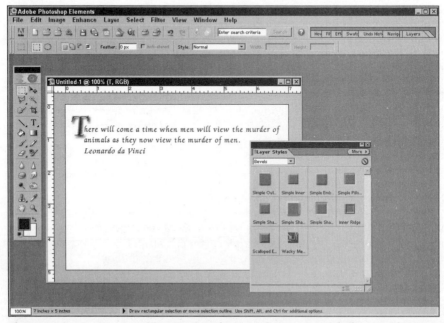

Figure 15-2: Create an exciting starting character for a paragraph that you don't want anyone to miss.

Note

Of course for long paragraphs, you're better off typing the text directly into your Web page by using your Web design application or text editor to create the paragraph. On the other hand, given the limited pool of fonts you can safely use on a Web page (as you want to use only fonts you're sure all of your visitors have on their computer), creating a text image in Photoshop Elements enables you to use interesting fonts, colors, fills, and effects and bring them to otherwise boring text on your Web page.

Navigating the Layer Styles Palette

The Layer Styles palette isn't terribly complicated, but it does have a lot of features. As shown in Figure 15-3, you can choose a style category, access supplementary menus, and view a sample of the style/s you applied right within the palette, as well as in the image window, which reflects the selections you made in the palette.

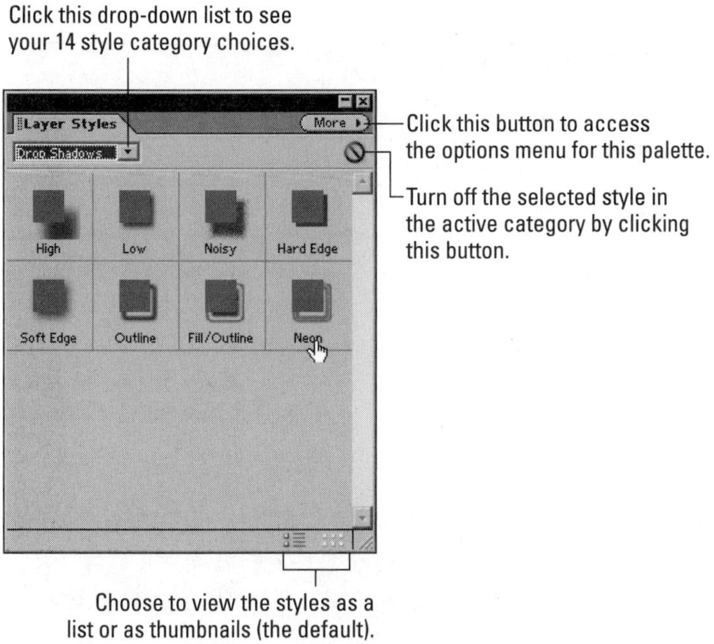

Click this drop-down list to see your 14 style category choices.

Click this button to access the options menu for this palette.

Turn off the selected style in the active category by clicking this button.

Choose to view the styles as a list or as thumbnails (the default).

Figure 15-3: Apply one or more styles to selected text with the easily-navigated Layer Styles palette.

Tip

The More button's name is sort of an overstatement. Within the menu that appears when you click the button are commands that open a Help window and choices for viewing the Layer Styles as a list or as an array of thumbnails. Yes, this is more than was visible in the palette, but most users expect more from the More menu.

Applying a Layer Style

To make applying layer styles easier, your image window displays the style/s you applied, showing how the text is affected by the choices you make in the Layer Styles palette. This isn't a preview, mind you—not as you've seen when working with Filters, where the image window displays the Filter's effect, but the Filter isn't really applied until you click OK in the given Filter's dialog box. Rather, as you click on various styles and see them applied to the text in the image window, you are actually applying them to the text. So essentially, all that's involved in applying a style—is selecting a category of styles (Drop Shadows, Bevels, Glass Buttons, whatever you prefer) and then clicking on the style you want in one or more of the categories. To assist you in choosing a Layer Style, review the samples in Table 15-1. A style from each of the 14 categories appears in the table, each applied to the same word on a background that allows the effect to be most clearly seen—glows, for example, show best on a dark background, whereas shadows show best on white or light backgrounds. Note that the name of the applied Layer Style appears in parentheses next to the style category for each row in the table.

Table 15-1
Layer Style Previews

Layer Style	Appearance
Bevels (Simple Sharp Outer)	*compassion*
Drop Shadows (Noisy)	*compassion*
Inner Glows (Simple)	*compassion*
Inner Shadows (Low)	*compassion*
Outer Glows (Small Noisy)	*compassion*

Layer Style	Appearance
Visibility (Ghosted shown here)	 *compassion*
Complex (Red, White, Blue Contrast)	 *compassion*
Glass Buttons (Deep Blue Glass)	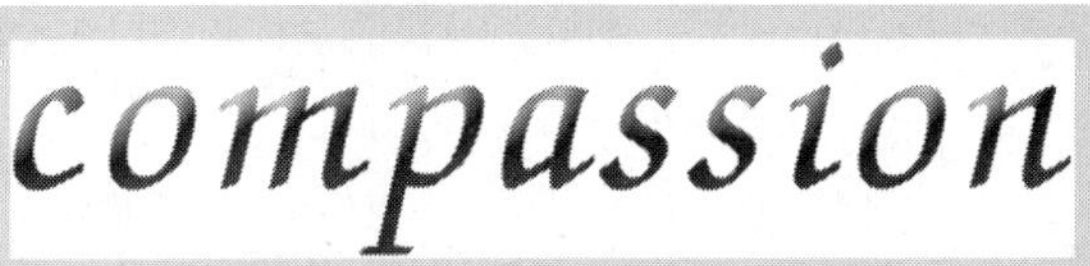 *compassion*
Image Effects (Puzzle)	 *compassion*
Patterns (Satin Sheets)	 *compassion*
Photographic Effects (Orange Gradient)	 *compassion*
Wow Chrome (Beveled Chrome)	 *compassion*
Wow Neon (Lt Blue Off)	 *compassion*
Wow Plastic (Plastic Purple)	 *compassion*

For clarity, however, I break the process of applying one or more of the Layer Styles down into a simple procedure, from selecting the type to be affected through removing styles you applied.

STEPS: Applying and Removing Styles

1. Select the type to which the style should apply. You can't apply the style to part of the text — rather; it must be applied to the entire type layer. You can select the text in one of two ways:

   • Double-click the T icon on the layer to select all of the text on the layer.

   • Click on the Move tool and then click on the layer — handles appear around the text content (see Figure 15-4) to indicate that it has been selected.

Figure 15-4: Whether selected with the Type tool or the Move tool, the entire type layer is affected by whatever style you choose to apply.

2. Display the Layer Styles palette. You can leave it on the docking well, or to keep it fully displayed on-screen the entire time you're using it, drag it off the docking well and bring it down onto the workspace, as shown in Figure 15-5.

3. Choose a Layer Style category by clicking the drop-down list at the top of the palette. Figure 15-6 displays the drop-down list.

4. From within the selected category, click on the style you want to apply.

5. View the results in the image window. As needed, move the Layers Palette (drag it by its title bar) so that it isn't obscuring any of text in the active type layer within the image window.

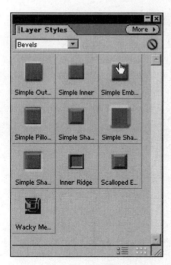

Figure 15-5: Keep the Layer Styles palette open and displayed by dragging it down from the docking well.

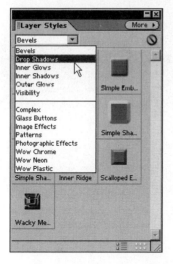

Figure 15-6: Want a 3D look? Use the Drop Shadows and/or Bevels categories.

6. If you want to apply more styles, switch to a new category (using the aforementioned drop-down list) and click on another style to apply. You can continue doing this until your text in the image window has the look you desire. Figure 15-7 shows text with a drop shadow, beveling, and a style from the Wow Plastic category applied.

7. To clear all styles and start over, click the Clear Style button (shown in Figure 15-8). All styles, from all categories you used, are cleared.

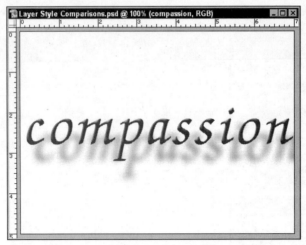

Figure 15-7: A combination of three different styles creates a glossy, 3D look.

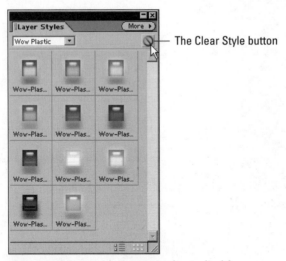

The Clear Style button

Figure 15-8: Get rid of every style applied from every category with the click of a single button.

Working with Text Effects

As I discussed in Chapter 13, Elements Effects palette contains Text Effects — special visual effects that apply only to type. The Effects palette, distilled to only the Text

Effects, is shown in Figure 15-9. In applying text effects, a type layer is changed to a regular content layer — the text is no longer editable and cannot be reformatted in terms of font or color. Text on such a layer is simply a graphic, as though you drew a shape and gave it a fill or drew with the Brush or Pencil tools.

Another detail that's important to know as you embark on using Text Effects is that you can't apply a second effect to text that's already had an effect applied. Text Effects can only be applied to a type layer, and as stated previously, if you applied a text effect, the type is no longer type. If you attempt to apply a second effect, a prompt appears (see Figure 15-10) telling you that the effect can only be applied to type.

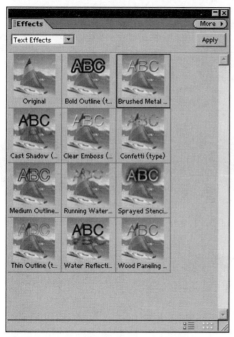

Figure 15-9: Choose from 11 different Text Effects for the type in your image.

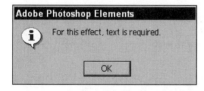

Figure 15-10: Text Effects can only be applied to type on a type layer.

The examples in the Effects palette are not always clear in terms of your forecasting how a particular Effect will change the appearance of your text. You can apply an effect and then if you don't like it, use Undo to return your text to its pre-effect state. This also returns the layer to a Type layer, so that the text can be edited and/or another Text Effect applied. Because the Text Effects in the Effects palette are not always clearly represented by the thumbnail images in the palette, Table 15-2 is provided to help you choose between effects. Each of the 11 effects are applied to the same word.

Table 15-2 Text Effects Preview	
Text Effect	**Appearance**
Bold Outline	**illusions**
Brushed Metal	*illusions*
Cast Shadow	**illusions**
Clear Emboss	*illusions*
Confetti	**illusions**
Medium Outline	*illusions*
Running Water	**illusions**

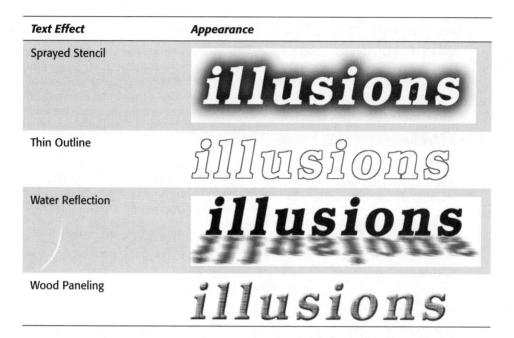

Text Effect	Appearance
Sprayed Stencil	
Thin Outline	
Water Reflection	
Wood Paneling	

It's important to note that when you apply an effect to text that's already been formatted—a color (applied from the Type tool's option bar or after one or more of the Layer Styles was applied), the results of the Text Effect you choose incorporates the existing formatting. As shown in Figure 15-11, if you had a Glass Button layer style applied and then choose a text effect that doesn't bring its own color effects with it, the color and bevel applied by the Glass Button style are included in the end result.

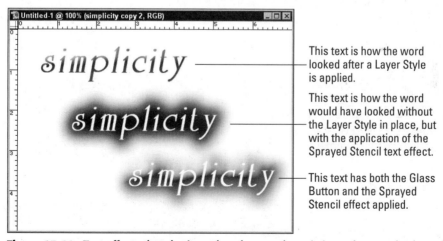

This text is how the word looked after a Layer Style is applied.

This text is how the word would have looked without the Layer Style in place, but with the application of the Sprayed Stencil text effect.

This text has both the Glass Button and the Sprayed Stencil effect applied.

Figure 15-11: Text effects that don't apply color use the existing color or color-based Layer Style, resulting in a combination of styles and effects.

Displaying Text Effects Thumbnails

Now that you have a sense of how the Effects can change the appearance of your text, you're ready to start applying them in your image. Before you can apply them, however, you need to display them. You can view them as a list, or you can view them as thumbnails, the latter being the default palette view (you saw it in Figure 15-9). Figure 15-12 shows the Effects palette, with all effects — not just those for text — displayed in List view. Of course, you have to scroll to see all 50+ effects — not all of them are visible simultaneously.

Click this drop-down list to choose to see Text Effects only.

Click the More button to get Help or to change your view from List to Thumbnails (or back again).

Click Apply after clicking on the Effect you want to use.

View a comparison between no effect (Original) and the selected Effect.

Click the Thumbnails View button to see an array of larger thumbnails for each effect.

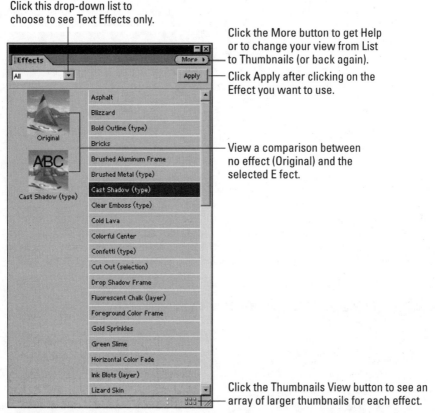

Figure 15-12: List view shows more effects at once and allows a comparison to the text with no effect applied.

If you click the drop-down list at the top of the palette, you can choose Text Effects — this distills the list of Effects down to just those that are designed for text. You could see them in the list of All effects (they had the word "Type" following the Effect name), but seeing only the Text Effects can make deciding on an effect much simpler.

Applying a Text Effect

You have two choices for applying a Text Effect to a selected type layer:

✦ Click once on the effect (in either List or Thumbnail view) and then click the Apply button on the right side of the Effects palette.

✦ Drag the Effect thumbnail out of the palette and onto the selected type layer.

In either case, moments later, the effect appears. Some effects take longer to apply than others, as there are sometimes more interim steps to take place — the combining of two or more filters or fills, the application of a layer style, application of color, and so on. Depending on your computer's processor and video card, you may see each step in the process of building the effect — you see layers appear and disappear in the layers palette, you may even see your text in each of the stages it goes through as the final effect is achieved. In the end, the effect you chose is applied, and your type layer is converted to a regular content layer, with Layer Styles applied (see Figure 15-13).

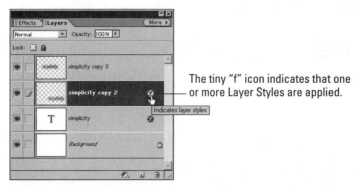

The tiny "f" icon indicates that one or more Layer Styles are applied.

Figure 15-13: View your layer, converted from a Type layer after Layer Styles were applied.

Tweaking Text Effects

After you apply a Text Effect, you can adjust its look. You can change the angle of a shadow or glow or change the depth or smoothness of a beveled edge. The number of features you can tweak depends on how many styles are applied, of course. Figure 15-14 shows the Style Settings dialog box for text to which the Brushed Metal effect is applied.

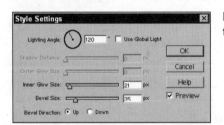

Figure 15-14: Adjust angles and light with the Style Settings dialog box.

To open the Style Settings dialog box, click the aforementioned "f" icon, the Layer Styles icon that appears on the far right of the layer to which an effect or layer style was applied. As soon as the dialog box is open, you can drag the sliders (those that aren't dimmed) and drag the radius in the Lighting Angle field to adjust the direction from which light should "shine" on your text. Figure 15-15 and 15-16 are before and after versions of the same text — the Sprayed Stencil effect is applied, and then the angle of light and depth of the beveled effect is adjusted.

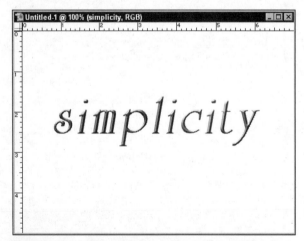

Figure 15-15: Here, the Brushed Metal Text Effect is applied in its default state.

Figure 15-16: After changing the direction of the light source and increasing the bevel depth, the text looks appreciably different.

Removing Text Effects

So what if you don't like the text effect after you apply it? You can't simply apply a new effect, because text effects only apply to Type and by having applied the now unwanted effect, your type is no longer seen as type but as graphic content to which Layer Styles have been applied. What to do? Get rid of the effect and start over. You have a few methods from which to choose:

✦ If you just applied the Text Effect, choose Edit⇨Undo to reverse your action. The text returns to being a Type layer and all signs of the effect and any Layer Styles it utilized are no longer applied.

✦ If you applied the Text Effect a while ago, use the Undo History palette (see Figure 15-17) and go back to the state just prior to "Brushed Metal (type)" where "Brushed Metal" can be the name of any Text Effect you applied.

Tip

The Undo History palette's list of states (actions you've taken, styles applied, and so forth) only goes back as far as the number of states you tell it to store through the Preferences dialog box (see Chapter 2 for more information on this), and is cleared when you exit Photoshop Elements. If you want to preserve your text as Type so that you can go back to it (and get rid of any reconsidered and later unwanted text effects) even after any kind of Undo is impossible, create duplicate Type layers and hide the one you're keeping as "backup." Apply the Text Effect to the visible Type layer and leave the hidden one alone. If you want to go back to pure Type and get rid of an Effect you applied, simply unhide the backup Type layer and throw out the version to which an Effect was applied.

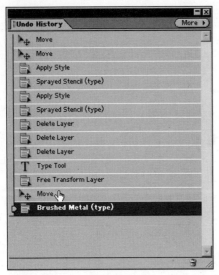

Figure 15-17: Go back in time and get rid of the Text Effect you applied.

✦   ✦   ✦

Sharing Your Elements Creations on Paper and Online

Chapter 16
Saving Your
Elements Images

Chapter 17
Printing Your Artwork
and Photographs

Chapter 18
Turning Images into
Web-Safe Graphics

Saving Your Elements Images

◆ ◆ ◆ ◆

In This Chapter

Saving Elements images for use in other applications

Saving multiple versions of a single image

Creating PDF files from your Elements images

Sending your Elements creations via e-mail

◆ ◆ ◆ ◆

PSD, which stands for Photoshop Document, is the native and default format for images created in Photoshop and Photoshop Elements. When you create an image in Photoshop Elements and choose File⇨Save (or File⇨Save As), it makes no difference when you're saving a new image for the first time. Elements assumes you intend to save in this format.

Saving Your Photoshop Elements Files

As shown in Figure 16-1, Elements selects the PSD format for you in the Save As dialog box.

If you edit an image of another format in Elements, when it comes time to save the file, Elements will assume you want to keep the original format and will offer options for that format within the Save As dialog box, shown in Figure 16-2. Here, a TIF/TIFF (Tagged Image File Format) image is being resaved after editing.

Figure 16-1: The Save As dialog box offers the PSD format as the default for images created in Elements.

Figure 16-2: Elements also enables you to edit files of other formats and save them in their original format, rather than forcing you to save them as PSD files.

When it comes to files of other formats, your desire to save them in their original format can be motivated by a number of factors:

✦ Wanting to keep the image in a format that another application can easily open

✦ Needing to keep the file small — PSD files are usually large, especially if there are multiple layers in the image

✦ The needs of another user, someone who may not have Photoshop or Elements, may dictate that you save the file in a format that person can open and edit

Whatever your motivation, you can accept the default format when saving (it will be whatever the file format was when you opened it in Elements), or you can save the file in several other formats, as shown in Figure 16-3. This figure displays the Save As dialog box Format list and shows a number of the available formats.

Figure 16-3: Choose a different format for your file, making a selection from the Format drop-down list.

If choosing a format that will be honored by another application is your goal, you may want to save the file in a format that a *vector*-based application (such as Adobe Illustrator or CorelDRAW) can open. By default, Photoshop and Elements only allow you to save files in a *bitmap* format, but some bitmap formats are acceptable to vector-based applications, at least for opening the file, after which the file will be converted to a vector image.

As stated, Elements, by default, creates bitmap files. These are files where the image information is stored in pixels, and a map of the image, in the form of an array of pixels is what makes up the image itself, as shown in Figure 16-4. This is clear when you look at a bitmap image at a high zoom percentage. You can see the individual pixels, the small dots I talk about throughout this book.

A curved edge isn't really a smooth curve, despite appearances at print size.

This line isn't really a line — it's a collection of pixels arranged to create the appearance of a line.

An individual pixel.

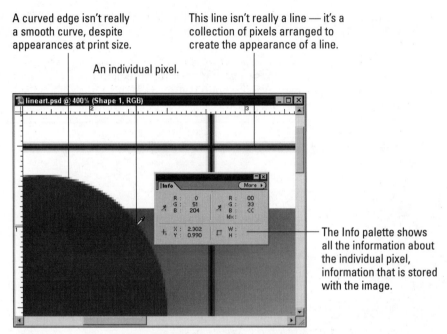

The Info palette shows all the information about the individual pixel, information that is stored with the image.

Figure 16-4: Tiny dots named pixels make up a bitmap image.

A vector image, on the other hand, is made up of mathematical information and measurements — the length of a line, the width of a box, the angle of a curve, and so on. Color information is also stored, but not in terms of pixels. Rather, the color information is stored relative to the size of the area filled with color, which reflects how much color is required to fill shapes or to color a line. Vector images, such as Adobe Illustrator images (.AI), can only be edited in graphics applications that support the vector file formats and the information stored in a vector image.

You can open a vector image in Elements, but it is converted to a bitmap image upon opening through a process known as *rasterizing*, which converts the vector data to a bitmap file. The same holds true for many other (but not all) graphics applications that create bitmap images. Figure 16-5 shows a vector image — not the lack of distinct pixels (even at a high zoom percentage). This is why vector images are often preferred for print work, because the lines, shapes, and curves are all crisp and clean — no jagged edges made up of pixels filling a shape.

A smooth curve with no jagged edge

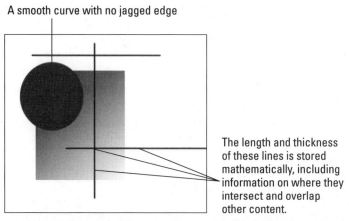

The length and thickness of these lines is stored mathematically, including information on where they intersect and overlap other content.

Figure 16-5: A vector image relies on mathematical information to store the fine details that determine the image content as displayed on-screen or printed on paper.

So what are your file format options when saving a file in Elements? Table 16-1 identifies common formats; all of them are available in the Elements Save As dialog box's Format drop-down list:

Table 16-1 Graphic File Formats		
Extension	**Format Name/Meaning**	**Notes/Additional Information**
BMP	Bitmap	This is the standard Windows image format, the default format for images created in Windows' Paint program.
EPS	Encapsulated PostScript	Use this format if your image is to be printed on a PostScript printer.
GIF	Graphics Interchange Format	Created by CompuServe to facilitate the transfer of images via the internet. The GIF format is best for simple images with solid colors and no photographic content and is one of three images considered "Web safe." Read more about GIF and its companion formats in Chapter 18.
JPG	Joint Photographic Experts Group	Created to support photographic content for the Web. Best used for complex images with a lot of colors in them and for photos. Not good for simple line art and images with large blocks of solid color.

Continued

	Table 16-1 (continued)	
Extension	**Format Name/Meaning**	**Notes/Additional Information**
PCX		This is a common bitmap format, acceptable in just about any bitmap application and in a variety of computer platforms.
PDF	Portable Document Format	Created by products such as Adobe Acrobat, this format turns images with text and/or graphics into easily transported, virtually universally acceptable files for viewing and printing. The format supports both vector and bitmap graphics.
PNG	Portable Network Graphics	This format is considered the "copyright-free" version of GIF, although you'd have to search a long time to find someone whose use of the GIF format was considered a copyright infringement (on CompuServe's patent on the format). It's considered a Web-safe format for line art and images with large areas of solid colors (where you'd typically use the GIF format), but PNG is not universally accepted by older Web browsers.
PSD	Photoshop Document	Photoshop and Elements' default file format
TIF (TIFF)	Tagged Image File Format	This format is great for transferring images between applications and computer platforms. Especially popular where Mac and PC users must share images.

Tip Not all bitmap formats support layers. PSD and TIF do, and you are prompted about whether or not you want to save your layers when saving a file in TIF format. Including layers increases file size, but if you don't include them, you lose the layers and the ability to edit portions of the image separately.

Resaving and Creating Multiple Image Versions

After you save your image — be it one you created in Elements or an existing image of any format that you opened and then edited in Elements, you can save it again. Of course, you should resave your image every few minutes while you're working, using the Ctrl + S shortcut for expediency, or by choosing File➪Save. Either technique updates the stored version of your file to include your latest changes and potentially save you hours of work redoing your edits or recreating content.

If you want to save your file with a different name than the one under which it is already saved, you can choose the File⇨Save As command. This command performs identically to the File⇨Save command on a first-time save—both commands, at that point, open the Save As dialog box because the file doesn't have a name yet. After a file has already been saved, however, the File⇨Save command won't open a dialog box—it simply updates the existing file. If you want to see the Save As dialog box again, you must choose File⇨Save As or use the Shift + Ctrl + S shortcut.

When you do resave your file and reopen the Save As dialog box, you can change the file name and/or choose a different place to store the file—a different drive or a different folder within the current drive. When you click Save to complete the resaving process, the previous version of the image is closed, leaving only this currently-renamed version open. This process can be invaluable if you want to maintain different versions of the same image. All you have to do is create a new name for each version and you're set. Each version is distinct, containing only the content that existed at the time it was last saved under its current name.

For example, Figures 16-6, 16-7, and 16-8 all started out the same, but each version has something different added. So what is the purpose of saving a series of images such as this? So you can go back to the basics as needed, and so that different versions of an image perhaps suited to different purposes, can be maintained without affecting each other.

Figure 16-6: The first version is simply a scanned photo with no editing or additional content included.

Figure 16-7: Here, I add some text to the image on a Type layer.

Figure 16-8: In the last version of the file, the text and photo are there, along with a frame, created using the Effects palette.

Now, of course, you can have one version of a file with the variable content on separate layers that can be hidden before printing a file or before saving the file for the Web. On the other hand, by maintaining separate versions, you don't have to worry about accidentally including unwanted content in a printout or when a file is optimized for the Web, and you can quickly go back to any version and work with that or share it with a coworker, all the while keeping the other versions intact and out of potential harm's way.

Saving Your Image As a PDF

If you want to share your Elements images with others and not have to worry whether or not they have Elements or some other graphics application, you can save your image in PDF format. This type of file, which can be opened by anyone with Adobe Acrobat Reader (a free application, available through the Adobe Web site, `www.adobe.com/products/acrobat/readstep2.html`), is a great choice for images, documents containing images, or documents that consist solely of text. Figure 16-9 shows a PDF file created from a Photoshop Elements image.

For Photoshop and Elements images, the PDF format is easy to use, and it couldn't be simpler to turn any Elements image into a PDF file.

STEPS: Saving an Elements Image As a PDF File

1. With the image that you want to save as a PDF open and active, choose File ➪ Save As.

2. From the Format drop-down list, choose Photoshop PDF from the list.

3. Use the File Name box, type a name for the file. If you want to keep the name that the file had in its PSD or other graphic file format, simply leave that name in place — the PDF extension is added to the name automatically (when you complete the save process).

4. Choose where to store the PDF file. You can save it to any drive or folder you desire, as long as there's room for the file, which you can establish by checking your desired location before beginning the saving procedure.

5. As needed, choose whether or not to save the image layers. To keep them, click inside the Layers check box to place a check there. Your alternative is to save the file as a copy, which adds the word "copy" to the file name, thus leaving any previously saved PDF intact with the original file name.

6. Click Save to save the file. A PDF Options dialog box appears (see Figure 16-10), through which you can establish the following options:

   - **Encoding method.** ZIP or JPG are your choices. If you choose JPG, you can set the quality of the image — the higher the number (set by typing a number or dragging the slider), the larger the resulting file will be.

   - **Turn on Image Interpolation.** This option allows a low-resolution image to print with anti-aliasing (smoothing of edges) in effect.

7. Click OK in the PDF Options dialog box, and your PDF file is created.

To check the quality of your PDF file, go to Windows Explorer or My Computer (or to your Desktop, if that's where you saved the file) and double-click the PDF file you created. Adobe Acrobat or Adobe Acrobat Reader (depending on which one you have installed and set as the first choice for opening PDF files) opens and displays your PDF file.

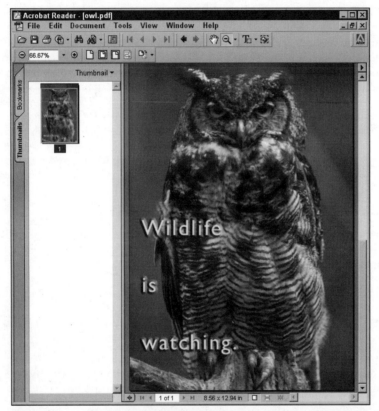

Figure 16-9: Other than the application in which the file is opened and displayed, you can't tell your original PSD file from this PDF version.

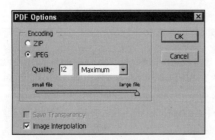

Figure 16-10: Set the rest of your PDF options in order to complete the saving process.

Creating a PDF Slideshow

A PDF Slideshow is a great tool for sharing a series of images with anyone — friends, family, a client, a prospective customer — anyone you want to show pictures to but don't know if they have Elements or any kind of slideshow viewer. As long as they have Adobe Acrobat Reader (and most people do) or are willing to download the free program, they are able to see your images, one by one, in a self-paced show.

To create a PDF slideshow, follow this simple procedure — you can prepare for it by either opening all the images you want to include in the slideshow, or making sure you know where they all are so that you can find them during the slide-show creation process.

STEPS: Create a PDF Slideshow of a Series of Elements Images

1. Choose File➪Automation Tools➪PDF Slideshow. The PDF Slideshow dialog box opens, as shown in Figure 16-11.

Figure 16-11: Use the PDF Slideshow dialog box to set up the slideshow and choose the images to include in it.

2. If you elected to open all of the images you want to include in the slideshow, click the Add Open Files check box. If not, or if you have images open that should not be included in the show, click the Browse button.

3. In the resulting Open dialog box (shown in Figure 16-12), navigate to the drive and folder containing the images you want to use in the show.

Figure 16-12: Locate the files you want to show.

4. Select the file/s you want to include in the slideshow. If there is more than one you want to include in the same folder, use the Ctrl key to gather the files, clicking on each one until all the desired files are selected.

5. Click Open to add the selected files to the PDF Slideshow dialog box, where they then appear in a list, as shown in Figure 16-13.

6. Repeat Steps 3, 4, and 5 for any images that are in a different folder than that which you chose the first time you clicked the Browse button.

7. If you didn't select your files in the order in which you want them to appear in the slideshow, you can rearrange them. Simply click and drag on any image in the list, dragging up to move it forward in the list, or down to make it appear later in the show. A horizontal bar, shown in Figure 16-14, accompanies the image listing as you drag it.

8. After all the files you want to include are listed in the dialog box, click the Choose button in the Output File section of the dialog box. This opens a Save dialog box (see Figure 16-15), through which you can choose an existing PDF slideshow file, or type the name of a new file (which you create in the next step).

Figure 16-13: Your selected files appear in a list that includes their path and file name.

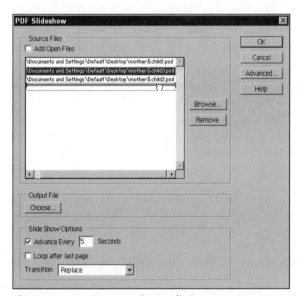

Figure 16-14: Drag your image listings to rearrange their order in the slideshow.

Figure 16-15: Establish an output file — the actual slideshow file, in PDF format — for your series of images.

9. Type the name of the file (if it's a new file) and click Save.

10. Using the Slide Show Options section of the dialog box, determine the delay between slides (it's set to five seconds by default), and if desired, set the show to loop (begin again) each time the last slide displays for the allocated number of seconds.

11. Click the Transition drop-down list to choose from a list of animated effects that transition one slide into another. Figure 16-16 shows the list displayed in the dialog box.

12. Click OK to close the dialog box and create the slideshow.

Tip

If you click the Advanced button, you'll see the same dialog box that appears as the last step in saving a file as a standard PDF — you can choose a ZIP or JPG encoding method and set the quality if you opt for the JPG option. If you leave the Interpolation option on, you'll be able to improve the visual quality of any low-resolution images in your show.

To run the show, go to the location where you chose to store the output file and double-click the file. This opens the file, and the slideshow begins — with the images you choose, in the order you established, at the speed and with the animation Transition effect you selected. Figure 16-17 shows a slideshow in progress — it runs full-screen, with a black background. Figure 16-18 shows the Acrobat Reader view of the show, with the Thumbnails panel showing all the images in the show.

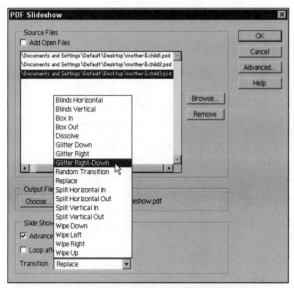

Figure 16-16: Choose a quick animation that segues from one slide to another during the show.

Figure 16-17: Share your images one at a time in an animated PDF slideshow.

Each image is a page within the PDF document.

Figure 16-18: After you finish watching the show, press Esc to return to the Acrobat Reader application window.

Attaching an Image to an E-Mail Message

When it comes to sharing images, e-mail has made it possible for people all over the world to go on vacation with loved ones, attend a wedding they couldn't get to, see a new baby just minutes after it was born, and entertain people with amusing and evocative images.

Typically, when you want to send a picture via e-mail, you use your e-mail program's Attach command, which enables you to choose and attach image files to your e-mail message, sending the files along with the e-mail to the intended recipient/s.

Through Photoshop Elements, you can accomplish this in one procedure — using the File⇨Attach to Email command, you can attach any saved file to an e-mail message, with Elements opening the e-mail application, opening a new message window, and attaching your image to it.

STEPS: Attaching an Image to an E-Mail Message

1. Be sure that the image you want to attach is open and active in the Elements workspace.

2. To save steps during this procedure, save the file in either JPG or GIF format, choosing a format based on the image content — choose JPG for photos and GIF for simple line art. You can also save the file in PSD format if you intend to edit it later.

3. Open the JPG or GIF version of the file and be sure it's the active open image in the Elements workspace.

4. Choose File⇨Attach to Email. A prompt appears, asking you to choose an e-mail profile. The Choose Profile dialog box appears in Figure 16-19.

Figure 16-19: Choose your e-mail application from the list of profiles. Only those applications installed on your computer appear in the list.

5. After you make a choice, a new message window appears, as shown in Figure 16-20. The image is attached, and the message window is ready for you to address the message, give it a subject, type a message, and send it.

If you typically keep your e-mail application open all day (or the entire time you're working on your computer), you may find the File⇨Attach to Email procedure through Elements to be less than convenient — unless, of course, you were already in Elements, working on the image you want to send. If you don't have Elements open, however, and have no need to edit the image before sending it, you may just as well use your e-mail application's Attach command in a new message window of your own and attach the image/s that way.

Tip   You read more about the JPG and GIF file formats and their uses on the Web in Chapter 18.

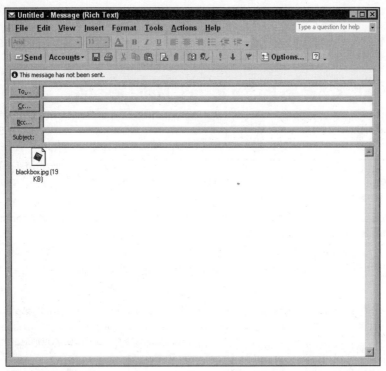

Figure 16-20: A new message window opens with your selected image already attached.

✦   ✦   ✦

Printing Your Artwork and Photographs

✦ ✦ ✦ ✦

In This Chapter

Understanding your printing options

Selecting a printer for the job

Previewing and setting up a print job

Printing your photos and original artwork

Using Elements' specialized print layout tools

✦ ✦ ✦ ✦

You scanned your photo or drew your own artwork, you edited the image, you applied special effects or filters, and now you're ready to create tangible evidence of all your hard work. If your image will be used on the Web, you can use the optimization techniques discussed in Chapter 18 to make sure the image looks great and loads quickly on your Web site.

Applying Your Artwork to Paper

If, on the other hand, your image is going to be printed, you have an entirely different set of concerns. Rather than worrying about file size (you don't want big files on the Web, because they take too long to load), you're going to be more concerned with the image quality—crisp edges, clean curves, clear details, accurate colors—all the details that printed output show. These aspects of the printed image involve several factors:

✦ **The image itself.** If your image was created at or is now set at a low resolution (lower than 300 pixels per inch), you may not like the printed output. You may see jagged edges on curves, *artifacts* (dots of random, unwanted color) along edges and where content in the image was resized, and the overall level of clarity and detail may not be very high. As discussed in earlier coverage on scanning, you should scan at a high resolution to get as much information into the image as possible, giving you more detail with which to work. If you're creating an image from scratch—painting or drawing it yourself—start with at least 300 ppi so that your content is as crisp and clean as possible, with as much detail and clarity as possible. Figure 17-1 shows you the New dialog box, with the Resolution field set to 300 ppi — the minimum you should have it set to for images that will be printed and that have to look great.

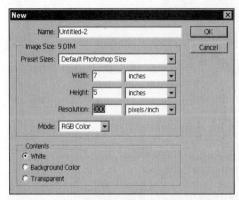

Figure 17-1: Choose File➪New to start a new image out on the right foot.

✦ **The printer you'll use to print out the image.** The printer, as you discover as you continue reading this chapter, can make or break your image. From inkjets to lasers to dye-sublimation printers to the printers that professional printing companies use, you have everything from the basics to the best at your disposal, one way or the other.

✦ **The paper you'll print on.** If you want the clearest, crispest, most detailed image possible, don't print on copier or plain inkjet paper. Always print on matte, satin, or photographic paper, in the brightest white you can find. This makes all the difference, as shown in Figures 17-2 and 17-3. In the first example, plain inkjet paper was used to print a photo. The same photo, with all the same resolution and other quality settings in place, was printed on glossy photo paper in the second example. The differences are obvious.

Why does the same photo look different if you print it on plain inkjet paper than it does on good photo paper? The porous nature of regular 20 lb. inkjet paper absorbs more of the ink, and this affects the reflective quality of the colors. Images will look darker, contrast will be lost, and overall quality will be diminished if you print on porous paper. If you print on glossy or matte photographic paper, a coating on the paper prevents absorption, so your photo's color and content really stand out, clearly, crisply, and in full detail.

Figure 17-2: Okay for a proof or rough draft, plain copier or inkjet paper doesn't allow your image to really shine.

Figure 17-3: Bright, white, glossy paper allows all of your image details to stand out.

Of course, you have different reasons to print out your artwork, and each one has different requirements in terms of quality. For example, if you're printing a copy of a photo to send to a friend who wasn't able to be at your bridal shower or birthday party, you probably don't care if it's the clearest, most beautiful photo you ever reproduced. On the other hand, if you've painstakingly restored a vintage photo and want to give the last known picture of your great grandfather to your great grandmother, you want it to be an absolutely perfect printout. Here are some other printing needs and the quality you most likely desire for them:

✦ You need to create a suitable-for-framing version of a photo that was too small or too damaged to be framed before you edited it. If it will be given as a gift or displayed prominently, you want a great quality print.

✦ You want to create a backup print of a very precious photo in case something happens to the original. Another reason for the best quality printout you can achieve with your printer or by perhaps borrowing someone else's or going to a professional printer.

✦ You're building a portfolio of your digital artwork, and you need a printed copy to show to prospective employers or clients. Of course, you want to put your best foot forward here, right?

✦ You require a *proof,* or printed image to be submitted for approval by someone who can't view the image online. This can be more of an average printout, without every little detail clearly and cleanly applied to paper. You just want an okay or a general reaction to the image from a boss or coworker.

✦ You require a proof and viewing the file electronically won't provide the information about print quality that is needed. Unless there is information in the image itself—text or numbers that have to be legible, someone's face that you need to be able to recognize—you can produce an average-quality printout for a job like this.

✦ Your photo ends up in printed marketing materials, such as ads, brochures, or flyers and you need to create camera-ready art for a professional printer to use in creating the finished materials. Here you want the best. For camera-ready images, you want to provide a pristine, top-quality image that the professional printer will use to reproduce your image. If your image will end up on marketing materials, you want to make the best impression you can, and a less-than-perfect image won't do that.

Tip   Because computer monitors aren't capable of displaying colors exactly as they'll appear in print, you want to print at least one "in progress" version of your image so that you can check for color, clarity, and other qualities before you commit the final version to a sheet of expensive photo paper. You can purchase lower-priced photo paper for your test prints (as printing on plain copier/inkjet paper may compound any color misconceptions), and then use the top-quality paper for your final output.

Choosing the Right Printer

When you go to print your image, you may have more than the paper to consider. As most of us only have one or maybe two types of printers, you may need to make use of a friend or colleague's printer, or take your print job (electronically) to a professional printer. To help clarify your printing options in terms of the printers you can obtain yourself or in all likelihood borrow from a friend, review Table 17-1.

Table 17-1		
Printer Comparison		
Type of Printer	*Price Range*	*Notes/Additional Information*
Inkjet	$75 - $350	Color inkjet printers can create near photo-quality images, assuming you use good quality photo paper for the output and make sure your ink cartridges aren't getting low on ink (colors can be distorted and blacks can be less dense if you're running low on ink). Price isn't necessarily an indication of print quality, and you should print a test page before making a purchase, or go on the recommendation of someone who owns the same model.
Laser	$600 - $3000	Color laser printers are more expensive than inkjets and black and white laser printers. If you're creating camera-ready art for very important, detailed publications, you probably want a color laser (assuming the images are in color) rather than an inkjet, but the image quality is not as good as what you'd get with a dye-sublimation printer.
Dye-Sublimation	$600 - $1000	Dye-sublimation printers provide an excellent image, especially for color photos. The subtle results are great for professional designers, artists, and photographers. The cost of the printer itself may be prohibitive for small businesses and home users, but the lower-priced models may be within your budget, and may be well worth the price depending on your needs.

Tip   Not sure if you should invest in a better printer (of any type) than the one you have now? Consider what you're printing and what you stand to gain from being able to generate great printed images. If the images will be used for marketing materials, you stand to gain customers who are impressed with your obvious concern for quality, especially if you're selling your services as a designer or in another creative pursuit. If the images are literally intended to be works of art — restored vintage or professional photos, items that will be displayed or given as gifts — consider what you'll save on having a professional create the printouts.

Understanding the Inkjet Printer

The name "inkjet" gives you an idea of how the inkjet printer works — assuming that the word "jet" makes you think of the water jets on a whirlpool bath. The way it works is rather simple — ink cartridges are vibrated by piezoelectric crystals (the crystals are sandwiched between two electrodes, which make them dance). Different levels of voltage cause the crystals to vibrate differently, adjusting the colors and amount of color sprayed through a nozzle onto the paper. The paper onto which the ink is sprayed often has more impact on the print quality than the printer itself does — if the paper absorbs most of the ink, much of the detail and clarity is lost. If the paper is coated and doesn't absorb all of the ink, the image will be crisper, cleaner, and have a much better overall appearance.

Looking Inside a Laser Printer

Laser printers work very much like photocopiers. A laser beam is aimed at a photo-electric belt or drum, building up an electrical charge. This happens four times, once each for the four colors used to make all the colors in your image — cyan, magenta, yellow, and black. The electric charge makes the colored toners stick to the belt, where it is then transferred to the drum, along which the paper rolls as it moves through the printer. The toner is transferred to the paper, and then either pressure, heat, or both are used to make the toner stick to the paper.

Working with Dye-Sublimation Printers

Here, the name of the printer doesn't really tell you very much about the way the printer works. Despite their enigmatic name, dye-sublimation printers work in a rel-atively straightforward way — a strip of plastic film, called a transfer ribbon, is coated with cyan, magenta, and yellow dye. When a print job is sent to the printer, a ther-mal print head heats up the page-sized (8.5" × 11") panel of plastic transfer ribbon and through variations in temperature across the expanse of the ribbon, controls the colors and amounts of colors that are applied to the paper. Because the paper has a special coating on it, the dye sticks.

Tip   You can find paper that's conducive to all these printer types at any well-stocked stationery or office-supply store. You can also look online, searching, for example, for "dye-sublimation printer paper" or "laser paper." Online resources are often lower in price than "brick and mortar" stores, although you have to pay to have the paper shipped to you.

Printing Your Image

When you're ready to commit your image to paper, you want to issue one of two commands to Elements:

✦ File➪Print

✦ File➪Print Preview

I recommend the latter approach, as you can go from previewing your image (and making changes to the printout itself) to the actual printing of the image, so no significant extra work is involved if you preview the image first. Previewing the image is always the smart move, unless you already printed the image once and made no changes to the image, the printer settings, or the paper since that last printout. If you have made any changes to any of those aspects of the print job, it's best to preview again, just to be sure nothing undesirable is about to end up on paper.

Previewing Your Printout

If you follow my advice and use the File➪Print Preview path, you'll enjoy some benefits — being sure that your image fits on the paper onto which you intend to print, and the ability to add helpful items, such as crop marks to the image. These marks can be very helpful if you'll be trimming the images after printing, or if you're giving the printed image to a professional printing company for reproduction from your camera-ready original. Figure 17-4 shows the Print Preview dialog box, ready to take you from preview to printing in just a few clicks.

Scaling the Print Job

If the print preview reveals that your Image is larger than the paper you're going to print on, you have two options, only one of which you find within the Print Preview dialog box:

✦ Exit Print Preview and go to the Image Size dialog box (choose Image➪ Resize➪Image Size) and change the dimensions of the image, as shown in Figure 17-5.

✦ Use the Scaled Print Size options in the Print Preview dialog box. Unlike the previous option, these adjustments don't affect the image — only its printed size on this particular print job.

Tip

Not sure if you want to make permanent changes to the image or just scale it for this one printout? Consider the future for this image. If you'll be printing it again and again, it might be easier to reduce the image height and width (be sure to maintain current width-height proportions) through the Image Size dialog box so that you never have to worry about the image fitting on the paper you typically use again. This can be a helpful approach if you won't be the only person printing the image, especially if the other user/s aren't as well-versed in Elements and won't know about the scaling options or if they might not do a print preview first.

The white box represents the printable area of the paper that your printer is currently set to use.

Tools for changing the placement of the image on the paper

The image to be printed

Use these options for adjusting the size of the printout.

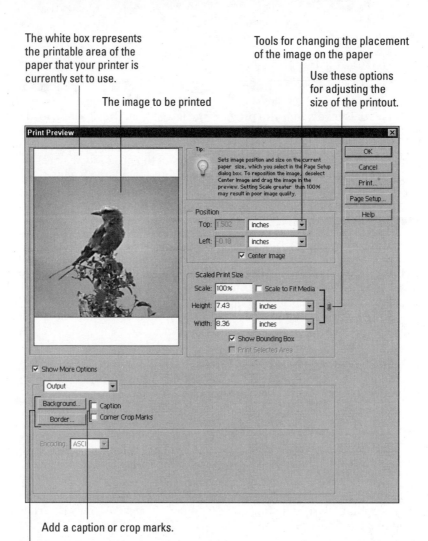

Add a caption or crop marks.

Click these buttons to apply a colored background (outside the image itself) or a border.

Figure 17-4: A preview is always a good idea before you potentially waste expensive photo paper.

Reducing image dimensions will also reduce file size.

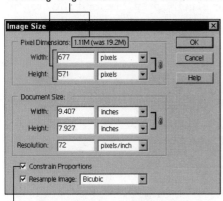

Keep the Constrain Proportions option on
so your image width-to-height ratio is not
changed as you shrink the image.

Figure 17-5: Don't raise the bridge, lower the river.
If your image is too big for the paper, you can shrink
the image so that it will fit on the paper now and in
any future printouts.

If you do decide to use the scaling tools, here's how it's done:

STEPS: Scaling an Image to fit on Letter Size Paper

1. With the image you want to print open and active in the Elements workspace,
   choose File⇨Print Preview. The Print Preview dialog box opens.

2. Using the Scaled Print Size section of the dialog box, choose how you want to
   resize the printed version of the image:

   • Enter a percentage of the actual size into the Scale field.

   • Choose Scale to Fit Media, which resizes the image to fit on the paper
     that Elements sees as the current paper size.

   • Enter a specific height and width for the print job (note the chain icon
     which indicates that entries in the Scale field adjust the Height and
     Width fields, and vice versa).

• Use the tiny handles (see Figure 17-6) on the corners of the image (visible only if the image is smaller than the printable area) and drag outward to increase the printed size of the image, or inward to make the printed size smaller.

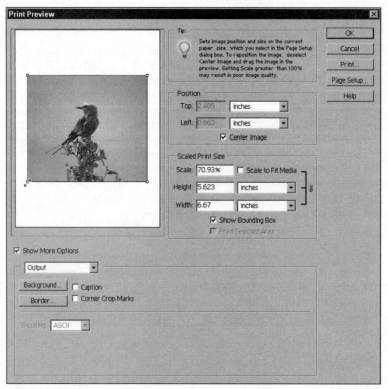

Figure 17-6: Make manual adjustments to the print size by dragging with your mouse.

Tip

The Show Bounding Box option must be on in order to see and use the handles on the previewed image.

3. Enter the scaling information that works for your image. Allow for half an inch on all four sides of the paper — so if your image is currently 9" × 12", you will have to reduce it so that it's no larger than 8" × 10.5" to print on letter size paper.

4. If you have no other changes to make — adding crop marks or a caption, which are discussed in the next section of this chapter, click Print. This opens the Print dialog box, through which you can establish settings for the printer to make sure you get the quality of printout that you need, and then finally print out your image.

Positioning the Print on the Page

If your image isn't the exact same size as the printable area of the paper (in either its width, height, or both), you can reposition the image on the paper. By default, it's set to print in the center of the paper, but you may want to make it print at the top or bottom of the paper to allow for other content you may adhere to the page (in a scrapbook, for example), or to hug the right or left side of the paper to make room for binding.

Tip

Be sure your printer is properly set up before executing any very important print job—the proper setup will allow Elements to work effectively with your printer, and you'll know that the image will be exactly where you want it on the page. Most printers come with an interface you can invoke to set up the printer's color, darkness, and proper image positioning. It's also a good idea to make sure you have the latest drivers for your printer, so that it will work with the latest operating systems, computer hardware, and other applications. You can usually download these driver files from the printer manufacturer's website.

To change the position of the printout on the paper, follow this quick procedure:

STEPS: Changing the Print Position of Your Image on the Paper

1. In the Print Preview dialog box, move to the Position section of the dialog box and turn off the Center Image option (click to remove the check mark), which is on by default.

2. Note that the image doesn't move within the preview box, but now the Top and Left measurement fields are available.

3. Enter measurements into one or both of the boxes that position your image at the desired location on the paper. For example, to move the image up on the page, reduce the Top setting. To make the image move closer to the right (to allow for left-sided binding), increase the number in the Left box, as shown in Figure 17-7. If it's currently a negative number, be sure your number is positive, or the image will move closer to the left side of the paper.

Tip

If you are framing the image and will have a mat around the image within the frame, allow for the size of the mat and the portion of the image that it may have to overlap. For example, if you'll be placing your printed image in a 5 × 7 frame with a mat that comes in from the edge of the frame by an inch all around, your image must fit within a 4 × 6 space, with a tiny amount of the image being under the mat—say .10 to .25 of an inch in excess of 4 × 6. Adjust the size of the printed image accordingly, using the Scaled Print Size options, and be sure not to position the printed image so close to any edge of the paper so as to not allow for that .10 to .25 of an inch you need for your framing needs.

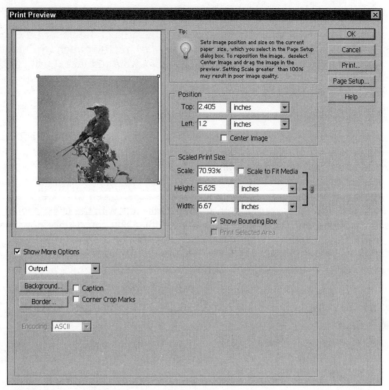

Figure 17-7: Reposition your image on the paper to allow for binding or any other requirements you may have for the printed image.

Applying Crop Marks, Captions, and Borders

While you're still in the Print Preview dialog box, you have some additional options for your printed image. If it's not already checked, click in the Show More Options check box to expand the dialog box. This expansion includes an Output field, two buttons, and two check boxes. Your options include:

✦ **Background.** Click this button to open the Color Picker and select a color for the background of the printout. This color fills the printable area of the paper, outside of the image itself, as shown in Figure 17-8.

✦ **Border.** Click this button to open the Border dialog box (see Figure 17-9), through which you can establish the width of a border that are adding to the printout. The border does not become part of the image itself — it will only appear in this particular printout.

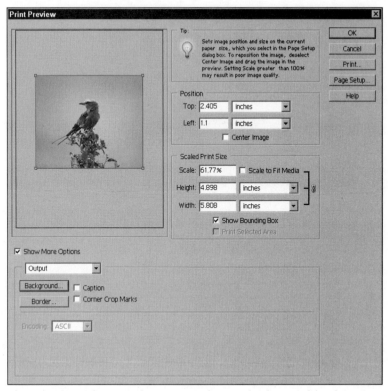

Figure 17-8: Pick a complementary color as a background for the printed image.

Figure 17-9: A border can create a nice finish for an image, or it can be a problem, especially if you're framing the image or will be cropping to the exact edges of the image.

✦ **Click in the Caption check box to print any caption text entered in the File Info dialog box.** Whatever caption you establish prints by default in 9 point Helvetica, or the closest font to that if you don't have Helvetica on your computer. Helvetica is a sans serif font that looks very much like Arial. To set up a caption, choose File➪File Info and enter the caption text you want into the Caption field (see Figure 17-10).

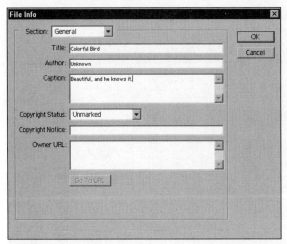

Figure 17-10: Create a caption for your image in the File Info dialog box.

✦ **Click the Corner Crop Marks option and turn it on.** This option is off by default, but crop marks can help you use a paper cutter to crop to the edges of the image after printing, or to help a professional printer position the image for reproduction or mass cropping (such printers typically have hydraulic paper cutters that can cut a huge stack of pages all at once). Figure 17-11 shows the Print Preview dialog box with an image that now includes crop marks on its corners.

Note   The Output field in the Show More Options area of the dialog box is actually a drop-down list, and it offers Color Management as its alternative. If you choose this, the dialog box expands further to offer you another drop-down list (Profile) through which you can choose from several monitor settings (as different monitors display colors differently). Typically, you leave this set to Same As Source, which means that the image prints based on your current monitor settings, with the color settings you established for the image when you scanned or created it from scratch.

Corner crop marks run vertically and horizontally on all four corners.

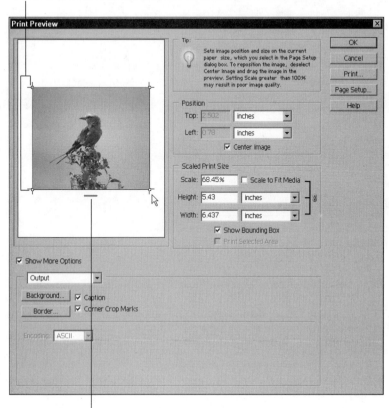

This small mark represents the location of the caption when this image is printed.

Figure 17-11: If you'll be cropping (cutting away) the edges of the paper to leave only the printed image, turn on Corner Crop Marks.

Working with Page Setup

You have times when you need to step out of the Print Preview process to make an adjustment to your image setup. This isn't the same as exiting Print Preview to resize the image — rather, you're opening the Page Setup dialog box while the Print Preview dialog box remains open, and you're simply changing the way the image relates to the paper. Figure 17-12 shows the Page Setup dialog box, which you open by clicking the Page Setup button on the right side of the Print Preview dialog box.

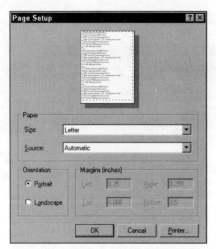

Figure 17-12: Change the settings for your page size and orientation with Page Setup.

In the Page Setup dialog box, you can make the following adjustments:

✦ **Choose a new Paper Size.** Letter is the default, but you have several options to choose from, as shown in Figure 17-13.

✦ **Enter a new Paper Source.** This is based on your printer's defaults and capabilities. If your printer has several trays from which to choose, all of them will be listed. If it only has one tray, Automatic will be selected and is your only option.

✦ **Change the Orientation of the paper,** switching from the default Portrait to Landscape or vice versa (if you already changed to Landscape and now Portrait is required). You switch to Landscape, for example, if your image is wider than 8.5".

Tip   Click the Printer button to open a Printer dialog box that shows you which printer you're set to send the print job to. This dialog box also contains a Properties button, which opens a dialog box that enables you to tell your printer what kind of paper you're printing on and what quality of print job (draft, normal, better, best) you're looking for. The options in this latter dialog box vary by your printer — the dialog box is typically a product of the printer software, provided by your printer's manufacturer.

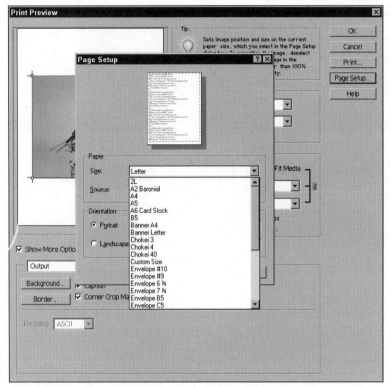

Figure 17-13: Find U.S., European, and Asian paper sizes from which to choose.

Setting the Print Quality

Whether you open the Properties dialog box for your printer through the Page Setup dialog box or by clicking the Properties button in the Print dialog box (see Figure 17-14), you're faced with a dialog box that enables you to set the quality of the current print job and to inform the printer of any changes in paper quality — going from plain copier/inkjet paper, for example, to glossy photo paper or card stock.

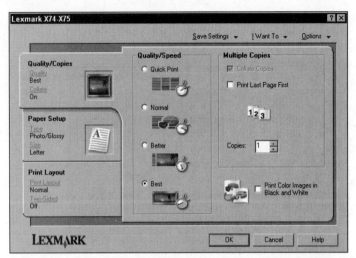

Figure 17-14: Tell your printer what you want and what you expect in terms of the quality of the print job it's about to do for you.

The dialog box shown in Figure 17-14 is one that "comes with" the Lexmark 75 printer, which is the author's default printer. Your printer may be from a different manufacturer, and therefore, the Properties dialog box will be different. The basic options are the same, however. You can choose from two or more print quality settings, and you can choose from a variety of types of paper. Your choices for paper type affect how the printer applies ink (if it's an inkjet printer) to the paper—the printer changes its settings internally to accommodate glossy versus plain paper, or to move thicker paper through its print and paper-handling mechanism. Note that the author's particular printer also does scanning, copying, and faxing, so those other options are visible as well. If your printer only prints, you won't see these options or any variations thereof.

Printing the Image

After you have all your print settings in place—the size of the image, the quality of the print job, the paper size and type you're using—it's time to print the image. Your print method varies based on where you are in the process. If you're in the Print Preview dialog box, click the Print button to open the Print dialog box. If you didn't do a preview first or have closed that dialog box, you can choose File⇨Print and your settings from within Print Preview (and Page Setup, if you went to that dialog box) should still be in place if you haven't exited Elements or opened any new images in the time since you closed the Print Preview dialog box.

In any case, when you tell Elements you're ready to print, the Print dialog box opens, as shown in Figure 17-15. Through this dialog box you can tell Elements how many copies of the image to print, what portions of the image to print (particular pages or just a selection from within the image), and you can switch to a different printer (if you're attached to more than one directly or via a network). Again, too, you can click the Properties button to access the aforementioned settings for your particular printer.

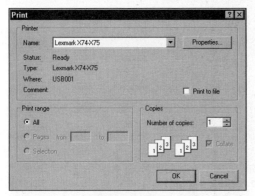

Figure 17-15: Ready to print? Tell Elements how many copies you want and then click OK.

Tip
The Print to File option creates a file that when double-clicked later, sends your image to the selected printer. You can do this without opening Elements and it is typically done when you're not attached to a printer now but will be later.

Choosing a Print Layout

While most of your printing will consist of a single image on a single sheet of paper, Elements doesn't restrict you to that. Through the File➪Print Layouts command, you can access tools for printing a *contact sheet,* which is a sheet of thumbnails of many different images (see Figure 17-16), traditionally used for selecting an image or images to use for publication. You can also use Elements' Picture Package, which creates a page filled with repetitions of a single image — similar to the proof sheets that you get from a portrait photographer, as shown in Figure 17-17.

Figure 17-16: Print several images out on a contact sheet to help you or a team of designers select the image you'll use for a print or Web publication.

Printing a Contact Sheet

When you print a contact sheet, you may need to do a little work in advance. The contact sheet feature assumes that all of your images that you want to include on the contact sheet are in the same folder or within the subfolders of a single folder. For example, if you have a "pictures" folder with subfolders under it, such as "family photos," "vintage scans," and "artwork," you can create a contact sheet from the main folder (pictures) all by itself, or you can make one from all the images in the main folder plus its subfolders.

Therefore, to prepare for printing the contact sheet, you need to either create such a folder/subfolder structure, or move all of the images you want to include in the contact sheet into one folder (and you can choose, therefore, not to include images in the subfolders, if there are any). Beyond that, there isn't much else you have to do — just follow this simple procedure to create the contact sheet, print it, and then use it to make your image selections.

Figure 17-17: Choose from a variety of sizes of the same image on a Picture Package printout.

STEPS: Printing a Contact Sheet

1. Choose File⇨Print Layouts⇨Contact Sheet. The Contact Sheet dialog box opens, as shown in Figure 17-18.

2. Click the Browse button to select the folder that contains the images you want to include on the contact sheet. The Browse for Folder dialog box opens, as shown in Figure 17-19.

3. As desired, leave the Include All Subfolders check box checked (it's on by default) so that any images filed in folders within your main folder are also included.

4. Using the Document section of the Contact Sheet dialog box, choose the size of the paper, the resolution of the images as they'll print on the page, and whether or not to print in grayscale or in color.

5. Use the Thumbnails section of the dialog box to establish the layout of the thumbnail images. You can determine the number of columns and rows, and what order the images appear in. The preview on the right side of the dialog box changes if you alter the number of rows and/or columns, so you can see the overall change in layout.

Set up the contact sheet's dimensions here.

View a preview of the layout here.

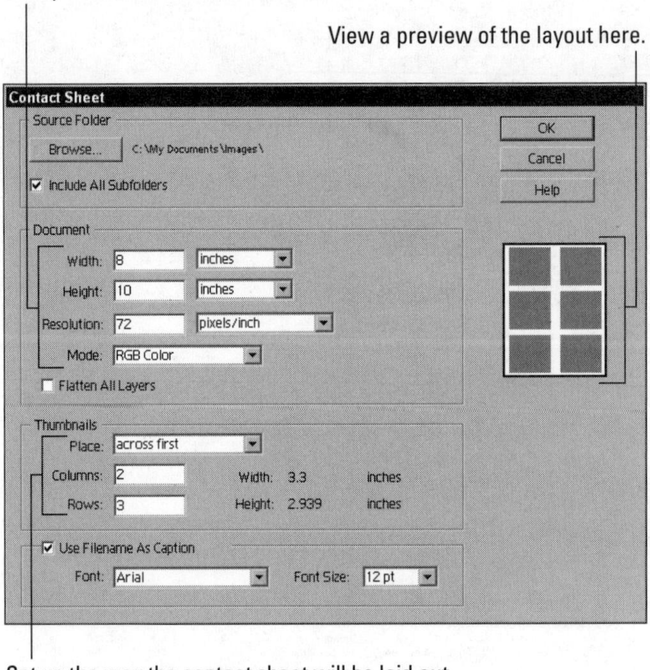

Set up the way the contact sheet will be laid out.

Figure 17-18: You find everything you need to create a contact sheet in this single dialog box.

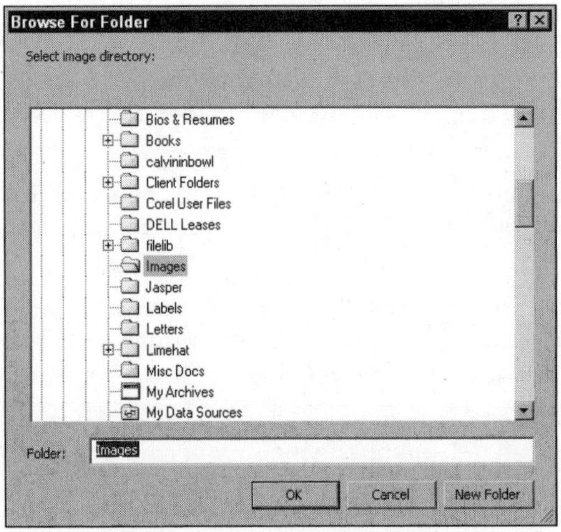

Figure 17-19: Use the expandable folder tree to find and select the folder containing the images you want.

Tip   The option to Flatten Layers pertains to the Picture Package document — not to the images you're placing in it. If you turn this default setting off, you increase the size of the Picture Package file, which may adversely affect your ability to send it as an e-mail attachment (most e-mail service providers only allow attachments of 2MB or less).

6. If you want the file names for each of the images to be included (placed under the images, like a caption), select Use Filename as Caption.

7. If you want to change the font and size of the caption text, use the Font and Font Size drop-down lists to make those changes.

8. Click OK to create the contact sheet.

As soon as you click OK, Elements goes to work. The images you selected (by selecting the folder/s containing them) open one by one, and they're added as thumbnails to a new image. You can see the Layers palette grow, layer by layer, with each image. Figure 17-20 shows the Layers palette for a contact sheet that contains six images.

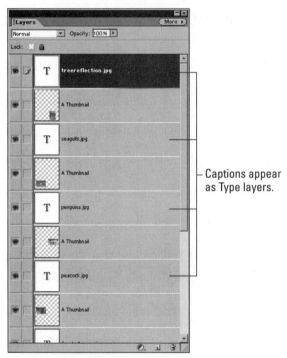

Captions appear as Type layers.

Figure 17-20: Each thumbnail in your contact sheet is on its own layer.

If you select a folder that contains many images, the contact sheet document will be multiple pages in length — enough pages to house a thumbnail for each image, using the layout (number of rows and columns) you specified. The documents are named Contact Sheet-001, 002, and so on, and they can be printed individually.

Using Picture Package

Whether your image is a school picture, a wedding portrait, or even a simple image of one of your pets or a shot taken on vacation, you can create a set of various sizes of the image — from a 5 × 7 portrait size to tiny wallet-size images, all printed on a single sheet of paper. After the sheet is printed, you can use a paper cutter to cut out individual images and strips of smaller images.

To create a Picture Package, follow this procedure — you should know in advance where the image you want to use is located on your computer, of course, but just to speed the process of selecting it. Unlike the contact sheet feature, there's no need to move images around within folders, as you're only printing a single image.

STEPS: Creating a Picture Package

1. Choose File⇨Print Layouts⇨Picture Package. This opens the Picture Package dialog box, shown in Figure 17-21.

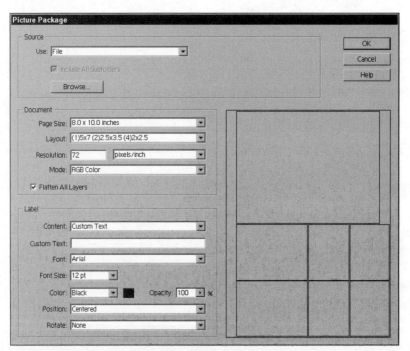

Figure 17-21: The Picture Package dialog box enables you to select the image you want to package and to set up the image sizes and layout on the page.

2. If the image you want to use is already open and on-screen, choose Frontmost Document (assuming your image was also the active image when you opened the Picture Package dialog box). If you don't have the image open, click Browse to find it.

3. Locate the image you want to use, click on it, and then click the Open button in the Select an Image File dialog box. You can also double-click the desired file in the dialog box to select the file and close the dialog box in one step.

4. To add another image to the package, click on one of the images in the preview (see Figure 17-22) to reopen the Select an Image File dialog box. Select an image, and it replaces the one you clicked on in the Preview.

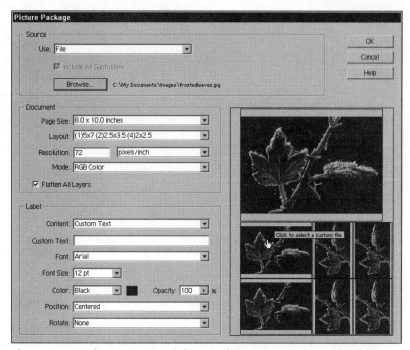

Figure 17-22: The image you click on in the preview is the image that is replaced by the next image you select.

5. Back in the Picture Package dialog box, establish your Document settings — choose a page size, set the layout for the images (see your choices in Figure 17-23), and choose a resolution to establish print quality for the images. You can also choose a color mode for the package — typically, people use color, but grayscale is a nice choice, too.

Figure 17-23: Choose the dimensions and quantity of repetitions of your selected image from the Layout drop-down list.

6. Turn the Flatten Layers option off (it's on by default) if you want the Picture Package document to retain a layer for each of the images it contains. This does NOT affect the images themselves, just the Picture Package document.

7. Set up a Label for your Picture Package by clicking the Content drop-down list, shown in Figure 17-24. Depending on your selection, fill in the rest of the options beneath this field. If you choose Custom Text, that field becomes available.

8. Click OK to create the Picture Package. Elements creates a new document (see Figure 17-25) that contains multiple versions of the image/s you chose to include in the package. You can print the image and/or save it for future use.

Tip

You can use several images in a Picture Package, although it's not as common a choice. In the Picture Package dialog box, click the Use drop-down list (that displays "File" by default) and choose Folder. This activates the Include All Subfolders option, and now the dialog box behaves like the Contact Sheet dialog box in that you include images from a folder and all its subfolders. This then populates the package sheet with many images, rather than just one. You can also choose more than one image without using this aspect of the feature — just use the Ctrl key as you browse for a File and click on multiple images that you want to use in the package.

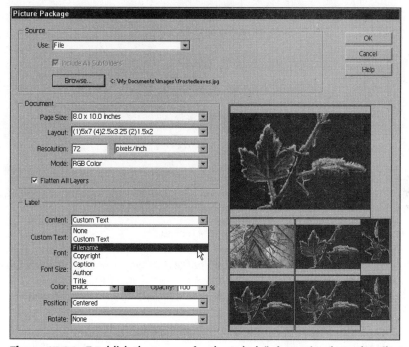

Figure 17-24: Establish the source for the Label (information from the File↪ File Info dialog box) and set the font, size, color, and position for the text.

Because Flatten Layers was left on, there is just one
layer for all the images included in the package.

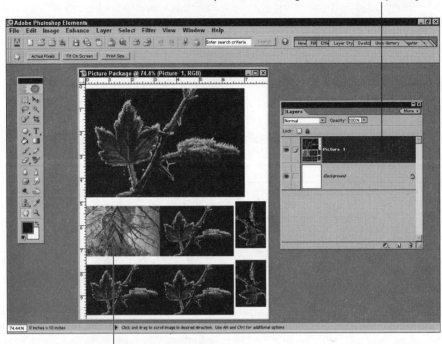

The single document contains two images, one repeated
several times, and a single image that appears only once.

Figure 17-25: After printed, your picture package becomes several images of varying sizes, suitable for framing, carrying in your wallet, or putting in a locket.

Printing a Panoramic Picture with Photomerge

So you stood and took a series of three or four photos of a sunset or a beautiful horizon, and you want to place them side by side to create the illusion of a panorama shot — one of those wide images that shows the entire view from left to right. If your camera doesn't take panorama shots, you have to make do with multiple shots taken along the span of the panorama as you could see it by eye, and hope that the images line up after developed.

While it can't make up for shots that weren't taken at the same distance or vertical angle along the span of the panoramic view you wanted to capture, Elements can help you place the series of shots you took in one long strip, capturing the look of a single panoramic photo. This is done with Elements' Photomerge feature, which you find in the File menu by choosing File⇨Create Photomerge.

In the Photomerge dialog box (shown in Figure 17-26), you can select the images you want to incorporate into a single wide shot, and then in the next phase of the process, move the images around so that they line up from left to right, in the proper order, positioned so that continuous content — clouds, a shoreline, whatever started in one shot and continued in the next — looks truly continuous.

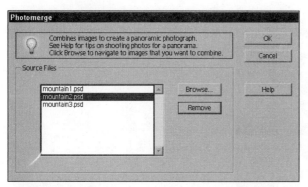

Figure 17-26: Start by clicking the Browse button to choose your series of images.

Tip   If you want, you can open the images before invoking the File➪Create Photomerge command, and as long as they're saved, you can jump right into the merge process without having to stop and Browse for the images. If you have an image open and don't want it to become part of the panorama, click once on it in the Photomerge dialog box and click the Remove button.

After selecting the images, you see them listed in the Photomerge dialog box. Click OK to move to the next step, wherein Elements gathers the images and then you can move the images around on-screen and make sure they line up properly. After seeing the images open in their original file names and then reopening them as Untitled images within the Elements workspace, the Photomerge window opens, as shown in Figure 17-27. If the images were all the same size, Elements will line them up, side-by-side, in the order you selected them. If they're not the same size, Elements places them in a single stack, and you can rearrange them as needed.

As soon as the images line up in as close to a seamless panoramic view as possible, you can use the Advanced Blending option (in the Composition Settings section of the dialog box) and Preview the effect — the dialog box doesn't change other than that you can see the merged images as one image, and you can't drag them around anymore. If there were any subtle gaps between images and their content, this feature can smooth them out. After previewing, choose Exit Preview to return the dialog box to a state wherein you can continue to edit your Photomerge.

Figure 17-27: If the images don't line up automatically, drag your images around to place them in the panoramic series you envisioned.

After the merged images look the way you like them to, click OK to return to the Elements workspace. An image file is now added, containing the panoramic shot you created (see Figure 17-28). You can print the image (perhaps in landscape mode, on legal size paper if it's a very wide image) on photographic paper, and you have that panoramic shot you wanted in the first place.

> **Tip**
>
> If you want to resize the image for available paper, choose Image⇨Resize⇨Image Size, or use the Print Preview dialog box to scale the image to the paper you're using for the final output of your merged images. Through specialty stationers, you should be able to special order larger sized specialized papers with glossy or matte coatings, making it possible to create a very large printout of your very wide image. Assuming the paper is only 8.5" wide, you can feed it through your inkjet printer with the page set to Landscape (choose File⇨Page Setup). If, of course, you need a printout that's not possible with your printer due to the print size or the quality required, consider using a professional printing company—including those who work online. Hiring a printing company will cost a bit more than doing it yourself, but you'll get the results you want.

Figure 17-28: Your multiple images are now smoothly combined into one wide shot, ready for preview, setup, and printing. Refer to the earlier sections of this chapter for details on this process.

✦   ✦   ✦

Turning Images into Web-Safe Graphics

✦ ✦ ✦ ✦

In This Chapter

Working with graphics on the Web

Saving images for use in Web pages

Understanding the optimization process

Animating your Elements images

✦ ✦ ✦ ✦

What is *Web optimization?* It's the process of trying to reduce an image to its smallest possible file size, while maintaining the highest level of clarity and fidelity.

Understanding the Web Optimization Process

Why optimize images? Because you're trying to create the best user experience for your visitors. Their browser downloads these images — consequently, the smaller the file size the faster the image appears in the browser window.

GIF? JPEG? PNG? Choosing the Right Web Graphic Format

At the time of this writing, three graphic file types are supported by Web browsers: These are the Graphics Interchange Format (GIF), the JPEG format (named for the Joint Photographic Experts Group), and the Portable Network Graphics format (PNG).

Graphic Interchange Format

When talking about image formats, it means talking about bits. *Bits* are the smallest unit of data computers work with, and the number of bits a format can devote to each pixel determines the maximum number of colors the format can display. *Bit depth* is the number of bits per pixel a format is capable of handling, and *color depth* is a maximum number of colors a format supports.

You can calculate a format's color depth by using a simple equation. Begin by taking the number of states a bit has (2, one state being on, the other being off) and raise that number to the power indicated by the format's bit depth.

GIF is an 8-bit format, making its color depth 2^8 — or $2 \times 2 \times 2 \times 2 \times 2 \times 2 \times 2 \times 2$ — which totals 256. Therefore, 256 are the maximum number of colors a GIF image can contain. This is the first of GIF's strengths — a low color depth helps ensure a low file size.

GIF's next major strength is how it compresses file data. GIF uses a compression method called LZW, after its creators Lempel, Ziv, and Welch. When turning an Elements image into a GIF file, this compression method exploits inefficiencies in the file's data structure, effectively removing unused space within the file. Consequently, no additional space is removed from the image, making LZW compression a "lossless" method.

If GIF only supports a maximum of 256 colors in an image, than it follows that you wouldn't try to optimize an image with thousands of colors into this format. GIF is best suited for images with a limited number of total colors, preferably with a high degree of contrast and where the edges at which two colors meet are sharply defined. Figure 18-1 shows a prime candidate for GIF optimization.

Figure 18-1: LZW compression favors images with larger zones of single colors.

JPEG File Interchange Format (JPEG)

Members of the Joint Photographic Experts Group represent a wide variety of companies and academic institutions throughout the worldwide that meet to discuss and create the standards for still image compression. The standards they developed for continuous tone images — images with an unlimited range of color or shades of gray — were used by C-Cube Microsystems to create the JPEG File Interchange Format.

JPEG has a bit depth of 24, giving it a color depth of 2^{24} or 16,777,215 colors. Its method of compression reduces file size by removing data from the image, capitalizing on the limitations of the human eye (the thing actually viewing these images).

Our eyes perceive minute changes in brightness better than they perceive equally minute changes in color. JPEG's compression method favors changes in brightness, discarding colors the eye won't necessarily miss, while still reproducing up to 16.7 million colors. Viewing the image on a 72 dpi monitor, we humans perceive an image we consider highly detailed.

Because JPEG compression removes data, it is referred to as a "lossy" compression method. The degree of compression is adjustable, allowing you to choose how much data is lost. The higher you compress the file, the smaller its size. The less you compress it, the better the image quality.

Images that are better handled using the JPEG format can be deduced from the format's name — photographs and photo-realistic images. Images with millions of colors or shades of gray, heavy degrees of gradation, where large zones of single colors are few. Figure 18-2 provides a good example.

Figure 18-2: Avoid using JPEG to optimize images with large zones of a single color. JPEG compression introduces distortions (called artifacts) when rendering them.

Portable Network Graphics (PNG)

The PNG format has an interesting history. When Unisys, the owners of the patent on LZW compression, began collecting royalties from manufactures that used it in their software, some confusion erupted and there were those who thought the royalties would be levied against anyone who so much as used a GIF image in their Web site. This confusion turned out to be a boon for graphics artists when the Internet Engineering Task Force produced their answer to GIF — PNG, a format that used a lossless compression method AND came in 8-bit and 24-bit flavors, effectively combining the best aspects of both GIF and JPEG.

Used in its 8-bit version, PNG and GIF are fairly even in their abilities to produce quality images with low file sizes. PNG tends to produce slightly large files, but only by a kilobyte or two and is fine for optimizing the same sort of images for which GIF should be used.

The 24-bit version of PNG does not, however, compare with JPEG. Because the compression method is lossless (removing no additional data from the image), files optimized in this format tend to be double in size than when optimized in the JPEG format.

Using the Save for Web Command

Elements' primary optimization interface is the Save For Web dialog box, shown in Figure 18-3. Here you preview your optimized image, selecting the format, compression, and color options. To display the Save For Web dialog box, choose File⇨Save for Web or click the Save for Web button in the shortcuts bar.

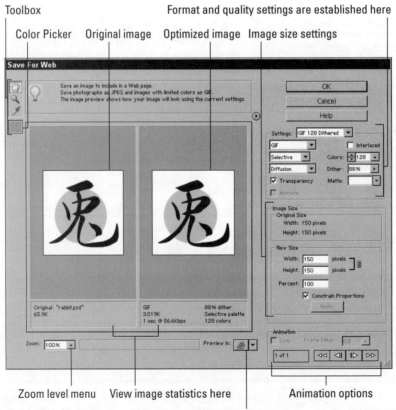

Figure 18-3: The Save for Web dialog box.

In the Save For Web dialog box you compare your original image, seen on the left, with the optimized results on the right, deciding which optimization settings prove best for your image.

The annotation area beneath the original image displays the file name and file size. Beneath the optimized image, the current optimization settings, file size, and estimated download time is shown.

The download time is based on the dialog box's currently selected Internet access speed. To change the selected Internet access speed, click the small arrow to the right of the optimized image to display the Preview pop-up menu, shown in Figure 18-4 and select the access speed of your choice.

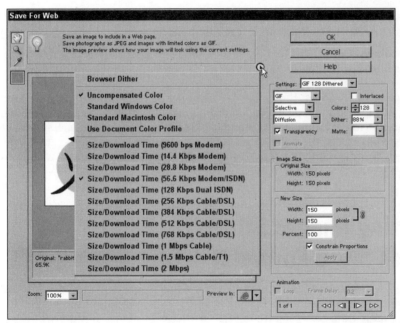

Figure 18-4: The Preview pop-up menu enables you to choose between multiple modem, ISDN, cable, or DSL speeds.

The Save For Web dialog box also lets you to view the differences in Gamma correction between platforms. Gamma measures the intensity to voltage response of a signal sent to a computer system's monitor. The technical specifics aren't terribly important to you as an Elements user, other than understanding that Gamma affects image contrast.

The Windows and Macintosh platforms, for example, use significantly different Gamma correction methods. Macintosh systems have partial gamma correction integrated into their hardware. Windows systems have no such gamma correction though some graphics card manufacturers do provide this functionality. Because Macintosh has Gamma correction, images created on Windows PCs look washed out on Macintosh systems. Conversely, images created on Macintosh systems look darker to Windows users.

To preview differences in Gamma Correction, access the Preview pop-up menu by clicking the small arrow to the right of the optimized image and choose one of the following display options:

✦ **Uncompensated Color:** This default option displays the image with no color adjustment.

✦ **Standard Windows Color:** Displays the image with the color adjusted to simulate the Gamma of a standard Windows monitor.

✦ **Standard Macintosh Color:** Displays the image with color adjusted to simulate the Gamma of a standard Macintosh monitor.

✦ **Document Color Profile:** Displays the image with its current color profile if has one.

These options only adjust the color display in the Save For Web dialog box alone. The original and optimized images are not physically modified in any way. Windows users should view their images in Standard Macintosh Color, Mac users in Standard Windows color, to see the differences. If the change in contrast is too great, the typical remedy is for Macintosh users to slightly lighten their images and Windows users to slightly darken their images.

Optimizing Images into GIF and PNG-8 Formats

GIF and PNG are both indexed color formats. When images are optimized into either format, Elements indexes the colors used, storing them in a *color lookup table* (CLUT). Limiting the color palette in this way helps to reduce file size while preserving image quality.

To reiterate, GIF and PNG-8 are best suited to images with a limited range of colors to begin with (under 256), where zones of color are crisply defined. Optimization settings are adjusted in the Settings area of the Save For Web dialog box, shown in detail in Figure 18-5.

File Format menu   Color Reduction Algorithm menu

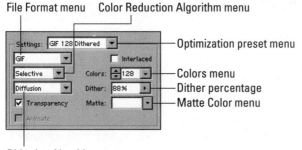

Optimization preset menu

Colors menu

Dither percentage

Matte Color menu

Dithering Algorithm menu

Figure 18-5: The options in the Settings area change based on the file format you choose. GIF and PNG-8 have identical Settings options.

Optimization Presets

The Optimization preset menu provides seven GIF presets and one PNG-8 preset. These are

- ✦ GIF 128 Dithered
- ✦ GIF 128 No Dither
- ✦ GIF 32 Dithered
- ✦ GIF 32 No Dither
- ✦ GIF 64 Dithered
- ✦ GIF 64 No Dither
- ✦ GIF Web Palette
- ✦ PNG-8 128 Dithered

The numbers 128, 64, and 32 represent total number of colors Elements maintains in the image. The Web Palette preset pushes each color in the image to its closest corresponding value in the Web Safe color palette — the palette of 216 colors identical to all browsers, operating systems, and monitors when running in 8-bit, 256 color mode.

In the color indexing process common to GIF and PNG, choosing Dithered or No Dither indicates whether some colors lost by optimization are simulated by alternating pixels in a checkerboard-like pattern by using colors left within the color lookup table.

Custom GIF and PNG-8 Optimization Settings

Custom optimization settings are adjusted by using the remaining menus, pop-ups, and sliders in the Settings area.

To specify your chosen file format, select GIF or PNG-8 from the File Format menu. Next, choose a method for establishing the color look-up table of the image by making a selection from the Color Reduction Algorithm menu.

In Elements, color look-up tables fall into three categories: Dynamic options, Fixed options, and Custom options.

Dynamic Color Palette Options

Using Elements' dynamic options, color lookup tables are based on colors present in the image and the number of colors chosen from the Colors menu.

The Color Reduction Algorithm menu's dynamic options are described.

Perceptual

The perpetual palette creates a customized color lookup table using colors in the image to which human eyes are more sensitive.

Selective

The selective palette — similar to the perceptual palette in its inclination toward colors favored by human visual response — creates a table that is more sensitive to areas of single flat colors. This algorithm prevents such colors from being merged with other colors in the image and preserves any existing Web-safe colors. This palette tends to be the best for Web graphics.

Adaptive

The adaptive palette creates a CLUT by sampling the predominant colors within the image. For example, if the image you're optimizing has a preponderance of yellows and greens, choosing the adaptive palette creates a CLUT slanted to those two colors.

Fixed Color Palette Options

Instead of using colors present in the image as the basis from which the CLUT is derived, Elements' fixed options use predefined palettes from which to build the CLUT.

The fixed options include:

Web
The Web palette consists of 216 colors common to Windows, Macintosh, Netscape Navigator, and Internet Explorer out of the 256 available in 8-bit mode. Choosing this option pushes the image's existing color to their closest Web palette equivalent.

Mac OS
Choosing this palette pushes existing colors to their closest equivalents in the default 256 system colors of the Macintosh operating system's 8-bit color mode.

Windows
Choosing this palette pushes existing colors to their closest equivalents in the default 256 system colors of the Windows operating system's in 8-bit color mode.

Custom Color Palette Options
When you select Custom from the Color Reduction Algorithm menu, this maintains your current color table as a fixed palette that doesn't update with changes to the image.

As soon as you select the Color reduction algorithm, choose the maximum number of colors you want the image to contain by using the Colors pop-up menu. The maximum number of colors available is 256 because you're creating an indexed color file when optimizing as GIF or PNG-8. The fewest colors possible is two.

If you chose either Web or Custom for the color reduction algorithm, you can choose Auto in the Colors menu, which tells Elements to decide the optimal number of colors in the color table based on the frequency of colors in the image.

Applying Dither Settings
Dithering creates the illusion of different colors and shades by varying a pattern of pixels by using colors within the image's existing palette. For example, Figure 18-6 shows how a simple checkerboard pattern of black and white pixel can appear gray.

 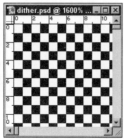

Figure 18-6: The image appears gray, but on closer examination we see it is actually made up of alternating black and white pixels.

Dithering can happen in one of two ways — either through Elements' optimization process (application dither), or via the Web browser if the user has their system set to 8-bit color mode (browser dither). The likelihood, however, that a contemporary computer user has their system set to 8-bit color mode when the typical graphics card is capable of 24 or 32-bit color is slim. Application dither, then, is your primary concern.

The reason to apply dither is to prevent colors from *banding* — where the chosen color reduction method has eliminated any continuous tone, leaving nothing but solid bands of color, as shown in Figure 18-7.

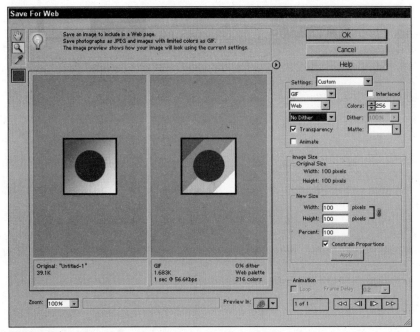

Figure 18-7: The original image on the left contains a gradient, which when pushed to the Web-safe palette without dither, creates the banded results on the right.

To dither an image in the Save For Web dialog box, simply make a selection from the Dithering Algorithm menu. The options are described next.

Diffusion

The Diffusion algorithm, instead of using an obvious checkerboard-like pattern, diffuses the pattern of dithered pixels. This algorithm works in conjunction with the Dither percentage slider. The higher the dither percentage, the more latent colors you simulate, increasing the overall file size.

Pattern

The Pattern algorithm dithers pixels in a clear, linear pattern.

Noise

The Noise algorithm creates a randomized pattern of dithered pixels.

Figure 18-8 shows a close-up of the differences between Diffuse, Pattern, and Noise.

Diffusion   Pattern   Noise

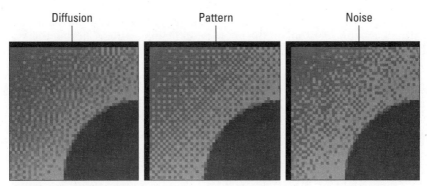

Figure 18-8: Where Diffuse creates a more random dither, Pattern creates a noticeable checkerboard-like effect. Noise generates a randomized pattern.

GIF and PNG-8 Transparency and Matte Settings

GIF and PNG-8 both support transparency. You typically leave transparent regions in an image so the background color or background image of the intended Web page can show through.

Unlike native Elements files, whose layers can have varying degrees of opacity, in a GIF or PNG-8 file a pixel is either opaque or transparent. This presents a dilemma when Elements needs to optimize a drop-shadow or anti-aliased edge. Here, Elements translates any pixels of partial transparency into a fully opaque pixel, calculating the appropriate color based on that of the original semi-opaque color and the color you choose for the matte.

To preserve transparent regions when optimizing images in GIF or PNG-8 formats, simply select the Transparency check box. Any completely transparent pixels remain so, while semi-transparent pixels are blended with your chosen matte color (typically, the intended Web page's background color) to simulate a gradual transition.

The matte color is selected using the Matte Color menu. The Matte Color menu provides the following options.

None

Disables matte color. Pixels of less than 50 percent transparency are made entirely opaque, while pixels of more than 50 percent transparency are made completely transparent.

Eyedropper Color

Uses the color last selected with Save for Web dialog box's eyedropper, shown beneath the eyedropper tool on the left side of the dialog box. Clicking this color swatch also invokes the Elements color picker from which to make a selection.

Black

Sets the matte color to black.

White

Sets the matte color to white.

Other

Invokes the Photoshop color picker from which to make a selection.

Also, clicking on the Matte Color menu's text field directly invokes Elements' color picker.

Interlacing Graphics

To interlace an image, check the Interlace check box in the Settings area. When an optimized image is interlaced, browsers start by displaying it at a lower resolution and bring it up to full resolution over seven progressive scans. The purpose of this is to get something to the site visitor's screen ASAP so there are no blank areas on the screen while the visitor waits for the entire page to download.

In the days of 14.4 Kbps and 28.8 Kbps modems, interlacing graphics was a common practice. While it resulted in insignificant increases in file size, at least the visitor wasn't staring at text with a bunch of square holes punched in it waiting for something to appear. With contemporary Internet connection speeds interlacing images isn't really necessary, and doing so can even hurt performance because imposing seven scans may take longer than simply allowing the image to download unencumbered.

Optimizing Images into JPEG and PNG-24 Formats

As mentioned previously, JPEG and PNG-24 are meant for optimizing continuous tone images. This is facilitated by their 24-bit color depth, supporting 16,777,216 colors. The JPEG File Interchange Format uses a "lossy" compression method, which removes color data, while PNG-24 (like PNG-8 and GIF) uses "lossless" compression, which results in significantly larger file sizes than JPEG.

Figure 18-9 shows the Save For Web dialog box's Settings area options for JPEG and PNG.

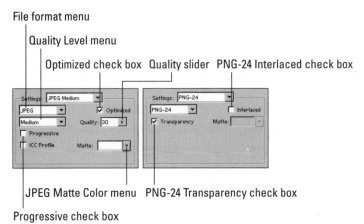

Figure 18-9: The left side shows JPEG settings and PNG-24 settings are on the right.

Optimization Presets

Elements offer three presets for JPEG and one preset for PNG-24:

✦ JPEG Low

✦ JPEG Medium

✦ JPEG High

✦ PNG-24

In Elements, a scale of 0 to 100 represents JPEG compression. The three presets of Low, Medium, and High represent compressions of 10, 30, and 60, respectively. The higher the number, the greater the degree of compression—which decreases the overall image quality. Your mission is to achieve a balance between image quality and file size.

Custom JPEG and PNG-24 Optimization Settings

The JPEG Quality Level menu (Figure 18-10) offers one setting not provided by the presets—Maximum—which equals a compression value of 80. The Quality slider manually adjusts the compression value to any point on the 0-100 scale.

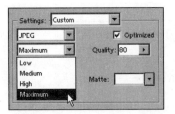

Figure 18-10: Use the Quality Level menu to quickly set the level of compression or adjust it manually by using the Quality slider.

The Optimized check box available for JPEG optimization should always be selected. It improves color optimization and produces smaller files.

JPEG and PNG-24 Transparency and Matte Settings

Unlike GIF and PNG-8, JPEG lacks transparency support, so a matte color must be used to fill such zones created in the original image. The JPEG Matte menu is identical to those used by GIF and PNG-8, described earlier in the chapter.

PNG-24 supports up to 256 levels of transparency by clicking the Transparency check box and consequently doesn't need a matte option. Unfortunately, while Netscape Navigator 7.x correctly renders PNG-24 transparency, Microsoft Internet Explorer never has.

Progressive JPEG and Interlaced PNG-24

Like GIF and PNG-8, PNG-24 provides an interlacing option, and the same rules apply. JPEG provides similar functionality with a feature referred to as Progressive JPEG.

Where interlacing GIF and PNG files increases their overall file size, using the progressive option results in smaller JPEG files. But again, forcing the image into a series of progressive scans can actually make the download take longer.

Resizing Images

Image dimension impacts over file size in rather obvious ways. Beneath the Save For Web dialog box's Settings area sits the Image Size area (see Figure 18-11), which enables you to adjust an image's dimensions without going back to the Elements workspace.

Width field   Original size

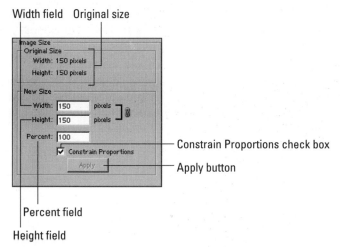

Constrain Proportions check box

Apply button

Percent field

Height field

Figure 18-11: The Image Size area resembles the Pixel Dimensions area of the Image Size dialog box.

The Original Size area shows the image's original dimensions with the New Size area beneath where you can enter new values. Adjust the image's dimensions proportionally by using the Constrain Proportions check box, which also actives the Percentage field.

Creating Animated GIF Images

If you ever made flipbook animations as a child, the concept of the animated GIF image will be easy to grasp. All animation creates the illusion of movement by displaying a sequence of images rapidly enough to trick the eye into perceiving uniform motion. In a flipbook, you draw one image after another, subtly changing each one. In elements, instead of using pages, you use layers — each layer acting as a single frame.

STEPS: Creating an Animation

1. Create an image in which each layer acts as an individual frame of the finished animation. The bottom-most layer represents the first frame, the upper-most layer is the last.

2. Choose Save for Web from the File menu.

3. Optimize the image in GIF format.

4. Select the Animate check box.

5. To make the animation repeat continuously, select the Loop check box.

6. Specify the duration of each frame by using the Frame Delay pop-up menu.

To preview your work, use either the VCR buttons along the bottom of the Animation Area (First Frame, Previous Frame, Next Frame, Last Frame) or open the file in a Web browser by choosing a browser from the Preview pop-up menu. There, you can use the browser's Stop and Refresh or reload buttons to stop and replay the animation.

✦   ✦   ✦

Keyboard Shortcuts to Speed Your Elements Activity

While you can always click the toolbox buttons to activate a tool, sometimes pressing a single button on the keyboard to switch between tools is faster and easier.

Toolbox Shortcuts

Table A-1 shows you the shortcuts for each button on the toolbox.

Table A-1
Keyboard Shortcuts

Shortcut	Tool Activated
M	Rectangular and Elliptical Marquee tools
V	Move tool
L	Lasso tool
W	Magic Wand tool
A	Selection Brush
C	Crop tool
U	Custom Shape tool
T	Horizontal or Vertical Type tool
K	Paint Bucket
G	Gradient fill tool
B	Brush
N	Pencil
E	Erase
Y	Red Eye Brush
R	Blur tool
P	Sharpen tool
Q	Sponge tool
F	Smudge tool
O	Dodge tool
J	Burn tool
S	Clone Stamp tool
I	Eyedropper tool
H	Hand tool
Z	Zoom tool
X	Switch the current Foreground and Background colors
D	Return to the default Foreground and Background Colors

Menu Command Shortcuts

Table A-2 lists all the keyboard shortcuts that issue menu and shortcuts bar commands.

Table A-2 Menu Command Shortcuts	
Shortcut	**Tool Activated**
Ctrl+N	Open a New file
Ctrl+O	Open an existing file
Ctrl+Shift+O	Browse for an existing file
Alt+Ctrl+O	Open a file in a specific format
Ctrl+W	Close the active image
Shift+Ctrl+W	Close all open images
Ctrl+S	Save the active image (if this is the first time the file's been saved, the Save As dialog box opens).
Shift+Ctrl+S	Opens the Save As dialog box for renaming or resaving an existing file
Alt+Shift+Ctrl+S	Opens the Save for Web dialog box
Ctrl+P	Opens a Print Preview window
Shift+Ctrl+P	Opens the Page Setup dialog box
Alt+Ctrl+P	Opens the Print dialog box with no preview
Ctrl+Q	Exits Photoshop Elements
Alt+Ctrl+Z	Undo
Ctrl+Y	Step Forward (Redo, or repeat last step)
Ctrl+Z	Step Backward (really the same as Undo)
Ctrl+C	Copy selection
Ctrl+X	Cut selection
Ctrl+V	Paste cut or copied selection
Shift+Ctrl+K	Open the Color Settings dialog box

Continued

Table A-2 *(continued)*

Shortcut	Tool Activated
Ctrl+K	Open the Preferences dialog box
Ctrl+T	Place the active layer in Free Transform mode
Ctrl+I	Invert the colors of the current selection
Shift+Ctrl+L	Apply Auto Levels command
Alt+Shift+Ctrl+L	Apply Auto Contrast command
Shift+Ctrl+B	Apply Auto Color Correction
Ctrl+U	Open the Hue/Saturation dialog box
Shift+Ctrl+U	Remove color
Ctrl+L	Open the Levels dialog box
Shift+Ctrl+F	Open the Fill Flash dialog box
Shift+Ctrl+N	Create a New Layer
Ctrl+A	Select everything on the current layer
Ctrl+D	Deselect whatever's currently selected
Shift+Ctrl+D	Reselect what you just deselected
Shift+Ctrl+I	Invert your selection (select everything but what's currently selected)
Alt+Ctrl+D	Open the Feather dialog box
Ctrl+F	Reapply the just-used Filter, with the settings used last time
Ctrl+ + (plus sign)	Zoom in
Ctrl+ – (minus sign)	Zoom out
Ctrl+0 (zero)	Fit the image on-screen
Alt+Ctrl+0 (zero)	Display image in actual pixels size
Ctrl+H	Display selection
Ctrl+R	Display ruler
F1	Open the Help window

Tip   To close all open images, hold the Shift key as you click the File menu. The Close command is now the Close All command.

✦   ✦   ✦

Finding Photoshop Elements Tools on the Web

✦ ✦ ✦ ✦

In This Appendix

Online resources

What is available for Photoshop professionals

Creating a Photoshop Elements gallery

✦ ✦ ✦ ✦

Finding information online about Photoshop Elements is rather simple. Just go to a search site (a good choice is www.Google.com) and type **"Photoshop Elements"** into the search field (be sure to use the quotes so that your search looks for both words). The results will be numerous, as shown in Figure B-1.

Finding Online Resources

Of course, you have to wade through sites that are selling the Elements software, which presumably, you already have. But, amongst the sites you find are pages that include information on using Photoshop Elements, tricks and tips posted by other users, experts, and even other authors of books such as this one. You also find photos and other images to inspire you — when you see what other people have done, you'll want to see if you can achieve similar (or even better) results.

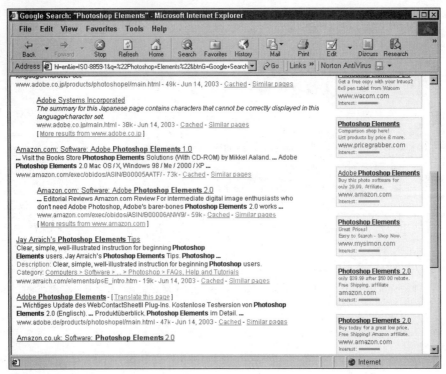

Figure B-1: So many choices, now that Photoshop Elements has been around for a little while

Of course, more Photoshop sites are available (and you get these mixed in with your search results if you don't put "Photoshop Elements" in quotes when you enter your search criteria). And there are tools for Photoshop users that you, as an Elements user, can't utilize — simply because of differences between the two applications. Also, because Photoshop Elements has only been available to the public for about two years, there aren't as many user groups or online organizations devoted to it as there would be for more long-standing applications such as Photoshop.

If you're interested, however, you can find many Photoshop-related sites that will contain information you can use — tips for achieving special effects by combining one or more Filters and other tools, ways to customize your brush settings to achieve interesting effects you may never have thought of, and so on. It's worth the time you take poking around.

When searching through Google or some similar search site, type **"Photoshop tips"** (again, use the quotes) into the search field and you find these sites and others like them.

Jay Arraich's Photoshop Elements Tips

Check out www.arraich.com/elements/psE_intro.htm (shown in Figure B-2).

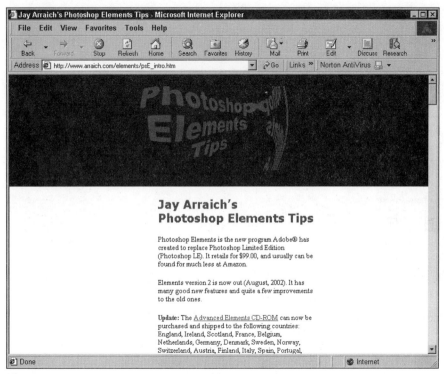

Figure B-2: www.arraich.com/elements/psE_intro.htm

Photoshop Tips & Tricks

Visit www.graphic-design.com/Photoshop (shown in Figure B-3).

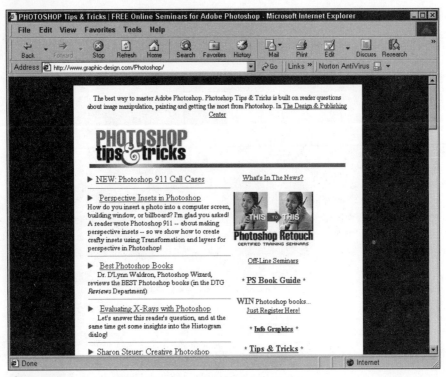

Figure B-3: www.graphic-design.com/Photoshop

Photoshop Elements Resources

You'll find a lot of useful information at `http://graphicssoft.about.com/cs/ photoshopelements` (shown in Figure B-4).

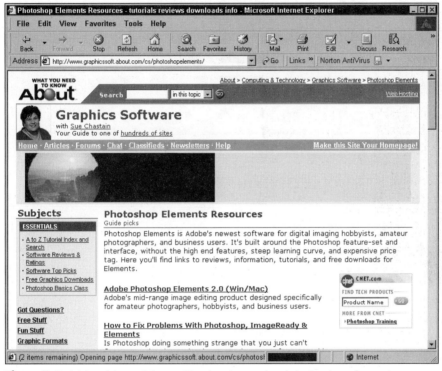

Figure B-4: `http://graphicssoft.about.com/cs/photoshopelements`

EyeWire

EyeWire is another great resource. Go to `www.eyewire.com/tips/photoshop` (shown in Figure B-5).

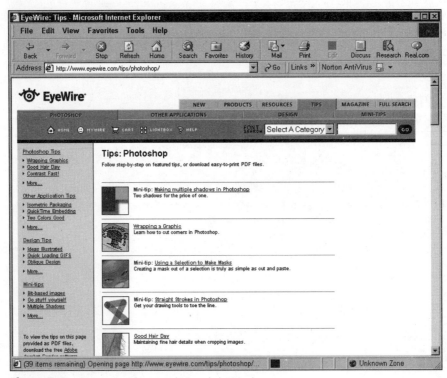

Figure B-5: `www.eyewire.com/tips/photoshop`

Photoshop Paradise

Visit www.desktoppublishing.com/photoshoptips.html (shown in Figure B-6).

From general design tips to photos you can purchase or download for free and use to experiment and practice, you can find a lot of interesting information at these sites.

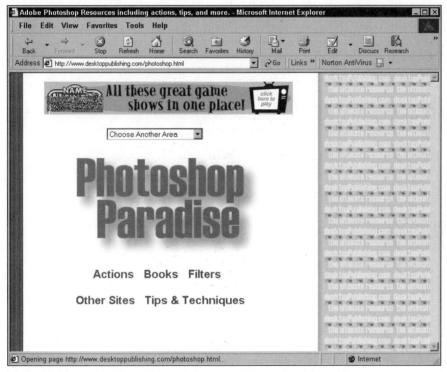

Figure B-6: www.desktoppublishing.com/photoshoptips.html

The National Association of Photoshop Professionals

Another site (www.photoshopuser.com) that's packed with Photoshop information is the National Association of Photoshop Professionals Web site. It's clear that this organization is focused on Photoshop, and not Photoshop Elements, but you can still find many tips and small tutorials, step-by-step procedures, and so forth of which you might want to make use. There is also a calendar of events that you might want to attend if the seminar in question will be held close to your home.

In addition to viewing some basic info on their Web site, if you join their organization, you'll have access to more of the site, and you'll be subscribed to their magazine, *Photoshop User*. To find out more about joining—the current membership fee and what you'll get for it, visit their Web site, shown in Figure B-7.

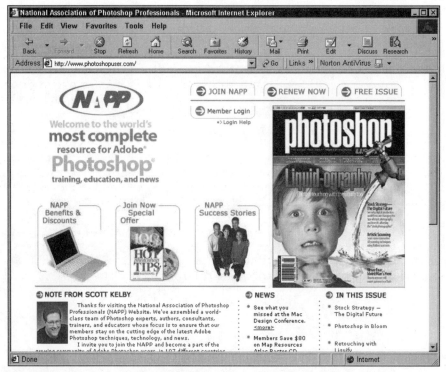

Figure B-7: Become an official Photoshop User, even though Elements is your weapon of choice!

Creating Your Own Photoshop Elements Gallery

If you have free Web space allocated to you by your ISP (Internet Service Provider, such as AOL, MSN, or a service such as Earthlink), you can share *your* Elements creations with the rest of the world. Just set up a Web page with a selection of your images on it, and post it to the Web. You can learn more about saving your Elements images for the Web in Chapter 18.

Now, you may be thinking that you can't possibly build your own Web page and post it to the Web, but think again. Most ISPs provide a simple interface through which to build a page and insert images — and if yours doesn't, there are books galore on simple and inexpensive applications that help you do it. You may already have some tools at your disposal, such as FrontPage, which came with certain versions/editions of Microsoft Office.

Tip   When you post your own Elements creations, share your knowledge — accompany each image with some short explanation of which tools you used, and if you created your own very special effects, explain how you did it. You can copyright your images, placing your name and the © date in the corner of the image and also repeating it on the Web page itself.

If you want to automate the process of putting several of your photos online, use the File➪Create Web Photo Gallery command. The resulting dialog box (see Figure B-8) allows you to choose the style of the gallery, which images to include, and how the accompanying text — the captions/descriptions/explanations I mentioned in the previous tip — is formatted.

Click the Destination button to choose where your gallery will be stored locally, and you can use that as the source for your online copy of the images. Figure B-9 shows a gallery with thumbnails of each image in the gallery and a single image shown full size. This is previewed in a browser window so you'll know how it will look online.

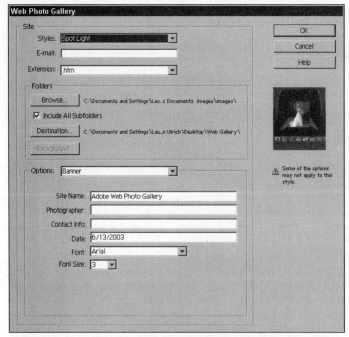

Figure B-8: Set up your Web gallery with these easy options.

Note

Uploading images to the Web (and the pages that house them) requires either the publishing tools in your Web design software, or a separate FTP program, such as WSFTP Pro, CuteFTP, or FTP Commander. You can find a lot of shareware and freeware FTP programs online, or you can purchase one of those I list here, for a very small fee. Do a search online for **"Free FTP software"** if you're on a budget, or **"FTP Software"** if you want a selection that includes packages you must purchase. FTP software is easy to use and usually comes with some level of help to get you started.

Figure B-9: Spotlight each of your images individually by clicking their thumbnail images along the bottom of the page.

Tip

As with any sharing of files, the risk of "catching" a virus from another computer cannot be overstated. If you're downloading programs (.exe, .zip, and other forms of executable files) or even documents or worksheets, be sure to have up-to-date virus software installed. Scan any downloaded files before executing or opening them, and be sure to get virus definition updates frequently—there are always new viruses being unleashed, and you'll want to have the latest tools to detect and defeat them. Virus definition updates can be downloaded from the virus protection software manufacturer's website, and most virus protection software has automatic tools for downloading the latest virus definitions.

✦   ✦   ✦

Restoring and Preserving Your Original Images

In This Appendix

Dealing with the signs of age

Getting rid of unwanted spots

Reducing moire patterns

Repairing torn images

Removing stains

An image that's been pitted and scuffed by dust, and/or attacked by mold and mildew, may have dulling clouds on the surface. If it's a glossy or modern matte-finish print, or in the case of vintage matte-finish images, the surface of the image (and its cardboard mat) may be pitted and dotted from where the dust has been ground in and where mold has grown and eaten into the surface. When you scan these images, the mold and mildew, along with any dust that has been engrained into the image, may be exaggerated as the scanner creates shadows within the pitted areas, and where the change in the surface texture of the image eliminates the scanner's ability to capture the details of the image.

Removing the Signs of Age and Improper Storage

When these things happen, you'll need to smooth out the textures, recreate the details, and where the small dots and scratches are so overwhelming, remove them. You may also want to use them — going for an interesting artistic effect that both masks the blemishes and creates an entirely new kind of image.

Using the Dust & Scratches Filter

The Dust & Scratches filter that is found in the Noise submenu of the Filter menu, works by changing adjacent pixels that are very different, and makes them more similar. This has a blurring, softening effect, as drastic differences between contiguous pixels are reduced. You can take a photo with lots of little dark dust and mold spots on it and soften the look of those spots to the point that they're nearly invisible if not completely eradicated.

The Dust & Scratches dialog box contains a Preview area, and two sliders: Radius, and Threshold. You can use these sliders (or their accompanying text boxes) to control the effects that the filter has:

✦ Radius determines how many contiguous pixels will be compared to each pixel. For example, a Radius of 10 will create a fairly blurry image and a Radius of 80 will create a virtually unrecognizable image, because pixels in groups of 80 are changed to a similar color. However, a Radius of 3 will have a much more subtle effect, with just a gentle softening of all the content, as every group of three pixels is adjusted to match each other.

✦ Threshold determines how varied the pixels compared within the established radius must be in order to be adjusted. A low Threshold will result in very subtle results and a high Threshold will result in a lot of pixels being adjusted, for more dramatic results.

Tip As you increase the Threshold, the Radius setting has less of an impact. The Radius setting that made the image disappear into blurry nothingness when a low Threshold was set will not have that same effect when the Threshold is set to 10 or more.

As you tinker with the settings, watch both the Preview window and the image window — if you move the dialog box aside, you'll be able to see more of the photo and see how the filter's settings are affecting it. Once you like what you see in both places (or only in the Preview window if it's not possible to see both), click the OK button to apply the filter to your image.

Using the Median Filter to Soften Light and Dark Spots

Another filter found in the Noise submenu is the Median filter. Instead of changing the color values of pixels that are deemed too different from one another, this filter blends the brightness levels of pixels within a selected area, or across the entire image. The dialog box allows you set the Radius for the filter, and as in the case of the Dust & Scratches filter, the higher the Radius, the more drastic the changes will be.

There is no Threshold setting in this filter, so you're leaving it to Elements to decide which pixels are too different in terms of their light levels. The results of these two filters are very similar, and depending on the nature of your image and its problems, you may find them to be interchangeable.

Note If your photo only has some areas that are affected by dust or mold, you can select those areas before using either of the filters. Be careful, though, when using the filters on selected areas rather than the whole image — if you create too much softness with either filter, the area will stand out and look blurry compared to the rest of the image. If you use the filters in subtle ways (with low Radius and/or Threshold settings), the area you've filtered won't stand out as much when you deselect it.

Blending Out Individual Marks

When it comes to tiny spots from dust or a good crop of mold that's eaten into your photo, you can attack the little blemishes individually if you have the patience or if there aren't that many of them. You can use the Brush tool, applying the color that the spot *should* be, or you can use the Smudge tool to drag some of the surrounding color onto the spot. These techniques have been discussed in previous chapters, but for our purposes here, we'll discuss the use of these tools to cover very small areas.

Before proceeding with any of the following tools or techniques, it is essential that you zoom in on your image. Zoom in to a very high magnification, so that you can see the spot clearly, and the surrounding pixels as well. You can use the Zoom tool, the Navigator palette, or the Ctrl + shortcut (Ctrl plus the plus sign key) to zoom in — use the shortcut over and over until you're in close enough to see the pixels.

Tip If you're using the Zoom tool, click on the spot you want to get closer to — and keep clicking until you're very, very close. If you're using the Navigator palette, drag the red box until it's over the area containing the spot, and then drag the slider to the right until you're right on top of the spot, with a clear view of it and the surrounding clean pixels.

Paint Dots on Unwanted Spots

When you use the Brush tool to get rid of a spot, you normally don't have to drag the mouse — you're just going to click once, maybe twice, on the spot, depositing a dot of paint. You can adjust the Brush size, choose a textured or solid preset, and tweak the Opacity so as to not apply an obvious glob of paint where a subtle, slightly see-through dot is all that's required.

To keep your painted dot or dots from standing out, try using a textured brush — one of the Charcoal or Dry Brush presets, or any preset that doesn't apply a round, discernable dot. It's a good idea to experiment (you can always Undo) with a few different Brush and color settings. Do this until you find the one that eliminates the dot without leaving an equally unsightly and obvious dot behind.

Tip Why use an Opacity setting that's less than 100%? Because if the area containing the spot is slightly textured, or there are many colors making up the look of a single, solid color, using a see-through Brush will allow you to apply color without masking those subtle details.

Doing a Quick Smudge

The Smudge tool smears color from one place to another, enabling you to smooth over blemishes much as you would with makeup on your face—spreading a dot of cover-up onto a freckle or other spot you don't want the world to see. When it comes to tiny spots on an image, the Smudge tool can be quite effective in that you don't need to select a color first to paint over the spot—you're dragging the color from adjoining pixels onto the spot, so there's no risk that the colors won't match. If you're zoomed in close enough, you will literally be smudging colors from the pixels right next to the spot, and you can use the Smudge tool's Strength setting to make sure the smudge is subtle. By adjusting the size of the brush with which you're smearing color, you can make sure you smudge just enough to cover the spot, and no more. A short, quick smudge should be all it takes.

Caution Be sure the Finger Painting option is OFF on the Smudge tool's options bar—otherwise you'll smudge in the current Foreground Color, and that may not enhance your results.

Dealing with Noise and Textures from Digital Captures

Digitally-captured images, taken with a digital camera or scanned from printed photos, can contain noise and textures that you won't want to keep—artifacts along the edges of shapes or within large fields such as skies or other backgrounds, and an odd pattern effect, called *moiré*, which is a distortion of colors and light. You can eliminate the possibility of the noise and artifacts by shooting or scanning at higher resolutions (300 ppi, minimum), and you can eliminate some moiré effects by not scanning offset-printed originals (pictures from magazines or brochures). If there's no way around the problem, either through settings on your digital device or the nature of the original, however, you're stuck with the problem, and have to use Elements to fix or mitigate its effects.

To get rid of artifacts, noise, and non-moiré textures, you can use a variety of filters, including:

✦ Add Noise

✦ Despeckle

✦ Median

These filters work by making the noise stand out less, just as they can help mitigate the effects of dust and mold. You can refine their effects through their dialog boxes, and through making a selection in the image before issuing the individual filter commands.

To get rid of offset moiré effects or the moiré that can occur due to different digital capturing methods, there blurring filters (Blur and Blur More) which can be followed by other filters to bring back detail without losing the pattern-softening effect of the blur. You can also use manual blurring tools to soften the moiré, and then clone the results of a small area all around the other spots that have an undesirable texture in them.

Using the Noise Filters

Noise filters work by adding or removing noise. When noise is added, the noise you have becomes less of a visual distraction, because there's more of it, and it's evenly distributed. It can also be an artistic effect, simulating photos taken on high-speed film, or giving the impression of age to a relatively new photo. When noise is taken away, it is done by making some or the entire photo blurry, either by closing the color gap between adjacent pixels, or reducing the difference in light levels throughout blocks of pixels.

Whether you choose to add noise or take it away, the results can be quite subtle or very dramatic. It all depends on the dialog box settings (if any) for the filters and how you adjust them, whether or not you restrict the filter to a particular area by making a selection first, and/or what filters or tools you use afterward.

Working with the Add Noise Filter

As the name implies, the Add Noise filter adds pixels to your image, increasing the number of differently-colored pixels. It's handy for hiding any kind of banding, where there are obvious strips of color, lighting effect, or a pattern created by previous retouching efforts, because it creates a random, yet evenly-distributed noise that keeps any noise or pattern effect from being too obvious or visually distracting.

The Add Noise dialog box offers two Distribution options — Uniform, where the distribution is — you guessed it — uniform, and Gaussian, where the distribution is less uniform, and more speckled.

Obviously, with either Distribution method, the Amount slider (or the text box into which you can enter any number from 0 to 400) will determine the number of noisy pixels added to your image. Higher numbers result in more noise, lower numbers in less noise. A very high setting will obliterate your image entirely, but it can be used on selected parts of the image (select them first) with those areas turned entirely to noise (like a snowy TV screen) for an interesting effect of contrasting noise levels.

Tip   If you turn on the Monochromatic option (it's off by default), your effects will use only the tones currently found in your image, and no colors will be changed.

Despeckling an Image

The Despeckle filter offers no dialog box, so you can't adjust its intensity or customize its effect. When you choose this filter, Elements detects the edges within the image and blurs everything but those edges. The results can be mixed, with some noise being added, along with the newly-defined edges. It may seem highly intuitive for the software to detect an edge, but it's done simply by comparing ranges of pixels. Where color and/or light are different over a series of several contiguous pixels, the lines where those differences are most extreme are seen as edges.

One of the benefits of this filter is that you preserve overall detail, or the illusion of it, by preserving the detail of the edges. This is a welcome advantage, as many of the techniques for removing noise and textures involve blurring, and you lose a lot of detail if you don't go back and add back some focus with sharpening tools. The Despeckle filter sort of does both things in one step, although nothing is sharpened — the edges just look sharper by comparison to the blurred areas.

Despeckling also saves the image from being so blurry that it looks totally out of focus. You'll find it helpful when you see color banding in scanned magazine or brochure photos, or where you've applied artificial coloring to black and white images and a "Colorized by Ted Turner" look has resulted. By heightening the impact of the edges, things don't look so flat.

Tip   Find out more about colorizing black and white images in Chapter 8, Perfecting Image Quality. You'll also find out about removing color, and creating sepia-tone images from both black and white and color images.

Using the Median Filter

The Median filter works by discarding any pixels that are substantially brighter or darker than the adjacent pixels, creating a more uniform lighting throughout an image or the selected portion thereof. You'll use the Radius slider to determine how many pixels are compared as a group, and obviously the fewer you compare at a time, the more subtle the effects of the filter will be.

Note   The overall effect of this filter is rather blurring, and at settings higher than 4 pixels (using the Radius slider), an great deal of detail can be lost.

Reducing the Impact of Moiré

Moiré is unlikely to occur in images with mostly solid colors, low contrast, and where you're scanning or taking a digital picture at a high resolution. Sometimes, however, you can't control the content of the image or the quality of the capture, and you'll end up with a pattern of shapes and edge distortions that you want to get rid of. As mentioned earlier, if you scan magazine or brochure images that were printed with an offset printer, you may get bands of color, these known as *offset moiré*. You'll want to get rid of these, too, because they'll make your image look striped, and the detail that depends on color will be lost.

The options for getting rid of moiré include the aforementioned Median filter, and you can also use the Blur, Blur More, and Smart Blur filters to get rid of the texture that moiré creates.

Using the Blur Filters

The Blur submenu in the Filter menu contains six filters, only a few of which really apply to the goal of removing noise and textures. You can try any of them, but you'll have the most success with the following three:

- ✦ Blur
- ✦ Blur More
- ✦ Smart Blur

The Blur and Blur More filters are essentially the same tool — the latter one does what the former does, but does more of it. First, how it works: blurring by filter is the same as blurring by Blur tool in that Elements averages the color values of the pixels over which the mouse is dragged (Blur tool) or within the image or selection (Blur/Blur More filter), resulting in a soft focus due to a lack of color diversity. When you zoom in on a blurred area, you can see the results on a pixel-to-pixel level, and compare them to an un-blurred area visible at the same time.

Neither of these filters have a dialog box, so you can't control their intensity. If you use the Blur tool and wish it had done more, you can repeat it (Ctrl + F for Windows, Command + F for Mac), or you can use the Blur More filter. I prefer to repeat the Blur filter until I get the desired result, because the Blur More filter often goes too far when it comes on the heels of the Blur tool. Bear in mind that you don't have to use Blur More after the Blur tool — it can be your first choice if you know you want substantial blurring.

The Smart Blur tool is very effective in that it's not so even or heavy-handed. It blurs more precisely, given the presence of a dialog box that allows you to control what's blurred and how much blurring is applied.

You can also choose a Quality for the filter's results, selecting Low, Medium, or High, and then use the Mode setting to choose a Normal, Edge Only, or Overlay Edge blur. Each image requires different settings, so it's good to experiment, taking advantage of the Preview window to see what happens at different settings. Generally, High Quality and Normal Mode give you the best results. The Edge Only and Overlay Edge settings create a very distinctive result, where the edges actually stand out so much that the image can be distorted, especially in images without a lot of colors or intense lights and darks in them.

Note   You may find that you can't tell any difference between the results of the Blur filters and the Noise filters, given that blurring or softening is the goal for most of them. If you feel like you're not observant or that you don't understand what's going on, don't—depending on the problems in your image, the colors or lack thereof in the photo, and the other retouching steps that you've taken previously, any of the filters discussed in this chapter can be used, often interchangeably. The key is to find the one that looks right to you—there are no "rules" to follow.

Blurring Manually

You can also use the Blur tool to rub over areas that are textured with moiré. Just select the area first (you want to confine yourself, so you don't drag the mouse over a non-textured area), and then scrub away with the mouse. The Blur tool's Strength setting will allow you to make your blurring very subtle (a low setting, typically at 30% or less) or more extreme (a high setting, or anything over 50%). By using a brush Size that's suited to the size area you're blurring, and by selecting the area first, you can have very specific effects on very specific areas.

 Tip   If, after deselecting, the edges of your blurred area stands out because it's drastically different than the surrounding areas, use the Blur tool again, set to a low setting (somewhere around 30%) and drag over the edges to make them blend in.

Reconstructing Torn Images

When a photograph is torn, the content along the tear is normally lost. If a corner or more of the image is torn and literally torn *off*, of course that content is gone, too. Before the advent of photo editing software, you'd have had to crop the image to what was untouched by the tear, and resign yourself to the loss of the torn or missing content. With Photoshop Elements, however, you have the tools to reconstruct and literally recreate the content that's been torn through or torn away. You can go from significant damage to restored and repaired, the degree of effort involved dependent solely on the amount of the image that's missing and what other content you have to work with in recreating the portions that are gone.

In the reconstruction process, you'll primarily utilize two features:

✦ The Edit menu's Copy and Paste commands, which enable you to take sections of any image and duplicate them for positioning elsewhere—somewhere else in the same image, or in another image entirely.

✦ The Layer Via Copy command, which creates a new layer in your image, based on content you select in the same or another image.

 Tip   For smaller tears, you can use the Clone Stamp to rebuild what's been damaged by the tear itself. Complete instructions for using this tool follow in this chapter, in the section entitled "Fixing Minor Rips, Tears, and Scratches." Generally, the Clone Stamp is not the best choice for rebuilding large sections of an image.

Of course, once your repairs are in place, you'll want to make them blend into their surroundings — you can do this with various lighting, color, and sharpening/blurring tools, making it possible to use content from just about anywhere to rebuild the content that is missing from your damaged photo.

Rebuilding Missing Content

The missing corner, the big chunk out of the middle of a photo, the strip of content lost to a huge rip — this content can be rebuilt by using other content within the same image, or by "borrowing" content from another image. Of course, to simplify your life, if you grab content from another image, it helps if that image is similar to the damaged one — the same age, similar lighting (indoor vs. outdoor), taken at a similar distance (to avoid having a lot of resizing to do), and so on. Images taken on the same day or at the same event provide a lot of potential content for rebuilding a damaged image (think of wedding photos, taken by the same photographer, shots taken on vacation) as do vintage photos that are the same shade of sepia, printed on the same kind of paper. The more things that your damaged photo and the "donor photo" have in common, the easier it will be to make the donated content blend in.

If another photo is not available for the rebuilding process, you'll have to use other content from within the same damaged image. This normally solves the problem of making content match, although one part of an image can have different lighting or focus than another part of the same image. When using content from within the same image, it can mean taking one of the undamaged corners and reusing it, rotated to fill in for a missing corner, or taking content right next to the rip or hole, and using it to make the rip or hole go away.

The process of using content from within the same image or from another image is the same — you're duplicating the patch material and positioning it over the damaged area, then making the repairs blend in. This three-phase process is made simple in Photoshop Elements, using selection tools to choose the content that will be reused, the Layer or Edit menus' commands to create the patch content, and Layers palette to position the patch content where it does the most good.

Using Copy and Paste

If you want to select a section of your image (or another image that's also open on the Elements workspace) to use as the patch for your repair or a portion thereof, you can use any selection tool and then choose Edit ➪ Copy to make a duplicate of the selection. Be sure, of course, that the appropriate layer is active, so that you get the content you want.

Once the copy is made, choose Edit ➪ Paste (in the image to be repaired), and the copied section appears on the image. If you've copied from the same image, the duplicate you paste appears on top of the original selection — making the duplicate nearly invisible. You'll only know it's there because a new layer appears in the Layers palette.

Tip When selecting the portion of the image that will serve as the patch, consider whether or not it will be easy to hide sharp corners or overly straight edges, such as you'll find if you use the Rectangular or Elliptical Marquee tools. I prefer to use the Lasso tool, or the Selection Brush tool, so that I select only what I need and can achieve an edge that's more natural—perhaps even managing to select a shape that matches the damaged area.

If you Paste into an image other than the one from which the copy was taken, you'll be able to spot the pasted content immediately, and you'll also see a new layer appear in the Layers palette.

Once the pasted content is on the damaged image, switch to the Move tool and drag the patch into position. It may not blend in seamlessly, as it is likely to have sharp edges, and if it came from a spot on the image or another image that isn't the same in terms of lighting, texture, and color, it will stand out until you tinker with those aspects. As we'll discuss later, you can make just about anything blend in— removing or adding color, changing contrast, adding or removing light, using tools to soften edges so that the pasted patch looks like a part of the original image.

Creating and Positioning New Layers

Another way to duplicate content from an image (the damaged one or another image) for use in patching a scratch, tear, or large hole, is to create a layer based on a selection. Using the appropriate selection tool, select the area to be used as the patch, and then choose Layer ➪ New ➪ Layer via Copy. This places the selected portion of the image (from whichever layer was active at the time) in a new layer. You can then drag the new layer onto the damaged area, using the Move tool.

Tip Any layers added through pasting or using the Layer via Copy command can be renamed to make them easier to find and use. If you have a lot of generically-named layers—"Layer 1," "Layer 2," and so on—double-click the name of the layer you created to serve as a patch, and type a new name for it. "Patch" or "Cover-up" are good choices. When you've typed a new name, press the Enter key to confirm it, and now you'll be able to spot the layer quickly whenever you need to select it for moving, resizing, or any other layer-specific treatment.

Making Repairs Blend into the Image

As soon as your patch is in place, you'll be able to assess its effectiveness. You may need to go get more patching material, selecting more content from the same or another image, and repeating whatever duplication and positioning procedure you used in the first place. Once all the patches are in place, however, it's time to make sure they do the best job they can. This often means:

✦ Changing the lightness levels

✦ Adjusting saturation and hue

✦ Tweaking the color levels

✦ Blurring the edges of the patches

✦ Using the Sharpen or Blur tools to create the same level of focus in the patch as exists in the surrounding content

Tip   All of the tools involved have already been covered to this point in this book — you can check Chapter 3 for more information on adjusting color, and Chapter 4 to learn more about adjusting light. For any tool you want to use, check Chapter 2, where all of the tools, option bars, and palettes are introduced and explained.

Adjusting Light Levels

To make the patch content blend in, you may have to make it darker or lighter, so that it matches the surrounding pixels. You can do this in a number of ways:

✦ Use the Dodge and Burn tools to apply more light or shadow with your mouse

✦ Work with the Adjust Lighting submenu, found in the Enhance menu

✦ Access the Quick Fix command, found at the top of the Enhance menu

✦ Use the Color Variations command, found by choosing Enhance ➪ Adjust Color ➪ Color Variations

Whichever tool you use, be sure to select the patch first, and make sure that the patch content layer is active before you make any changes. You don't want to accidentally lighten or darken the main image, leaving the patch untouched. On the other hand, if only the pixels immediately surrounding the patch are not a good match for the patch content, you can lighten or darken those pixels, making the patch blend in as well as solving a lighting discrepancy that already existed in the original image.

Tip   If you're adding something new to the image to cover damage — say a shrub or a person, or a slab of grass or roadway — don't forget to make changes to the surrounding area. The new landscaping is bound to cast a shadow, and you'll want to use the Burn tool to create it. You can make anything appear to be sitting heavily in its new spot by creating a shadow beneath it, or by darkening surrounding content just a little bit, so that the new content seems more at home.

Softening the Edges

When the patch is first positioned over the damage, it will probably stand out like a sore thumb by virtue of its crisp, sharp edges. You can eliminate them by using the Blur and/or Smudge tool to soften them, scrubbing over the edges until they blend in with the rest of the image.

If the image you're patching is sharper or softer-focused than the patch content, use the Blur or Sharpen tools to make things match — adjusting the focus of the patch to match its new surroundings or adjusting the focus of the damaged image to match the patch. Whichever is less work (requiring less tinkering) is the way to go — if you can make a slight adjustment to a small area, that's always a better idea than making intense changes to a large area.

One exception—imagine that your patch comes from an image that's very sharp and crisp and you're using it in an image that's very much out of focus. In such a case, it may be impossible to use the Sharpen tool or Sharpen Filter to make the entire image sharp enough to match the patch—you can end up with bright spots and odd coloration if you overuse the sharpening tools and filters. If this happens, it might make more sense to soften the patch so that it's as out of focus as the rest of the image—again, taking a path of least resistance.

As you work with your damaged photos and the patches you bring in to repair them, each situation will direct you, and you'll find the right combination of tools and techniques to solve individual problems if you experiment and refer to guides such as this book.

Merging the Patch Layers

Once you've added a layer to patch your image and done whatever's needed to make that patch blend in with the surrounding pixels, you may want to merge the patch with the original image. Why? So that you can deal with the image as a single unit, simplifying any resizing, moving, or editing that will involve the damaged area and its patch. You only want to do this if your patch is perfect (or as close to perfect as possible) in terms of blending in—the lighting, focus, and texture adjusted to make it a seamless repair. Once this is achieved, choose Layer ➪ Merge Visible.

This will make one layer out of all the layers that can be seen in the image, and allows you to hide any layers that you don't want to include in the merge, such as any Type layers you may have added. Of course, you'll want to hide the layers that shouldn't be merged before you issue the Merge Visible command.

Fixing Minor Rips, Tears, and Scratches

Unlike big tears that result in completely mangled or missing content, you'll find that minor scratches, tears, wrinkles, and rips are far more commonplace, and luckily, far easier to repair. Instead of having to recreate missing content, you simply need to eradicate the small signs of damage.

The tools you can use to make these simple repairs include:

- ✦ Clone Stamp
- ✦ Paint brush
- ✦ Smudge tool

Through these tools, you can patch any kind of simple tear or rip, eliminating any sign that your photo was at one time torn in two, ripped along a fold (which you can also get rid of), or seriously scuffed. You can also paint out the signs of damage, applying a solid color or pattern to the image, covering up the signs of damage.

Finally, if your damage is slight — tiny spots, very small scuff-marks — you can Smudge them away, utilizing Photoshop Elements' Smudge tool to literally smear the spots away.

These restorative tools can be applied to extremely small areas, eliminating signs of damage one pixel at a time, or to larger areas if the damage is widespread or is repeated in several contiguous areas. Because all three tools are brush-based, you can decide how much of your image to repair with each click or drag of the mouse by setting the brush Size before using the tool.

Tip   If any single site of damage takes up more than 1 or 2% of your image, don't use the Clone Stamp, paint Brush, or Smudge tool to fix it. If you try to use these tools to repair a large area or to reconstruct a great deal of missing content, you'll find that your restorative measures will be too obvious, and the image will look "doctored." Tools like these, which can be used to tinker with very small areas, don't lend themselves to large seamless repairs.

Painting Out Scratches

Sometimes, the answer to your image restoration challenges is much easier or more straightforward than you thought it would be. When it comes to photo editing, one of the simplest tools to use is the paint Brush, because it works very much like the real-life version of the same thing, applying color wherever you want it. You can pick the color you'll paint with, and you can set the Size and style of the brush (by selecting a brush Preset), and you paint over the scratch, scuff mark, or other type of small mark on your image.

Another thing to remember when painting out scratches — the scratch needn't only traverse parts of the image that are the same color or texture. You can paint over just a few pixels, then switch to a new color, paint a bit more, and keep going along the length of the scratch, tear, or scuff-mark, until you've obliterated it, one section at a time. You can change brush sizes and shapes when the scratch/scuff changes thickness and texture, and by the end of the process, the scratch is gone, and the repairs should be virtually (if not entirely) invisible. If you mess up along the way, Undo what you've done to the point where things went awry, and then redo. Depending on the scratch in question, the process might require some painstaking steps, but overall, the tool and its options are your easiest retouching solution.

So – when you're ready to take the easy way out, follow these steps with the Brush tool — you can even use a Pencil tool if your scratch is very thin:

1. Click on the brush for larger areas or damage with edges that are soft — like scuff marks, abrasions, tears. Use the Pencil tool if your scratches are very fine and sharp-edged.

2. When the tool becomes active, so do its options. You can adjust the size, shape, and style of the brush or pencil tip, which controls how and how much color it applies.

3. Next, set the color that the paintbrush or pencil will apply. You can do this by sampling pixels next to the damaged area, using the Eye dropper, or open the Color Picker by clicking the Foreground Color button on the toolbox.

4. When the right color is selected, go back to the Brush or Pencil and begin painting or drawing out the unwanted scratches, scuffs, and spots. You can click to get rid of a small dot, or drag to get rid of a scratch.

Tip If you find that your painting appears obvious no matter what you do, try painting with your Brush set to a lower Opacity. By not applying dense paint (even thin, textured lines can look painted on, sort of like a face with too much make-up), you allow just a little of the content underneath the paint to show through. If the scratch still shows too much, put another very see-through layer on, perhaps an even thinner line, if possible. Keep layering it, experimenting with brush sizes and textures, and always keeping the Opacity low, until you get coverage that doesn't look like coverage!

Smudging Blemishes Away

The Smudge Tool works like your fingertips do when you're blending make-up or if you're softening the edges between two areas in a pastel or chalk drawing. By mixing color from one area of the image onto another area, you make divisions between differently-colored areas less obvious. You can use this tool to blend hard edges, to soften or smudge away blemishes when actually patching them would be too obvious or might rob the image of too much texture. You can use the tool in black and white or color images, and by utilizing its options, even add a third color — the current Foreground color — to the smudge.

Smearing with the Finger Painting Option

The Finger Painting option, which is off by default, allows you to smear the current Foreground color into the area you're smudging (6.20). You can use this option to incorporate new colors, or brighter, more vibrant versions of existing colors by finger-painting them in.

Tip The Smudge tool may mimic the effects of finger painting or fingertip smearing, but it is a brush-based tool. You can set the size and texture of your fingertip by using the Size option, and by choosing from the same group of Brush Presets that are available when you're using the actual Brush tool. Sometimes, a textured fingertip can achieve a more natural-looking result than a smooth one.

Getting Rid of Spots and Stains

When my aunt was a little girl, she took great delight in drawing on photos — especially those that had my mother (her sister) in them. Consequently, the family has a lot of photos with pen, pencil, and crayon streaks across them. We also have the normal number of photos on which someone rested a coffee-cup, photos that got wet and developed water "rings," and photos that picked up the tannins from a leather wallet pocket or from the paper to which they were taped.

The stains and spots that result from accidents, poor storage decisions, and vandalism can be just as damaging as rips and tears — the stain may entirely obscure image content, or it may render a previously frame-worthy image fit only for the back of a drawer. If you have a stained or spotted photo, however, don't despair. The same tools you'd use to get rid of scratches, dust spots, and the changes in color that occur with age can be used as the "detergent" to make your photos look clean again.

Washing Out Stains with the Sponge Tool

If the spot in question is a brown, rust, or some other-colored stain, you can wash out its color by selecting it (using the Magic Wand, if possible, so that only the stain is selected) and then using the Sponge tool set to Desaturate mode. With the Sponge tool, you can literally scrub away the color with your mouse, hopefully leaving the image intact beneath it. If it also washes away the color from the image, you can reapply that color using the surrounding un-stained content to supply the color information.

To use the Sponge tool to remove a stain, follow these steps:

1. Activate the Magic Wand tool, and set its Tolerance option so that when you click on the stain, only the stain (or a portion thereof) is selected. If the stain's color or intensity is not uniform, you may have to perform this and the subsequent steps for each varied area of the stain, or by pressing and holding the Shift key, you can keep clicking on areas in the stain to add to the selection.

2. With as much of the stain selected as you can get without selecting other parts of the image, activate the Sponge tool.

3. Change the Mode to Desaturate, so that instead of increasing color saturation, the tool will reduce it.

4. Reduce the Flow to 50%–you may move up or down from there when you see the results, but reducing it is a good idea so that you don't wash out all the color — the stain and the image beneath it — as you drag over the stain.

5. Continue selecting and desaturating sections of the stain if you can't do it all in one fell swoop — it may be a better idea to do it in sections anyway, so that you can adjust the Sponge tool's Flow to match the intensity of the stain's color — more Flow will remove more color with each drag of the mouse.

Tip

After you've used the Sponge tool to remove as much of the stain as you can, you may be left with remnants of the stain to deal with. Based on the nature of the remnants, their placement, and how much of a problem you still have, you can use the Eraser, set to a low Opacity, to remove more of the stain, or you can use the Clone Stamp to cover up the stain with content from surrounding, unstained areas of the image.

Selecting and Recoloring Stained Content

If the Sponge tool isn't working or has removed the color (and not just the stain) from your image, you can recolor the stain to get rid of it. The first step in this process is much the same as the Sponge tool procedure discussed previously — you want to select the stain (and none of the surrounding pixels, if you can avoid it) and therefore focus your recoloring tools on the stain alone.

Once the stain is selected — in whole or in part — you can use any of the following tools/commands to eradicate the unwanted wash of color:

+ Use the Color Variations dialog box to remove the color of the stain — reduce the amount of Red to get rid of a brownish or rust-colored stain, or reduce one or more of the other reducible colors (Yellow, Green, or Blue) and experiment to see which one/s get rid of the stain or a portion thereof. The dialog box is opened by choosing Enhance ➪ Adjust Color ➪ Color Variations.

+ Use the Enhance ➪ Adjust Color ➪ Color Cast command to get rid of the stain's color. You'll use the eye dropper button (active by default in the Color Cast dialog box, to select gray, white, or black areas within the selection, helping Elements to determine which color is overwhelming the others.

+ Use the Enhance ➪ Adjust Color ➪ Hue/Saturation command to open the Hue/Saturation dialog box. With the dialog box open and the stain selected, use the sliders to reduce the Saturation, increase Lightness, and with the color of the stain selected from the Edit drop-down list, adjust the Hue setting until the stain is mitigated.

When All Else Fails: Spot and Stain Camouflage

Some stains are stubborn, and amount to more than an unwanted wash or smear of color — sometimes they have texture, and sometimes their removal leaves (or would leave, if you pursued it) a big hole in your image — the content would be removed right along with the stain.

If you've opted to skip removing the stain or if you've attempted to do so and have damaged the image beneath it, the next best solution is to cover up the stain. You can use the following tools and techniques to camouflage the stain, hopefully eliminating any sign of it:

+ Use the Clone Stamp to apply content from the surrounding areas to the stained area. If the stain is small, this can happen with just a few clicks of the Clone Stamp. You can extend an area into the area of the stain, or you can duplicate undamaged portions of the content that's partially obscured by the stain, and use that duplicate content as cover-up.

✦ Select and duplicate undamaged content using the Layer ➪ New ➪ Layer Via Copy command to create a layer that can be positioned on top of the stain. You'll find complete coverage of this and the Clone Stamp earlier in this chapter, where major rips, tears, and missing areas of content were covered.

Tip

If the stain is on a non-crucial part of the image and the photo's composition won't suffer for it, consider cropping to just inside the area where the stain ends. While you may end up with a smaller photo, it can be worth it to avoid a potentially difficult restoration process. Most stains and spots can be eradicated, however, so if the cropping will ruin your composition or if the stain involves an important component of the photo, use the recoloring and camouflage techniques discussed in this section to get rid of the stain as best as you can.

Understanding the Special Needs of Vintage Photos

Vintage photographs present some very common problems. Over the years, images fade due to the passage of time, developing procedures, the paper that the image was printed on, exposure to the sun, and exposure to extreme heat or dampness. Dampness can cause even more harm, because you can get mold, and that eats away the coating on the photos and can damage the paper as well. In many cases, multiple culprits have been and are at work, and you'll have multiple problems — faded image content along with scuffs, scratches, stains, mold, dust, and outright damage in the form of rips, tears, and missing corners.

When faced with an image with more than one problem, you need to perform triage — the process of deciding which "injuries" are the most serious, and which ones should be addressed first. Should you repair the scratches and scuffs before you adjust the color? Will it help to replace the corner before you tinker with the exposure or saturation? The order in which you deal with an image that exhibits multiple problems really depends on the location and severity of the problems, and which one/s bother you the most.

Consider these scenarios when determining the right order in which to deal with a vintage image and its problems — you may not have the exact same problems, but these situations may still help you make decisions about your images:

✦ If there are multiple problems in a single area, solving one might solve the other, or make it a moot point. Consider a torn corner, with a big stain on it. You can paste content from the opposite corner over it (rotating the pasted content with the Image ➪ Transform ➪ Free Transform command and your mouse), and in that process, you may get rid of the stain, too.

✦ If there's a portion of the edge or frame missing, you can simply crop around the image to eliminate the need to replace the missing corner or side. If the missing portion includes part of the image, consider whether or not that portion is important to the composition of the image. You may be able to crop away the damage and leave the important parts, eliminating hours of restoration work.

✦ If you can't crop, decide whether or not the damage is really that bad. This may sound like a cop-out or some giant rationalization, but does the damage lend an air of history to the picture? Part of the charm of vintage photos is that they look old — the places and people depicted are old — their clothes worn by people in the image, the scenery, the architecture, etc. If the photo was taken in the 1800's, there's no harm (perhaps) in it looking like an image that's over 100 years old. However, if the damage is on someone's face or across front of the family home, yes, try to fix it. If the damage is on the periphery or doesn't detract from the overall appeal of the image, consider leaving it alone.

✦ If you've decided to fix the problem/s, tackle the structural ones first. After you've replaced the corner or filled in the hole or scratch, then go about improving color quality, eliminating tiny scratches and spots, or bringing out detail lost to fading or bad lighting. There's no sense making these changes to the overall image and then having to do them again to make a patch blend in.

✦ Work slowly and deliberately. Don't try to do too many things at once. If the picture is that precious or historically important, it's worth laboring over it, working zoomed in to get things right, editing pixel by pixel.

Tip Be patient, and don't be surprised if it takes many hours to get the picture "just right." For photos that may be the only tangible evidence that a now-deceased relative ever lived, or for photos that depict special events such as weddings or vacations to places that don't exist anymore, it's worth it to take whatever time is required to bring the photo back to its original glory. Don't make yourself crazy, however, and do give yourself breaks. There's no harm in taking several hours or even a few days off between retouching sessions — give your eyes a rest, and come back to the task refreshed and ready to do the best job you can.

Preserving Your Original Photos

Many of your original photographs, whether taken by you or someone else, are precious to you. The fact that you're reading this appendix in particular, proves that — you want to keep your images safe from damage, age, and loss. as you read on, you'll learn some tips for storing different kinds of photos, and how to maintain an electronic "back-up" of your photos so that if the worse happens — your originals are lost or destroyed — you have printable copies on your computer.

Storing Vintage Photos

Vintage photos, which I consider to be any photo taken before cameras were something that "regular people" owned and used on a regular basis, present some challenges:

✦ Many photos were printed on porous, matte-finish paper, making them susceptible to damage from moisture, dust, dirt, oils from people's hands. The card stock on which the photos were pasted is also susceptible to drying out and breaking — this accounting for all the old photos you see with broken corners and chipped edges. Over time the cardboard dries out, and it simply doesn't stand up to handling very well.

✦ When exposed to sunlight, vintage photos paper turns brown, and the photos themselves fade.

✦ Water absorbs easily into the card stock on which photos were printed, and the water marks and rings are impossible to get rid of.

✦ Nobody has the negatives for these photos, so reprints from the original film are not possible.

To remedy the problems related to the paper on which the photos are printed, great care must be taken in the methods you employ to store and display vintage photos. First, never store them loose in boxes or drawers. Always store them in such a way as to prevent them banging into each other, scraping against other photos or the box in which they're stored. Some options include:

✦ Store them in photo albums, made from acid-free paper, with plastic sheeting that goes over the photos but that does not seal the pages. You don't want any moisture to build up under the plastic, but you want the protection from scuff marks that the plastic provides.

✦ Store them in envelopes, again using acid-free paper, and keep the envelopes, which should be sized to match the size of the photos, in a box.

✦ Have the photos professionally dry-mounted and framed, using acid-free paper. The glass will protect them from physical damage, and the framing makes them easy to display. Do not put the framed photos in the sun, or leave them where the sun may shine for any length of time. Choose a shady corner of the room where very little light will hit the photos.

✦ Store your photos in a cool, dry place. Don't put them in the attic or basement, because the attic is likely to get very hot during the summer and dry heat from your house will rise into the attic during the winter. Basements tend to be damp, so unless yours is dry all year round, don't store photos there, either. Good choices are closets and file cabinets, places where the photos won't be handled excessively, where temperatures remain fairly constant, and where dampness is unlikely to be a problem.

Why "acid-free"? Because paper with acids in it will damage the photos—you'll see staining and the paper will begin to disintegrate. It's not hard to find acid-free photo albums and framing materials these days, so don't worry that you won't be able to find the right storage and display paraphernalia at your local store.

If your area is prone to flooding, store your photos as high as you can—on top shelves, on upper floors of the house (but not the attic, for reasons mentioned earlier), anywhere water won't go if you get a few feet of floodwater in your home during a storm.

Most fireproof file cabinets will prevent paper inside them from charring in the event of even the hottest fire—you can get safes and cabinets that meet different standards, and the prices go up as the fire-proof qualities increase. In even the best cabinets and safes, however, the heat may get high enough to melt plastic, so if you store your photos in a fire-proof safe or cabinet, don't put them in plastic bags, sleeves, or envelopes—the plastic will melt and get stuck to your photos.

Keeping New Images in Mint Condition

Photos taken in the last few decades are much more likely to survive rough handling than their predecessors, many of which will fade and discolor with time. The paper used by current photo processing labs is also more durable than the paper used in, say, 1960. The older your photos are, the more careful you need to be in storing and displaying them, and for your photos taken before 1960, it's a good idea to follow the suggestions for storage and display of vintage photos.

For photos taken in the 1970's through today, you don't have to be quite so cautious. You still don't want to handle them with wet or oily hands, as the water and oils in your skin will break down the emulsion on the photos, but you don't have to be as afraid of incidental damage from the photos being stacked in a single envelope, or stored in a drawer. You want to reduce the amount of jostling and scraping against each other that the photos endure, however, just to eliminate scuff marks and any accidental damage from spilled liquids, fire, and rough handling by children.

The same rules for storage in terms of heat, dampness, and risk of loss to flood apply to new photos—while the paper and processing make them hardier than their predecessors, it's still a good idea not to expose photos to any extremes—of temperature or humidity.

Some cats find the emulsion on photos to be quite delicious. You'll find them licking the coating off your photos, leaving a sticky mess behind, and usually ruining the photo. More importantly, the chemical coating isn't good for the cat, so don't leave photos lying around unattended—when you've finished looking at them, put them back in the envelope.

Creating Electronic Archives

A good backup plan for your most precious originals is to scan them at the highest resolution you can (1200 dpi, for most scanning applications), and store them on CDs. More durable than floppy or zip disks, CDs also hold more information, making it possible to store the huge files that high-resolution scanning will create. You may end up with individual files that exceed 50 megabytes, so being able to store several on one CD is quite convenient. You can read more about the scanning process — setting up your scanner, installing scanning software, scanning photos in color, etc. in Chapter 2.

Tip

If the photos are extremely precious, depict famous people, or document an important event — historically, personally, professionally — and you can't imagine life going on if the photo were lost, scan it, store it on CD, and put that CD in your bank safe deposit box. It will be safe from fire, theft, flood, and accidental loss or damage there.

✦   ✦   ✦

Index

SYMBOLS & NUMERICS

... (ellipsis), 20
3D effects filters
    Clouds, 358
    Difference Clouds, 359
    Lens Flare, 359–360
    Lighting Effects, 360
    overview of, 357
    Texture Fill, 360–361
    3D Transform, 357
3D Transform filter, 357

A

.ABR extension, 227
Accented Edges filter, 324
accessing
    help, 54–55
    presets for tools, 38–39
    shortcut menu, 265
    tool options, 98, 99
acid-free paper, 523, 524
Acrobat Reader (Adobe), 431
activating
    layer, 262
    tool, 98
Actual Pixels size view and Zoom tool, 28
adaptive palette (Color Reduction Algorithm
        menu), 481
Add Noise dialog box, 509–510
Add Noise filter, 351, 509–510
Add to option (Shape tool), 281, 282
Add to Selection button, 106, 111
adding text to photo or image, 9–10
Adjust Backlighting tool, 181–182
Adjust Color Intensity slider (Color Variations
        window), 180
Adjust Fill Flash dialog box, 182
adjusting
    automatically
        Auto Levels command, 190
        Quick Fix command, 189–190
    blur, 123–127
    brightness in Brightness/Contrast dialog box,
        183–184
    color and contrast, 5–6
    contrast in Brightness/Contrast dialog box, 183,
        184–186

    highlights, 187–188
    hue, 174–175, 182
    intensity of color, 180, 326
    light level, 515
    opacity for Brush tool, 232–234
    pixel dimensions and depth, 204–205
    saturation, 174–175, 182
    shadow, 187–188
    sharpness, 123–127
adjustment layer, improving image with, 190–191
Adobe
    Acrobat Reader, 431
    color picker, 59, 60, 166
    Illustrator, 11, 12, 426
    online, sunflower icon and, 35
    Web site, 71
After image (Color Variations window), 179
.AI extension, 426
Airbrush mode (Brush tool), 234–235
All Elements Shapes option (Custom Shape tool),
        279–280
Alt key and dragging, 100
Alt+Ctrl+O (Open As dialog box), 80
alternate tool, 18, 19, 34–35
Alt+F4 (Exit Elements), 73
Always Maximize Compatibility for Photoshop (PSD)
        Files option (Saving Files), 62
Amount slider (Add Noise dialog box), 509
Angle gradient, 301
Angled Strokes filter, 325
animated GIF image, creating, 487–488
animation for PDF Slideshow, choosing, 436, 437
anisotropic, definition of, 362
Anti-aliased option
    Magic Eraser tool, 254
    Magic Wand tool, 110
    Paint Bucket tool, 292
anti-aliasing, definition of, 391
appending
    group of patterns to existing group, 295
    set of presets to Brush tool, 229
Apply button (Filters and Effects palettes),
        313, 416
applying
    Artistic filters, 315–322
    directional or shape gradient, 301–302, 303

Continued

applying *(continued)*
    effects
        image or text, 378–380
        to photo or drawing, 10–11
        steps for, 313–314
    filter
        by double-clicking or dragging, 45
        to part of image, 335
        steps for, 313–314
    Foreground or Background color, 48
    image and text effects, 378–380
    Layer Style
        by clicking, 47
        effects of, 305
        image window and, 408
        steps for, 410–412
    multiple Layer Styles, 305
    Pattern fill, 292–295
    PSD file as texture, 370
    special effects to photo or drawing, 10–11
    Text Effect
        to formatted text, 415
        steps for, 378–380
        to Type layer, 417
Area option (Impressionist Brush tool), 244
arrow keys, 289
artifacts
    description of, 441, 475
    eliminating
        Noise filters and, 509–510
        options for, 508–509
Artistic filters
    Brush Stroke filters
        Accented Edges, 324
        Angled Strokes, 325
        Crosshatch, 325
        Dark Strokes, 326
        Ink Outlines, 326
        overview of, 315, 322–323
        Spatter, 327
        Sprayed Strokes, 327
    Colored Pencil, 315
    dialog boxes for, 321–322, 323
    Dry Brush, 316
    Film Grain, 316
    Fresco, 317
    Neon Glow, 317
    overview of, 315
    Palette Knife, 318
    Plastic Wrap, 318
    Poster Edges, 319

Rough Pastels, 319
Sketch filters
    Bas Relief, 328
    Chalk & Charcoal, 329
    Charcoal, 329
    Chrome, 330
    Conte Crayon, 330
    Graphic Pen, 331
    Halftone Pattern, 331
    Note Paper, 332
    overview of, 315, 323, 328
    Photocopy, 332
    Plaster, 333
    Reticulation, 333
    Stamp, 334
    Torn Edges, 334
    Water Paper, 335
Smudge Stick, 320
Sponge, 320
Underpainting, 321
artwork, creating original, 8, 9
Ask Before Saving Layered TIFF Files option (Saving
        Files), 62
aspect ratio, 217
attaching image to e-mail message, 438–440
Auto button (Levels dialog box), 188
Auto Color Correction command, 183
Auto Contrast command, 186
Auto Erase option (Pencil tool), 247–248
Auto Levels command (Enhance menu), 188,
        190, 197

B

background. *See also* background color
    patterned, creating, 155–158
    for Web page, designing, 8, 9
background color
    applying, 48
    Auto Erase option and, 247–248
    choosing, 167
    Pointillize filter and, 356
    restoring, 167–168
    swapping with foreground color, 168–169
Background Eraser tool, 250–252
Background layer
    applying Layer Style and, 305
    description of, 50
    using erasers on, 252
Background option (Print Preview dialog box),
        452, 453

banding, 482
Bas Relief filter, 328
Beep When Done option (General Preferences), 61
Before image (Color Variations window), 179
Behind mode (Brush tool), 193
Bend slider (Warp Text dialog box), 396, 397
Bevel Layer Style, 408
Bicubic option (Image Size dialog box), 204, 205
Bilinear option (Image Size dialog box), 204
bit, 473–474
bit depth, 474
bitmap (BMP) format, 427, 428
bitmap image, 12, 425–426
black, 170
black and white photograph
    colorizing, 7–8
    Film Grain filter and, 316
    scanning, 82, 86, 90–91
Black option (Matte Color menu), 484
blemish, eliminating
    with Brush tool, 507–508
    with Smudge tool, 143–145, 508, 518
blending
    color, 193
    repairs, 514–515
blur, adjusting, 123–127
Blur filters
    Blur
        dialog box, 336
        moiré and, 511–512
        using, 129
    Blur More, 336, 511
    Gaussian Blur, 129, 337
    Motion Blur, 337
    motion or radial, applying, 130–132
    overview of, 128, 335
    Radial Blur, 129, 337, 338
    Smart Blur, 338, 511
    types of, 129
    uniform, soft blur, creating, 129
Blur More filter, 336, 511
Blur tool
    Blur filters compared to, 335
    Strength setting, 37
    using, 126–127
BMP (bitmap) format, 427, 428
Bold Outline (Text Effects), 414
Border dialog box, 452, 453
Border Selection dialog box, 112
borders, selecting, 362
bounding box, 219

Brick effect, 380
brightness
    Accented Edges filter and, 324
    adjusting in Brightness/Contrast dialog box,
        183–184
Brightness/Contrast dialog box, 183–186
Browse for Folder dialog box, 461, 462
browser and Web-safe format, 7
Brush Name dialog box, 41, 239
brush preset, creating, 40–43
Brush size painting cursor, 64, 66
Brush Stroke filters
    Accented Edges, 324
    Angled Strokes, 325
    Crosshatch, 325
    Dark Strokes, 326
    Ink Outlines, 326
    overview of, 315, 322–323
    Spatter, 327
    Sprayed Strokes, 327
Brush tool (paint brush)
    Airbrush mode, 234–235
    Brush Mode settings, 229–232
    creating preset, 239–240
    customizing existing preset, 237–239
    More Options button, 37–38
    More Options dialog box, 225–226, 236–237
    Opacity slider, 232–234
    overview of, 225–226
    red eye, eliminating with, 162
    selecting size and preset options, 226–229
    spot, painting dot on unwanted, 507–508
    tips for using, 240–242
brush-based tools
    Impressionist Brush, 242–244
    Mode options, 191–196
    options for, 35, 36
    Strength setting, 37
    switching between while drawing or painting, 242
Brushed Metal (Text Effects), 414, 418
Burn tool
    overview of, 143
    using, 145–148

C

camera, digital, capturing image with, 93
camera-ready image, 444
canvas size, changing, 206
Canvas Size dialog box, 206–207
Caption check box (Print Preview dialog box), 453

capturing image
    with digital camera, 93
    from scanner, 84–85
Cast Shadow (Text Effects), 414
CD, storing photographs on, 525
Center Document Windows option (General
        Preferences), 62
Chalk & Charcoal filter, 329
Change the Text Orientation button (Type tool),
        400–401
Channels palette (Photoshop), 14, 15
character, selecting in text, 393, 401
Charcoal filter, 329
choke, definition of, 371, 373–374
Choose Profile dialog box, 439
Chrome filter, 330
circle icon and Lasso tools, 102, 103
Clear Emboss (Text Effects), 414
Clear mode (Brush tool), 193
Clear Style button (Layer Styles palette), 47, 307,
        411, 412
Clear Undo History button, 49
clip art, 12
clipping away, 208
Clone Stamp tool
    damaged image and, 92
    filling in hole with, 154
    removing scratch, tear, or other damage with,
        139–142
    replacing and editing content with, 150, 151
    spot or stain, eliminating with, 143, 520–521
    using, 145
Close All command (File menu), 492
closing
    all open images, 492
    floating palette, 51
    free-form selection, 102, 103–104
    palette to Docking Well, 310
Clouds filter, 358
color. *See also* background color; foreground color
    adjusting, 5–6
    correcting, 171–172, 183
    density of, setting for Brush tool, 232–234
    erasing specific, 253–254
    for font, choosing, 391
    hue, adjusting, 174–175
    inverting, 200
    removing, 175–176
    replacing, 176–178
    sampling from existing content, 169–170
    saturation, adjusting, 174–175

    scanning and, 90–91
    swapping foreground and background, 168–169
    Text Effect and, 415
    Web Safe color palette, 479
Color Burn mode (Brush tool), 193
color cast, correcting, 172–174
color depth
    GIF and, 474
    JPEG and, 475
Color Dodge mode (Brush tool), 194
Color Halftone filter, 353, 354
color lookup table
    categories of, 480
    Custom options, 481
    description of, 478
    Dynamic options, 480
    Fixed options, 480–481
Color mode (Brush tool), 195
Color Picker dialog box
    choosing from, 59–60
    gradient fill and, 300
    mouse pointer and, 169
    opening, 165–166
    painting mask and, 119
    RGB and HSB levels, 170
    Shape tool and, 275
    Web-safe color and, 167
Color Variations command, 150
Color Variations dialog box, 520
Color Variations window
    quality and color levels of photograph, adjusting,
        178–180
    saturation, adjusting, 182
color wheel, 173
Colored Pencil filter, 315
Colorize option (Hue/Saturation dialog box), 175
colorizing black and white photograph, 7–8
column size, setting, 69
combining selections, 105–107
commands
    Auto Color Correction, 183
    Auto Contrast, 186
    Auto Levels (Enhance menu), 188, 190, 197
    Brush tool, preset-related, 227
    Close All (File menu), 492
    Color Variations, 150
    Contract, 112
    Cut, 115, 116
    Define Brush (Edit menu), 41
    Delete Layer (shortcut menu), 267
    Distort (Image menu), 213

Duplicate Layer (shortcut menu), 263, 264
Fill Flash (Enhance menu), 182
Free Transform (Image menu), 213, 214–216
Gradient Map (Image menu), 197, 198–199
Gradient tool, 301
Import, 84–88, 93
keyboard shortcuts for, 491–492
Load Brushes (Brush tool), 227, 229
Next (Preferences dialog box), 57
palette and, 21
Pattern, 294
Perspective (Image menu), 213
Posterize (Image menu), 200–201
Previous (Preferences dialog box), 57
Quick Fix (Enhance menu), 189–190
Reset Tool, 38
Save for Web (File menu), 69
Sharpen More, 133
Simplify Layer (shortcut menu), 265
Skew (Image menu), 213
Threshold (Image menu), 201–202
Transform (Image menu), 213–214
Undo, 48, 60, 240
undoing, 20
committing text, 61
Complex Layer Style, 409
compression
    GIF and, 474
    JPEG and, 475
Confetti (Text Effects), 414
Constrain Proportions option (Image Size dialog box), 204, 449
Contact Sheet dialog box, 461–462, 463
contact sheet, printing, 460–463
Conte Crayon filter, 330
content
    layer, creating from existing, 258–260
    of layer, rotating, 214–216
    of photograph
        covering up unwanted and filling in hole, 154–155
        duplicating and patching tear with, 513
        replacing and editing, 150–151
        selecting, moving, and removing, 152–154
    sharing between images, 115, 116, 268–269
context sensitivity
    of help in Hints palette, 54
    of palette, 21–22
Contiguous option
    Background Eraser tool, 251
    Magic Eraser tool, 254

Contract command, 112
contrast, adjusting
    in Brightness/Contrast dialog box, 183, 184–186
    overview of, 5–6
convolution, 373
copying
    content from one image into another, 115, 116, 513–514
    content to new layer, 258–260
copyrighting image, 501
CorelDRAW, 11, 12
Corner Crop Marks option (Print Preview dialog box), 454
correcting
    color, 171–172, 183
    color cast, 172–174
    light level, 180–182
Craquelure filter, 368
Create New Fill or Adjustment Layer button (Layers palette), 190–191
Create New Folder button (Save As dialog box), 94
Create New Layer button
    dragging existing layer to, 113, 114
    Layers palette, 263
Create Warped Text tool, 394–400
Crop tool, 209–211
cropping image
    with Crop tool, 209–211
    to eliminate damage, 521, 522
    manually, 212
    overview of, 208–209
Crosshatch filter, 325
Crystallize filter, 354
Ctrl++ and Ctrl +- (zoom in and zoom out), 26
Ctrl key, selecting images for Picture Package with, 467
Ctrl+A (Select All), 267
Ctrl+Alt+P (Print), 60
Ctrl+F (repeat last-used filter), 133, 336
Ctrl+O (Open dialog box), 77–78
Ctrl+P (Print with Preview), 60
Ctrl+S (Save), 60, 93–94, 428
Ctrl+V (Paste), 151
Ctrl+X (Cut), 152
Ctrl+Y (Forward), 60
Ctrl+Z (Undo), 48, 60
cursors
    Color Picker dialog box and, 169–170
    for painting, 64–67
    for text, 393
Custom filter, 372, 373

custom options (Color Reduction Algorithm menu), 481
custom shape, drawing, 279–280
customizing
    brush preset, 237–240
    display and cursors, 64–67
    Edit ⇨ Preferences and, 57–58
    General Preferences, setting, 58–62
    grid, 70–71
    Layer Style, 306
    memory and image cache, 73–74
    plug-ins and scratch disks, 71–72
    presets for tools, 40–44
    save settings, 62–64
    tool, 35
    transparency settings, 67–68
    units and rulers, 68–69
Cut command, 115, 116
Cutout filter dialog box, 322
cutting content to new layer, 258–260

D
damaged photograph
    prioritizing multiple problems, 521–522
    restoring
        overview of, 4–5, 136
        scratch, scuff, or tear, eliminating, 136–142, 505–506
        spot or stain, eliminating, 142–150, 518–521
    scanning, 92
    torn, reconstructing
        blending repairs, 514–515
        copy and paste method, 513–514
        layer, creating based on selection, 514
        overview of, 512–513
Dark Strokes filter, 326
Darken mode (Brush tool), 193
darkening image content to remove stain, 147–148
Darker slider (Adjust Backlighting dialog box), 181–182
decreasing. See reducing
default configuration
    Paint Bucket tool, 292
    resolution for new document, setting for, 69
    restoring for foreground and background color, 167
    returning tool to, 38
    3D Transform filter, 357
    tools, 35
    of workspace, 17–18
Default Foreground and Background Colors button, 167–168

Default set (Custom Shape tool), 279
Define Brush command (Edit menu), 41
De-Interlace filter, 371, 372
Delete Layer command (shortcut menu), 267
deleting
    color, 175–176
    edges of image by cropping, 208–212
    layer, 267–268
    Layer Style, 307
    pattern, 297–298
    saved selection, 122
    selected content, 117
    text, 401
    Text Effect, 419–420
density of color, setting for Brush tool, 232–234
Desaturate mode (Sponge tool), 148
designing Web page background and navigational tools, 8, 9
Despeckle filter, 350, 351–352, 510
Diamond gradient, 301
Difference Clouds filter, 359
Difference mode (Brush tool), 195
Diffuse filter, 362
Diffuse Glow filter, 342
Diffusion algorithm (Dithering Algorithm menu), 482, 483
digital camera, capturing image with, 93
directional gradient, applying, 301–302, 303
Discontiguous option (Background Eraser tool), 251, 252
Displace filter, 342
Display & Cursors preferences, 64–67
displaying
    custom shapes, 279–280
    Filters and Effects by category, 311
    grid, 30–31
    layer, 261–262
    palette, 21, 51
    Ruler, 29–30
    Text Effects thumbnails, 416–417
    tool tip, 32, 33
Dissolve mode (Brush tool), 193
Distort command (Image menu), 213
Distort filters
    Diffuse Glow, 342
    Displace, 342
    Glass, 343, 370
    Liquify, 341, 343, 344
    Liquify window compared to, 350
    Ocean Ripple, 345
    overview of, 341

Pinch, 345
Polar Coordinates, 346
Ripple, 346, 370
Shear, 347
Spherize, 348
Twirl, 348
Wave, 349
ZigZag, 349
distorting image, 219–220. *See also* Distort filters
Dither option (Gradient tool), 299
dithering, 481–483
Docking Well
    closing palette to, 310
    opening palette in, 51
    palettes excluded from, 21
    rearranging tabs in, 52–53
    reattaching palette to, 52
    uncrowding, 53
Document Color Profile option (Save For Web dialog
        box), 478
Document section (Contact Sheet dialog box), 461
document, setting default resolution for new, 69
document size, 203
Document Size setting (Image Size dialog box),
        204–206
Dodge tool
    overview of, 143
    using, 145–148
double-clicking
    to force selection closure, 104
    layer, 265, 266
    Type layer, 401
    word to select, 393, 394
downloading file
    interlacing and, 484, 486
    virus and, 503
dragging
    to apply effect, 379
    cloned content and, 142
    Gradient tool and, 302, 303
    layer to create duplicate, 113, 114, 263, 264
    with Marquee tools, 99–100
    to paint selection, 108
    Pattern Stamp tool and, 158
    perspective, changing, and, 222
    to resize layer, 117
    to resize workspace, 24, 25
    rotation mode and, 216
    Shape layer, 289
    Shape tool and, 275, 276
    thumbnail to apply filter or effect, 313, 314
    Transform command and, 213

drawing. *See also* Sketch filters
    Accented Edges filter and, 324
    applying special effects to, 10–11
    Colored Pencil filter and, 315
    custom shape, 279–280
    line, 280–281
    polygon, 277–278
    rectangle or ellipse, 275–277
    scanning, 91
    tips for, 240–242
driver for printer, 451
Drop Shadows Layer Style, 408
Dry Brush filter, 316
duotone, 175
Duplicate Layer command (shortcut menu),
        263, 264
duplicating layer, 113, 114, 263–264
Dust & Scratches dialog box, 137, 506
Dust & Scratches filter, 136–138, 352, 505–506
dye-sublimation printer, 445, 446
dynamic options (Color Reduction Algorithm
        menu), 480

E

E (Eraser tool shortcut key), 249
edge
    Accented Edges filter and, 324
    definition of, 324
    Despeckle filter and, 510
    Find Edges filter and, 362, 364
    Glowing Edges filter and, 364
    High Pass filter and, 373
    of image, cropping, 208–212
    Ink Outlines filter and, 326
    of paint, softening, 234–235
    softening, 515–516
    Trace Contour filter and, 366
Edit button (Gradient tool), 302
Edit drop-down list (Hue/Saturation dialog box), 175
Edit ⇨ Copy
    creating layer from selection, 113
    filling in hole with, 154
    layer, creating using, 258–260
    sharing content between images, 115, 269,
        513–514
Edit ⇨ Cut
    deleting layer and, 267
    layer, creating using, 258–260
    moving content between images with, 115
    replacing and editing content with, 151, 152–154

Edit ➪ Define Brush
    brush preset, creating, 41
    Brush tool preset, creating, 239
    Pencil tool preset, creating, 247
Edit ➪ Define Pattern, 43, 296
editing
    custom brush, 240
    existing text
        overview of, 389, 390
        on Type layer, 392–394
    mask-made selection, 121
    paragraph content, 401–402
    Text Effects, 418–419
Edit ➪ Paste
    creating layer from selection, 113
    replacing content with, 151
    sharing content between images, 115, 269, 513–514
Edit ➪ Preferences
    customizing and, 57–58
    grid size, setting, 32
    ruler units, setting, 30
Edit ➪ Undo, 20, 48
effects. *See also* Effects palette; Text Effects
    applying
        image or text, 378–380
        to photo or drawing, 10–11
        steps for, 313–314
    Frames, 381–382
    reversing, 126
Effects palette. *See also* Text Effects
    categories, 376–377
    displaying options by category, 311
    overview of, 46–47, 309–310, 375–376
    viewing options as list, 311–313, 416
    Wood Frame effect, 375, 377
Elements
    exiting, 73
    functions list, 4–11
    limitations of, 11–13
    overview of, 3
    Photoshop compared to, 13–15
    uninstalling and reinstalling, 83
eliminating
    artifacts
        with Noise filters, 509–510
        options for, 508–509
    blemish
        with Brush tool, 507–508
        with Smudge tool, 143–145, 508, 518
    moiré
        Blur filters and, 511–512
        blurring manually, 512
        options for, 509

red eye
    automatically, 158–160
    with Brush tool, 162
    with Eyedropper tool, 161
    manually, 161–163
    scratch, scuff, or tear, 136–142
    spot or stain, 142–150
eliminating noise. *See* Noise filters
ellipse, drawing, 275–277
Ellipse tool. *See* Shape tool
ellipsis (...), 20
Elliptical Marquee tool, 99–100, 514
e-mail message, attaching image to, 438–440
Emboss filter, 362, 363
Encapsulated PostScript (EPS) format, 427
Encoding method (PDF Options dialog box), 431
Enhance menu tools, 171–172
Enhance ➪ Adjust Brightness/Contrast ➪ Levels, 187
Enhance ➪ Adjust Color, 171
Enhance ➪ Adjust Color ➪ Color Cast, 172, 520
Enhance ➪ Adjust Color ➪ Color Variations, 150, 178, 520
Enhance ➪ Adjust Color ➪ Hue/Saturation, 174, 520
Enhance ➪ Adjust Color ➪ Remove Color, 175
Enhance ➪ Adjust Color ➪ Replace Color, 176
Enhance ➪ Adjust Lighting, 180–181
Enhance ➪ Adjust Lighting ➪ Adjust Backlighting, 181
Enhance ➪ Adjust Lighting ➪ Fill Flash, 182
Enhance ➪ Auto Color Correction, 183
Enhance ➪ Auto Contrast, 186
Enhance ➪ Auto Levels, 190
Enhance ➪ Quick Fix, 189
enhancing detail with filter, 128–135
Enter key, typing text and, 389
EPS (Encapsulated PostScript) format, 427
equalizing image, 197, 198
Eraser tools
    Background Eraser, 250–252
    Magic Eraser, 253–254
    overview of, 248–249
    standard, 249–250
Exclude Overlapping Shape Areas option (Shape tool), 281, 282
Exclusion mode (Brush tool), 195
exiting Elements, 73
Expand Selection dialog box, 112–113
Export Clipboard option (General Preferences), 61
Extrude filter, 363
eye, adding sparkle to, 163
eye icon (layer), 261, 262
Eyedropper Color option (Matte Color menu), 484

Eyedropper tool
    pixel, finding level of color in, 49
    red eye, eliminating with, 161
EyeWire site, 498

F

F1 (Help), 54
f icon (Layer Styles), 417, 418
face, creating pattern from, 297
Facet filter, 355
Fade option (Brush tool), 236
Feather, adding, and Brightness/Contrast dialog
            box, 186
File Browser, opening, 78–79
File Info dialog box, 454
file type. *See* format
File ⇨ Attach to Email, 439
File ⇨ Automation Tools ⇨ PDF Slideshow, 433
File ⇨ Create Photomerge, 468
File ⇨ Create Web Photo Gallery, 501
File ⇨ Exit, 73
File ⇨ File Info, 453
File ⇨ Import
    capturing image with, 84–85
    scanner and, 83
File ⇨ Import ⇨ Image from Digital Camera, 93
filename extensions
    .ABR, 227
    .AI, 426
File ⇨ New, 442
File ⇨ Open As, 80
File ⇨ Open Recent, 62, 63, 77, 80
File ⇨ Page Setup, 470
File ⇨ Print, 447
File ⇨ Print Layouts, 459–460
File ⇨ Print Layouts ⇨ Contact Sheet, 462
File ⇨ Print Layouts ⇨ Picture Package, 464
File ⇨ Print Preview, 447
files
    bitmap, 426
    downloading, 503
    moving layers between, 268–269
    size of
        merging layers and, 271
        PSD format and, 425
    TIFF, saving, 62, 63
File ⇨ Save, 93–94, 428
File ⇨ Save As, 93–94, 95, 429
File ⇨ Save for Web, 476
Fill Flash command (Enhance menu), 182
filling in hole, 154–158

fills
    gradient
        color, choosing for, 300
        creating presets for, 42
        directional and shape, applying, 301–302, 303
        overview of, 298–299
    pattern
        applying, 292–295
        choosing different set of, 293–295
        creating, 296–298
        creating from selection within image, 42–44
        presets, creating for, 42
Film Grain filter, 316
Filter Options dialog box, 45, 46
Filter ⇨ Blur ⇨ Motion Blur, 131–132
Filter ⇨ Blur ⇨ Radial Blur, 131, 132
Filter ⇨ Noise, 136
filters. *See also* Filters menu; Filters palette
    applying
        by double-clicking or dragging, 45
        overview of, 313–314
        to part of image, 335
    Artistic
        Colored Pencil, 315
        dialog boxes for, 321–322, 323
        Dry Brush, 316
        Film Grain, 316
        Fresco, 317
        Neon Glow, 317
        overview of, 315
        Palette Knife, 318
        Plastic Wrap, 318
        Poster Edges, 319
        Rough Pastels, 319
        Smudge Stick, 320
        Sponge, 320
        Underpainting, 321
    Blur
        Blur, 336, 511–512
        Blur More, 336, 511
        creating uniform, soft, 129
        Gaussian Blur, 129, 337
        Motion Blur, 337
        motion or radial, applying, 130–132
        overview of, 335
        Radial Blur, 129, 337, 338
        Smart Blur, 338, 511
    Brush Stroke
        Accented Edges, 324
        Angled Strokes, 325
        Crosshatch, 325

Continued

filters *(continued)*
  Dark Strokes, 326
  Ink Outlines, 326
  overview of, 322–323
  Spatter, 327
  Sprayed Strokes, 327
Distort
  Diffuse Glow, 342
  Displace, 342
  Glass, 343, 370
  Liquify, 341, 343, 344, 350
  Ocean Ripple, 345
  overview of, 341
  Pinch, 345
  Polar Coordinates, 346
  Ripple, 346, 370
  Shear, 347
  Spherize, 348
  Twirl, 348
  Wave, 349
  ZigZag, 349
Noise
  Add Noise, 351, 509–510
  Despeckle, 350, 351–352, 510
  Dust & Scratches, 136–138, 352, 505–506
  Median, 352, 506, 510
  overview of, 350
Other
  Custom, 372, 373
  High Pass, 373
  Maximum, 373–374
  Minimum, 373, 374
  Offset, 375
  overview of, 371
overview of, 128–129
Pixelate
  Color Halftone, 353, 354
  Crystallize, 354
  Facet, 355
  Fragment, 353
  Mezzotint, 355
  Mosaic, 356
  overview of, 353
  Pointillize, 356
reapplying last, 336
Render
  Clouds, 358
  Difference Clouds, 359
  Lens Flare, 359–360
  Lighting Effects, 360
  overview of, 357

  Texture Fill, 360–361
  3D Transform, 357
Sharpen
  overview of, 335, 339
  Sharpen, 339
  Sharpen Edges, 340
  Sharpen More, 339, 340
  Unsharp Mask, 341
sharpness
  of edges, increasing, 133, 134
  overall, increasing, 133
Sketch
  Bas Relief, 328
  Chalk & Charcoal, 329
  Charcoal, 329
  Chrome, 330
  Conte Crayon, 330
  Graphic Pen, 331
  Halftone Pattern, 331
  Note Paper, 332
  overview of, 323, 328
  Photocopy, 332
  Plaster, 333
  Reticulation, 333
  Stamp, 334
  Torn Edges, 334
  Water Paper, 335
Stylize
  Diffuse, 362
  Emboss, 362, 363
  Extrude, 363
  Find Edges, 362, 364
  Glowing Edges, 364
  overview of, 361
  Solarize, 365
  Tiles, 365–366
  Trace Contour, 366
  Wind, 367
Texture
  Craquelure, 368
  Grain, 368
  Mosaic Tiles, 369
  overview of, 367
  Patchwork, 369
  Stained Glass, 370
  Texturizer, 370–371
Unsharp Mask, 133, 134–135
Video
  De-Interlace, 372
  NTSC Colors, 372
  overview of, 371

Filters menu
    categories, 128
    overview of, 312
Filters palette
    dialog boxes and, 312
    displaying options by category, 311
    overview of, 45
    viewing options as list, 311–313
Filter ⇨ Sharpen, 133
Filter ⇨ Sharpen ⇨ Unsharp Mask, 133, 134–135
Find Edges filter, 362, 364
Finger Painting option (Smudge tool), 508, 518
Fit on Screen view
    moving on-screen tools when using, 29
    uses of, 28
Fit to Page view and Hand tool, 28
fixed options (Color Reduction Algorithm menu),
        480–481
Flatten Layers option
    Contact Sheet dialog box, 463
    Picture Package dialog box, 466, 468
flattening
    image, 262
    image layer before adding frame, 381–382
    layer, 271
floating palette, 51–52
fly-out toolbar, 18, 19
folder, creating in Save As dialog box, 94–95
font, choosing, 391, 392
forcing selection closure, 104
foreground color
    applying, 48
    Auto Erase option and, 247–248
    choosing, 167, 292
    Paint Bucket tool and, 291
    restoring, 167–168
    swapping with background color, 168–169
Foreground-to-Background gradient, 300
format
    BMP, 427, 428
    color depth, calculating, 474
    EPS, 427
    GIF
        animated image, creating, 487–488
        description of, 427, 473–474
        optimizing image into, 478–484
    JPEG
        description of, 427, 474–475
        digital camera and, 93
        optimizing image into, 485–486
    PCX, 427

    PDF, 427, 428, 431–432
    PNG
        description of, 427, 428, 475–476
        optimizing image into PNG-8, 478–484
        optimizing image into PNG-24, 485–486
    PSD
        description of, 428
        Save As dialog box and, 94
        saving file and, 423, 424
    Save As dialog box and, 423–424
    saving file in original, 423–425
    saving image and, 84
    TIFF
        description of, 427, 428
        saving files in, 62, 63
    Web graphic, 7, 473
formatting text, 388–389, 403
Fragment filter, 353
frame overlay, turning shape into, 217
Frames effects, 381–382
framing image, 451
Free Transform command (Image menu)
    rotating layer and, 214–216
    Skew, Distort, and Perspective commands
            compared to, 213
free-form area
    closing, 102, 103
    selecting, 101–102
    Selection Brush tool and, 107–109
Fresco filter, 317
FrontPage (Microsoft), 501
FTP software, 502
Fuzziness slider (Replace Color dialog box), 176–177

G
gallery, posting to Web through ISP, 501–503
Gamma correction, 477–478
garbage can icon, 267, 268
Gaussian Blur filter, 129, 337
General Preferences, setting
    Color Picker, 59–60
    keyboard shortcuts, 60–61
    Options list, 61–62
    overview of, 58
geometric shape, selecting, 99–100
GIF (Graphics Interchange Format)
    animated image, creating, 487–488
    description of, 427, 473–474
    optimizing image into, 478–484
Glass Buttons Layer Style, 409

Glass filter, 343, 370
Glowing Edges filter, 364
Google search site, 493
Gradient Editor dialog box, 302–304
gradient fills. *See also* Gradient tool
    color, choosing for, 300
    creating presets for, 42
    directional and shape, applying, 301–302, 303
    overview of, 298–299
Gradient Map command (Image menu), 197, 198–199
Gradient Map dialog box, 199
Gradient tool
    dragging and, 302, 303
    Gradient Editor dialog box, 302–304
    options bar, 298–299
    preset, selecting, 300–301
    shape, filling with, 284
Grain filter, 368
graphic. *See* image
Graphic Pen filter, 331
Graphics Interchange Format. *See* GIF
grayscale
    gradient maps and, 197
    scanning and, 90–91
Grayscale mode, 175
grid
    displaying, 30–31
    hiding, 32
    sizing, 32
Grid Preferences dialog box, 70-71

H

Halftone Pattern filter, 331
Hand tool and Fit to Page view, 28
handles. *See also* dragging
    bounding box and, 219
    Print Preview dialog box, 450
Hard Light mode (Brush tool), 194
Help menu, 54
Help window, 54–55
hiding
    grid, 32
    layer, 261–262
    Ruler, 30
    Type layer, 419
High Pass filter, 373
highlights, adjusting, 187–188
high-resolution scan, 86
Hints palette
    location of, 21
    overview of, 54

histogram, 187
History states, setting level of, 60
hole, filling in, 154–158
Horizontal Distortion slider (Warp Text dialog box), 396, 398
Horizontal radio button (Warp Text dialog box), 398, 400
Horizontal Type Mask tool, 387
Horizontal Type tool, 385, 386, 387
hotspot, 8
How To palette
    location of, 21
    overview of, 54
HSB (Hue, Saturation, and Brightness) level, 170
hue, adjusting, 174–175
Hue mode (Brush tool), 195
Hue/Saturation dialog box, 174–175, 182

I

Illustrator (Adobe), 11, 12, 426
image. *See also* image size; scanning
    adding text to, 9–10
    attaching to e-mail message, 438–440
    camera-ready, 444
    capturing with digital camera, 93
    clipping away, 208
    copyrighting, 501
    creating new and setting resolution for, 203
    creating pattern from selection within, 42–44
    damaged or low-quality, scanning, 92
    existing, opening, 77–81
    flattening, 262
    masking area of, 118–122
    moving content between, 115, 116–117
    optimizing
        into GIF and PNG-8 formats, 478–484
        into JPEG and PNG-24 formats, 485–486
        overview of, 473
    printing, 458–459
    saving
        first time, 93–94
        new version of existing, 95, 428–431
        as PDF file, 431–432
    sending to printing company, 84
    sharing content between, 115, 116, 268–269
    vector compared to bitmap, 12
    Web-safe format for, 7
image cache, 72

Image Effects Layer Style, 409
image size
    canvas size and, 206–208
    definition of, 203
    pixel dimensions and depth, adjusting,
        204–205
Image Size area (Save For Web dialog box), 487
Image Size dialog box, 447, 449
image window
    applying Layer Style and, 408
    resizing, 80–81
Image ⇨ Adjustments, 196
Image ⇨ Adjustments ⇨ Equalize, 197
Image ⇨ Adjustments ⇨ Gradient Map, 197, 198
Image ⇨ Adjustments ⇨ Invert, 197, 200
Image ⇨ Adjustments ⇨ Posterize, 200–201
Image ⇨ Adjustments ⇨ Threshold, 201–202
Image ⇨ Crop, 212
Image ⇨ Mode, 175
Image ⇨ Resize ⇨ Canvas Size, 206
Image ⇨ Resize ⇨ Image Size, 69, 204, 447
Image ⇨ Transform, 213
Image ⇨ Transform Shape, 286
Image ⇨ Transform ⇨ Distort, 219
Image ⇨ Transform ⇨ Free Transform, 215, 278
Image ⇨ Transform ⇨ Perspective, 220
Image ⇨ Transform ⇨ Skew, 218
Import command
    fine-tuning scan, 86–88
    Image from Digital Camera submenu, 93
    overview of, 84–85
    previewing image, 85–86
Impressionist Brush tool, 242–244
"in progress" version of image, printing, 444
increasing
    canvas size, 206–208
    memory, 205
    overall sharpness, 133
    sharpness of edges, 133, 134
Info palette
    overview of, 49–50
    pixels and, 426
Ink Outlines filter, 326
inkjet printer, 445, 446
Inner Glow Layer Style, 408
Inner Shadows Layer Style, 408
installing scanner, 82–84
intensity of color, adjusting
    Color Variations window, 180
    Ink Outlines filter, 326

interlacing image, 484, 486
Internet access speed, changing, 477
Internet Service Provider (ISP), 501
interpolation method, 204
Intersect Shape Areas option (Shape tool), 281,
    282, 283
Intersect with Selection button, 106
inverting color, 200
ISP (Internet Service Provider), 501

J
Jay Arraich's Photoshop Elements Tips site, 495
JPEG (Joint Photographic Experts Group) format
    description of, 427, 474–475
    digital camera and, 93
    optimizing image into, 485–486

K
keyboard shortcuts
    Alt+Ctrl+O (Open As dialog box), 80
    Alt+F4 (Exit Elements), 73
    Ctrl++ and Ctrl +- (zoom in and zoom out), 26
    Ctrl+A (Select All), 267
    Ctrl+Alt+P (Print), 60
    Ctrl+F (repeat last-used filter), 133, 336
    Ctrl+O (Open dialog box), 77–78
    Ctrl+P (Print with Preview), 60
    Ctrl+S (Save), 60, 93–94, 428
    Ctrl+V (Paste), 151
    Ctrl+X (Cut), 152
    Ctrl+Y (Forward), 60
    Ctrl+Z (Undo), 48, 60
    E (Eraser tool), 249
    F1 (Help), 54
    L (Lasso tools), 34
    Mac, 61
    menu commands, 491–492
    overview of, 34
    setting, 60
    Shift+Ctrl+O (File Browser), 78–79
    toolbox, 490
Keyboard Zoom Resizes Windows option (General
    Preferences), 61

L
labeling Picture Package, 466, 467
Landscape orientation, 470
laser printer, 445, 446
Lasso tool button, 34

Lasso tools
    L keyboard shortcut for, 34
    Lasso
        selecting with, 105, 106, 514
        shape, creating with, 284, 285
    location on toolbox, 98
    Magnetic Lasso, 102, 103
    Polygonal Lasso
        options, 99
        shape, creating with, 284, 285
        using, 102
    using, 101
layer
    creating
        from existing content, 258–260
        new, blank, 257–258
        overview of, 256–257
        from selection, 113–114, 514
        Type or Shape, 260–261
    deleting, 267–268
    deleting selected content and, 117
    duplicating, 263–264
    erasing content from, 250, 252
    hiding and displaying, 261–262
    linking and unlinking, 269–270
    merging or flattening, 270–271
    moving between files, 268–269
    order of stacking, 266–267
    overview of, 255
    renaming, 265
    resizing, 117, 216–217
    rotating content of, 214–216
    selecting, and Marquee tools, 99–100
    skewing, 218–219
Layer Properties dialog box, 265–266
Layer Styles palette
    applying Layer Style, 305–306, 410–412
    Clear Style button, 47, 307, 411, 412
    customizing Layer Style, 306
    dragging from Docking Well, 411
    f icon, 417, 418
    navigating, 407
    overview of, 47
    previews, 408–409
    removing Layer Style, 307
    style categories, 406, 411
    Style Settings dialog box, 418
    working with, 405–406
layer thumbnail, 389

Layer ⇨ Flatten Image, 262, 271
Layer ⇨ Merge Linked, 271
Layer ⇨ Merge Visible, 271, 516
Layer ⇨ New ⇨ Layer, 257, 266
Layer ⇨ New ⇨ Layer Via Copy, 113, 114, 258, 259, 514
Layer ⇨ New ⇨ Layer Via Cut, 113, 114, 258, 259
Layers palette
    Create New Fill or Adjustment Layer button, 190–191
    overview of, 44, 50–51, 255–256
    rearranging layers in, 266–267
Lens Flare filter, 359–360
letter, hand-written, scanning, 91
Levels dialog box, 187–188
light
    Lens Flare filter and, 359–360
    level, correcting, 180–182, 515
    Neon Glow filter and, 317
Lighten mode (Brush tool), 194
lightening image content to remove stain, 147–148
Lighting Effects filter, 360
line
    drawing, 280–281
    straight, painting, 241
line art, 11–12
Line tool. See Shape tool
Linear Burn mode (Brush tool), 193
Linear Dodge mode (Brush tool), 194
Linear gradient, 301
Linear Light mode (Brush tool), 195
linked layer, hiding, 262
linking layers, 269–270
Liquify filter
    Distort filters compared to, 350
    selecting and, 343
    window, 341, 344
List View button (Filters and Effects palettes), 311, 313, 377, 378
Load Brushes command (Brush tool), 227, 229
Load dialog box (Brush tool), 227, 229
Load Patterns dialog box, 294, 295
Load Selection dialog box, 122
location for file, choosing when saving, 94
lossless compression, 474
lossy compression, 475
Luminosity mode (Brush tool), 195
LZW compression, 474, 475

M

Mac OS palette (Color Reduction Algorithm menu), 481
Macintosh
    Gamma correction and, 477–478
    keyboard shortcuts for, 61
Magic Eraser tool, 253–254
Magic Wand tool
    location on toolbox, 98
    using, 109–110
Magnetic Lasso tool, 102, 103
magnification and red eye elimination, 163
Marquee tools
    Elliptical Marquee tool, 99–100
    Rectangular Marquee tool
        cropping image manually using, 212
        location on toolbox, 98
        options bar, 35, 36
        using, 99–100
    selections and, 105, 106
mask
    creating, 118
    Horizontal Type Mask tool, 387
    painting, 118–120
    saving, 120–121
    turning into selection, 388
    Vertical Type Mask tool, 387, 388
Matte menu (JPEG), 486
matte settings for GIF and PNG-8, 483–484
Maximize button, 23
maximizing workspace, 23
Maximum filter, 373–374
Median filter, 352, 506, 510
Medium Outline (Text Effects), 414
memory
    allocation of, 73
    increasing, 205
    virtual, and image cache, 72
Memory & Image Cache Preferences dialog box, 73–74
menu bar, 20
menu command shortcuts, 491–492
merging layers, 270–271, 516
Mezzotint filter, 355
Microsoft
    Office Clip Organizer, 94
    Windows and Gamma correction, 477–478
Minimize button, 81
minimizing image window, 81
Minimum filter, 373, 374
Mode options
    brush-based tools, 191–196
    Layers palette, 258

modifying selection, 111–113
moiré
    description of, 508, 510–511
    eliminating
        Blur filters and, 511–512
        blurring manually, 512
        options for, 509
mold on photograph, dealing with, 505–506
monitor setting, printing and, 454
monotone pen, sketching with, 331
More button
    Effects palette, 416
    File Browser, 78, 79
    Layer Styles palette, 407
    Layers palette, 257
More Options button (Brush tool), 37–38
More Options dialog box
    Brush tool, 225–226, 236–237
    Impressionist Brush tool, 243–244
Mosaic filter, 356
Mosaic Tiles filter, 369
motion blur, applying, 130–132
Motion Blur dialog box, 132
Motion Blur filter, 337
motion, creating appearance of
    Motion Blur filter, 337
    Radial Blur filter, 129, 337, 338
mouse. *See also* dragging
    double-clicking
        to force selection closure, 104
        layer, 265, 266
        Type layer, 401
        word to select, 393, 394
    pointer
        Color Picker dialog box and, 169–170
        for painting, 64–67
        for text, 393
        within Preview window (Dust & Scratches dialog box), 138
Move tool
    resizing layer using, 216–217
    rotating using, 216
    Shape layer and, 289
    turning mask into selection with, 388
    type layer and, 385
    typing text and, 389
moving
    content, 152–154
    content between images, 115, 116–117
    layers between files, 268–269

Continued

moving *(continued)*
    linked layers, 269
    on-screen tools when using Fit on Screen view, 29
    options bar, 19
    palette, 51
    palette tabs in Docking Well, 52–53
    shape, 289–290
    toolbox, 32, 33
    workspace items, 24
Multiply mode (Brush tool), 193

N

naming. *See also* renaming
    custom brush, 239, 240
    custom pattern, 294
    folder, 94–95
    layer, 257
    pattern, 296–297
    selection, 122
    Shape layer, 260
    Type layer, 261, 385, 386
    version of image, 429
National Association of Photoshop Professionals, 500
navigational tools for Web page, designing, 8, 9
Navigator palette
    Brush tool and, 507
    overview of, 49
    zooming in using, 26, 27
Nearest Neighbor option (Image Size dialog box), 204
Neon Glow filter, 317
New Brush dialog box, 238
New dialog box, 442
New Layer dialog box, 257, 258
New Selection button, 106
Next command (Preferences dialog box), 57
noise
    definition of, 350
    eliminating, 508–509
Noise algorithm (Dithering Algorithm menu), 483
Noise filters
    Add Noise, 351, 509–510
    artifacts, eliminating with, 509–510
    Despeckle, 350, 351–352, 510
    Dust & Scratches, 352, 505–506
    Median, 352, 506, 510
    overview of, 350
None option (Matte Color menu), 484
Normal mode (Brush tool), 193
Note Paper filter, 332
NTSC Colors filter, 371, 372

O

Ocean Ripple filter, 345
OCR (optical character recognition), 82
Offset filter, 375
offset moiré. *See* moiré
OK button (Warp Text dialog box), 398
online. *See also* Web sites
    preparing image for use, 205
    resources, finding, 493–494
Only Web Colors option (Color Picker), 167
Opacity setting
    Brush tool, 507, 508, 518
    Eraser tool, 250
    Magic Eraser tool, 254
Opacity slider (Brush tool), 232–234
Open As dialog box, 80
Open dialog box
    overview of, 77–78
    PDF Slideshow, 433–434
opening
    Color Picker, 165–166
    Color Variations dialog box, 520
    existing image, 77–81
    File Browser, 78–79
    palette in Docking Well, 51
    Save As dialog box, 429
operating system and color picker, 59–60
optical character recognition (OCR), 82
optimizing image
    GIF and PNG-8 formats
        custom optimization settings, 480–484
        overview of, 478–479
        presets, 479
    JPEG and PNG-24 formats, 485
    overview of, 473
options bar
    Background Eraser tool, 251
    Blur tool, 127
    Brush tool, 225–227
    brush-based tools, 191–195
    Burn tool, 146
    Clone Stamp tool, 140
    Crop tool, 209, 211
    Dodge tool, 146
    Eraser tool, 249
    Free Transform, 216
    Gradient tool, 299, 302
    Impressionist Brush, 243
    Lasso tool, 105, 106

Magic Eraser tool, 254
Magic Wand tool, 109–110
Marquee tool, 105, 106
More Options button, 37–38
moving, 19
overview of, 18, 19
Paint Bucket tool, 291–292
Pencil tool, 245–246
Polygon tool, 278
preset sample (Brush tool), 236, 237
Rectangular Marquee tool, 35, 36
Red Eye Brush tool, 160
Rounded Rectangle tool, 276–277
Selection Brush tool, 107–108, 118
Shape tool, 261, 273, 274–275, 282
Sharpen tool, 125
Smudge tool, 144, 508
Sponge tool, 149
Type tool, 391
Options Menu button, 41
orientation
Landscape, 470
of paper, changing, 456
of text, changing, 400–401
Other filters
Custom, 372, 373
High Pass, 373
Maximum, 373–374
Minimum, 373, 374
Offset, 375
overview of, 371
Other option (Matte Color menu), 484
Outer Glow Layer Style, 408
Overlay mode (Brush tool), 194

P

page layout, 13
Page Setup button (Print Preview dialog box), 455
Page Setup dialog box, 455–457
PageMaker
column size and, 69
page layout and, 13
paint brush (Brush tool)
Airbrush mode, 234–235
Brush Mode settings, 229–232
creating preset, 239–240
customizing existing preset, 237–239
More Options button, 37–38
More Options dialog box, 236–237
Opacity slider, 232–234
overview of, 225–226
red eye, eliminating with, 162
selecting size and preset options, 226–229
tips for using, 240–242
Paint Bucket tool
Mode list, 192
overview of, 291–292
Pattern commands, 294
Pattern fill option, 292–295
Pattern presets for, 38, 39
shape, filling with, 284
Paint Daubs filter dialog box, 321, 322
painting
Dry Brush filter and, 316
Fresco filter and, 317
mask, 118–120
method of, and Impressionist Brush tool, 244
Palette Knife filter and, 318
Rough Pastels filter and, 319
scratch, 517–518
selection, 107–109
Sponge filter and, 320
tips for, 240–242
Underpainting filter and, 321
Painting Cursors, options for, 64–67
Palette Knife filter, 318
Palette Options dialog box, 50
palettes
context sensitivity of, 21–22
displaying, 51
Docking Well
rearranging tabs for in, 52–53
reattaching to, 52
Effects
categories, 376–377
displaying options by category, 311
overview of, 46–47, 309–310, 375–376
viewing options as list, 311–313, 416
Wood Frame effect, 375, 377
Filters
dialog boxes and, 312
displaying options by category, 311
overview of, 45
viewing options as list, 311–313
Hints, 21, 54
How To, 21, 54
Info, 49–50, 426

Continued

palettes *(continued)*
    Layer Styles
        applying Layer Style, 305–306, 410–412
        Clear Style button, 47, 307, 411, 412
        customizing Layer Style, 306
        dragging from Docking Well, 411
        f icon, 417, 418
        navigating, 407
        overview of, 47
        previews, 408–409
        removing Layer Style, 307
        style categories, 406, 411
        Style Settings dialog box, 418
        working with, 405–406
    Layers
        Create New Fill or Adjustment Layer button,
            190–191
        overview of, 44, 50–51, 255–256
        rearranging layers in, 266–267
    moving, 24, 51
    Navigator, 26, 27, 49, 507
    overview of, 21, 44–45
    resizing, 310
    Save Palette Locations option (General
        Preferences), 61
    Swatches, 48
    Undo History
        Open state, 49
        overview of, 48–49
        undoing adjustment using, 126
        undoing command using, 20
Pan tool (Liquify dialog box), 344
panoramic picture, printing, 468–471
paper
    acid-free, 523, 524
    orientation of, changing, 456
    for panoramic image, 470
    for printing, 442–443, 446
Paper size option (Page Setup dialog box), 456
paragraph, editing, 401–402
pasting
    copied content, 155, 514
    cut content, 153
    text in layer, 403
Patchwork filter, 369
Pattern algorithm (Dithering Algorithm menu), 483
pattern fills. *See* patterns
Pattern Name dialog box, 43, 296
Pattern Stamp tool, creating background with,
    155–158

patterns
    applying, 292–295
    choosing different set of, 293–295
    creating
        overview of, 296–298
        from selection within image, 42–44
    presets, creating for, 42
Patterns Layer Style, 409
PCX format, 428
PDF Options dialog box, 431–432
PDF (Portable Document Format), 427, 428, 431–432
PDF Slideshow, creating, 433–438
PDF Slideshow dialog box, 433, 434, 435, 436
Pencil tool
    Auto Erase option, 247–248
    overview of, 245
    preset, creating, 247
    size and preset, selecting, 245–247
perpetual palette (Color Reduction Algorithm menu), 481
perspective, changing, 220–222
Perspective command (Image menu), 213
Photocopy filter, 323, 332
photograph
    adding text to, 9–10
    applying special effects to, 10–11
    bitmap-based product and, 12
    black and white
        colorizing, 7–8
        Film Grain filter and, 316
        scanning, 82, 86, 90–91
    capturing with digital camera, 93
    content of
        covering up and filling in hole, 154–155
        replacing and editing, 150–151
        selecting, moving, and removing, 152–154
    creating texture from, 360–361
    damaged
        prioritizing multiple problems, 521–522
        restoring, 4–5, 136
        scanning, 92
        scratch, scuff, or tear, eliminating, 136–142,
            505–506, 517–518
        spot or stain, eliminating, 142–150, 518–521
        tear, repairing, 512–515
    electronic archive for, 525
    Impressionist Brush tool and, 242–244
    preserving new, 524
    quality of
        enhancing detail with filter, 128–135
        scratch, scuff, or tear, eliminating, 136–142

sharpness and blur, adjusting, 123–127
spot or stain, eliminating, 142–150
red eye
eliminating automatically, 158–160
eliminating manually, 161–163
scanning, 4, 92
turning into puzzle, 366
vintage
special needs of, 521–522
storing, 523–524, 525
Photographic Effects Layer Style, 409
Photomerge dialog box, 469
Photomerge feature, 468–471
Photoshop (Adobe), Elements compared to, 3,
13–15
Photoshop Document format. See PSD format
Photoshop Elements. See Elements
Photoshop Elements Resources site, 497
Photoshop Paradise site, 499
Photoshop Tips & Tricks site, 496
Picture Package, creating, 464–468
Picture Package dialog box, 464, 465, 466, 467
Pin Light mode (Brush tool), 195
Pinch filter, 345
pixel
bitmap format and, 426
color cast and, 173
filter and, 128
finding level of color in, 49
Info palette and, 426
replacing color and, 176
sampling and, 109–110
sharpening, 133, 134–135
pixel dimensions
adjusting, 204–205
description of, 203
reducing, 205
Pixel Doubling, turning on, 64
Pixelate filters
Color Halftone, 353, 354
Crystallize, 354
Facet, 355
Fragment, 353
Mezzotint, 355
Mosaic, 356
overview of, 353
Pointillize, 356
Plaster filter, 333
Plastic Wrap filter, 318
Plug-Ins & Scratch Disks Preferences dialog box, 71–72

PNG (Portable Network Graphics) format
description of, 427, 428, 475–476
optimizing image into
PNG-8, 478–484
PNG-24, 485–486
Pointillize filter, 356
Polar Coordinates filter, 346
polygon, drawing, 277–278
Polygon tool. See Shape tool
Polygonal Lasso tool
options, 99
shape, creating with, 284, 285
using, 102
Portable Document Format. See PDF
Portable Network Graphics format. See PNG format
Position section (Print Preview dialog box), 451, 452
positioning image on page before printing, 451–452
Poster Edges filter, 319
Posterize command (Image menu), 200–201
Posterize dialog box, 201
Precise painting cursor, 64, 65, 66
Preferences dialog box
Display & Cursors version, 64–67
General version of, 58–62
grid and, 32
Grid version, 70–71
Memory & Image Cache version, 73–74
Plug-Ins & Scratch Disks version, 71–72
Previous and Next commands, 57
Ruler and, 30
Saving Files version, 62–64
Transparency version, 67–68
Units & Rulers version, 68–69
preparing image for use online, 205
presets
appending set of to Brush tool, 229
Brush tool
creating, 239–240
customizing existing, 237–239
selecting, 226–229
for gradient fills, creating, 42
Optimization
GIF and PNG-8, 479
JPEG and PNG-24, 485–486
for Paint Bucket tool, 38, 39
for pattern fills, creating, 42
for tools
accessing, 38–39
customizing, 40–44
Preview pop-up menu (Save For Web dialog box), 478

Preview window (Dust & Scratches dialog box), 136, 138
previewing
    animated GIF image, 488
    image before printing, 447–455
    warped text, 394, 396
Previous command (Preferences dialog box), 57
Print dialog box
    printing from, 458–459
    Properties button, 457, 458
Print Preview dialog box
    Background option, 452, 453
    Border option, 452, 453
    Caption check box, 453
    Corner Crop Marks option, 454
    Page Setup button, 455
    Position section, 451, 452
    Scaled Print Size option, 447–448
    Show Bounding Box option, 450
    Show More Options check box, 452, 454
Print Size view, 28
Print to File option (Print dialog box), 459
printer
    choosing, 445
    interface for, 451
    overview of, 442
    types of, 446
Printer button (Page Setup dialog box), 456
printing. See also Print dialog box; Print Preview dialog
        box; printer
    applying crop marks, captions, and borders,
        452–455
    changing image size for, 205–206
    clipping away and, 208
    contact sheet, 460–463
    hidden layer and, 262
    image, 441, 458–459
    "in progress" version of image, 444
    Page Setup dialog box, 455–457
    panoramic picture, 468–471
    paper for, 442–443
    positioning image on page, 451–452
    quality issues, 444
    quality, setting, 457–458
    scaling image, 447, 449–450
    shortcuts, establishing, 60
Progressive JPEG, 486
proof, 444
Properties button (Print dialog box), 457, 458, 459

Properties dialog box (printer), 457–458
PSD compatibility options, 62
PSD (Photoshop Document) format
    description of, 428
    file, applying as texture, 370
    Save As dialog box and, 94
    saving file and, 423, 424
puzzle, turning photo into, 366

Q
quality
    of PDF file, checking, 432
    of photograph
        enhancing detail with filter, 128–135
        scratch, scuff, or tear, eliminating,
            136–142
        sharpness and blur, adjusting, 123–127
        spot or stain, eliminating, 142–150
    of printout, 444
Quality Level menu (JPEG), 486
QuarkXPress
    column size and, 69
    page layout and, 13
Quick Fix command (Enhance menu), 189–190

R
radial blur, applying, 130–132
Radial Blur dialog box, 132
Radial Blur filter, 129, 337, 338
Radial gradient, 301
radius, definition of, 327
Radius field (Rounded Rectangle tool), 277
Radius setting
    Dust & Scratches dialog box, 137, 506
    filters, 327
    Gaussian Blur filter, 337
    Median filter, 506
    Smart Blur filter, 338
rasterizing, 426
reapplying last filter, 336
rearranging
    layers in Layers palette, 266–267
    order of images in slideshow, 434, 435
    palette tabs in Docking Well, 52–53
reattaching palette to Docking Well, 52
Recent File List Contains option (Saving Files), 63
Recipes, 54
rectangle, drawing, 275–277
Rectangle tool. See Shape tool

Rectangular Marquee tool
  cropping image manually using, 212
  location on toolbox, 98
  options bar, 35, 36
  using, 99–100
red box and Navigator palette, 49
Red Eye Brush tool, 159–160
red eye, eliminating
  automatically, 158–160
  manually, 161–163
Redo button (Color Variations window), 179
redraw, speeding up, 72
reducing
  canvas size, 208
  image to number of specified colors, 200–201
  pixel dimensions and resolution, 205
Reflected gradient, 301
reinstalling Elements, 83
Relaxed Text Selection option (General Preferences), 62
removing
  color, 175–176
  edge of image by cropping, 208–212
  layer, 267–268
  Layer Style, 307
  pattern, 297–298
  saved selection, 122
  selected content, 117
  text, 401
  Text Effect, 419–420
renaming. See also naming
  folder, 94–95
  hidden layer, 262
  layer, 265
  pattern, 298
Render filters
  Clouds, 358
  Difference Clouds, 359
  Lens Flare, 359–360
  Lighting Effects, 360
  overview of, 357
  Texture Fill, 360–361
  3D Transform, 357
repairing damaged photograph. See restoring
        damaged photograph
Replace Color dialog box, 176–178
replacing
  color, 176–178
  text, 389, 390
resaving image, 428–431
Reset Image button (Color Variations window), 179

Reset Tool command, 38
resizing. See also sizing
  image
    memory and, 205
    panoramic, 470
    for Web, 487
  image window, 80–81
  layer, 117, 216–217
  palette, 310
  pasted content, 153
  shape, 287
  type layer, 385, 387
  workspace, 23–25
resolution
  default, setting for new document, 69
  image size and, 203
  printing and, 441
  reducing, 205
  for scan
    color mode and, 90–91
    damaged photo and, 92
    overview of, 82
    setting, 86–87
    time to complete scan and, 89
Resolution field (New dialog box), 442
Resolution setting (Image Size dialog box), 205
resources, finding, 493–494. See also Web sites
restorative filters. See also Blur filters; Sharpen filters
  Dust & Scratches, 136–138
  motion or radial blur, applying, 130–132
  overview of, 128–129
  sharpness
    of edges, increasing, 133, 134
    overall, increasing, 133
  uniform, soft blur, creating, 129
  Unsharp Mask, 133, 134–135
Restore button, 81
restoring damaged photograph
  overview of, 4–5, 136
  prioritizing multiple problems, 521–522
  scratch or scuff, eliminating, 136–142, 505–506,
        517–518
  spot or stain, eliminating, 142–150, 518-521
  tear
    blending repairs, 514–515
    copy and paste method, 513–514
    eliminating, 136–142, 505–506, 517–518
    layer, creating based on selection, 514
    overview of, 512–513
result color, 193

Reticulation filter, 333
Reverse option (Gradient tool), 299
reversing effect, 126
Revert button (Liquify dialog box), 344
RGB (Red, Green, and Blue) level, 170
RGB (Red, Green, and Blue) mode
    converting to, 175
    scanning and, 91
right-clicking layer, 265
Ripple filter, 346, 370
rotating
    image to be cropped, 211
    layer content, 214–216
    pasted content, 153
    polygon, 278
    shape, 287
Rough Pastels filter, 319
Rounded Rectangle tool. *See* Shape tool
Ruler
    displaying, 29–30
    hiding, 30
    units for, choosing, 68
running PDF Slideshow, 436, 437
Running Water (Text Effects), 414

S

Same As Source option (Print Preview dialog box), 454
sampling
    Clone Stamp tool and, 139
    color
        from existing content, 169–170
        to use as foreground color, 292
    overview of, 109–110
saturation, adjusting
    Adjust Fill Flash dialog box and, 182
    Hue/Saturation dialog box and, 174–175
Saturation mode (Brush tool), 195
Save As dialog box
    format and, 423–424
    Format list, 425, 427–428
    opening, 429
    saving image first time and, 93–95
Save dialog box
    gradient, adding to presets group, 303, 304
    PDF Slideshow, 436
Save for Web command (File menu), 69
Save For Web dialog box
    displaying, 476
    Dither settings, 481–483
    Gamma correction and, 477–478
    Image Size area, 487
    Preview pop-up window, 477

Settings area, 478–479, 485
    Web-safe format and, 7
Save Palette Locations option (General Preferences), 61
Save Selection dialog box, 121–122
saving. *See also* Save As dialog box; Save dialog box;
        Save For Web dialog box
    Custom filter, 372
    custom pattern, 294
    image
        first time, 93–94
        formats for, 84, 423–425
        new version of existing, 95, 428–431
        PDF and, 431–432
        PSD format and, 423, 424
    location for file, choosing when, 94
    mask selection, 120–122
    scanned image, 89
    setting options for, 62–64
    version of image, 95, 428–431
Saving Files dialog box, 62, 63
Scaled Print Size options (Print Preview dialog box),
        447, 448
scaling print job, 447, 449–450
scanner. *See also* software, for scanner
    keeping glass plate clean, 85
    setting up, 82–84
scanning. *See also* scanner
    color versus black and white, 90–91
    damaged or low-quality image, 92
    Import command
        fine-tuning scan, 86–88
        overview of, 84–85
        previewing image, 85–86
    overview of, 81–82
    photograph, 4
    results of, 88–89
Scatter option (Brush tool), 236, 237
Scratch Disks, setting up, 71
scratch on photograph, eliminating, 136–142, 517–518
Screen mode (Brush tool), 194
screen tip, 279
scuff mark on image, dealing with, 350
Select Move Tool After Committing Text option
        (General Preferences), 61
Select ➭ Delete Selection, 122
selecting
    area
        to scan, 85–86
        to use filter on, 507
    borders, 362
    content, 152–154
    existing text on Type layer, 392–394

free-form area, 101–102
geometric shape, 99–100
part of image to use as patch, 514
stain, 149
Select ➪ Inverse, 130
selection. *See also* mask
applying effect and, 379
Brightness/Contrast dialog box and, 186
creating layer from, 113–114
creating pattern from, 296–298
deleting, 117
Liquify dialog box and, 343
naming, 122
saving, 122
sharing content between images, 115, 116
turning mask into, 388
Selection Brush tool
location on toolbox, 98
mask, creating, 118
using, 107–109, 111
selection tools
adding to, subtracting from, and combining
selections, 104–107
modifying selection, 111–113
overview of, 97–98
painting selection, 107–109
sampling and, 109–110
shape, creating with, 284–285
selective palette (Color Reduction Algorithm
menu), 481
Select ➪ Load Selection, 122
Select ➪ Modify, 111–113
Select ➪ Save Selection, 121
Set Background color tool, 165–166
Set Foreground color tool, 165–166
Settings area (Save For Web dialog box), 485
shadow, adjusting, 187–188
shape
creating with selection tools, 284–285
moving, 289–290
see-through, placing on top of image, 217
transforming, 286–288
shape gradient, applying, 301–302, 303
Shape layer
creating, 260–261
double-clicking, 265
working with, 281–284
Shape Selection tool, 289
Shape tool
alternate buttons, 273, 274
custom shape, drawing, 279–280

line, drawing, 280–281
options bar, 261, 273, 274–275, 282
options drop-down list, 287–288
overview of, 273–274
polygon, drawing, 277–278
rectangle or ellipse, drawing, 275–277
sharing content between images, 115, 116, 268–269
Sharpen Edges filter, 133, 340
Sharpen filters
overview of, 335, 339
Sharpen
applying, 339
overview of, 128
using, 133
Sharpen Edges, 133, 340
Sharpen More, 339, 340
Unsharp Mask, 339, 341
Sharpen More command, 133
Sharpen More filter, 339, 340
Sharpen tool
Sharpen filters compared to, 335
using, 124–126
sharpness
adjusting, 123–127
of edges, increasing, 133, 134
overall, increasing, 133
Shear filter, 347
Shift key
closing all open images and, 492
dragging and, 100
painting straight line and, 241
resizing
layer and, 217
type and, 385
rotating layer and, 216
selecting text one character at a time with, 393
Shape tool and, 276
switching between grouped tools using, 6
Shift+Ctrl+O (File Browser), 78–79
shortcut menu
Delete Layer command, 267
Duplicate Layer command, 263, 264
right-clicking layer and, 265
Simplify Layer command, 284, 289–290
shortcuts. *See* keyboard shortcuts
shortcuts bar, 20
Show Asian Text Options option (General
Preferences), 61
Show Bounding Box option (Print Preview dialog
box), 450

Show Font Names in English option (General Preferences), 61
Show More Options check box (Print Preview dialog box), 452, 454
Show Tool Tips option (General Preferences), 61
Sides field (Polygon tool), 278
Simplify button (Shape tool), 275, 276, 278
Simplify Layer command (shortcut menu), 265
simplifying Shape layer, 284
size of font, choosing, 391
Size slider
    Brush tool, 227, 228
    Pencil tool, 247
sizing. *See also* resizing
    Brush tool, 227, 228
    grid, 32
    workspace, 23–25
Sketch filters
    Bas Relief, 328
    Chalk & Charcoal, 329
    Charcoal, 329
    Chrome, 330
    Conte Crayon, 330
    Graphic Pen, 331
    Halftone Pattern, 331
    Note Paper, 332
    overview of, 315, 323, 328
    Photocopy, 332
    Plaster, 333
    Reticulation, 333
    Stamp, 334
    Torn Edges, 334
    Water Paper, 335
Skew command (Image menu), 213
skewing image content, 218–219
Smart Blur filter, 338, 511
smart quotes, 62
Smooth Selection dialog box, 112
Smudge Stick filter, 320
Smudge tool, 143–145, 508, 518
Snap to Grid (View menu), 30, 31
Soft Light mode (Brush tool), 194
softening edge, 515–516
software
    anti-virus, 503
    for digital camera, 93
    FTP, 502
    for scanner
        Import command and, 84–85
        installation and, 82–83
        quality adjustment tools, 87–88

Solarize filter, 365
source image, 268
Spacing option (Brush tool), 236, 237
Spatter filter, 327
special effects. *See* effects; Effects palette
Special Effects group (Brush tool), 228
spelling, checking, 402–403
Spherize filter, 348
Spin blurring, 338
Sponge filter, 320
Sponge tool
    overview of, 143
    using, 145–146, 148–150
    washing out stain with, 519
spot on photograph, eliminating, 142–150, 505–506
Sprayed Stencil (Text Effects), 415
Sprayed Strokes filter, 327
spread, definition of, 371, 373–374
stacking order of layers, 266–267
stain on photograph, eliminating, 142–150, 518–521
Stained Glass filter, 370
Stamp filter, 334
Standard Macintosh Color option (Save For Web dialog box), 478
Standard painting cursor, 64, 65
Standard Windows Color option (Save For Web dialog box), 478
storing
    large images, 205
    photographs, 523–524, 525
Strength setting
    Blur tool, 127, 512
    brush-based tools, 37
    Sharpen tool, 125
    Smudge tool, 145
Style option (Impressionist Brush tool), 244
Style Settings dialog box, 306, 418
Stylize filters
    Diffuse, 362
    Emboss, 362, 363
    Extrude, 363
    Find Edges, 362, 364
    Glowing Edges, 364
    overview of, 361
    Solarize, 365
    Tiles, 365–366
    Trace Contour, 366
    Wind, 367
Subtract from option (Shape tool), 281, 282, 283
Subtract from Selection button, 106, 111
Sumi-E filter, 323

sunflower icon, 35
swapping foreground and background colors, 168–169
Swatches palette, 48
switching
    between brush-based tools when drawing or
        painting, 242
    between grouped tools using Shift key, 62

T

T icon (Type layer), 260, 389
tablet and pen device, enabling support for, 226
Tagged Image File Format (TIFF)
    description of, 428
    saving files in, 62, 63
target image, 268
tear on photograph, getting rid of, 136–142, 512–515
text. *See also* Text Effects
    adding to photo or image, 9–10
    anti-aliasing and, 391
    applying Text Effect to formatted, 415
    character, selecting, 401
    committing, 61
    formatting, 388–389, 403
    Layer Style and, 405, 406
    orientation, changing, 400–401
    spelling, checking, 402–403
    Type layer
        preserving as, 419
        selecting and reformatting on, 392–394
    typing, 388–390
    typing into Web page, 407
    warping, 394–400
Text Effects
    applying, 378–380, 415, 417
    categories, 413
    displaying thumbnails, 416–417
    overview of, 412–413
    previews, 414–415
    removing, 419–420
    tweaking, 418–419
Texture Fill filter, 360–361
Texture filters
    Craquelure, 368
    Grain, 368
    Mosaic Tiles, 369
    overview of, 367
    Patchwork, 369
    Stained Glass, 370
    Texturizer, 370–371
Texturizer filter, 370–371
Thin Outline (Text Effects), 415

3D effects filters
    Clouds, 358
    Difference Clouds, 359
    Lens Flare, 359–360
    Lighting Effects, 360
    overview of, 357
    Texture Fill, 360–361
    3D Transform, 357
3D Transform filter, 357
Threshold command (Image menu), 201–202
Threshold dialog box, 202
Threshold setting
    Dust & Scratches dialog box, 137, 506
    Smart Blur filter, 338
thumbnail
    applying Layer Style and, 305
    in contact sheet, 463
    dragging to apply filter or effect, 313, 314
    Effects palette, 309–310, 375, 376
    replacing color and, 176, 177, 178
    Text Effects, displaying, 416–417
Thumbnail View button (Filters and Effects palettes),
        311, 313, 416
Thumbnails section (Contact Sheet dialog box), 461
TIFF (Tagged Image File Format)
    description of, 428
    saving files in, 62, 63
Tiles filter, 365–366
Tolerance option
    Background Eraser tool, 252
    Impressionist Brush tool, 244
    Magic Eraser tool, 254
    Magic Wand tool, 110
    Paint Bucket tool, 292
    Red Eye Brush tool, 160
tool tip
    displaying, 32, 33
    options, 62
toolbox
    keyboard shortcuts, 490
    moving, 24, 32, 33
    overview of, 18, 19, 32
    selection tools on, 98
tools. *See also specific tools*
    activating, 98
    customizing, 35
    More Options button, 37–38
    options
        accessing, 98, 99
        setting, 35–37

Continued

tools *(continued)*
    presets for
        accessing, 38–39
        customizing, 40–44
    returning to default settings, 38
    working with, 32
Torn Edges filter, 323, 334
torn image, reconstructing, 512–515
Trace Contour filter, 366
Transform command (Image menu), 213–214
transforming
    frame, 381
    shape, 286–288
transparency options
    GIF and PNG-8, 483
    Gradient tool, 299
    PNG-24, 486
    Preferences dialog box, 67–68
triangle icon on toolbox button, 18, 19, 34
Turn on Image Interpolation option (PDF Options
        dialog box), 431
turning on Pixel Doubling, 64
Twirl filter, 348
twisting image, 348
Type formatting tools, 14
Type layer
    applying Text Effect to, 417
    creating, 260–261, 385–387
    double-clicking, 265, 266
    preserving text as, 419
    selecting existing text on, 392–394
    text effects and, 413
    typing on existing, 389, 390
Type tools
    Create Warped Text, 394–400
    overview of, 387
    Type
        Change the Text Orientation button, 400–401
        options bar, 391
        overview of, 9–10
        using, 389
type, units for, choosing, 68
typing text, 388–390

U

Uncompensated Color option (Save For Web dialog
        box), 478
Underpainting filter, 321
Undo button (Color Variations window), 179

Undo command
    drawing or painting and, 240
    Undo History compared to, 48
    use of, 60
Undo History palette
    Open state, 49
    overview of, 48–49
    undoing adjustment using, 126
    undoing command using, 20
undoing. *See also* Undo command; Undo History
        palette
    adjustment, 126
    command, 20
    deletion, 268
uninstalling Elements, 83
Unisys (company), 475
Units & Rulers Preferences dialog box, 68–69
unlinking layers, 270
Unsharp Mask dialog box, 133, 134–135
Unsharp Mask filter, 339, 341
uploading image to Web, 502
Use All Layers option
    Magic Eraser tool, 254
    Magic Wand tool, 110
    Sharpen tool, 125
Use Filename as Caption option (Contact Sheet dialog
        box), 463
Use Shift Key for Tool Switch option (General
        Preferences), 61
Use Smart Quotes option (General Preferences), 62

V

vector image, 12, 426–427
vector-based application, 425
version of image, saving, 95, 428–431
Vertical Distortion slider (Warp Text dialog box), 398,
        399
Vertical radio button (Warp Text dialog box), 398, 400
Vertical Type Mask tool, 387, 388
Vertical Type tool, 385, 386, 387
Video filters
    De-Interlace, 372
    NTSC Colors, 372
    overview of, 371
View menu
    options, 28
    overview of, 26
    Snap to Grid, 30, 31
View ⇨ Grid, 30, 69

viewing options
    Effects palette, 46
    Filters and Effects as list, 311–313, 377, 378
    overview of, 25–28
    size of image window and, 81
View ➪ Ruler, 29, 30
views
    Actual Pixels size and Zoom tool, 28
    Fit on Screen
        moving on-screen tools when using, 29
        uses of, 28
    Fit to Page and Hand tool, 28
    Print Size, 28
vintage photograph
    special needs of, 521–522
    storing, 523–524, 525
virtual memory and image cache, 72
virus, protecting against, 503
Visibility Layer Style, 409
Vivid Light mode (Brush tool), 195

W

Warp Text dialog box, 394–400
Water Paper filter, 335
Water Reflection (Text Effects), 415
Watercolor filter dialog box, 321, 323
Wave filter, 349
Web graphic format
    GIF (Graphics Interchange Format), 473–474
    JPEG (Joint Photographic Experts Group), 474–475
    PNG (Portable Network Graphics), 475–476
Web optimization, 473
Web page
    anti-aliasing and, 391
    designing background and navigational tools for, 8, 9
    Layer Style and, 405
    posting gallery through ISP, 501–503
    typing text into, 407
Web palette (Color Reduction Algorithm menu), 481
Web Photo Gallery dialog box, 502
Web Safe color palette, 479
Web sites
    Adobe, 71
    Adobe Acrobat Reader, 431
    EyeWire, 498
    Google, 493

Jay Arraich's Photoshop Elements Tips, 495
National Association of Photoshop
        Professionals, 500
    Photoshop Elements Resources, 497
    Photoshop Paradise, 499
    Photoshop Tips & Tricks, 496
Web-safe format
    Color Picker and, 167
    overview of, 7
white, 170
White option (Matte Color menu), 484
Wind filter, 367
Window ➪ Reset Palette Locations, 24
Windows (Microsoft) and Gamma correction, 477–478
Windows palette (Color Reduction Algorithm menu),
        481
Wood Frame effect, 375, 377
Wood Paneling (Text Effects), 415
word processor, checking spelling through, 402–403
workspace
    canvas, 206
    default configuration, 17–18
    Docking Well, 21
    menu bar, 20
    options bar, 18, 19
    palette, 21
    Photoshop compared to Elements, 13–14
    shortcuts bar, 20
    sizing, 23–25
    toolbox, 18, 19
Wow Chrome Layer Style, 409
Wow Neon Layer Style, 409
Wow Plastic Layer Style, 409

Z

zero point, setting, 29
ZigZag filter, 349
Zoom blurring, 338
Zoom percentage setting, 28
Zoom tool
    Actual Pixels size view, 28
    Brush tool and, 507
    Liquify dialog box, 344
    using, 26, 27
zooming in and out
    drawing detailed item and, 242
    options for, 25–28